Semantic Web Services

T0189979

M. Brian Blake • Liliana Cabral
Birgitta König-Ries • Ulrich Küster
David Martin
Editors

Semantic Web Services

Advancement through Evaluation

 Springer

Editors
M. Brian Blake
University of Miami
Coral Gables, FL
USA

Birgitta König-Ries
University of Jena
Jena
Germany

David Martin
Apple, Inc.
Cupertino, CA
USA

Liliana Cabral
The Open University
Knowledge Media Institute - KMI
Milton Keynes
UK

Ulrich Küster
University of Jena
Jena
Germany

ISBN 978-3-642-42664-3   ISBN 978-3-642-28735-0 (eBook)
DOI 10.1007/978-3-642-28735-0
Springer Heidelberg New York Dordrecht London

ACM Codes: H.3, I.2, D.2, C.4

Springer is part of Springer Science+Business Media (www.springer.com)

Foreword

This book is about evaluating semantic web services. Obviously, this is a task for Heroes and most of us would rather clean up the Augean stables than perform this task. Nevertheless, it has been done, and I have been asked to provide my insight on it. As every child knows, big things should become understandable by breaking them into pieces. Obviously, this book is about the following elements: Evaluation, Semantics, Web, Services, Semantic Web, Web Services, Semantic Web Services, and Evaluating Semantic Web Services. Let's go through them step by step.

Evaluation is a tricky task. In the last millennium I attended a workshop on it (during a very hot summer in Budapest). There they evaluated heuristic search methods. In order to prevent any artificial bias, they used randomized data for it. At first, this sounded very reasonable, especially because the workshop chair had such an impressive and marvelous Oxford English accent – giving you the impression that you were actually speaking to Newton himself. Still, I was a bit surprised about the documented and mostly negative results. I started to wonder whether random data are the right resource to evaluate heuristics. Heuristics make certain assumptions about domain and task specific regularities in order to outperform generic search methods. Obviously the data used in this workshop prevented us from any bias, but is it not precisely a certain bias that makes heuristics work if the bias is chosen well? In other words, could you measure the added value of intelligence in a completely randomized (or alternatively completely frozen) universe? It was evolution that granted our bias the ability to survive in the environment with which we are confronted and which we continue to form according to this bias. In the end, I started to wonder whether not having a bias is actually a very powerful way of actually having one without being able to talk about it. From this experience I learned that you cannot escape your bias; your perception is focused, and something completely random has a rather limited bias and focus. You should rather make your bias explicit and an object of discourse. With this you do not escape it but you can partially observe and rationalize it. Quite an insight for a hot summer that smelted away objectivity as an illusion of people that seem to negate but actually absolute their subjectivity as a matter outside of any discourse!

Semantics is an even stranger beast. In [1] we made an effort to define it by using some others words in a structured, natural language sentence. Unfortunately, we ended up with a set of other words that were just as difficult to understand. Recursively expanding their natural language definitions brought us back in no more than seven steps from our point of departure. In the end, semantics seems to be defined through being semantics. In a certain sense, this should not really be a surprise. If you have a limited number of words to define their meanings, you quickly return to the word you are trying to define. This should not be a problem for most words, but slightly disappointing for words that are about meaning. Now what is the Origin of Meaning? When do I think you understood what I was talking about? When you perform in the way that I had hoped you should act. The meaning of the act of communication is rooted outside the sphere of communication, reflecting the fact that communication is just a partial aspect of structured cooperation process. Or, in the words of Bill Clinton: "It is the cooperation, stupid!" In the end, it is the usage of something that defines its meaning for the subject that is using it (and, by the way, also for the object).

Capturing the essence of the **Web** seems to be rather trivial compared to evaluating semantics. It was invented by Sir Tim just as he invented hypertext, the internet, computers, electricity, and gravitation. More seriously spoken, it was a more focused innovation and somehow a tiny step. He allowed pointers to point beyond the borderlines of existing hypertext systems and he used the internet protocol to implement these links. This was a small step for him but a significant step for mankind. He generated a new mass media on a global scale, with 404 as its bug and major feature. It is currently evolving from a web of documents into in a web of data and hopefully soon into a web of services, processes, sensors, streams, devices and many more. Some of us have become gray haired whilst waiting for this "Future Internet" that is more than just a large pile of static documents and data. When these gray haired people talk about the web they mean it as a synonym for large, decentralized, distributed, and heterogeneous networks no matter which specific protocol instance is used to implement them.

Services started as a verbal cover for a statistical anomaly. Economic activities that could neither be classified as primary nor secondary (agriculture and manufacturing) needed a label, especially because this exception slowly started to become the major economic activity in developed countries. Similar to the case of IBM when it gave up its traditional core business and needed a name and a vision to justify its future, covering with a slogan, a new and not very well understood area does not necessarily lead to good definitions of the field. According to Wikipedia, Services are the "soft parts of the economy"[1] and many of its characterizations read "soft", too, mostly only concrete in what services are not. I tend to understand services as a certain functionality that is provided in abstraction of the infrastructure that is providing it. In conclusion, when you are describing a service as a service you focus on what it is providing (its functionality) and not on how it is implemented.

---

[1] http://en.wikipedia.org/wiki/Tertiary_sector_of_the_economy

Therefore, services are not about tangible products but about an organized way to use these things as a means of achieving certain goals.

In contrast to their name **Web Services** do not have much to do with the web other than using XML as exchange syntax. However, they come with their own protocol (SOAP), and use a message-centric paradigm. Finally, most of them are not used on the web but in intranets neither being open available nor using a web protocol. Meanwhile, this is slightly chanced by a number of services being directly accessible on the web using HTTP as their protocol. However, this introduces a new difficulty. In the old days, one could argue that a web service is a URI described by a WSDL file. The new type of services usually does not have such a machine readable description. It is hard to distinguish an ordinary web site and a web service. Somehow this is not surprising since we inherit this difficulty from the vague definition of what a service is. Still, we can identify two major characteristics of services:

• They are means to encapsulate data. Take the multiplication of two digits as an example. Instead of materializing all possible results in a large and potentially infinite matrix one can publish a function that does these calculations when needed.
• They are means to perform transactions like buying a book or booking a journey.

The **Semantic Web** applies semantics to the web. Therefore, its first generation was document-centric. It provides annotations for describing web content. With the web of data, it evolved towards a means of directly providing data on the web without being structured as documents. Indeed, a SPARQL endpoint in the web of data could be viewed as a service, however, as a pure data delivery service. **Semantic Web Services** provide semantic annotations for web services. Since the field of web services is still in its infancy, semantic web services are nevertheless mostly an academic exercise compared to the huge take-up of the semantic web and the web of data. Also, they are tackling a much more difficult problem. They do not simply annotate a piece of data but a piece of software with potentially real world activities following their usage. Clearly, pragmatic assumptions must be made to save us from the impossibility of automatic programming.

Therefore, **Evaluating Semantic Web Services** is obviously a difficult task. A first step in this direction was made by Petrie et al. [2] and I congratulate the editors and authors of this issue for making a second one. It provides a complete and up-to-date survey of the field by integrating results from all major evaluation initiatives such as the Semantic Service Selection contest, the Semantic Web Service Challenge, and the Web Service Challenge. In conclusion, I can strongly recommend this book and it is a pleasure to provide a Foreword for it.

Innsbruck   Dieter Fensel

References

1. J. Domingue, D. Fensel, J.A. Hendler, Introduction, in *Handbook of Semantic Web Technologies*, ed. by J. Domingue, D. Fensel, J.A. Hendler, vol. 1 (Springer, Heidelberg/New York, 2011)
2. C. Petrie, T. Margaria, H. Lausen, M. Zaremba (eds.), *Semantic Web Service Challenge* (Springer, New York, 2009)

Preface

This book compiles the perspectives, approaches and results of the research associated with three current Semantic Web Service (SWS) evaluation initiatives, namely the Semantic Service Selection (S3) contest,[1] the Semantic Web Service Challenge (SWS Challenge)[2] and the Web Service Challenge (WS Challenge).[3] The book will contain an overall overview and comparison of these initiatives as well as chapters contributed by authors that have taken part in one or more of these initiatives.

In addition, the participants are given the opportunity to focus on a comparative analysis of the features and performance of their tools with respect to other contest entries.

The goals of this book are to:

- Report results, experiences and lessons learned from diverse evaluation initiatives in the field of Semantic Web Services.
- Enable researchers to learn from and build upon existing work (SWS technology) and comparative results (SWS technology evaluation).
- Provide an overview of the state of the art with respect to implemented SWS technologies.
- Promote awareness among users and industrial tool providers about the variety of current Semantic service approaches.
- Provide information to enhance future evaluation methodologies and techniques in the field.

This book is aimed at two different types of readers. On the one hand, it is meant for researchers on SWS technology. These researchers will obtain an overview of existing approaches in SWS with a particular focus on how to evaluate SWS technology. In this community, the book will also encourage more thorough and

---

[1]http://dfki.uni-sb.de/~klusch/s3/index.html

[2]http://sws-challenge.org

[3]http://wschallenge.org/

methodological evaluation of new approaches. On the other hand, this book is meant for potential users of Semantic Web service technology and will provide them with an overview of existing approaches including their respective strengths and weaknesses and give them guidance on factors that should play a role in evaluation.

We hope the broader community will benefit from the insights gained from the experimental evaluation of the presented technologies. This book will extend the state of the art, which is concerned with developing novel technologies but often omits the experimental validation and explanation of their merits.

We would like to thank all the participants of the evaluation initiatives, who through their contributions promoted advances in the Semantic Web Service area.

The Editors (alphabetically):
M. Brian Blake
Liliana Cabral
Birgitta König-Ries
Ulrich Küster
David Martin

Contents

Chapter 1
Introduction

M. Brian Blake, Liliana Cabral, Birgitta König-Ries, Ulrich Küster, and David Martin

This introduction will provide the necessary background on Semantic Web Services and their evaluation. It will then introduce SWS evaluation goals, dimensions and criteria and compare the existing community efforts with respect to these. This allows comprehending the similarities and differences of these complementary efforts and the motivation of their design.

Finally, in the last section, we will discuss lessons learned that concern all of the evaluation initiatives. In addition, we will analyze open research problems in the area and provide an outlook on future work and directions of development.

1.1 Organization of the Book

The remainder of the book is divided into four parts. Each part refers to one of the evaluation initiatives, including an introductory chapter followed by chapters provided by selected participants in the initiatives.

M.B. Blake (✉)
University of Miami, Coral Gables, FL, USA
e-mail: M.Brian.Blake@miami.edu

L. Cabral
KMi, The Open University, Milton Keynes, UK
e-mail: l.s.cabral@open.ac.uk

B. König-Ries · U. Küster
Department of Computer Science, University Jena, Jena, Germany
e-mail: Birgitta.Koenig-Ries@uni-jena.de; Ulrich.Kuester@uni-jena.de

D. Martin
Apple, Inc., Cupertino, CA, USA
e-mail: david_martin@apple.com

M.B. Blake et al. (eds.), *Semantic Web Services*, DOI 10.1007/978-3-642-28735-0_1,
© Springer-Verlag Berlin Heidelberg 2012

Part I will cover the long established first two tracks of the Semantic Service Selection (S3) Contest – the OWL-S matchmaker evaluation and the SAWSDL matchmaker evaluation. Part II will cover the new S3 Jena Geography Dataset (JGD) cross evaluation contest. Part III will cover the SWS Challenge. Finally, Part IV will cover the semantic aspects of the WS Challenge.

The introduction to each part provides an overview of the evaluation initiative and overall results for its latest evaluation workshops. The following chapters by the participants, in each part, will present their approaches, solutions and lessons learned.

1.2   SWS in a Nutshell

Semantic Web Services (SWS) has been a vigorous technology research area for about a decade now. As its name indicates, the field lies at the intersection of two important trends in the evolution of the World Wide Web. The first trend is the development of Web service technologies, whose long-term promise is to make the Web a place that supports shared activities (transactions, processes, formation of virtual organizations, etc.) as well as it supports shared information [3]. In the shorter term, the driving objective behind Web services has been that of reliable, vendor-neutral software interoperability, across platforms, networks, and organizations. A related objective has been the ability to coordinate business processes involving heterogeneous components (deployed as services), across ownership boundaries. These objectives, in turn, have led to the development of widely recognized Web service standards such as the Web Services Description Language (WSDL[1]) for specification of Web services and Universal Description, Discovery and Integration (UDDI[2]) for the advertisement and discovery of services. At least initially, Web services based on WSDL have been widely adopted in industry practices where interoperation could only be achieved through syntactic approaches. Inter-organization use of Web services, operated either by SOAP[3] or Representational State Transfer (REST) protocols, were limited to pre-established understanding of message types or shared data dictionaries.

Consequently, the second trend, the Semantic Web, is focused on the publication of more expressive metadata in a shared knowledge framework, enabling the deployment of software agents that can make intelligent use of Web resources or services [1]. In its essence, the Semantic Web brings knowledge representation languages and ontologies into the fabric of the Internet, providing a foundation for a variety of powerful new approaches to organizing, describing, searching for, and reasoning about both information and activities on the Web (or other networked environments).

---

[1] http://www.w3.org/TR/wsdl

[2] http://www.uddi.org/pubs/uddi_v3.htm

[3] http://www.w3.org/TR/soap

The central theme of SWS, then, is the use of richer, more declarative descriptions of the elements of dynamic distributed computation – services, processes, message-based conversations, transactions, etc. These descriptions, in turn, enable fuller, more flexible automation of service provision and use, and the construction of more powerful tools and methodologies for working with services.

Because a rich representation framework permits a more comprehensive specification of many different aspects of services, SWS can provide a solid foundation for a broad range of activities throughout the Web service lifecycle. For example, richer service descriptions can support greater automation of service discovery, selection and invocation, automated translation of message content (mediation) between heterogeneous interoperating services, automated or semi-automated approaches to service composition, and more comprehensive approaches to service monitoring and recovery from failure. Further down the road, richer semantics can help to provide fuller automation of such activities as verification, simulation, configuration, supply chain management, contracting, and negotiation of services. This applies not only to the Internet at large, but also within organizations and virtual organizations.

SWS research, as a distinct field, began in earnest in 2001. In that year, the initial release of OWL for Services (OWL-S, originally known as DAML-S) was made available[4] [14]. Other major initiatives began work not long thereafter, leading to a diverse array of approaches including the Web Services Modeling Ontology (WSMO[5], WSMO-Lite[6]), the Semantic Web Services Framework (SWSF[7]), MicroWSMO[8], and the Internet Reasoning Service (IRS [5]).

In the world of standards, a number of activities have reflected the strong interest in this work. Two of the most visible of these are Semantic Annotations for WSDL (SAWSDL[9]), which received Recommendation status at the World Wide Web Consortium (W3C) in August 2007, and SA-REST[10].

1.3 Evaluation in General

Evaluation has been part of science and scientific progress for a long time. In this section, we will have a brief look at evaluation in general before we focus on the much shorter history of evaluation in computer science.

---

[4]http://www.w3.org/Submission/OWL-S/

[5]http://www.wsmo.org/

[6]http://www.w3.org/Submission/2010/SUBM-WSMO-Lite-20100823/

[7]http://www.w3.org/Submission/SWSF/

[8]http://www.wsmo.org/TR/d38/v0.1/

[9]http://www.w3.org/2002/ws/sawsdl/

[10]http://www.w3.org/Submission/SA-REST/

1.3.1   Benefits and Aims of Evaluation

Lord Kelvin reportedly said more than 100 years ago, "If you can not measure it, you can not improve it". This sentence provides one of the main motivations for evaluations in a nutshell: By defining criteria that measure how good a system is, it becomes possible to objectively find strengths and weaknesses of this system and to systematically identify areas that need improvement. The German Evaluation Society puts it a bit more formally [2]:

> Evaluation is the systematic investigation of an evaluand's worth or merit. Evaluands include programs, studies, products, schemes, services, organizations, policies, technologies and research projects. The results, conclusions and recommendations shall derive from comprehensive, empirical qualitative and/or quantitative data.

When looking at the evaluation of software, [7] offers a useful summary of possible goals of an evaluation: It may aim at comparing different software systems ("Which one is better?"), at measuring the quality of a given system ("How good is it?") and/or at identifying weaknesses and areas for improvement ("Why is it bad?").

Despite it being obvious that asking the questions above makes sense and will contribute to advancing computer science, evaluation is – in general – rather neglected in computer science. While benchmarks etc. have long been used systematically in some areas of computer science, overall, systematic experimentation has only recently gained importance in other areas of computer science. This may be due to the fact that this is a very young discipline which didn't have much time yet to establish its scientific standards. Several independent studies show that compared to other sciences experimental papers and meaningful evaluations are less frequent in computer science [6, 16]. This hinders progress and makes adaptation of research results in industry more difficult since often no proven benefits exist [17]. An area of computer science where this has been recognized early on and has been overcome by a community effort, namely the establishment of the TREC conference, is Information Retrieval. This is particularly interesting in the context of this book, as Information Retrieval (IR) and Semantic Web Service Discovery have a number of obvious similarities (albeit also differences) that are leveraged by some of the initiatives described in this book. Many Semantic Web Service evaluation techniques duplicate and extend established IR quality measures.

1.3.2   Quality Criteria for Evaluation

Before delving into evaluation for Semantic Web Services, we will take a closer look at evaluation in general in this section. More particularly, we will review research on criteria that make an evaluation meaningful. Which criteria does an initiative need to meet in order to come up with results that are useful and will really achieve the aims pursued by evaluations?

More systematically, the evaluation standards by the German Evaluation Society identify 25 requirements categorized in four groups that evaluations need to meet. Very briefly, these requirements are:

- Utility Requirements: Stakeholders should be identified and be able to become involved; the purpose of the evaluation needs to be explicitly identified; evaluators need to be trustworthy and competent; information needs of different parties need to be taken into consideration; evaluation results shall be timely reported in a complete and understandable manner.
- Feasibility Requirements: Evaluations shall be carried out in a cost-effective manner and in a way that maximizes acceptance by the stakeholders.
- Propriety Requirements: Obligations of the involved parties need to be made explicit; the rights of all stakeholders need to be preserved, the evaluation and reporting shall be fair, complete and unbiased;
- Accuracy Requirements: It should be explicitly described what is to be evaluated and in which context, what purposes and procedures are relevant and which information sources are being used; the collected data shall be systematically examined with respect to errors, qualitative and quantitative information; findings shall be justified; the evaluation itself should be evaluated.

It has been shown that community efforts are a good basis for meeting at least some of these criteria. The main advantages of community efforts are that they distribute the significant burden of evaluation and the development of appropriate test sets, criteria, measures, and so on, required by many participants. This is often the only feasible way to manage the overall burden and the most likely approach for the evaluation effort to be complete. Also, community efforts by their nature include many different aspects and view points and thus have a much better chance at being fair and unbiased than any effort by a single group or person. Additionally, community efforts offer a certain guarantee that all findings – and not only those convenient to a specific evaluator – will be reported on. Finally, by the involvement of a significant part of a research community in the evaluation initiative, a deeper understanding of the goals of a certain endeavor, appropriate means to quantify and measure achievement of these goals and of the area in general, will be widespread – and will further future progress in that area.

1.4 Evaluation for SWS

Now, that we have set the stage, let us have a closer look at SWS evaluation by first reexamining the aims of such an evaluation and then identifying dimensions for evaluation.

1.4.1 Aims of SWS Evaluation

Over the last decade, a vast amount of funding has been spent on the development of Semantic Web Service frameworks. Numerous description languages, matchmaking and composition algorithms have been proposed. Nevertheless, when faced with a real-world problem, it is, today, very hard to decide which of those different approaches to use. The situation was even worse 5 years ago, when there was basically the same plethora of approaches, but very few evaluations. To make things worse, these evaluations were done by different groups for their respective technologies without a common set of services or measures. So even where there existed evaluations, they could not be used to compare different approaches. This had at least two negative effects: First, it was (and to a degree still is) a major hurdle on the way to real-life adaptation of SWS technology. Potential users just did not know which technology was suitable for their problem – and they had no way of finding it out. Second, the lack of measurements and comparisons hindered the further advancement of science [13].

This situation is quite similar to the one observed by the IR community several decades ago:

> First [..] there has been no concerted effort by groups to work with the same data, use the same evaluation techniques, and generally compare results across systems. [...] The second missing element, which has become critical [..] is the lack of a realistically-sized test collection. [...] The overall goal of the Text REtrieval Conference (TREC) was to address these two missing elements. It is hoped that by providing a very large test collection, and encouraging interaction with other groups in a friendly evaluation forum, a new thrust in information retrieval will occur [8].

The enormous effect the concerted effort towards evaluation had on the IR community – but also similar effects observed in other communities creating benchmarks – is a strong incentive for similar efforts in SWS evaluation.

1.4.2 Dimensions of SWS Evaluation

Before we can start to evaluate, we need to decide on what we actually want to evaluate. In [12] a number of dimensions for evaluation of SWS, i.e., interesting aspects, were identified. For each of these aspects, an evaluation initiative will have to determine appropriate measurements and how they can be obtained. The dimensions are performance/scalability, usability/effort, correctness/automation, coupling, and functional scope/context assumptions, as described in the following.

Performance/Scalability This is probably the most obvious of the five dimensions and also the one where existing methods can probably be most easily adapted. It measures the resource consumption. Possible measures include runtime, memory consumption etc.

Usability/Effort The best solution does not help, if no one (or only few experts) can use it or if the effort of setting up the system is prohibitively high, thus, this effort should be measured by an evaluation. Quite obviously, it is not easy to find appropriate measures to capture this.

Correctness/Automation One of the most obvious criteria for a solution is that the results returned by a framework are correct. Here, IR-like measures including precision and recall (or variants thereof that take the subtle differences between IR and SWS into account) are used.

Coupling Here, criteria are needed that measure whether service offers and requests can be developed independently of another or not.

Functional Scope/Context Assumptions SWS frameworks differ widely in the functional scope they support: This ranges from static discovery over contracting and negotiation capabilities to automatic invocation and mediation.

1.5 Comparison of Current SWS Evaluation Initiatives

Now that we know the nature of the evaluations and what are the most meaningful criteria to regard with respect to SWS, let us briefly introduce the existing SWS evaluation initiatives and compare them according to the criteria and dimensions described in the previous sections. The initiatives will be described in detail in the introduction of the following parts.

For each of these initiatives, we will summarize their approach and give a short overview on the dimensions they address. We will also discuss how well they fit with the quality criteria for evaluation. The results of the comparison are summarized in Table 1.1 which has been adapted from [10]. In the latter, you'll find a much more detailed discussion of this topic.

1.5.1 The SWS Challenge

The SWS Challenge, originally founded by STI Innsbruck and the Stanford Logic Group, has been running as a series of workshops since 2006. As published in [15], its aim is to "develop a common understanding of various technologies and to explore the trade-offs among existing approaches".

The SWS Challenge provides a set of scenarios focusing on different aspects of the SWS problem space. Participants develop solutions to these scenarios and present these – including a code inspection – at the SWSC workshops. The scenarios fall in two broad categories namely mediation and discovery. For most of the scenarios, a testbed has been implemented. Solutions are supposed to be programmed against this testbed and need to actually call and execute the appropriate services. A lot of effort went into defining the evaluation methodology which was continuously adapted and refined over the course of the workshops.

Table 1.1 Existing initiatives in comparison

		SWS challenge	S3 contest	WS challenge
Dimension	Performance and scalability	n/a	Runtime for matchmaking	Runtime for composition
	Usability and effort	Adaptation effort	Description effort (cross eval track)	n/a
	Correctness and automation	No notion of partial correctness	Retrieval correctness	Correctness of algo, but not semantics
	Coupling	n/a	Decoupled setting, explicit in cross eval track	n/a
	Functional scope	Hierarchy of scenarios	Static discovery	Static composition
Criteria	Utility	++	++	+
	Feasibility	+	+	0
	Propriety	+	0	0
	Accuracy	−	0	+

In particular, measures were sought to capture the effort involved in adapting solutions to slight changes in the scenario. Initially, the idea was, that ideally, this should be possible without any programming effort by just changing declaration. However, it proved difficult to distinguish the two in practice.

The SWS Challenge concentrates on evaluating the functional scope of a framework. To a certain degree usability/effort are taken into consideration as well. Correctness/Automation are not measured; a proposed solution is either correct (i.e., provides the expected results) or not. There is no notion of a partially correct solution in the SWS Challenge. The other dimensions are not covered by the SWS challenge. Coupling has been paid no attention to at all (in general, offers and requests are written by the same people). Concerning performance/scalability this has not been an issue either. On the one hand, from a philosophical point of view the initiators of the SWSC did not deem them as important as other dimensions, on the other hand, the design of the SWSC is not suitable to measure performance. This is mainly due to the small number of scenarios which does not allow for statistically relevant performance measures.

Concerning the criteria for evaluations, the SWSC does pretty well with respect to utility, feasibility, and propriety requirements (with the exception of the need for formal agreement of stakeholders tasks). Its design results in less good marks concerning accuracy requirements. Since a lot of the evaluation is done in an interactive process at the workshops with manual code inspections and discussions, not all of the information is as "hard" as the accuracy requirements would like to see. Also, a meta-evaluation has been lacking, albeit that has been partially done by Küster [10].

1.5.2   The S3 Contest

The S3 (Semantic Service Selection) Contest was founded in 2006 by Mathias Klusch from DFKI Saarbrücken (Germany) and has been run annually together with groups from France Telekom Research, SRI International, NTT DoCoMo Research Europe, and the Universities of Zurich, Southhampton, and later on also Jena. It has an open call; results are presented annually at a workshop. The S3 contest performs evaluation in a number of tracks related to static discovery. These tracks either investigate the runtime performance and correctness of matchmakers in a single formalism or compare results across different formalisms. The S3 contest provides an extensive (albeit artificial) collection of semantically described services in different formalisms (OWL-S, SAWSDL) and a testing platform. Participants program their matchmaker against this platform. The platform will run the test and compute measures like run time, precision, recall and so on.

The S3 Contest uses an evaluation methodology that has long been agreed upon in the IR community. However, the adaptation to the SWS context raises some issues: First of all, the quality of the evaluation results depends strongly on the quality of the test collections. While OWLS-TC and SAWSDL-TC are no doubt the most comprehensive SWS test collections available and have been put together with considerable effort, there has been some concern about their quality. A more realistic collection would certainly be beneficial. Also, there exists a wide variety of measures for precision and recall or variants thereof. Up to now, a careful evaluation of which of these measures are best suited for SWS evaluation and what influence the measures have on the outcomes of the evaluation is largely lacking.

The focus of the S3 contest is on the evaluation of performance/scalability on the one hand and correctness/automation on the other. While the first is quantified with a number of runtime measures, the latter are compared by IR like measures. The recent cross-evaluation track of the S3 contest explicitly addresses coupling and to a certain degree (albeit rather informally) usability/effort. The functional scope considered is that of static discovery. The S3 contest does not take into consideration whether a framework could do more.

With respect to the evaluation criteria, the S3 contest fares similarly to the SWS Challenge concerning the utility and feasibility requirements. It has weaknesses regarding propriety and accuracy requirements. The latter is due mainly to the lack of reflection on the appropriateness and influence of the measures used. First steps to overcome this have been taken in the context of the cross-evaluation track [11].

1.5.3   The WS Challenge

The IEEE Web Service Challenge was founded in 2004 by M. Brian Blake of the University of Notre Dame. The challenge, itself, has been held annually since 2005. The event has been funded annually by the National Science Foundation.

The first event, initially named the IEEE EEE-05 Challenge, was organized by M. Brian Blake and William Cheung. While it started with evaluation of traditional web service frameworks and web service composition from a software engineering perspective, it has included composition via semantic services over the last several years. Evaluation measures used over time include the speed of the composition process, the correctness of the composition (measured in terms of accuracy, completeness, and minimal composition length), the execution time of the composed process (rewarding exploitation of parallelism), and the overall solution architecture.

An advantage of the WS Challenge compared, e.g., to the SWS Challenge is the unambiguous problem description provided. The WS Challenge has developed over two dozen different web service repositories from smaller, manually-created services (with realistic interfaces) to very large repositories with randomly generated semantic services. This approach is somewhat unique with respect to the other challenges. For the WS Challenge, it is also important to traverse a huge search space as efficiently as possible.

With respect to the evaluation dimensions, the WS Challenge measures a number of performance indicators and evaluates correctness of the algorithm, albeit not necessarily of the semantic reasoning. The functional scope is restricted to static composition. Coupling and usability/effort are not taken into account.

Regarding the criteria for good evaluations, the WS Challenge fares better than the other two when it comes to the accuracy requirements; it is almost comparable to them with regard to utility and propriety and is a bit less effective in determining the feasibility of real-life services. Since the initiative is a competition, sharing of approaches is less explicit than in the other challenges. Solutions are not generally developed through collaboration, but individual participants create their approaches separately and as a part of the forum techniques are discussed and perhaps incorporated individually for the next year. The other challenges seem to more encourage mutual understanding and learning.

The following parts will contain more detailed descriptions of the individual initiatives as well as experience reports from their participants. Most of the issues raised here will be touched upon in those chapters again.

1.6 The Future of the Initiatives

All three initiatives in which this book is based on are still running and are continuously being improved.

The S3 contest will continue to conduct annual events at least through 2013, with the existing tracks focused on the use of OWL-S and SAWSDL. It is anticipated that the OWL-S and SAWSDL test collections, which are used by the contest, will continue to grow and become further refined by the existing community effort that has been established.

The Semantic Web Service Challenge continues to be available online and has been collaborating with the SEALS project and running workshops in conjunction with the SEALS campaigns. As SEALS approaches the completion of its platform, there is also an opportunity to make the benchmarks from the SWS Challenge available in this platform. The SWS Challenge also counts on expanding its number of problem scenarios by contribution from the community.

The WS Challenge will continue to run annually. There are four newly anticipated aspects of the challenge in the coming years. The challenges will work on new dimensions of defining "what is good" with respect to quality of service. In previous challenges, all dimensions (performance, accuracy, efficiency, etc.) were treated equally. The challenge will apply weights in real time that competitors will need to acquire and leverage in their compositions. Also, the WS Challenge will incorporated dynamism in the service repositories. Instead of having a repository that is static throughout the evaluation process, we will remove and insert services in real time. This will prevent competitors from making one-time indexes for all challenge sets. The WS-Challenge will develop sets for security. Competitors will have to comply with a specific protocol in executing the sets. Finally, a challenge will be developed for service mashups. Instead of composing web services in workflows, the solution will be a set of services that creates mashups that are relevant to a specific purpose.

Regarding related initiatives that are contributing to a change in the evaluation landscape in the Semantic Web realm, the SEALS (Semantic Evaluation at Large Scale) project[11] is undertaking the task of creating a lasting reference infrastructure for semantic technology evaluation (the SEALS platform). The SEALS Platform will be an independent, open, scalable, extensible and sustainable infrastructure that will allow online evaluation of semantic technologies by providing an integrated set of evaluation services and a large collection of datasets. Semantic Web Services are one of the technologies which are supported by SEALS. The platform will support the creation and sharing of evaluation artifacts (e.g. datasets and measures) and services (e.g. retrieving data sets from repositories and automatic execution of tools), making them widely available according to problem scenarios, using semantic based terminology. A description of the results of SEALS for Semantic Web Service technologies and its relation with the current initiatives has been published in several deliverables (available from the website) and also in [4]. It is expected that the SEALS infrastructure, together with some of the outcomes of the project, such as a new dataset for WSMO-Lite [9], will benefit evaluation participants and organizers and advance the state-of-the-art of SWS evaluation.

---

[11]http://about.seals-project.eu/

1.7 Summary

We hope that we have convinced you by now – if you weren't from the beginning – that evaluations in computer science are important in order to advance the state of the art and to promote adoption of research results in real life applications. We have shown that this is also – or maybe even particularly – true for Semantic Web Services.

While necessarily short, we have introduced quality criteria that evaluations should meet and have compared existing evaluation initiatives for SWS with these criteria. We have also given a brief overview of the dimensions of evaluation for SWS and of which initiative addresses which of these dimensions.

Without having a closer look at the initiatives we can already conclude that while they do not meet all the criteria and do not address all dimensions equally, they offer a good starting point and are valuable.

In the next parts, you will find detailed reports on the initiatives supporting this view. There will be introductions by the organizers of the respective campaigns and in depth experience reports from participants.

We believe that one can learn three things from this book: It gives a good overview of existing approaches to SWS and discusses their respective weaknesses and strengths as found by the evaluations. It can thus serve as a guideline, if you are looking for a platform to use. Second, it gives a detailed overview of the state of the art in evaluation of SWS. If you are a developer of an SWS framework, the dimensions discussed and the experiences made by participants in the evaluation campaigns might guide you towards improvements of your solution. Better yet, of course, take part in one of the campaigns yourself. This book will help you identify the one that addresses the issues that you are most concerned about. Third, we hope to contribute to the progress of evaluation in computer science in general. This book should give a good impression on what to consider when planning an evaluation campaign and which results to expect.

References

1. T. Berners-Lee, J. Hendler, O. Lassila, The semantic web. Sci. Am. **284**(5), 34–43 (2001)
2. W. Beywl, Selected comments to the standards for evaluation of the german evaluation society – English edition. Technical report, German Evaluation Society (DeGEval), (2003)
3. M.B. Blake, H. Gomaa, Agent-oriented compositional approaches to services-based cross-organizational workflow. Decis. Support Syst. **40**(1), 31–50 (2005)
4. L. Cabral, I. Toma, Evaluating semantic web services tools using the SEALS platform, in *Proceedings of IWEST Workshop at ISWC 2010*, Shanghai, 2010
5. J. Domingue, L. Cabral, S. Galizia, V. Tanasescu, A. Gugliotta, B. Norton, C. Pedrinaci, IRS-III: a broker-based approach to semantic web services. J. Web Semant. **6**(2), 109–132 (2008)
6. N. Fenton, S.L. Pfleeger, R.L. Glass, Science and substance: a challenge to software engineers. IEEE Softw. **11**(4), 86–95 (1994)

7. G. Gediga, K.-C. Hamborg, I. Düntsch, Evaluation of software systems, in *Encyclopedia of Computer Science and Technology*, vol. 45, ed. by A. Kent, J.G. Williams (Marcel Dekker, Inc., CRC, New York, 2002), pp. 127–153
8. D. Harman, Overview of the first Text REtrieval Conference (TREC-1), in *Proceedings of the First Text REtrieval Conference (TREC-1)*, Gaithersbury, 1992
9. J. Kopecky, T. Vitvar, WSMO-Lite: lowering the semantic web services barrier with modular and light-weight annotations, in *Proceedings of 2nd IEEE International Conference on Semantic Computing (ICSC)*, Santa Clara, CA, USA, 2008
10. U. Küster, An evaluation methodology and framework for semantic web services technology, University of Jena, Berlin Logos, 2010
11. U. Küster, B. König-Ries, Relevance judgments for web services retrieval-a methodology and test collection for sws discovery evaluation, in *2009 Seventh IEEE European Conference on Web Services* (IEEE, Los Alamitos, 2009), pp. 17–26
12. U. Küster, B. König-Ries, C. Petrie, M. Klusch, On the evaluation of semantic web service frameworks. Int. J. Semant. Web Inf. Syst. **4**(4), 31–55, (2008)
13. H. Lausen, C. Petrie, M. Zaremba, W3C SWS testbed incubator group charter (2007), Available online at http://www.w3.org/2005/Incubator/swsc/charter
14. D. Martin, M. Burstein, D. McDermott, S. McIlraith, M. Paolucci, K. Sycara, D.L. McGuinness, E. Sirin, N. Srinivasan, Bringing semantics to web services with OWL S. World Wide Web **10**(3), 243–277 (2007)
15. C. Petrie, U. Küster, T. Margaria-Steffen, W3C SWS challenge testbed incubator methodology report. W3c incubator report, W3C, (2008), Available online at http://www.w3.org/2005/Incubator/swsc/XGR-SWSC/
16. W.F. Tichy, Should computer scientists experiment more? IEEE Comput. **31**(5), 32–40 (1998)
17. M.V. Zelkowitz, D.R. Wallace, Experimental models for validating technology. Computer **31**(5), 23–31 (1998)

Part I
Results from the S3 Contest: OWL-S and SAWSDL Matchmaker Evaluation Tracks

Chapter 2
Overview of the S3 Contest: Performance Evaluation of Semantic Service Matchmakers

Matthias Klusch

Abstract This chapter provides an overview of the organization and latest results of the international contest series on semantic service selection (S3). In particular, we introduce its publicly available S3 evaluation framework including the standard OWL-S and SAWSDL service retrieval test collections OWLS-TC and SAWSDL-TC as well as its retrieval performance evaluation tool SME2. Further, we classify and present representative examples of Semantic Web service matchmakers which participated in the S3 contest from 2007 to 2010. Eventually, we present and discuss selected results of the comparative experimental performance evaluation of all matchmakers that have been contested in the past editions of the S3 series.

2.1 Introduction

In the rapidly growing Internet of services, efficient means for service discovery, that is the process of locating existing services based on the description of their (non-)functional semantics are essential for many applications. Such discovery scenarios typically occur when one is trying to reuse an existing piece of functionality (represented as a Web service) in building new or enhanced business processes. Matchmakers [6] are tools that help to connect a service requestor with the ultimate service providers. The process of service selection or matchmaking encompasses (a) the pairwise semantic matching of a given service request with each service that is registered with the matchmaker, and (b) the semantic relevance ranking of these services. In contrast to a service broker, a service matchmaker only returns a ranked list of relevant services to the requestor together with sufficient provenance

M. Klusch (✉)
German Research Center for Artificial Intelligence (DFKI), Stuhlsatzenhausweg 3,
Saarbruecken, Germany
e-mail: klusch@dfki.de

M.B. Blake et al. (eds.), *Semantic Web Services*, DOI 10.1007/978-3-642-28735-0_2,
© Springer-Verlag Berlin Heidelberg 2012

information that allows to directly contact the respective providers. A matchmaker neither composes nor negotiates nor handles the execution of services.

Semantic matching of services determines the degree of semantic correspondence between the description of a desired service, that is the service request, and the description of a registered service, that is the service offer. For this purpose, both service request and service offer are assumed to be described in the same format. In this chapter, we focus on semantic service matchmakers [5] that are capable of selecting semantic services in formats such as OWL-S,[1] SAWSDL[2] or WSML,[3] that is services whose functionality is described by use of logic-based semantic annotation concepts which are defined in one or multiple formal ontologies [4]. The processing of such semantic annotations for service selection by a matchmaker bases either on a global ontology it is assumed to share with service consumers and providers, or on the communication of sufficient ontological information on service annotation concepts to the matchmaker for this purpose. The performance of any service matchmaker can be measured in the same way as information retrieval (IR) systems are evaluated for decades, that is in terms of performance measures like recall, average precision and response time.

Though many implemented semantic service matchmakers exist, there was no joint initiative and framework for the comparative experimental evaluation of their retrieval performance available until a few years ago. For this reason, the international contest series on semantic service selection (S3) has been initiated in 2006 by DFKI together with representatives of several other institutions and universities in Europe and USA. Since then it has been organized annually based on a publicly available S3 evaluation framework for semantic service selection which actually consists of the standard test collections OWLS-TC[4] and SAWSDL-TC,[5] as well as the evaluation tool SME2.[6] The participation in the contest is by online submission of a matchmaker plugin for the SME2 tool while the final results of each edition of the contest are presented at a distinguished event such as at a major conference of the Semantic Web or relevant community and/or on the official Web site of the S3 contest.[7] The S3 contest series has been exclusively funded by the German ministry of education and research (BMB+F) under project grants 01IW08001 (MODEST, http://www.dfki.de/-klusch/modest/) and 01IW08005 (ISReal, http://www.dfki.de/-klusch/isreal/).

The remainder of this chapter is structured as follows. We briefly introduce the S3 evaluation framework in Sect. 2.2. This is followed by a classification of all participants of the contest from 2007 to 2010 together with brief descriptions of

---

[1]http://www.w3.org/Submission/OWL-S/

[2]http://www.w3.org/2002/ws/sawsdl/

[3]http://www.wsmo.org/wsml/wsml-syntax

[4]http://projects.semwebcentral.org/projects/owls-tc/

[5]http://projects.semwebcentral.org/projects/sawsdl-tc/

[6]http://projects.semwebcentral.org/projects/sme2/

[7]http://www.dfki.de/-klusch/s3/

some of them as representative examples in Sect. 2.3. Eventually, we provide and discuss selected evaluation results in Sect. 2.4 before we conclude the chapter in Sect. 2.5.

2.2 The S3 Evaluation Framework

The S3 evaluation framework consists of two components: Semantic service retrieval test collections, especially OWLS-TC and SAWSDL-TC, and the S3 evaluation tool for comparative experimental evaluation of retrieval performance of semantic service matchmakers.

2.2.1 Service Retrieval Test Collections

The semantic service retrieval test collections that are currently used in the S3 contests are OWLS-TC and SAWSDL-TC. Both collections are publicly available at the Semantic Web software portal semwebcentral.org and were initially created at DFKI in 2004 (OWLS-TC1) and 2007 (SAWSDL-TC1). Since their creation these collections have been continuously revised and extended with support of many colleagues from different institutions and universities worldwide. Though the collections are commonly considered as standards in the domain of Semantic Web services today, they do not have the degree of maturity of the prominent TREC (text retrieval conference) collections that have been used in the IR domain for the same purpose for several decades. To achieve this requires a significant increase of joint efforts by the community than it did invest in the building of both collections so far.

OWL-S Service Retrieval Test Collection OWLS-TC. The first version of the collection OWLS-TC [10] was created at DFKI in 2004 and released at semwebcentral.org in 2005. It consisted of only 500 service offers in OWL-S, each of which judged by only four users on their binary relevance for only a few service requests in OWL-S. Five years later, the latest edition of the collection, OWLS-TC4, contains already 1,083 OWL-S services from multiple domains such as travel, sport, business and healthcare, and 42 queries together with their binary and graded relevance set. These sets of relevant services were determined by more than a dozen users. Each semantic service of the OWLS-TC4 is grounded in a Web service in WSDL 1.1. The semantic annotations of all services are based on references to 34 OWL ontologies in total.

Most of the services of OWLS-TC4 were directly retrieved from the Web while a few others were created in addition by semi-automated transformation of WSDL services in the Web into OWL-S services. Each semantic service in the OWLS-TC is grounded with a WSDL service; for those OWL-S services for which we did not find any grounding in the Web, we created one by its semi-automated transformation to WSDL service by use of our OWLS2WSDL tool.[8] In addition, the descriptions of 160 OWL-S service offers and 18 OWL-S service requests in the OWLS-TC4 include logical specifications of preconditions and effects in PDDL 2.0 (Planning Domain and Description Language) and SWRL (Semantic Web Rule Language). The choice of these logical languages was motivated by their widespread use for this purpose and respective recommendations in the OWL-S specification documents. With more than eleven thousand downloads as of February 14, 2011, the OWLS-TC appears to be the by far most widely used semantic service retrieval test collection.

SAWSDL Service Retrieval Test Collection SAWSDL-TC. The retrieval performance of SAWSDL service matchmakers in the S3 contest is measured over the test collection SAWSDL-TC [12]. In its current version, the SAWSDL-TC3 consists of 1,080 services and 42 requests with both binary and graded relevance sets while the semantic annotations of services are based on references to 38 ontologies in total. Most of the services of SAWSDL-TC3 were created by semi-automated transformation of all OWL-S services in OWLS-TC3 with the OWLS2WSDL tool (available at semwebcentral.org) to WSDL services which are then transformed to SAWSDL services by manually editing the semantic annotations suggested by the tool without taking service preconditions and effects into account. SAWSDL services that were directly retrieved from the Web or have been contributed by the community to this collection currently make up only two percent of its size in total. The collection has been downloaded more than 400 times as of February 14, 2011.

Binary and graded relevance sets of OWLS-TC and SAWSDL-TC. The measurement of the performance of semantic service retrieval requires any test collection to include a set of relevant services for each service request in the collection. Both collections, OWLS-TC and SAWSDL-TC, are providing such relevance sets based on two different types of relevance assessments. The binary relevance of a service offer S to a request R is judged by human users in terms of S being either relevant (relevance score: 1) or not (relevance score: 0). In contrast, the graded relevance of a service is judged by human users on the standard four-graded relevance scale of the NTCIR test collection for IR systems.[9] In this case, the degrees of semantic relevance of a service S to a request R range from "highly relevant" to "relevant" and "partially relevant" to "not relevant at all" with corresponding relevance scores of 3 to 0. In particular, partially relevant services are assumed to overlap with the service request, that is, the service provides functionality that has been requested and some that has not while the functionality of relevant services is supposed to be subsumed by but not equal to the requested one. The semantic relevance set for each service request is determined by union average pooling of relevance assessments provided by human users: A service S is considered relevant to R if S is judged relevant to R by at least one user, and considered not relevant otherwise, that is, if it is not included in the relevance set

---

[8]http://projects.semwebcentral.org/projects/owls2wsdl/
[9]http://research.nii.ac.jp/ntcir/index-en.html

of R or has not been rated yet. The graded relevance sets for service requests in OWLS-TC and SAWSDL-TC are available since 2009, respectively, 2010 only.

2.2.2   Evaluation Tool SME2

The evaluation tool SME2 (Semantic Service Matchmaker Evaluation Environment) [2] is part of the S3 evaluation framework. It enables the user to perform an automated comparative evaluation of the retrieval performance of any given set of semantic service matchmakers over given test collections with respect to classical retrieval performance measures.

Retrieval performance measures. The SME2 tool determines the retrieval performance of matchmakers over a given test collection with binary relevance sets by measuring the macro-averaged precision at standard recall levels (MAP), the average precision (AP), the R-precision and precision@k as known from the IR domain. In case of graded relevance, the tool computes the values of the classical measures Q and nDCG (discounted cumulative gain).

For example, the average precision measure determines for each query how many services retrieved are also relevant and averages this ratio over the set of queries. The standard recall measure determines how many services which are relevant to a query have been retrieved. In addition, the SME2 tool measures the average query response time, that is the elapsed time per query execution, and the number of accesses by matchmakers to service annotation ontologies, that is their number of respective http-requests during the query-answering test phase. For reasons of space limitation, we omit the comprehensive definition of used performance measures but recall only some of them in Fig. 2.1 and refer the interested reader to the extensive literature on the topic in the IR domain as well as publicly available software packages on the subject.

SME2 user interface. The SME2 evaluation tool provides an easy to use graphical user interface for configuration, execution and analysis of comparative experimental performance evaluation of any set of plugged in matchmakers over a given test collection. In particular, the tool allows users to tailor summary reports of the evaluation results for archival and printing purposes. Figure 2.2 shows screen shots of the SME2 user interface for an example configuration and the display of evaluation results.

The SME2 evaluation tool was developed at the German Research Center for Artificial Intelligence (DFKI) and is publicly available since April 2008 at the portal for Semantic Web software semwebcentral.org. It has been implemented in Java, uses an embedded Jetty Web server and interacts with any semantic service matchmaker through its XML-based plug-in API. The latest version 2.2 of the SME2 evaluation tool also comes with the test collections OWLS-TC4 and SAWSDL-TC3 together with the plugins of all matchmakers that click cancel participated in the 2010 edition of the S3 contest.

For binary relevance: Average precision

$$AP = \sum_{R \in RS} \frac{1}{|\operatorname{Rel}_R|} \sum_{r=1}^{|L_R|} isrel(r) \frac{count(r)}{r}, \; L_R \text{ rank list of services retrieved for request } R$$

$$isrel(r) = \begin{cases} 1 & \text{if service in } L_R \text{ at rank } r \text{ is relevant} \\ 0 & \text{else} \end{cases}, \quad count(r) = \sum_{i=1}^{r} isrel(i)$$

For binary relevance: Macro-averaged precision at standard recall levels

$$MAP_n = \frac{1}{|RS|} \sum_{R \in RS} \max\{\operatorname{Prec}_{R,o} : \operatorname{Rec}_{R,o} \geq \operatorname{Rec}(n), (\operatorname{Prec}_{R,o}, \operatorname{Rec}_{R,o}) \in Obs_R\},$$

$$n \text{ - th recall level } \operatorname{Rec}(n) = \frac{n}{\lambda}, n = 1..\lambda, (\lambda = 20); \text{ Ceiling interpolation}$$

For graded relevance: nDCG-measure (normalized discounted cumulative gain)

$$nDCG_l = \sum_{R \in RS} \frac{1}{|\operatorname{Rel}_R|} (\sum_{r=1}^{\max\{|L_R|,l\}} DCG(r) / \sum_{r=1}^{l} DCG_{ideal}(r))$$

$$DCG(r) = \begin{cases} \dfrac{g(r)}{\log_a(r)} & \text{if } r > a \; (=2) \\ g(r) & \text{else} \end{cases}, \quad \text{Cut - off value } l \; (=100)$$

For graded relevance: Q-measure

$$Q = \sum_{R \in RS} \frac{1}{|\operatorname{Rel}_R|} \sum_{r=1}^{|L_R|} isrel(r) \frac{\omega CG(r) + count(r)}{\omega CG_{ideal}(r) + r}, \; \omega = 1 \text{ (robustness)}, \; \omega = 0 : Q \cong AP,$$

$$CG(r) = \sum_{i=1}^{r} g(i), \; CG_{ideal}(r) \equiv CG(r) \text{ for perfect service rank list } L_R \text{ for } R$$

Fig. 2.1 SME2: examples of service retrieval performance measures

2.3 Contest Organization and Participants

2.3.1 Organizational Issues

The international S3 contest series was jointly initiated in late 2006 by Matthias Klusch (DFKI, Germany), Ulrich Kuester (University of Jena, Germany), Alain Leger (France Telecom Research, France), David Martin (SRI International, USA), Terry Payne (University of Southampton, UK), Massimo Paolucci (NTT DoCoMo Research Europe, Germany) and Abraham Bernstein (University of Zurich, Switzerland). Since 2007, Patrick Kapahnke and Matthias Klusch at DFKI coordinated four annual editions and presented each of their results at the SMR2 (Service Matchmaking and Resource Retrieval in the SemanticWeb) workshops at different locations world wide: 2007 in Busan (South Korea), 2008 in Karlsruhe (Germany), 2009 in Washington D.C. (USA), and 2010 in Shanghai (China).

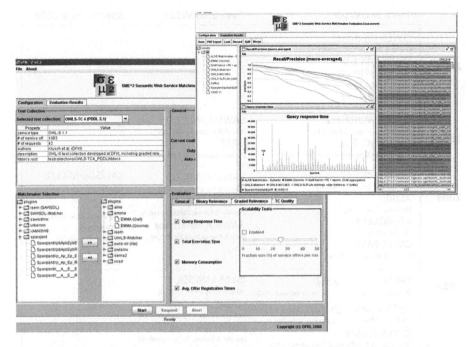

Fig. 2.2 SME2 user interface screen shots for configuration and display of evaluation results

Actually, the contest consists of two tracks that are devoted to the comparative performance evaluation of matchmakers for OWL-S, and SAWSDL services over the standard service retrieval test collections OWLS-TC and SAWSDL-TC, respectively (cf. Sect. 2.2). The contest is open to the comparative evaluation of matchmakers for other kinds of semantic service description as well, if there are respective test collections publicly available for this purpose. This concerns, for example, the evaluation of implemented WSML service matchmakers of which a few are publicly available such as WSMO-MX, but the WSML test collection required for testing them still remains to be created by the community. The same holds for the evaluation of linked (open) services[10] discovery tools like iServe.

The 2009 edition of the contest also offered a special track on an initial cross-evaluation of matchmakers and has been organized by Ulrich Kuester (University of Jena). This track aimed at the evaluation of different matchmakers for different service description formats over respective variants of the same test collection, that is the special collection JGD (Jena Geographic Data Set) of geoservices. We omit the description of the JGD, the evaluation results and lessons learned of this special track since they are presented elsewhere in this book.

---

[10]linkedservices.org

	Track 1: OWL-S	Track 2: SAWSDL	Special Track 2009
2007	OWLS-iMatcher (Kiefer & Bernstein, U Zurich, D) OWLS-MX 1.0 (Klusch & Fries, DFKI, D) JIAC-OWLSM (Masuch, TU Berlin, D)		
2008	OWLS-iMatcher2 (Kiefer & Bernstein, U Zurich, D) OWLS-MX 2.0 (Klusch, Fries & Kapahnke, DFKI, D)	SAWSDL-MX 1.0 (Klusch & Kapahnke, DFKI, D) URBE (Plebani, Politecnico di Milano, I)	
2009	Opossum (Toch, Gal & Dori, Technion, IL) ALIVE (Andreou, U Bath, UK) SPARQLent (Sbodio, HP, I) OWLS-MX3 (Klusch & Kapahnke, DFKI D)	SAWSDL-MX 2.0 (Klusch & Kapahnke, DFKI, D) COM4SWS (Schulte & Lampe, TU Darmstad, D) SAWSDL-iMatcher (Wei & Bernstein, U Zurich, CH)	SAWSDL-MX1/2 SAWSDL-iMatcher IRS-III (Cabral et al, Open U, UK) Themis-S (Müller, U Münster, D) WSColab (Gawinecki, U Modena, I)
2010	SeMa^2 XSSD (Masuch, TU Berlin, D) (Li & Chu, U Beihang, PRC) iSeM (Klusch & EMMA (Garcia, Ruiz & Kapahnke, DFKI, D) Ruiz-Cortez, U Seville, ES) OWLS-SLRlite (Meditskos & Bassiliades, U Thessaloniki, GR)	iSeM-SAWSDL (Klusch & Kapahnke, DFKI, D) LOG4SWS.KOM (Schulte & Lampe, TU Darmstad, D) COV4SWS.KOM (Schulte & Lampe, TU Darmstadt, D)	

Fig. 2.3 Participants of the S3 contest series (showing first appearance only for each)

The 2010 edition has been organized in collaboration with the semantic technology evaluation campaign of the European research project SEALS project[11] but has not been funded by or made use of any infrastructure of this project. The collaboration included mutual presentations of the initiatives at the International Semantic Web conference (ISWC 2010).

The participation in the S3 contest is continuously open, without any costs and by online submission of a matchmaker code plugin to the SME2 tool together with essential information on the matchmaker itself; the contest Web site provides a short guideline of participation. In its first four editions, the S3 contest received 25 submissions in total including 14 OWL-S service matchmakers and 8 SAWSDL service matchmakers. Of these the special track of the 2009 edition received three additional submissions, which were IRS-III [1] (Open University, UK), Themis-S (University of Muenster, Germany) and WSColab (University of Modena and Reggio Emilia, Italy). Figure 2.3 summarizes all entries in the order of their first appearance in the contest from 2007 to 2010; all matchmakers except OPOSSUM and ALIVE remained entries for subsequent contest editions.

---

[11]http://www.seals-project.eu/

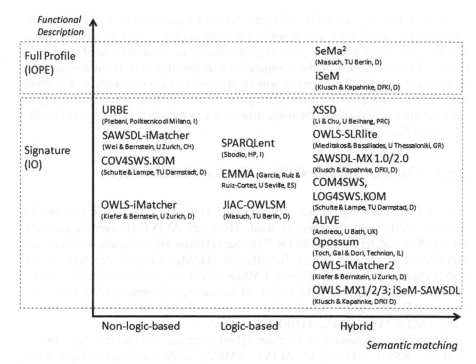

Fig. 2.4 Classification of semantic service matchmakers of the S3 contest from 2007 to 2010

In the following, we classify all participants of the contest from 2007 to 2010 according to a classification of semantic service matchmakers proposed in [5].

2.3.2   Classification of Contest Participants

Current semantic service matchmakers including those which participated in the S3 contest can be classified according to (a) the kind of semantic selection they perform, and (b) what parts of the semantic service description they exploit for this purpose. In particular, we may distinguish between means of logic-based, non-logic-based and hybrid semantic service selection based on the service signature (input/output, IO), the specification (preconditions/effects, PE), the full functional profile (IOPE), a monolithic service description in logic, with text or tags, the non-functional service parameters (NF), and combinations of the latter with any part of the functional service description (NF-IOPE). These terms are introduced in Sect. I of this volume and in [5]. The classification of all contest participants from 2007 to 2010 is summarized in Fig. 2.4: Since all of them perform semantic matching on either the service signature or the full profile, the figure does not show the remaining levels of the dimension of semantic service description parts. Further, the majority of contested matchmakers performs hybrid semantic matching of service annotations.

In the following, we briefly describe selected matchmakers of the contest as representative examples together with an indication of only their best performance results for average precision and response time that were measured in the S3 contest. Selected results of the comparative experimental performance evaluation of all matchmakers of the contest will be presented in the next section. For more information on the participants of of the past editions of the contest before 2010, we refer the interested reader to the respective summary reports that are available at the S3 contest Web site.[12]

2.3.3   Contest Track 1: OWL-S Service Matchmakers

The OWL-S matchmaker track of the S3 contest editions 2007–2010 received 14 different OWL-S matchmakers in total. These are ALIVE (University of Bath, UK), OWLS-iMatcher1 and OWLS-iMatcher2 (University of Zurich, Switzerland), OPOSSUM (Technion, Israel), SPARQLent (Hewlett-Packard Research, Italy), XSSD (Beihang University, China), EMMA (University of Seville, Spain), JIAC-OWLSM and SeMa2 (Berlin University of Technology, Germany), OWLS-SLR lite (Aristotle University of Thessaloniki, Greece), and OWLS-OWLS-MX1, OWLS-MX2, OWLS-MX3 and iSeM (DFKI, Germany).

Most of these matchmakers perform hybrid semantic selection (SeMa2, OWLS-SLR lite, XSSD, OPOSSUM, ALIVE, EMMA) while only two of them focus on non-logic-based, respectively, logic-based semantic selection (OWLS-iMatcher, SPARQLent). Notably, the evaluated OWL-S matchmakers OWLS-MX3, iSeM and OWLS-iMatcher2 perform an adaptive hybrid semantic service selection, that is, they apply machine learning techniques to find the most relevant services to given requests. The matchmaker EMMA does a special kind of logical prefiltering of services before calling the OWLS-MX matchmaker. As representative examples for each of these classes, we now in very brief describe the functionality of of some of these matchmakers together with their best average precision for binary and graded (nDCG measure) relevance and average response times.

Examples of (non-)logic-based matchmakers: OWLS-iMatcher, SPARQLent. The logic-based semantic matchmaker SPARQLent [13] considers the full semantic service profile. It assumes that preconditions and effects are described in SPARQL and computes their query containment relations, in particular RDF entailment rule-based matching of I/O concepts in OWL. SPARQLent has been developed by Marco Luca Sbodio (Hewlett-Packard EIC, Italy) and achieved a high average precision of 0.72 (0.82) with notably low average response time of 0.8 s.

The non-logic-based semantic matchmaker OWLS-iMatcher [3] performs signature matching based on the text similarities of service signatures and names. For this purpose, it offers a set of classical token-based and edit-based text similarity

---

measures. OWLS-iMatcher has been developed by Christoph Kiefer and Abraham Bernstein (University of Zurich, Switzerland) and achieved its best average precision of 0.67 (0.72) in 2.1 s of response time in average.

Examples of hybrid matchmakers: XSSD, OWLS-SLR lite, SeMa2, OPOS-SUM. The service matchmaker XSSD performs hybrid semantic signature matching based on the computation of logical I/O concept subsumption relations and additional text similarity of service description tags. Service relevance ranking is determined by the degree of logic-based matching followed by the degree of text similarity. XSSD has been developed by Jing Li and Dongjie Chu (U Beihang, China) and achieved a good average precision of 0.79 (0.88) with the second lowest response time of 0.12 s measured in the contest (the lowest one was 0.08 s measured for the matchmaker OPOSSUM).

OWLS-SLR lite is similar to XSSD but computes non-logic-based semantic matching scores as aggregated edge and upward co-topic distances between I/O concepts in the respective service annotation ontologies. OWLS-SLR has been developed by Georgios Meditskos and Nick Bassiliades (U Thessaloniki, Greece) and achieved a comparatively low average precision of 0.69 (0.72) but quite fast with an average response time of 0.46 s.

In contrast to both matchmakers above, the matchmaker SeMa2 (the successor of JIAC-OWLSM) performs a full profile-based service selection. Its hybrid semantic matching of signatures bases on computing logical I/O concept subsumption relations each of which represented by a fixed numeric score and simple string-based similarity of the concept names. The relevance ranking values are determined through linear weighted aggregation of the scores of both types of matching. Logic-based service sepcification matching by SeMa2 is restricted to the structural comparison of preconditions and effects in SWRL, in particular their instance-based containment relations. Since the service ontologies of the test collections used in the contest do not provide any concept instances (ABox), only the performance of SeMa2's signature matching could be evaluated. SeMa2 has been developed by Nils Masuch (TU Berlin, Germany) and achieved a reasonably high average precision of 0.74 (0.89) but with a high average response time of 4.44 s.

The hybrid semantic service matchmaker OPOSSUM [14] combines logic-based with non-logic-based semantic matching of service I/O concepts. The numerical score of the logic-based matching of concepts is combined with the values for their shortest path distance and concept depth (avg. ontology depth) for subsequent ranking. OPOSSUM has been developed by Eran Toch (CMU, USA), Avigdor Gal, Dov Dori (Technion, Israel) and Iris Reinhartz-Berger (Haifa University, Israel). Although its best precision of 0.57 (0.71) is comparatively low it did outrun all other participants in the 2009 edition of the contest with an average response time of 0.08 s.

The matchmaker OPOSSUM is described in more detail in a separate chapter of this part of the volume.

Examples of adaptive hybrid matchmakers: OWLS-MX3, iSeM, OWLS-iMatcher2. The matchmakers OWLS-MX3, iSeM and OWLS-iMatcher2 are the only adaptive hybrid semantic matchmakers that have been evaluated in the S3 contest series so far. While OWLS-MX3 [7] restricts its hybrid semantic selection to semantic service signatures, its successor iSeM processes the full (IOPE) profile of services. OWLS-MX3 adopts the four logic-based I/O concept matching filters of its predecessors OWLS-MX2 and OWLS-MX1 [8], that are logical equal, plugin, subsumes, subsumed-by matching degrees, and applies four different text similarity measures to pairs of unfolded I/O concepts. In addition, it computes numeric scores for ontology-based structural concept similarities. The optimal weighted aggregation of these logic-based and non-logic-based semantic matching filters for relevance decisions and ranking is learned off-line in advance for a given training collections (taken from the test collection) by utilizing a SVM-based (support vector machine) classifier. OWLS-MX3 has been developed by Matthias Klusch and Patrick Kapahnke (DFKI, Germany) and achieved a very high average precision of 0.83 (0.84) but at the cost of a high average response time of 5.37 s.

The adaptive hybrid semantic matchmaker iSeM significantly improves upon the OWLS-MX3 by the utilization of additional non-logic-based matching filters and an evidential coherence-based pruning of the given training set during off-line learning of semantic relevance. Notably, iSeM achieved the best average precision of 0.92 (0.84) that has ever been measured in the S3 contest so far, but with only moderately low response time of 2.34 s in average. The matchmaker iSeM is described in more detail in a separate chapter of this part of the volume.

The adaptive variant of the matchmaker OWLS-iMatcher, the OWLS-iMatcher2, learns off-line in advance which of its token- and edit-based text similarity measures performs best when applied to pairs of semantic service signatures each of which represented as a weighted keyword vector. OWLS-iMatcher2 also performs a hybrid semantic selection in the sense that it computes the text similarities of signatures based on the logical unfoldings of the respective annotation concepts in the shared ontologies. Notably, OWLS-iMatcher2 achieved the second highest average precision for binary relevance (0.84) in the 2009 edition of the S3 contest.

2.3.4 Contest Track 2: SAWSDL Service Matchmakers

The SAWSDL matchmaker track of the S3 contest editions 2007–2010 received eight different SAWSDL matchmakers in total. These are LOG4SWS.KOM, COV4SWS.KOM and COM4SWS (Darmstadt University of Technology, Germany), SAWSDL-MX1, SAWSDL-MX2 [9] and iSeM-SAWSDL (DFKI, Germany), URBE (Politecnico di Milano, Italy) and SAWSDL-iMatcher3 (University of Zurich, Switzerland).

Remarkably, these matchmakers perform either non-logic-based or hybrid semantic service selection. There has been no logic-based semantic service matchmaker submitted to the contest. Since the standard SAWSDL focuses on the annotation of service signatures only, the contested SAWSDL matchmakers perform semantic I/O-based selection only. In the following, we briefly describe some of them as representative examples together with an indication of their best average precision for binary and graded (nDCG measure) relevance and average response times.

Examples of non-logic-based matchmakers: SAWSDL-iMatcher, URBE. The SAWSDL service matchmakers URBE [11] performs non-logic-based signature (I/O) matching based on bipartite graph matching of service (request and offer) operations. In particular, the signature similarity values are computed by means of (a) ontology-based structural I/O concept similarity based on path lengths in a given reference ontology, and (b) WordNet-based text similarity for property class and XSD data type matching of WSDL service elements. The service operation rankings rely on a weighted aggregation of these structural and text matching scores. URBE has been developed by Pierluigi Plebani (Politecnico di Milano, Italy) and has won the SAWSDL track of the contest in 2008 and 2009. It achieved its best average precision with 0.75 (0.85) but also the worst average response time ever measured in this contest (40 s).

SAWSDL-iMatcher3 performs non-logic-based signature matching by applying classic vector model-based text similarity metrics to given pairs of semantic annotations of service I/O parameters. This matchmaker has been developed by Dengping Wei and Avi Bernstein (U Zurich, Switzerland), and its best precision of 0.74 (0.85) was as good as URBE but with significantly better response time in average (1.8 s).

Examples of hybrid semantic matchmakers: LOG4SWS.KOM, iSeM-SAWSDL. The hybrid semantic matchmaker LOG4SWS.KOM performs first a logic-based matching by computing the logical I/O concept subsumption relations represented as numeric scores. This is complemented by means of non-logic-based matching based on the computation of ontology-based structural I/O concept similarities as the shortest path lengths between concepts and using the WordNet distance as a fallback strategy for missing modelReference-tags of element names. The matchmaker has been developed by Stefan Schulte and Ulrich Lampe (Darmstadt University of Technology, Germany). It achieved the second highest precision of 0.837 for binary relevance and the best precision of 0.89 ever measured for SAWSDL matchmakers in the contest and with even the fastest response time in average (0.24 s). The LOG4SWS.KOM matchmaker is described in more detail in a separate chapter of this part of the volume.

The adaptive hybrid semantic matchmaker iSeM-SAWSDL is a variant of the matchmaker iSeM for OWL-S service selection described in the previous section. It processes SAWSDL services and, in contrast to iSeM, performs no specification matching. With an average precision of 0.842 (0.80) this matchmaker won the latest contest by performing slightly better than LOG4SWS.KOM for binary relevance sets, but with an significantly higher response time of 10.7 s in average. Notably, despite its adaptation to the given test collection, for the case of graded relevance the matchmaker iSeM-SAWSDL performed worse in terms of precision than all other tested SAWSDL matchmakers. The analysis of this relatively surprising result is ongoing.

2.4   Selected Results of Comparative Evaluation

The comparative experimental evaluation of the retrieval performance of matchmakers that participated in the S3 contest was done by using the SME2 tool and based on the test collections OWLS-TC and SAWSDL-TC (cf. Sect. 2.2). In this section, we provide selected results of this evaluation focusing on the potential trade offs between average precision and response time for binary and graded relevance, and those for adaptive and non-adaptive semantic service selection. For more detailed results of all editions and those of the special cross-evaluation track of the 2009 edition of the S3 contest, we refer the interested reader to the respective summary reports available at the S3 contest Web site.

Average precision Vs. average response times. The average precisions, nDCG and Q-values, and average query response times of selected OWL-S and SAWSDL matchmakers for editions 2009 and 2010 are summarized in Fig. 2.5.

Please note that the graded relevance sets in the OWLS-TC and SAWSDL-TC are only available since 2009 and 2010, respectively, and some matchmakers like ALIVE and OPOSSUM did not participate in the 2010 edition anymore. We refer to the summary reports of both editions for details. With regard to the measured performance of participants of the S3 contest, there has been a remarkable progress in the development of highly precise semantic service matchmakers since the first edition of the contest in 2007. For example, the best average precision of matchmakers improved from about 0.7 in 2007 to more than 0.9 in 2010. On the other hand, one can observe from Fig. 2.5 that there still is a large trade off between precision and response time: In both tracks, the fastest matchmakers were not necessarily the most precise ones, and vice versa. Another point to make regarding the results shown in Fig. 2.5 is that hybrid semantic matchmakers perform generally better than non-hybrid ones in that they offer service selection with a reasonable trade off between precision and response time like XSSD, LOG4SWS.KOM and iSeM.

However, as it has been shown for the popular semantic service matchmaker OWLS-MX in [8], the evaluation results for the COM4SWS matchmaker variants in the 2009 edition of the contest revealed that hybrid semantic matching may also be less precise than mere logic-based matching. This is particularly the case if the latter is complemented by rather than integrated with syntactic matching in terms of, for example, ontology-based structural or text similarity-based semantic filtering of services.

The average query response times of all contested matchmakers largely differed from 40 s in the worst case for URBE to 0.08 s in the best case for OPOSSUM. Actually, the hybrid matchmaker XSSD whose matching filters are similar to OWLS-MX (cf. Sect. 2.3) seems to offer the comparatively best balance of performance by achieving a moderately high degree of average precision (0.79) and running very fast (0.12 s). As can be seen from Fig. 2.5, its precision has been significantly improved only by (a) the adaptive variant of OWLS-MX, that is OWLS-MX3, and (b) the adaptive hybrid matchmaker iSeM which additionally performs ontology-

2010 (2009)	For binary relevance: AP	For graded relevance: nDCG / Q	Response Time AQRT (in secs)
OWL-S matchmakers:			
iSeM	**0.922**	0.841 / 0.821	2.34
OWLS-MX3	0.831	0.899 / 0.834	5.37
SeMa²	0.741	0.83 / 0.73	4.42
Hybrid XSSD	0.795	0.881 / 0.788	0.12
ALIVE	0.5	0.42 / 0.64	0.26
Opossum	0.57	0.71 / 0.51	0.08
OWLS-SLRlite	0.609	0.723 / 0.57	0.46
Logic SPARQLent	0.718	0.82 / 0.576	0.57
EMMA (OWLS-MX2)	0.803	0.881 / 0.815	11.54
Non-logic OWLS-iMatcher	0.846	0.719 / 0.671	2.15
SAWSDL matchmakers:			
LOG4SWS.KOM	0.837	0.896 / 0.851	0.24
Hybrid COV4SWS.KOM	0.823	0.884 / 0.825	0.30
iSeM-SAWSDL	0.842	0.803 / 0.762	10.66
SAWSDL-MX1	0.747	0.839 / 0.767	3.86
Non-logic URBE	0.749	0.85 / 0.777	40.01
SAWSDL-iMatcher	0.764	0.855 / 0.784	1.79

Fig. 2.5 Best average precisions, nDCG and Q-values with response times

based structural and approximated logical subsumption-based matching – but in any case at the cost of significantly higher response times.

The contest results also revealed that the precision of most matchmakers increase when they are measured against the test collections with graded (using both nDCG and Q measures) rather than binary relevance sets. In particular, by using the discounted cumulative gain (nDCG) most matchmakers perform more precisely for the top positions of their service rank lists.

Another lesson learned was that the full-fledged testing of some of the submitted matchmakers was not possible due to the actual characteristics of the test collections. For example, since none of the annotations of services in the OWLS-TC refer to ontologies with assertional knowledge (ABoxes), the matchmakers SeMa2 and SPARQLent could not perform their kind of specification (PE) matching by means of query containment checking over ABoxes. In addition, we observed only a low increase of precision of full-profile (IOPE) matchmakers compared to those which perform signature matching only. The main reason for that is that only 15% of the service profiles in the OWLS-TC4 include logical preconditions and effects. In fact, the number of cases in which a matchmaker could avoid false positives of semantic I/O matching by additional checking of service specifications (PE) turned out to be that low such that no significant difference in performance between service IOPE- and IO-based matchmakers has been measured. Thus, the call to the community is for extending the test collections with more full service profiles, in particular adding complex logical specifications of preconditions and effects to the semantic annotations of service requests and offers.

With regard to the performance of adaptive and non-adaptive matchmakers, one may observe from the contest results that the former type outperformed the latter in terms of precision in general. Besides, the tested adaptive matchmakers iSeM, OWLS-MX3 and OWLS-iMatcher2 clearly have an edge over the non-adaptive ones by being able to automatically learn offline the best performing combination of their individual matching filters. Though this obviously comes at the cost of prior training time over any given test collection, this apparent disadvantage has to be put into perspective of the potentially huge costs of finding the best filter combination by hand and every time the test collection changes.

Ontology caching strategies. In addition to the selected evaluation results above some further lesson has been learned by mere observation of the tested matchmaker code behavior: Some matchmakers try to reduce their number of time consuming accesses to service annotation ontologies by internal caching of (parts of) ontologies. In fact, according to the results of the experimental http-request behavior analysis of the tested matchmakers with the SME2 tool, one may conclude that different ontology caching strategies did account in part for significant differences in their measured average response times.

For example, the matchmakers XSSD, SeMa2 and OWLS-iMatcher are internally caching the complete set of service annotation ontologies during service registration. This may drastically reduce the number of potentially frequent and high number of external accesses (http-requests) to ontologies during the query processing phase. In fact, the matchmaker only has to get external access to those ontologies it requires to understand the comparatively much fewer service requests of the considered test collection. For the same reason the matchmakers iSeM and OWLS-MX3 are caching not the complete but only the relevant parts of ontologies for matching, that are the logically unfolded, thus self-contained definitions of the service annotation concepts.

2.5 Conclusions

We presented an overview and selected results of the international contest on semantic service selection (S3). The contest runs since 2007 on an annual basis and provides the publicly available S3 evaluation framework that actually includes the standard test collections OWLS-TC and SAWSDL-TC as well as the SME2 tool for automated comparative performance evaluation of semantic service matchmakers.

In general, the progress of development that has been made in the area of semantic service matchmakers is impressive regarding the significant increase of average precision from around 0.6 in 2007 to 0.92 in 2010. Since this increase in precision for most matchmakers is due to the application of more elaborated and complex matching filters and processing of semantic service annotations, this gain comes at the cost of increased average response time, despite reported streamlining of matchmaker implementations. The application of ontology caching strategies by some of the contested matchmakers showed promising results in this respect. Actually, the best trade off between precision and speed that has been achieved in the S3 contest is an average precision of around 0.8 with 0.1 s response time in average. Hybrid semantic matchmaking appears to be established now, while adaptivity appears to be one of the next trends of development in this domain; it certainly provides the developers with a higher degree of freedom by letting matchmakers automatically learn the best performing combination of given service matching filters.

The S3 contest has been exclusively funded by the German Ministry for Education and Research (BMB+F) in the national projects SCALLOPS, MODEST and ISReal. In 2010 the results of the S3 contest were additionally presented at the first SEALS evaluation campaign workshop. The international S3 contest will be further actively supported on demand by its organizational board (cf. Sect. 2.2), in particular by DFKI until 2013 at least.

References

1. S. Dietze, N. Benn, J. Domingue, A. Conconi, F. Cattaneo, Two-fold semantic web service matchmaking – applying ontology mapping for service discovery, in *Proceedings of 4th Asian Semantic Web Conference*, Shanghai, 2009
2. M. Dudev, P. Kapahnke, J. Misutka, M. Vasileski, M. Klusch, SME2: Semantic Service Matchmaker Evaluation Environment. Latest version 2.2 was released on Dec 2, 2010, at semwebcentral: http://projects.semwebcentral.org/projects/sme2/. First version of SME2 was released at semwebcentral on 17 Apr 2008. Online support for the SME2 tool is provided by Patrick Kapahnke DFKI (2007)
3. C. Kiefer, A. Bernstein, The creation and evaluation of iSPARQL strategies for matchmaking, in *Proceedings of the 5th European Semantic Web Conference (ESWC)*, Tenerife, 2008
4. M. Klusch, Semantic web service description, in *CASCOM – Intelligent Service Coordination in the Semantic Web*, ed. by M. Schumacher, H. Helin, Chapter 3 (Birkhäuser Verlag, Springer, Basel, 2008)
5. M. Klusch, Semantic web service coordination, in *CASCOM – Intelligent Service Coordination in the Semantic Web*, ed. by M. Schumacher, H. Helin, Chapter 4 (Birkhäuser Verlag, Springer, Basel, 2008)
6. M. Klusch, K. Sycara, Brokering and matchmaking for coordination of agent societies: a survey, in *Coordination of Internet Agents*, ed. by A. Omicini et al., Chapter 8 (Springer, London, 2001)
7. M. Klusch, P. Kapahnke, OWLS-MX3: an adaptive hybrid semantic service matchmaker for OWL-S, in *CEUR Proceedings of 3rd International Workshop on Semantic Matchmaking and Resource Retrieval (SMR2)*, Washington, 2009
8. M. Klusch, B. Fries, K. Sycara, OWLS-MX: a hybrid semantic web service matchmaker for OWL-S services. Web Semant. **7**(2), 121–133 (2009), Elsevier
9. M. Klusch, P. Kapahnke, I. Zinnikus, Adaptive hybrid semantic selection of SAWSDL services with SAWSDL-MX2. Semant. Web Inf. Syst. **6**(4), 1–26 (2011), IGI Global
10. OWLS-TC: OWL-S service retrieval test collection. Latest version OWLS-TC 4.0 (OWLS-TC4) published on 21 Sept 2010, at semwebcentral: http://projects.semwebcentral.org/projects/owls-tc/. First version of OWLS-TC was created by Benedikt Fries, Mahboob Khalid, Matthias Klusch (DFKI) and published at semwebcentral on 11 Apr 2005

11. P. Plebani, B. Pernici, URBE: web service retrieval based on similarity evaluation. IEEE Trans. Knowl. Data Eng. **21**, 1629–1642 (2010)
12. SAWSDL-TC: SAWSDL service retrieval test collection. Latest version SAWSDL-TC 3.0 (SAWSDL-TC3) published on 22 Sept 2009, at semwebcentral: http://projects.semwebcentral. org/projects/sawsdl-tc/. First version of SAWSDL-TC was created by Patrick Kapahnke, Martin Vasileski, Matthias Klusch (DFKI) and published at semwebcentral on 28 July 2008
13. M.L. Sbodio, D. Martin, C. Moulin, Discovering semantic web services using SPARQL and intelligent agents. Web Semant. **8**(4), 310–328 (2010), Elsevier
14. E. Toch, A. Gal, I. Reinhartz-Berger, D. Dori, A semantic approach to approximate service retrieval. ACM Trans. Internet Technol. (TOIT) **8**(1), 2-es (2007)

Chapter 3
SeMa²: A Hybrid Semantic Service Matching Approach

N. Masuch, B. Hirsch, M. Burkhardt, A. Heßler, and S. Albayrak

Abstract The SeMa² software module is a hybrid semantic service matchmaker based on OWL-S service descriptions and SWRL rules that participated in the S3 Contests 2008–2010. It provides syntactical as well as semantical matching techniques. Besides classifying input and output parameters it offers an approach to precondition and effect rule matching and reasoning. In this chapter we describe the architecture and the workflow of our approach and the results that have been evaluated during the last S3 Contest and with experimental test runs. Finally, we discuss the benefits and drawbacks of our implementation and propose future steps on our work.

3.1 Introduction

The process of service matchmaking is an important issue not only in the context of the Internet and its large quantity of services, but also within other distributed systems, where software programs offer services to other parties. Our intention for the development of a service matchmaker emerged while developing the multi-agent framework JIAC V[1] [6], which eases the development and the operation of large-scale, distributed applications and services. The least requirements to an agent based system and to an agent in particular are autonomy, social ability, reactivity and pro-activeness [12]. Especially the attribute of autonomy indicates that an agent should be able "to operate without the direct intervention of humans or others". This means that agents have to be able to autonomously decide which actions to process, or in

---

[1] www.jiac.de

N. Masuch (✉) · B. Hirsch · M. Burkhardt · A. Heßler · S. Albayrak
DAI-Labor, TU Berlin, Ernst-Reuter-Platz 7, 10587, Berlin, Germany
e-mail: Nils.Masuch@dai-labor.de; Benjamin.Hirsch@dai-labor.de;
Michael.Burkhardt@dai-labor.de; Axel.Heler@dai-labor.de; Sahin.Albayrak@dai-labor.de

M.B. Blake et al. (eds.), *Semantic Web Services*, DOI 10.1007/978-3-642-28735-0_3,
© Springer-Verlag Berlin Heidelberg 2012

other words, which service to select for invocation to reach desired goals. Therefore it is crucial to develop a service matchmaking algorithm that takes semantic service descriptions into account, in order to reach a higher level of precision than by solely considering the syntactic attributes of a service.

Since the ambition of JIAC V is to utilize standardized technologies, we use OWL-S service descriptions [1] into our system, which offer a clear distinction between service profiles based on OWL and service invocation details. Doing so, our matchmaker SeMa^2 matches different OWL-S service descriptions with each other following a hybrid approach by using both, syntactic and semantic matching techniques. In the following we will initially present our approach, which participated in the S3 Contest for the last 3 years (2008–2009 under the name of JIAC-OWLSM), regarding its architecture and the different, underlying matching algorithms. Further we will describe our implementation in detail by addressing the issue of the evaluation function, which accumulates the results of the different matching approaches, and is the basis for ranking the proposed services. We then will evaluate the impact of the different strategies of our matchmaker on the matching preciseness, and we will give a discussion about our evaluation function and its influence on the results. Finally, we point out the advantages and disadvantages of our matchmaker and conclude with improvements that are planned for the future.

3.2 Approach: Hybrid Service Matching

3.2.1 The SeMa^2 Architecture

Figure 3.1 provides an overview of the SeMa^2 architecture. The basic structure of our matching system is quite simple. The interfaces are illustrated as *Sensors* and *Effectors*. The principles of them are the reception of service advertisements and service requests and the return of matching results. In order to apply the matching algorithms to the OWL-S files, they have to be analyzed and serialized based on its relevant parameters, which is realised by the *OWLS-ServiceAnalyser*. All the service advertisements are being stored in memory after the initializing process, allowing a fast access to the description parameters at request time. The matching procedure itself is coordinated by the *MatcherController* instance. It selects the different matching strategies and is responsible for the aggregation of the partial results.

3.2.2 Matching Techniques

Different techniques for matching services with each other have been developed during the last years. When starting our work, it was unclear which approach might lead to the best results. Further, it became clear that service requests might be incomplete in their description and certain techniques would not be

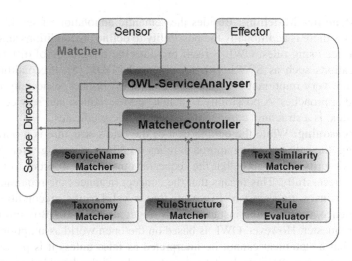

Fig. 3.1 Architecture of SeMa²

applicable in that case. Therefore our aim was to develop a service matchmaker that combines syntactic as well as semantic matching algorithms, which should – after an aggregation process – lead to sufficiently precise results. In the following we present the different matching approaches implemented in SeMa².

- **Service Name Matching:** The service name usually reflects a short identifier of a service, which is described in one, sometimes artificially concatenated, word. The comparison of different service names can be an indicator for their similarity, however it can also lead to misinterpretations, since many services with different functionalities share typical name fragments, such as *GetPriceOf....*. Therefore the syntactical service name matching approach is only utilized in combination with other matching techniques.

- **Text Similarity Matching:** Service descriptions provide additional information to the functionality of a service. In OWL-S a separate tag is defined for it within the profile. The description usually is much longer than the service name and is intended to describe the functionality with service specific nouns embedded in regular sentences. The comparison of entire sentences demands for more complex algorithms than service name matching. These will be presented in Sect. 3.3.

- **Taxonomy Matching:** Input and output parameters can either be simple data types or more complex concepts defined in referenced ontologies. These concepts are structured hierarchically and therefore the matching algorithms are not only able to check for the exact equality of requested and advertised input and output (IO) parameters but also for further taxonomic dependencies between them. The principal techniques for a logic-based matching of the IO parameters are well known [10], however the aggregation of logical results of single parameter comparisons can be implemented by different strategies.

- **Rule Structure Matching:** Besides the semantic annotation of services using ontologies there is additionally the possibility to define preconditions and effects of a service using rules. OWL-S itself provides the integration of different rule specifications such as SWRL [8], KIF [4] and PDDL [5]. Preconditions and effects are very important for the interpretation of services, especially in goal-oriented approaches. A possibility to match service request and service offer in that context is a structural comparison of single rule predicates.
- **Rule Reasoning:** While the comparison of the rule's structure is a pure TBox matching, the rule reasoning approach relies on ABox matching. Preconditions usually describe constraints that the requester must fulfill in order to invoke a service successfully. This means that the concept instances the requester wants to use for invocation must be in a state that is valid to the precondition. As a consequence, the matching instance needs to get all relevant ABox information by the requester. However, OWL is based on the open world assumption, which means that a statement cannot be interpreted as false unless it is proven to be false. This can sometimes lead to wrong results if the knowledge passed to the matcher is incomplete. On the other hand, it seems to be more important to actually recognize requests that do not fulfill the precondition and to filter services avoiding failed invocations.

3.3   Solution: SeMa^2 in Practice

3.3.1   Technological Basis

For the realization of our approach we employed different tools. For the parsing of OWL-S files and the extraction of relevant parameters we used OWL API [7], the taxonomic and rule reasoning algorithms are processed with the help of the Pellet Reasoner [11]. Our text similarity matching approach relies on different text comparison techniques, such as Levenshtein, JaroWinkler and Jaccard. All these algorithms have been integrated with the help of the SimMetrics^2 library.

3.3.2   Process Workflow

Figure 3.2 presents the process workflow of a service request for SeMa^2 as a BPMN diagram. After a query reception the request is analyzed regarding its relevant parameters and is compared with each of the registered service descriptions. At first the amount of requesting and advertising IO parameter are compared with each other. For example, if the number of requesting input parameter is less than

---

^{2}http://staffwww.dcs.shef.ac.uk/people/S.Chapman/simmetrics.html

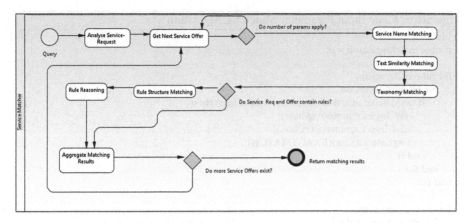

Fig. 3.2 The SeMa² workflow as a BPMN diagram

the advertising ones, the process skips to the next service offer. In other cases the process moves on to the different syntactic and semantic matching algorithms. Finally the partial results are aggregated to a complete rating of a request/offer pair and the process continues with the next service offer.

In the following we are showing how the different matching techniques that have been described in the Approach section are implemented within SeMa².

- **Service Name Matching:** The service names of service request and service offer are being processed by using simple string comparison techniques. Four different results can be evaluated: *EXACT* (request and offer are identical), *CONTAINS* (request name is part of the service offer name), *ISCONTAINED* (request name contains service offer name), *FAILURE* (request and offer differ in their names).
- **Text Similarity Matching:** The SeMa² text similarity measurement is based on different distance techniques, such as Levenshtein, Jaro-Winkler and Jaccard [2]. Each of these algorithms compare two string arrays and return a similarity measurement result between 0 and 1. In our approach we compute the arithmetic average of all the single results. The resulting value is then mapped to a overall text similarity result.
- **Taxonomy Matching:** The input and output parameter of a service on the one hand indicate which information is technically needed for a service invocation and on the other hand the parameter can specify which topic the service belongs to. By using OWL ontologies for the definition of input and output parameters there are different possibilities of computing taxonomic dependencies between them. SeMa² follows the approach of Paolucci et al. [10] by categorizing the degrees of a match into *EXACT, PLUGIN, SUBSUMES* and *FAILED*. In contrast to Paolucci's approach input and output matching results are rated equally. Further, as Algorithm 1 shows, when comparing services with multiple parameters there is not a categorization into one of the matching degrees. In fact, each matching level is mapped to a numerical value and after matching all

---

Algorithm 1 The Input Parameter Matching Algorithm

List singleResults;
double matchingResult = 0;

for all reqClasses **do**
    for all advClasses **do**
        if taxMatcher.exactMatch(reqClass, advClass) **then**
            reqClasses.remove(reqClass);
            advClasses.remove(advClass);
            singleResults.add(EXACTMATCH);
        end if
    end for
end for

for all reqClasses **do**
    for all advClasses **do**
        if taxMatcher.subMatch(reqClass, advClass) **then**
            reqClasses.remove(reqClass);
            advClasses.remove(advClass);
            singleResults.add(SUBMATCH);
        end if
    end for
end for

for all reqClasses **do**
    for all advClasses **do**
        if taxMatcher.superMatch(reqClass, advClass) **then**
            reqClasses.remove(reqClass);
            advClasses.remove(advClass);
            singleResults.add(SUPERMATCH);
        end if
    end for
end for

for all reqClasses **do**
    singleResults.add(FAILED);
end for

for all singleResults **do**
    matchingResult += overallResult;
end for

matchingResult = matchingResult / singleResults.size;

return matchingResult;

---

parameters the arithmetic average is computed. This leads to more differentiated results neglecting a clear categorization into one of the matching degrees.

- **Rule structure matching:** The rule structure matching, similar to the IO parameter matching algorithm, checks whether the structure of the preconditions and (main) effects of the service request correspond to the ones of the service offer. Doing so, this matching technique can evaluate whether the proposed service might fulfill the requester's goals. In our approach, preconditions and effects are represented by the Semantic Web Rule Language (SWRL). SeMa² parses this information with the help of the OWL API libraries and categorizes the rules into preconditions and effects. SWRL rule bodies are structured as conjuncts of atoms, which themselves can consist of Classes, Object Properties, Datatype Properties or SWRL built-ins. A simple example is the following precondition for a valid Email service:

$$EmailAddress(?a), hasStringIdentifier(?a, ?b), contains(?b, "@")$$

SeMa² extracts the atoms of a rule and compares the ones of a service request rule and of a service offer rule with each other. In doing so the atoms are being compared regarding its taxonomic dependencies (like input/output matching). Furthermore a theta-subsumption verification [3] is being processed, which checks whether the variables of the atoms are set correspondingly and the atoms of one rule are subsumed by the other. The result of a rule structure match is evaluated by checking which of the requesting atoms has the worst taxonomical match to the corresponding service offer's atom provided that the theta-subsumption verification has been positive. The corresponding matching value regarding the taxonomical similarity is returned as the rule structure result.

- **Rule reasoning:** The goal of the rule reasoning algorithm is to recognize whether the requesting instance fulfills the services' preconditions before the invocation of the service. Therefore the requester transmits all relevant knowledge for service invocation (parameter individuals) to the service matcher. In order to perform rule reasoning with the help of the Pellet reasoner the rule has to be modified. For all variables a generic predicate "fulfills" is inserted into the head of the rule. For the example of the rule structure matching algorithm the rule would look as follows:

$$EmailAddress(?a), hasStringIdentifier(?a, ?b), contains(?b, "@") ->$$
$$fulfills(?a), fulfills(?b)$$

SeMa² adds the requesters' knowledge and the relevant rule to Pellet's knowledge base and starts the classification. If any individuals (the requester's parameter instances) do fulfill the rule they will be extended with the temporary predicate "fulfills". If so, the rule reasoning is rated successfully. Like mentioned before, our algorithm expects that the requester transmits all necessary knowledge to the service matcher instance. This might not always be possible due to security issues or large data structures, but in all other cases the rule reasoning technique provides a solid solution to verify that the requester fulfills the preconditions to invoke a certain service successfully.

- **Evaluation Function:** The evaluation function computes an aggregated matching quality rating between service request and service offer. This value is the basis for sorting the service options regarding its suitability. Since the SeMa² matcher follows a hybrid matching approach, different partial results have to be concentrated to one overall result. In our case we calculate the result by aggregating the partial results weighting them regarding the importance of each matching technique. In our actual implementation the determination of the weighting has been done by steadily evaluating the impact of each matching technique to the result quality when using the OWLS-TC four test collection[3] for matching. As a result the input and output parameter matching are each being weighted by 25%, the service name matching by 10% and the text similarity matching by 40%. The rule structure and the rule reasoning matching modules have not been considered into the evaluation function for the S3 Contests since in the years 2008 and 2009 the Test Collection did not provide any rules for matching and the structure of the rules within the 2010 S3 Contest had a syntactic structure that our API was not able to read. Therefore we have not yet evaluated which weighting impact these matching techniques should have.

3.4   Lessons Learned

3.4.1   Evaluation Results

3.4.1.1   S3 Contest 2010

SeMa[2] participated in the S3 Contest 2010 for OWL-S Services and achieved middle-ranking results regarding its accumulated precision.[4] But when regarding the detailed Recall/Precision curves of the different participants, it becomes apparent that the precision for low recall values of SeMa[2] is very high. It actually has the best precision values until a recall value of about 0.125. This means that the quality of the first results to a request is quite good. As in most practical scenarios the requesting instance is just searching for the best matched service offer, this indicates that our approach might be appropriate for the usage in a realistic context. Furthermore the results reveal that the Average Query Response Time is quite high with 4.4 s per request. We will analyze that issue in one of the following subsections.

3.4.1.2   Evaluation Results of Different Matching Techniques

In order to evaluate, which matching techniques of our hybrid approach do have which impact on the overall results, we tested different setups of SeMa[2] by using the SME2[5] tool and OWLS-TC 4. Figure 3.3 shows the results of the test runs.

---

[3]http://projects.semwebcentral.org/projects/owls-tc/
[4]http://www-ags.dfki.uni-sb.de/~klusch/s3/s3c-2010-summary-report-v2.pdf
[5]http://projects.semwebcentral.org/projects/sme2/

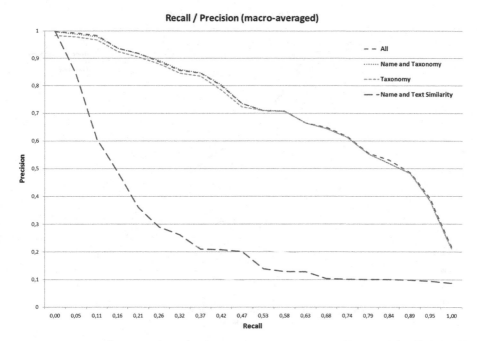

Fig. 3.3 The SeMa² recall/precision results

Altogether four different configurations have been evaluated:

- **SeMa2_Name_TextSim:** *Service Name Matching* and *Text Similarity Matching* are activated
- **SeMa2_Taxonomy:** *Taxonomy Matching* is activated
- **SeMa2_TaxSName:** *Service Name Matching* and *Taxonomy Matching* are activated
- **SeMa2_All:** *Service Name Matching*, *Text Similarity Matching* and *Taxonomy Matching* are activated

The configuration SeMa2_Name_TextSim, which only relies on text similarity measurements, indeed starts with a high precision value, but falls off very quickly. In contrast to that the curves of the other three configurations continue very similar on a much higher precision level, which makes them hard to distinguish in the diagram. Figure 3.4 takes a deeper look at these curves for low recall values. It shows that the taxonomy matching on IO parameters is the fundament for the overall results. However, the results become better (especially for low recall values) when adding service name and text similarity matching to the configuration. This indicates that the combination of different matching techniques might be superior than the concentration on a single approach.

The matching techniques *Rule Structure Matching* and *Rule Reasoning* have not been evaluated in these test runs, since the syntax of the SWRL rules within the

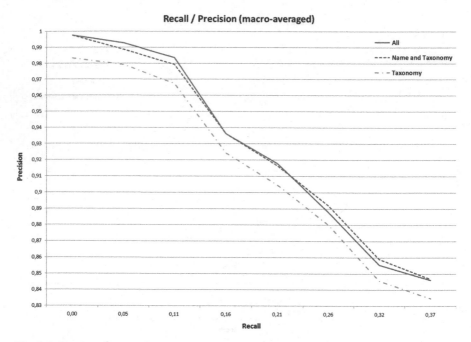

Fig. 3.4 The SeMa^2 recall/precision results for low recall values

test collection is not the one that is expected by the OWL API. Therefore we were not able yet to test these matching techniques on a large test collection but only on specific services for development purposes.

3.4.1.3 Time Consumption

As described before, the average response time of SeMa^2 is quite high. Therefore we analyzed our approach by measuring the time needed for different tasks and modules. Table 3.1 presents the results of the test run. The most time consuming task by far within SeMa^2 is the Taxonomy Matching of Input and Output parameters with more than 80% of the overall query time. Since the initialization and loading of ontologies into the reasoner has been measured separately and was fairly low with a time consumption of 7.7%, it indicates that the taxonomic reasoning itself might be the bottleneck.

3.4.2 Advantages and Disadvantages

The evaluation of SeMa^2 has shown that it provides one of the best precision values for the first few rankings of a result list, which means that the probability to automatically invoke an appropriate match is very high. On the other hand the

Table 3.1 Time effort of the different matching tasks

Description	Time in ms	Time in %
Service request analysis	1,453	1.1
Reasoner initialization	10,213	7.7
Service name matching	63	<1.0
Text similarity matching	11,093	8.4
Taxonomy matching	105,259	80.1
Overall query processing time	131,382	100.0

precision is declining faster than the best matchmakers for higher recall values. The question arises how important it is to find all possible matches, when the requesting instance will probably only need the best ones.

The SeMa² registration phase of the service offers is actually very fast. Since this value is not measured by the SME2 test environment, we do not have any comparisons, but in our case it took about 10 s to register the 1,083 services of the OWLS-TC 4 on a Lenovo Thinkpad T410s. However, as described before, the average query response time is quite high.

The modular structure of SeMa² allows the flexible integration of additional matching techniques. The actual evaluation function seems to be quite good adapted to the test collection, although the weighting has been done manually by multiple test runs. Therefore it is unclear if this truly has led to the best aggregation of the different modules. Furthermore the rule matching techniques are actually not integrated into the evaluation function, which comes apparent when the test collection rules can be parsed by SeMa².

3.4.3 Conclusions and Future Work

The results of SeMa² and other service matchers within the S3 Contest 2010 have shown that hybrid matching approaches seem to be the most competitive ones regarding the precision. However, a tradeoff for a good precision value seems to be a higher average response time, which in our case is caused by the taxonomical reasoning of the IO parameters. We will further investigate if there is a possibility to reduce the processing time by simplifying the taxonomic matching approach. On the other hand the taxonomic matching might become more precise if we do not just check for subsumption or plugin of concepts, but also check the depth of dependence between them.

Another open issue is the optimal aggregation of the different matching techniques. At present SeMa² is based on a weighted, linear aggregation that has been evaluated by manually testing different weightings on the OWLS-TC. It would be desirable to develop a machine learning algorithm that adapts its weighting by training. Klusch et al. [9] already proposed adaptive techniques within their matchmakers OWLS-MX3 and iSeM 1.0.

SeMa² already provides techniques for the reasoning on preconditions and effects. In the future we plan to integrate these techniques into the evaluation function. Especially for the intended usage of SeMa² within the multi-agent framework JIAC it is very important to reason on PE parameters, since we want to support goal-oriented algorithms and service composition strategies. Further the PE matching could solve some of the ambiguity issues between services.

3.5 Summary

In this chapter we proposed SeMa², a hybrid service matchmaker that is based upon OWL-S service descriptions with additional rule information in SWRL. For the evaluation it uses different service data, such as service name, service description and the input/output/precondition/effect (IOPE) parameters. Syntactic as well as semantic matching techniques are being processed and finally aggregated to a matching result.

We proposed the modular architecture and the process workflow of SeMa² and interpreted the results of the S3 Contest 2010 as well as of autonomous experiments on the impact of the different matching techniques and the time consumption. We showed that the semantic matching technique has a large impact on the quality of the result with the tradeoff of a slower average query response time. Further we presented our matching approaches on SWRL rules, which have not been tested on a large test collection yet due to syntactic incompatibilities.

References

1. A. Barstow, J. Hendler, M. Skall, J. Pollock, D. Martin, V. Marcatte, D.L. McGuinness, H. Yoshida, D. De Roure, OWL-S: semantic markup for web services (2004), http://www. w3.org/Submission/OWL-S/
2. J. Euzenat, P. Shvaiko, *Ontology Matching* (Springer, Berlin, 2007)
3. P.A. Flach, Logical approaches to machine learning – an overview. Think **1**, 25–36 (1992)
4. M. Genesereth. Knowledge interchange format. Proposed Draft, 1998
5. A. Gerevini, D. Long, Plan constraints and preferences in PDDL3 – the language of the fifth international planning competition. Technical report, University of Brescia, Italy, 2005
6. B. Hirsch, T. Konnerth, A. Heßler, Merging agents and services – the JIAC agent platform, in *Multi-Agent Programming: Languages, Tools and Applications*, ed. by R.H. Bordini, M. Dastani, J. Dix, A. El Fallah Seghrouchni (Springer, Berlin, 2009), pp. 159–185
7. M. Horridge, S. Bechhofer, O. Noppens, Igniting the OWL 1.1 touch paper: the OWL API, in *OWLED 2007: Proceedings of the Third International Workshop on OWL: Experiences and Directions*, Innsbruck, 2007
8. I. Horrocks, P.F. Patel-Schneider, H. Boley, S. Tabet, B. Grosof, M. Dean, SWRL: a semantic web rule language combining OWL and ruleML. *W3C Member Submission*, World Wide Web Consortium, 2004
9. M. Klusch, P. Kapahnke, iSem: approximated reasoning for adaptive hybrid selection of semantic services, in *ESWC (2)*, ed. by L. Aroyo, G. Antoniou, E. Hyvönen, A. ten Teije,

H. Stuckenschmidt, L. Cabral, T. Tudorache. Lecture Notes in Computer Science, vol. 6089 (Springer, Berlin/New York, 2010), pp. 30–44

10. M. Paolucci, T. Kawmura, T. Payne, K. Sycara, M. Paolucci, T. Kawamura, T.R. Payne, K. Sycara, Semantic matching of web services capabilities. in *The Semantic Web – ISWC 2002: First International Semantic Web Conference*, ed. by I. Horrocks J. Hendler. Proceedings, LNCS, vol. 2342, Sardinia, 9–12 June 2002

11. E. Sirin, B Parsia, B.C. Grau, A Kalyanpur, Y Katz, Pellet: A practical OWL-DL reasoner. J. Web Semant. **5**(2), 51–53 (2007)

12. M. Wooldridge, N.R. Jennings, Intelligent agents: theory and practice. Knowl. Eng. Rev. **10**(2), 115–152 (1995)

Chapter 4
OPOSSUM: Indexing Techniques for an Order-of-Magnitude Improvement of Service Matchmaking Times

Eran Toch

Abstract Indexing is a primary technique for enhancing the performance of search engines, databases and other data-intensive applications. In this chapter, we show how ontology-based indexing can be used to enhance the performance of matchmakers for semantic Web services. We provide an overview of the indexing architecture, and describe how ontologies can be used as the basis of index structures that enable sub-linear query inference process. We describe several key tradeoffs that characterize the index, such as the tradeoff between scalability and precision. We demonstrate our method by describing OPOSSUM, an index-based matchmaker, which was the fastest matchmaker at the 2009 International Semantic Service Selection Contest (S3).

4.1 Introduction

One of the great challenges in semantic Web service (SWS) matchmaking is the response time in which service advertisements are matched with service queries. A slow matching process would limit the possible applications of service matchmaking, while a quick matching process would enable new usage scenarios such as iterative matching and selection. SWS matchmaking methods are mostly based on online algorithms, which create in-memory data structures. These include works such as LARKS by Sycara et al. [8], OWLS-MX by Klusch et al. [7], iSPARQL by Kiefer et al. [4] and SAM [1]. In contrast, our approach relies on service and ontology indexing to cache possible outcome of matchmaking results. The ontology indexing allows service matching queries to be efficiently processed, resulting in sub-linear runtime complexity for service matchmaking.

E. Toch (✉)
Tel Aviv University, Tel Aviv, Israel
e-mail: erant@post.tau.ac.il

M.B. Blake et al. (eds.), *Semantic Web Services*, DOI 10.1007/978-3-642-28735-0_4,   49
© Springer-Verlag Berlin Heidelberg 2012

OPOSSUM (Object-PrOcess-SemanticS Unified Matching), the implementation of our indexing and matching approach, is an index-based hybrid matchmaker, based on standard relational database technologies. The advantages of service indexing are exemplified by the performance of OPOSSUM, which was the fastest matchmaker at 2009 International Semantic Service Selection Contest (S3). Our indexing approach indexes the service, including the concepts from the underlying ontologies of each service. Queries for semantic Web services are transformed to queries about ontology concepts, and are evaluated against the indexed ontology. Approximate matching is achieved by broadening the set of annotating ontology concepts of the service parameters with semantically related concepts. Additional approximation is achieved by text matching techniques.

The evaluation of our indexing approach in the context of the SWS matching contest provides insightful information about the design of our index. We discuss the scalability of OPOSSUM, relying on data collected in the process of the contest. We show that under several straightforward assumptions, OPOSSUM's index size is linear to the number of indexed services. These assumptions, which can intuitively defined as the sparsity of semantic relations in the ontology, are fully supported by all the OWL ontologies in the OWLS-TC test collection.[1] The scalability of the index is related to the characteristics of the services' underlying ontologies: the more concepts shared between services, the more compact is the index, as concepts are indexed once for several services.

We start this chapter by providing an overview of our indexing approach, the data structures that are used by the indexing algorithm, and the way the matching certainty is calculated and used to rank matching results. We follow by providing a detailed description of the implementation of OPOSSUM, showing how relational databases can be used for SWS indexing. We then describe several results regarding the scalability and complexity of OPOSSUM, highlighting the advantages and disadvantages of our approach. We conclude the chapter by providing directions for future research, specifically calling attention to open questions in SWS indexing for hybrid matchmakers.

4.2 Approach: Ontological Service Indexing

Our approach aims to optimize service matching response times while providing good precision and recall. It strive to fulfill this goal by matching services using a **service index** that caches the service parameters and their underlying ontology model. The theoretical model and supporting experimental evidence is presented

---

[1]The OWL-S service retrieval test collection OWLS-TC v2 consists of more than 570 services specified in OWL-S 1.1 covering seven application domains, and obtained from public IBM UDDI registries and semi-automatically transformed from WSDL to OWL-S. The collection can be found at: http://projects.semwebcentral.org/projects/owls-tc/

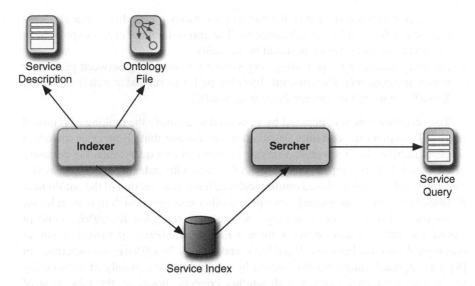

Fig. 4.1 The architecture of SWS indexing mechanism. The **Indexer** and the **Searcher** work independently to create index entries for new services and ontologies and to match queries with services using the index

in [9]. The main data structure used for matching single services is a hash-based index that maps concepts to their associated services, allowing efficient evaluation of service queries.

The matchmaking architecture is based of two independent components: **Indexer** and **searcher**. As depicted in Fig. 4.1, the indexer crawls semantic Web services descriptions in OWL-S and their associated ontologies, indexing all annotating concepts (concepts related to the service parameters,) keeping their mapping to the original services. The results are stored in *ServiceIndex*, a relational database that holds the index. When a query is sent to our matchmaker, in the form of a set of input and output service parameter concepts, the searcher tries to find matching concepts in *ServiceIndex*, and retrieves the relevant services that are mapped to this query's concepts.

A major challenge for SWS indexing is matching approximation. As increasing evidence shows, usable SWS matchmaking should include measures of approximation [6, 10]. In our approach we support hybrid matchmaking, according to the classification provided by Klusch [5]. The framework distinguishes between matchmaking based on ontological processing and matchmaking based on other method (such as text matching.) Our approach combines both methods, and therefore it is classified as hybrid approach. Our approach provides two mechanisms for approximation:

• Relaxing ontological relations when retrieving services according to I/O (inputs and outputs) queries. This is achieved by expanding the *ServiceIndex* with concepts which are related to the parameter concepts, including super concepts (on the is-a hierarchy) and sub concepts. The approximation level is expressed as a certainty measure which is stored in the index.

- Relaxing matching by providing very simple text matching between parameter names and concepts. The retrieval algorithm performs subtext search (i.e., finding *TaxedPrice* when the concept *Price* is queried).

The certainty function, denoted by γ, is used to quantify the ranking of returned results. To explain the certainty calculation, we assume that all services include a single parameter. If an advertised service is identical to a query, then the certainty of the match is 1, the upper bound for the function. Our indexing schema provides certainty evaluation for relaxed ontological relations, as a function of the ontological distance between the annotated concept and other concepts which may be relevant to the query. For example, matching a service that returns a *TaxedPrice* concept would also match a service that returns a *EuropeTaxedPrice*, if there is a strong ontological relation between *TaxedPrice* and *EuropeTaxedPrice*. As described in [9], our approach quantifies this notion by measuring the certainty of substituting the service parameter concept with another concept, based on the relaxation of ontological relations. In the version of OPOSSUM used in the evaluation, the subsumption is relaxed in both generalization directions: concepts can be exchanged with concepts which are subsumed or more general. This type of approximation was tested and found feasible in a user study [10]. For example, *TaxedPrice* can be exchanged with *EuropeTaxedPrice* or *Price*, as long as the certainty is above a constant threshold.

Given a concept C_1 representing a service parameter, let C_i be a concept i steps away from C_1 in the corresponding subsumption hierarchy. The certainty of relevance of the concept C_i is given by:

$$\gamma_{C_1}(C_i) = 1 - log(1 + i) \tag{4.1}$$

γ attaches a decreasing logarithmic value to the number of steps from C_1 to C_i. C_1 is the service parameter concept and C_i is a referring concepts. If the value of $\gamma_{C_1}(C_i)$ is high enough, then a service which has a parameter of C_i can substitute the original service, and can be returned by the matchmaker to answer a user's query. The indexing mechanism calculates $\gamma_{C_1}(C_i)$ for every feasible concept C_i in the knowledge base, which contains all the known ontologies to the matchmaker. The concept C_i is indexed in the services index as related to C_1 if the certainty of that match is higher than a threshold, T, such that $\gamma_{C_1}(C_i) > T$. Thresholding is a straightforward way to trim the index size by not including concepts which are too distanced, and thus, too uncertain for matching. T is constant, identical in the whole index, and is set in our implementation to 0.3. This value was experimentally evaluated to maximize the precision and recall of the matchmaker.

4.3   Solution: OPOSSUM Search Engine

OPOSSUM implements our indexing approach using simple relational database technologies.[2] As OPOSSUM was intended to be used as a reference implementation of our approach, we had focused on simplicity and standardization. We believe that SWS matchmaking can be implemented using standard information system technologies such as relational databases, Web services and object oriented programming. Therefore, the implementation is based on MySQL 5.0 as a database server, Apache Tomcat as a Web application server, and the Java programming language. The experimental results presented in this paper were obtained on a personal computer, with a 2.4 GHz Intel Core 2 Duo processor and 2 GB of memory.

The index is based on a hash table, where each entry represents a concept, pointing to a service. The index is described in Fig. 4.2 and exemplified in Fig. 4.3. Formally, *ServiceIndex* embodies a mapping function, which we define as:

$$ServiceIndex : C \times \{in, out\} \rightarrow G_N$$

C defines the keys of the index: a set of concepts that are stored in the concepts table. The tuple $\{in, out\}$ is stored in the attributes table and defines the type of the attribute: input or output attribute. G_N is a set of service entries in the services table. Each mapping is associated with a certainty function, $\gamma : ServiceIndex \rightarrow [T, 1]$, reflecting the semantic affinity between the query concept and the concepts of the service. Concepts that serve as keys of *ServiceIndex* are derived from the service model. For instance, *Price* is associated with an output parameter of the *ToyotaCar Price Service* service, with a certainty of $\gamma = 1$. The certainty is at its upper bound as the service is directly annotated by the *Price* concept, as can be seen in the visual depiction of the ontology in Fig. 4.4. *MaxPrice* is associated with the same service as an output parameter of *ToyotaCar Price Service*, with $\gamma = 0.562$. In this case, γ reflects a lower certainty, originating from the fact that *MaxPrice* is not connected directly to the service, but is a descended class of *Price*. The distance between the *MaxPrice* concept and the *Price* concept is 1, because *MaxPrice* is a direct descendant of *price*.

ServiceIndex is expanded with additional concepts that convey a broader meaning, in order to retrieve approximate services. For example, in Fig. 4.3, the concept *Price* is expanded with other concepts (e.g., *MaxPrice, RecommendedPrice, TaxedPrice*), each with different ontological distance and relation type. We call these concepts represented in the index as **reference concepts**. The relation type property in the concepts table captures the type of semantic relation used for approximation. (e.g., Self is the concept itself, descend is a descendant class, ascend is a parent class.) The distance column stores the distance between the referenced and

---

[2]The code of OPOSSUM is distributed under open-source license, and can be downloaded from http://projects.semwebcentral.org/projects/opossum/. A description of OPOSSUM's indexing and retrieval methods is presented at [9].

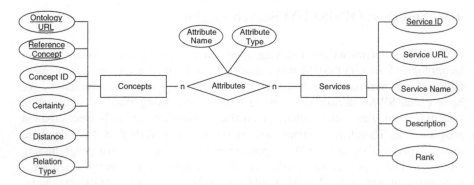

Fig. 4.2 A relational model of the main parts of the service index, using entity relationship diagram. The services table stores information about the services, the attributes table maps services to the concepts by way of their parameter types, and the concepts table stores information about the concepts. Semantic approximation is achieved by adding relevant concepts in the concepts table. Note that the concepts table is de-normalized, in order to provide fast text search over the table without using joins

Ontology Url	ReferenceConcept	ConceptId	Relation Type	Distance	Certainty
http://...	Price	101950	Self	0	1.000
http://...	MaxPrice101950		Descend	1	0.562
http://...	RecommendedPrice	101950	Descend	2	0.562
http://...	TaxedPrice	101950	Descend	2	0.562
http://...	TaxFreePrice	101950	Descend	2	0.562
http://...	EuropeTaxedPrice	101950	Descend	2	0.401
http://...	GermanTaxedPrice	101950	Descend	2	0.401

Concepts Table

Service ID	Concept ID	Element Type	Param Name
5308	101950	Output	_PRICE
5312	101950	Output	_PRICE
5314	101950	Output	_PRICE
5359	101950	Output	_PRICE
5360	101950	Output	_PRICE
5362	101950	Output	_PRICE
5364	101950	Output	_PRICE
5365	101950	Output	_PRICE

Attributes Table

Service	URL	ServiceName	rank
5307	http://...	CannonCameraPriceService	4
5308	http://...	WallmartCPriceService	3
5312	http://...	Red Ferrari price service	3
5314	http://...	ToyotaCar Price service	3
5359	http://...	MianMarkt ShoppingService	3
5360	http://...	Car Price service	2
5362	http://...	Car Price service	2
5364	http://...	Car Price service	1
5365	http://...	Car Price service	1

Services Table

Fig. 4.3 An example of *ServiceIndex*, including all the three tables modeled in Fig. 4.2. The tables exemplifies the way approximation is achieved by adding multiple references (e.g., *MaxPrice*, *RecommendedPrice*, *TaxedPrice*) to the concept **Price** in the Concept Index table

annotated concept, in terms of the interconnected concepts. The relation type and distance properties are served primarily for calculating the certainty value.

Expanding the index is carried out through the index construction process, in which a basic set of concepts is expanded with concepts that increase the retrieval scope of the index. At the first step the indexing algorithm traverses all the parameters of an service, adding the parameter's concept to the index. At the second

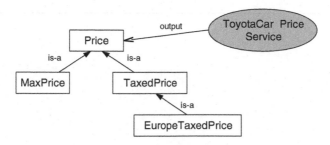

Fig. 4.4 A partial depiction of the *Concept* OWL ontology in the OWLS-TC collection. The service *ToyotaCar Price Service* has an output concept of *Price*. The concept *Price* has too sub-concepts, *TaxedPrice* and *MaxPrice*, and *TaxedPrice* has a sub-concept of its own: *EuropeTaxedPrice*

step, the algorithm recursively adds index entries for concepts that are connected to the parameter's concepts, until all concepts with a certainty higher than the threshold T are found.

4.4   Lessons Learned

In this section, we analyze the lessons learned from the SWS evaluation process. In particular, we discuss the index space complexity analysis, and tradeoffs between index design and matching performance.

4.4.1   Evaluation Results

In this section, we will highlight some results obtained by testing OPOSSUM in the SWS evaluation contest. We start by analyzing the time and space complexity of our solution. As indexing shifts complexity from time to space, we are interested to examine the size of the index and the patterns of index growth. Figure 4.5 depicts the relation between the number of indexed services and the total number of entries in the concepts index. The graph was obtained when adding OWLS-TC 2 services to the index. The graph shows that the growth of the index is linear to the number of services indexed with a steady rate of $\sim$30 index entries per service. The worst case scenario of indexing space is much higher. Imagine the following scenario: each service parameter is annotated using a concept in an individual ontology, and each ontology is a fully connected component. In this case, given n services, m parameters per service, and $O(k)$ concepts in each ontology, the number of index entries would be $nmO(k)$. Given that each service have an average of two parameters, and the average number of concepts in an ontology in the contest collection is 150, we can expect at the worst case 180,000 index entries per 600

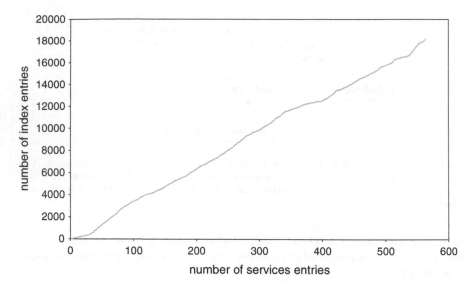

Fig. 4.5 A chart of the number of index entries as a function of the number of indexed services, showing a linear growth of the index when adding new services

services. Instead, there is one tenth of that number. What are the reasons? We attribute this ratio to two aspects of the indexing approach:

1. Concept sharing: concepts are shared by several services, and thus eliminate the need to index them multiple times. For example, is several services have an output parameter of *Price*, this concept can be indexed only once.
2. Bounded ontology expansions: thresholding trims the index size by eliminating concepts which would have low certainty from being indexed. This process bounds the size of the index with respect to the structure of the ontology.

In evaluating OPOSSUM, we observe that the services in the contest share ontologies and concepts by a large degree. Concept sharing has two aspects: first, and as mentioned above, parameters which are shared by several services are indexed only once. Only 8.3% of the service parameters are not reused by other services. Therefore, 91.7% of the service parameter concepts are shared between at least two parameters.

Second, as semantically-related concepts (referencing concepts) are indexed with service parameter concepts, the indexing algorithms stores the referencing concepts only once for each service parameter concept. We define the set of reference concepts that are indexed in reference to an individual annotated service's parameter concept, as the **concept neighborhood** of the annotated concept. As displayed in Table 4.1, the average size of the concept neighborhoods is 54.46.

Investigating the index structure and content shows a power law distribution of the concept's neighborhood size, as Fig. 4.6 exemplifies. Some concepts, such as the generic "Artifact" or "Position" in the SUMO ontology, or "PreparedFood" in

Table 4.1 Descriptive statistics about the Service Index

Property	Mean	SD
Distance between concepts	1.72	1.35
Certainty	0.55	0.23
Indexing neighborhood size	54.46	198.13

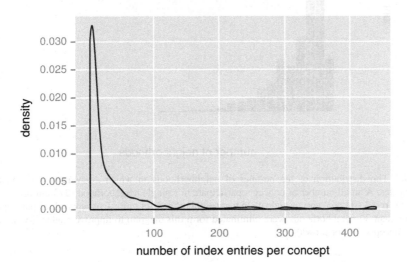

Fig. 4.6 The density graph of index entries per a service's parameter concept. The graph depicts the proportions of concepts with one index entries, two index entries, three index entries and so forth. The graph also represents the size of the concepts' indexed neighborhood

the Mid-Level ontology, are indexed hundreds of times more than other concepts. Some concepts are shared by many services, while others are shared by only a few, or sometimes a single service. The hierarchical nature of ontologies is also echoed in the index. Concepts which are higher up the abstraction levels are indexed as relevant to more services.

The amount of sharing in the system can be analyzed using Fig. 4.7. A small number of concepts participate in a single neighborhood (273 out of 3,284), while the rest 3,011 concepts participate two neighborhoods or more. Nine hundred thirty nine concepts are shared between two neighborhoods – the most common distribution, followed by 578 concepts that are shared between three neighborhoods. The characteristics of concept sharing depends on the semantics of services and the structure of ontologies. The index structure reflects the contest evaluation dataset, in which most service parameter are annotated by shared concepts. This property is not arbitrary, and originate from the common domains that services are based upon. As common domains are essential for interoperation, a major characteristic of Web services, it is likely that the indexing approach can produce compact indexes in real world service repositories.

Another reason for the bounded index size originates from the small world features of the ontology. In a small world graph, the diameter of the graph (the

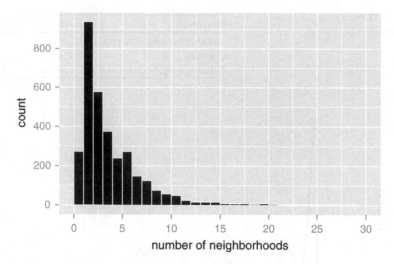

Fig. 4.7 The distribution of the number of neighborhoods in which every reference concept participates. A small number of concepts participate in a single neighborhood (273 out of 3,284), while the rest 3,011 concepts participate in two neighborhoods or more. Concepts which participate in more than 30 neighborhoods were eliminated form this diagram to improve readability (a total of 64 concepts are not shown)

greatest distance between any pair of vertices) is bounded. In other words, most nodes in small world graphs are not neighbors of one another, but can be reached from every other by a small number of steps. The ontologies in OWLS-TC are small world graphs, which means that the average distance between every two concepts is small. Furthermore, the number of semantic relations is small, resulting in a sparse graph. These two features allows us to bound the size of the index as the number of referencing concepts for each service parameter is relatively small.

Figure 4.8 depicts the ratio between semantic distance and certainty. The ratio follows (4.1), which defines the certainty for the indexed concepts. The certainty depends on the semantic distance between the annotated service parameter concept (C_1) and the referred concept (C_i). Table 4.1 provides some description on the semantic distance in the index, which has an average of 1.72, pointing to a relatively short paths of indexed services. Longer paths might improve recall but harm the scalability of the index. However, the longest path found in all of OWLS-TC 32 ontologies is 5, which limits considerably the size of the index.

The size of the index depends on the characteristics of the matching function. As the matching algorithm used in OPOSSUM is monotonic, indexing a concept which is n steps away from the annotated concepts will always have a lower certainty than a concept which is $n - 1$ steps away from the annotated concept (on the same ontological path). Therefore, a threshold will be efficient in trimming all of the low certainty ontological relations without substantially harming the precision or recall of the matchmaker. In an index that serializes a non-monotonic matching algorithm, such as described by Noia et al. [2], this property might not hold, and thresholding would be less effective.

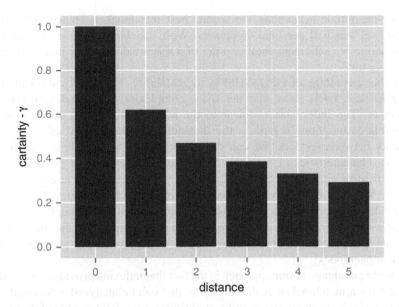

Fig. 4.8 The graph depicts the certainty of a matching a reference concept versus the ontological distance between the reference concept and the service parameter's concept. The certainty decline is logarithmic and monotonic

Finally, we report on the time complexity of query evaluation. Our experimental results show a constant query evaluation time, while the number of services increased from 1 to 10,000. The results of the 2009 International Semantic Service Selection Contest (S3) reflect this observation. In analyzing the time complexity, we explain these results theoretically. The complexity of query evaluation is given by:

$$O(p \cdot \mathscr{I}) + O(|\mathscr{R}| \log |\mathscr{R}|)$$

The complexity depends on the number of parameters, p, each of them processed by retrieving the indexed entries in $\mathscr{I}$ steps. The complexity of $\mathscr{I}$ is evaluated using a single select statement on a single relational database table, indexed using a hash index. While the full complexity analysis of running such a query is elaborate, the literature considers the practical complexity to be $O(1)$ [3]. The complexity of ranking of the results depends on the number of results (R) and is $|R| \log |R|$. The This is encouraging, as it exemplifies a possible path for scaling SWS matching to the scale of the Web, matching queries against tens of millions of services.

4.4.2 Advantages and Disadvantages

Query processing time is the apparent advantage of our indexing approach as evident from the SWS evaluation results. The difference is significant. OPOSSUM is an order-of-magnitude faster than the second best matchmaker. These results were obtained on standard personal computers. With scalable hardware and software infrastructure we anticipate another order of a magnitude improvement in average processing time.

Another advantage of OPOSSUM is its scalability. The empirical results presented in Sect. 4.4.1, show that the space complexity of the indexing solution is efficient. The index size is linear to the number of indexed services, under reasonable assumptions regarding the threshold and the amount of ontological similarity between services. We call these assumptions reasonable as they follow the basic characteristics of semantic Web: that a massive set of documents can be described using a relatively small dictionary. For example, a large number of semantic Web services can be described using hundreds of ontologies. The strength of our indexing approach lies at the inter-connectedness of the ontologies. The more ontologies are interconnected, and the more the concepts within the ontology are interconnected, the better precision and recall our approach can promise, with a more compact index.

A subtle advantage of our approach is the fact that indexing provides a static data structure for a matchmaker. A data structure that can be analyzed, optimized, and discussed. Unlike in-memory solutions, static indexing serializes some of the hidden characteristics of a matchmaker. The size of the indexing neighborhood can teach engineers about the anticipated recall of the matchmaker and the certainty values can predict precision. In fact, in many cases, the index structure and content can define the algorithm of the matchmaker. Specifically, matchmakers can be compared by comparing the certainty and distance values of their respected index structures.

OPOSSUM had exemplified how logical approximation can be efficiently indexed. However, it falls short in supporting non-logical methods for SWS matchmaking. As the general contest results show, hybrid matchmakers outperform logic-based matchmakers. While OPOSSUM supports sub-text matching, the precision and recall of OPOSSUM is basically similar to that of logic-based matchmaking. Specifically, OPOSSUM exhibit a recall problem. It did not recognize some of the services that were retrieved using text-based matching, resulting in mediocre precision and recall performance.

The question of monotonicity introduces an interesting trade-off between precision and scalability. Thresholding is an efficient method in trimming all of the low certainty ontological concepts, and not harm the precision. However, this observation will only hold if the underlying assumptions of monotonicity are effective for judging the matchmaking results. As the contest had proved that non-logical methods improve the performance of matchmaking, pure monotonicity has limitations with respect to precision and recall. Non-logical methods are non-monotonic in most cases, as they do not insure a decreasing matching function. However, there is no index size guarantee for non-monotonic matching functions, which may result in an unscalable index.

4.4.3   Conclusions and Future Work

In this chapter, we explain how indexing can be used to acquire an order-of-magnitude improvement in matching query evaluation time. We show how standard technologies, mainly relational databases, can serve as an efficient infrastructure for indexing. Implementing an indexing solution for SWS matchmakers reveals an interesting set of questions: how scalable is the index? What is the relation between index size and the matching algorithm? What is the relation between approximation and scalability? While we are far from answering those questions, in this chapter we presented and analyzed results regarding the structure and characteristics of our index. Our results show that the space complexity of the indexing solution is efficient, due to two properties of our index: thresholding and concept sharing. Thresholding insures that concepts which are not relevant to the service's parameters will not be indexed in reference to those parameters. Concept sharing is the process of combining concept indexes for parameters that refer to the same concepts.

We believe that the major challenge in SWS indexing is in providing a full indexing solution for hybrid matchmakers. OPOSSUM uses mainly logic-based methods for determining certainty for the index, and determining which services to match for a given query. However, as the evaluation results have shown, hybrid methods outperform logic methods for precision and recall. It is reasonable that hybrid matchmakers that use indexing can outperform other types of matchmakers with regard to response time, precision and recall. In order to provide a full indexing solution for SWS matching, the whole range of hybrid matchmaking should be indexed and accessed using a single interface. There are numerous solutions for indexing text, such as latent semantic indexing, which are widely used in Information Retrieval. Combining them with ontology indexing is a challenging and an interesting problem.

4.5   Summary

In this chapter, we reported on the use of Indexing to enhance the performance of semantic Web services matchmakers in an order-of-magnitude. We demonstrate our method by describing OPOSSUM, an index-based matchmaker, which is the fastest matchmaker at the 2009 International Semantic Service Selection Contest (S3). Our approach is based on indexing the service parameters for I/O matching, and provides approximation by indexing the concept substitution tree. We calculate a certainty function that incorporates logic-based matching method between the references concepts and the service parameter concepts, and rank the retrieved services according to the summarized certainty. Additional textual approximation is carried out by allowing sub-text retrieval from the index. OPOSSUM implements this approach using standard relational database (MySQL) and code written in Java.

This report presents results about the properties of the index through the evaluation in the course of the 2009 International Semantic Service Selection

Contest. The results show a linearity of space complexity of the index with respect to the number of indexed services. We highlight challenges and open questions for employing indexing solutions in SWS matching. Some of the challenges are theoretical. For example, whether indexing can be applied to matchmakers that include several strands of matching algorithms. Capturing the results of multiple matching algorithms requires additional space, which may harm the scalability of the index, as well as decision algorithms that can provide the final ranking of the results. Other challenges are empirical. In order to evaluate the scalability of SWS indexing solutions, new measures for evaluation should be introduced, such as indexing time, index growth, and index efficiency. Furthermore, the scale of test collections should reach millions of services, which simulate Web-scale service repositories.

References

1. A. Brogi, S. Corfini, R. Popescu, Semantics-based composition-oriented discovery of web services. ACM Trans. Internet Technol. **8**(4), 1–39 (2008)
2. T. Di Noia, E. Di Sciascio, F.M. Donini, Semantic matchmaking as non-monotonic reasoning: a description logic approach. J. Artif. Intell. Res. **29**, 269–307 (2007)
3. G. Graefe, Query evaluation techniques for large databases. ACM Comput. Surv. **25**, 73–169 (1993)
4. C. Kiefer, A. Bernstein, The creation and evaluation of isparql strategies for matchmaking. in *5th European Semantic Web Conference (ESWC2008)*, Tenerife, pp. 463–477, June 2008
5. M. Klusch, Semantic service coordination. in *CASCOM – Intelligent Service Coordination in the Semantic Web*, Chapter 4, ed. by H. Schuldt M. Schumacher, H. Helin (Birkhaeuser Verlag, Basel/Springer, London, 2008)
6. M. Klusch, P. Kapahnke, B. Fries, Hybrid semantic web service retrieval: a case study with owls-mx, in *International Conference on Semantic Computing* (IEEE Computer Society, Washington, 2008), pp. 323–330
7. M. Klusch, B. Fries, K.P. Sycara, Owls-mx: a hybrid semantic web service matchmaker for owl-s services. J. Web Semant. **7**(2), 121–133 (2009)
8. K. Sycara, S. Widoff, M. Klusch, J. Lu, Larks: dynamic matchmaking among heterogeneous software agents in cyberspace. Auton. Agent Multi-Agent Syst. **5**(2), 173–203 (2002)
9. E. Toch, A. Gal, I. Reinhartz-Berger, D. Dori, A semantic approach to approximate service retrieval. ACM Trans. Internet Technol. **8**(1), 2 (2007)
10. E. Toch, I. Reinhartz-Berger, D. Dori, Humans, semantic services and similarity: a user study of semantic web services matching and composition. Web Semant. **9**(1), 16–28 (2011)

Chapter 5
Adaptive Hybrid Selection of Semantic Services: The iSeM Matchmaker

Patrick Kapahnke and Matthias Klusch

Abstract We present the intelligent service matchmaker iSeM, which exhaustively exploits functional service descriptions in terms of logical signature annotations in OWL and specifications of preconditions and effects in SWRL. In particular, besides strict logical matching filters, text and structural similarity, it adopts approximated reasoning based on logical concept abduction and contraction for the description logic subset SH with information-theoretic valuation for matching inputs and outputs. In addition, it uses stateless logical specification matching in terms of the incomplete but decidable θ-subsumption algorithm for preconditions and effects. The optimal aggregation strategy of the above mentioned matching aspects is adapted off-line by means of a binary SVM-based service relevance classifier in combination with evidential coherence-based pruning to improve ranking precision with respect to false classification of any such variant on its own. We demonstrate the additional benefit of the presented approximation and the adaptive hybrid combination by example and by presenting an experimental performance analysis.

5.1 Introduction

Semantic service selection is commonly considered key to the discovery of relevant services in the semantic Web, and there are already quite a few matchmakers available for this purpose as for example the summary given in [7] and the annual international *Semantic Service Selection* (S3) contest[1] show. In this paper,

---

[1]http://www-ags.dfki.uni-sb.de/~klusch/s3/

P. Kapahnke (✉) · M. Klusch
German Research Center for Artificial Intelligence (DFKI), Stuhlsatzenhausweg 3,
Saarbruecken, Germany
e-mail: klusch@dfki.de; patrick.kapahnke@dfki.de

M.B. Blake et al. (eds.), *Semantic Web Services*, DOI 10.1007/978-3-642-28735-0_5,
© Springer-Verlag Berlin Heidelberg 2012

we present the first adaptive semantic service IOPE (inputs, outputs, preconditions and effects) matchmaker.[2] In essence, its innovative features are (a) approximated logical signature (IO) matching based on non-monotonic concept abduction and contraction in the description logic subset SH^3 together with information-theoretic similarity and evidential coherence-based valuation of the result to avoid strict logical false negatives, (b) stateless strict logical specification (PE) plug-in matching to avoid failures of signature matching only, and (c) SVM (support vector machine)-based semantic relevance learning adopted from [8] but extended to full functional service profile (IOPE) matching and use of approximated IO matching results to prune the feature space for precision. Performance evaluation results particularly indicate that this kind of approximated logical matching performs close to its logical and non-logical counterparts (text and structural matching) and significantly improves ranking precision in adaptive hybrid combination with those.

The remainder of the paper is structured as follows. We motivate our matchmaker iSeM and shortly comment on related work in the remainder of this Section followed by an overview of our approach in Sect. 5.2. A detailed description of its signature matching filters with focus on approximated logical matching is given in Sect. 5.3.1, while Sect. 5.3.2 discusses its stateless, logical specification matching filter. Section 5.3.3 describes the SVM-based service relevance learning for selection, while evaluation results and conclusions drawn from it are provided in Sect. 5.4. Finally, we conclude in Sect. 5.5.

5.1.1 Motivation

The specific problems of semantic service selection the matchmaker iSeM has been particularly designed to cope with are motivated by the following service example, which is used throughout the paper.

Example 5.1. Consider the semantic profiles of service request R and offer S in Fig. 5.1, taken from the standard test collection OWLS-TC4 according to which S is relevant to R. The desired service R is supposed to purchase a book for a given person by debiting his own debit account, shipping the book to him and eventually acknowledging the completed deal. The e-shopping service S like amazon.com offers arbitrary articles including books that are requested by some customer whose own credit card account gets respectively charged while sending an invoice for and pricing information about the deal. Both services are written in OWL-S with semantic signature concept definitions in description logic OWL-DL and their logical preconditions and effects in SWRL. In the following, we assume

---

[2]This chapter is a revised version of [9] with shortened descriptions of the approach and extended evaluation and discussion of results.

[3]http://www.cs.man.ac.uk/~ezolin/dl/

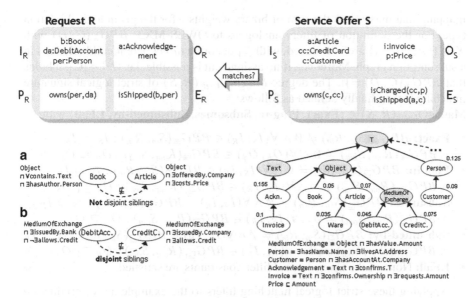

Fig. 5.1 Service request (*book purchasing*) and relevant service offer (*article purchasing*)

the matchmaker to have an appropriate shared ontology and a service registry available over which semantic service selection is performed.   ○

False negatives of strict logical signature matching. The majority of semantic service matchmakers perform logical signature matching (see [7] and S3). One prominent set of strict logical matching filters for this purpose is provided below [11, 18]. Each of these filters requires (a) each service input concept to be more generic than or equal to those provided in the request and (b) the complete requested output to be covered by that of the service in terms of different types of logical subsumption relations.

Definition 5.1. Strict logical signature matching.
Let S, R be semantic service offer and request and $S_{in}, S_{out}, R_{in}, R_{out}$ the multisets of input and output concepts of the semantic signatures of S and R defined in a shared OWL ontology O. The logical filter definitions used in iSeM are inspired by OWLS-MX3 [8] but are more strict with respect to the mapping of matching request and offer parameters. While each element of R_{in} (S_{out}) could have more than one matching part in S_{in} (R_{out}) in OWLS-MX3, iSeM requires strictly injective concept assignments for logical matching filters. This refinement was based on previous observations regarding cases of false positives in OWLS-MX3 due to this characteristic. To accomplish this, $BPG_\sqsubseteq(\bar{C}, \bar{D})$ is defined as the set of concept assignments (C, D) with $C \in \bar{C}$ and $D \in \bar{D}$ that form an injective mapping as valid solution of bipartite graph matching on a graph with $\bar{C}$ and $\bar{D}$ as nodes and weighted edges between them. The weights v between concepts C and D indicate whether $C \sqsubseteq D$ holds: $v = 1$ iff $C \sqsubseteq D$ else $v = 0$. That is, $BPG_\sqsubseteq(\bar{C}, \bar{D})$ is the

mapping that maximizes the sum of binary weights v for the given logical relation type. For the definition of filters analogous to OWLS-MX3, $BPG_X(\bar{C}, \bar{D})$ with $X \in \{(\equiv, \sqsubseteq_1, \sqsupseteq_1\}$ are introduced, with $\sqsupseteq_1$ denoting *direct* parent/child relations in a subsumption graph. Moreover, if no assignment is possible, i.e. $|\bar{D}| < |\bar{C}|$, it holds that $BPG_X(\bar{C}, \bar{D}) = \emptyset$. The degree MatchIO$_{Logic}(R, S)$ of strict logical signature matching is then finally defined as follows:

MatchIO$_{Logic}(R, S) \in \{$**Exact, Plug-in, Subsumes, Subsumed-by, LFail**$\}$ with

- **Exact:** $BPG_{\equiv}(S_{in}, R_{in}) \neq \emptyset \wedge \forall(I_S, I_R) \in BPG_{\equiv}(S_{in}, R_{in}) : I_S \equiv I_R$
  $\wedge\ BPG_{\equiv}(R_{out}, S_{out}) \neq \emptyset \wedge \forall(O_R, O_S) \in BPG_{\equiv}(R_{out}, S_{out}) : O_R \equiv O_S$
- **Plug-in:** $BPG_{\sqsupseteq}(S_{in}, R_{in}) \neq \emptyset \wedge \forall(I_S, I_R) \in BPG_{\sqsupseteq}(S_{in}, R_{in}) : I_S \sqsupseteq I_R$
  $\wedge\ BPG_{\sqsupseteq_1}(R_{out}, S_{out}) \neq \emptyset \wedge \forall(I_S, I_R) \in BPG_{\sqsupseteq_1}(R_{out}, S_{out}) : O_R \sqsupseteq_1 O_S$
- **Subsumes:** $BPG_{\sqsupseteq}(S_{in}, R_{in}) \neq \emptyset \wedge \forall(I_S, I_R) \in BPG_{\sqsupseteq}(S_{in}, R_{in}) : I_S \sqsupseteq I_R$
  $\wedge\ BPG_{\sqsupseteq}(R_{out}, S_{out}) \neq \emptyset \wedge \forall(I_S, I_R) \in BPG_{\sqsupseteq}(R_{out}, S_{out}) : O_R \sqsupseteq O_S$
- **Subsumed-by:** $BPG_{\sqsupseteq}(S_{in}, R_{in}) \neq \emptyset \wedge \forall(I_S, I_R) \in BPG_{\sqsupseteq}(S_{in}, R_{in}) : I_S \sqsupseteq I_R$
  $\wedge\ BPG_{\sqsubseteq_1}(R_{out}, S_{out}) \neq \emptyset \wedge \forall(I_S, I_R) \in BPG_{\sqsubseteq_1}(R_{out}, S_{out}) : O_R \sqsubseteq_1 O_S$
- **LFail:** None of the above logical filter constraints are satisfied.   ◇

Applying these strict logical matching filters to the example above produces a logical fail (LFail), hence a false negative. The reasons are that (a) the inputs book and article are not strictly logically disjoint siblings in the ontology, that is (*Book* $\sqcap$ *Article* $\not\sqsubseteq \perp$), and (b) the inputs debit account and credit card are strictly logically disjoint, that is (*DebitAccount* $\sqcap$ *CreditCard* $\sqsubseteq \perp$).

Such cases of logical signature mismatches may appear quite often, in fact, applying the above filters to the de facto standard collection OWLS-TC4 yields a relatively high number of strict logical false negatives for each request in the order of 45% of the size of its relevance set in average. As shown, for example, in [8, 11, 12] and the contest S3, some hybrid combination of strict logical with non-logic-based approximated signature matching methods may avoid failures of strict logical signature matching filters defined above in practice.[4] But how can logical matching itself be improved, and by what kind of complementary approximation (cf. Sect. 5.3.1)? Also, how well can such an approach perform compared to and in combination with its non-logic-based counterparts in practice (cf. Sect. 5.4.1)?

Failures of signature matching only. It is well known that matching of semantic signatures only may fail in many cases, since they do not capture the functional behavior commonly encoded in logical service preconditions and effects (PE). There are different approaches to logical PE-matching [7] – but which one can most effectively be used in a third-party matchmaker that usually has no access to concept instances describing the states of service providers and requesters (cf. Sect. 5.3.2)?

---

[4] Avoidance and higher (lower) ranking of false negatives (positives) increases average precision of ranked result lists.

Best combination of semantic matching filters. How to best combine different kinds of semantic service matching filters in terms of precision? One option proposed, for example, in [6, 8, 12] is to let the matchmaker learn the optimal aggregation of different matching results for its semantic relevance decision – rather than to put the burden of finding and hard-coding the solution by hand on the developer. Though this turned out to be quite successful in the S3 contest restricted to semantic signatures, how can approximated logical matching be used to improve the learning for better precision of service selection (cf. Sect. 5.3.3)?

5.1.2   Related Work

iSeM is the first adaptive, hybrid semantic service IOPE matchmaker, and there are quite a few other matchmakers available [7]. For example, the strict logical and the non-logic-based semantic signature matching filters as well as the SVM-based learning process of iSeM are adopted from the adaptive signature matchmaker OWLS-MX3 [8]. However, unlike iSeM, OWLS-MX3 neither performs approximated logical signature matching, nor PE-matching, nor is its adaptive process applicable to IOPE matching results and the feature space is not evidentially pruned. The same holds for the adaptive hybrid semantic signature matchmaker SAWSDL-MX2 [12]. Besides, SAWSDL-MX2 performs structural matching on the WSDL grounding level only which significantly differs from the semantic structural matching performed by iSeM. The use of abduction for approximated logical signature matching is inspired by DiNoia et al. [2, 3]. However, their non-adaptive matchmaker MaMaS performs abduction for approximated matching of monolithic service concept descriptions, while iSeM exploits it for significantly different approximated structured signature matching and its use for learning. Besides, MaMaS has not been evaluated yet.

5.2   Approach: The iSeM Matchmaker

Before delving into the technical details of the matchmaker iSeM, we shall first provide an overview of its functionality.

Matchmaking algorithm in brief. For any given service request R and service offers $S \in SR$ described in OWL-S or SAWSDL, with SR being the service registry of iSeM, the matchmaker returns a ranked set of relevant services as its answer set to the user. For this purpose, it first learns the weighted aggregation of different kinds of service IOPE matching results off line over a given training set of positive and negative samples by means of SVM-based binary relevance classification with ranking. These different kinds of matching approaches include strict and approximated logical, text similarity-based and structural semantic matching of service signatures (IO) in SH,[5] as well as stateless, logical plug-in matching of service preconditions and effects (PE) in SWRL, if they exist. Once learning has been done, the same filters are used by the learned relevance classifier for selecting relevant services for previously unknown requests. iSeM may be classified as an adaptive, hybrid semantic service IOPE matchmaker [7].

Hybrid signature (IO) matching. Logical signature matching of iSeM comes in two complementary flavors: Strict logical matching and approximated logical matching. For every service pair (R, S) for which strict logical signature matching $MatchIO_{Logic}(R, S)$ as defined above (Sect. 5.1.1, Definition 5.1) fails, iSeM computes the approximated logical matching degree $MatchIO_{ALogic}(R, S)$ based on approximated subsumption relations $(C \sqsubseteq_{AC} D)$ between I/O concepts C, D via contraction and structured abduction together with their information-theoretic valuation. This leads to two hypotheses of approximated logical signature matching, that are approximated logical plug-in (H_1) and subsumed-by (H_2), both of which weighted by their averaged informative quality $v \in [-1, 1]$. Eventually, the degree $MatchIO_{ALogic}(R, S) = (H, v)$ of approximated logical service signature matching is determined as the hypothesis H with maximal valuation v. The approximated logical matching results are used in the learning process over a given training set of service pairs to prune the respective feature space restricted to logic-based matching to compensate for strict logical false negatives. In addition, iSeM performs non-logic-based approximated matching, that are text and structural semantic similarity-based signature matching for which purpose it applies the respective filters of OWLS-MX3 [8] (cf. Sect. 5.3.1).

Logical specification (PE) matching. To cope with failures of signature matching only and to allow for third-party matchmaking without having access to service concept instances, iSeM performs stateless, logical plug-in matching $MatchPE(S, R)$ of service preconditions and effects by means of approximated theorem proving, that is theta-subsumption, of required logical PE-implications, similar to the approach in LARKS[18] (cf. Sect. 5.3.2).

Learning of full service profile (IOPE) selection. To combine the results of its different IOPE matching filters for optimal precise service selection, iSeM performs binary SVM-based semantic relevance learning off line over a given training set of positive and negative samples (S, R) each of which is represented as a vector x in the 10-dimensional feature space of different matching filters. This space gets particularly pruned by exploiting the approximated logical signature matching results to compensate for strict logical false negatives. Once that has been done, the learned binary classifier d with ranking r is applied by iSeM to any service pair (S, R) with unknown request R to return the final result: $MatchIOPE(S, R) = (d, r)$ (cf. Sects. 5.3.3 and 5.4.1).

---

[5]Restriction to annotation in SH is due to respective limitation of the adopted concept abduction reasoner [3]; its extension to $SHOIN$ is ongoing.

5.3 Solution: Adaptive Hybrid Service Selection

In the following, the matching procedure of iSeM is presented, providing details
on each of the aspects introduced before. Regarding hybrid signature matching, in
addition to the approximation approach, the application of structural and text-based
methods from OWLS-MX3 in context of iSeM are recapitulated.

5.3.1 Hybrid Semantic Signature Matching

Semantic signature matching in iSeM is performed by means of both logic-
based and non-logic-based matching. While the first type basically relies on
strict logical (cf. Definition 5.1) and approximated logical concept subsumptions
(cf. Sect. 5.3.1), the second exploits text and structural similarities of signature
concepts (cf. Sect. 5.3.1). Both the approximated logical and non-logic-based
matching are performed by iSeM in particular to compensate for strict logical
signature matching failures and contribute to the relevance classification learning
phase (cf. Sect. 5.3.3).

Approximated Logical Matching

Inspired by [2, 3, 14], approximated logical signature matching of a given service
pair (S, R) relies on the combined use of logical contraction and abduction of
signature concepts for approximated concept subsumption (cf. Definition 5.2) which
is valuated in terms of the information gain and loss induced by its construction
(cf. Definition 5.3). Eventually, we extend both means of approximation and valuation on the concept level to its application on the signature level (cf. Definition 5.4).

Definition 5.2. Logical concept contraction and abduction.
Let C, D be concepts of an ontology O in SH. The *contraction* of C with respect
to D is $CCP(C, D) = (G, K)$ with $C \equiv G \sqcap K$ and $K \sqcap D \not\sqsubseteq \bot$.[6] The abducible
concept K^h is derived from concept K through rewriting operations [3]:
$K^h = h_0 \sqcap rew(K)$, $rew(A) = A$, $rew(\neg A) = \neg A$, $rew(C_1 \sqcap C_2) = rew(C_1) \sqcap$
$rew(C_2)$, $rew(\exists R.C) = \exists R.(h_i \sqcap rew(C))$ and $rew(\forall R.C) = \forall R.(h_i \sqcap rew(C))$;
where i is incremented per application of rew, A is a primitive component (in the
logical unfolding of K in O), C_i are concepts in SH, and $\bar{H} = (h_0, \dots, h_n)$ denotes
variables in the resulting concept structure, where additional definitions are added
for approximation. The *Structural abduction* of concept K with respect to D is
$SAP(K, D) = H = (H_0, \dots, H_n)$ with $\sigma[\bar{H}, H](K^h) \sqsubseteq D$ and $\sigma[\bar{H}, H](K^h) \not\sqsubseteq \bot$.
The *approximated concept* $C' := \sigma[\bar{H}, H](K^h)$ of C with respect to D is

---

[6] K ("keep") denotes the compatible part of C with respect to D, while G ("give up") denotes the
respectively incompatible part.

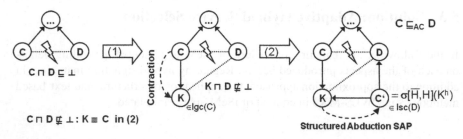

Fig. 5.2 Approximated logical concept subsumption. *Arrows* denote subsumption relations, dashed lines concept (in-)compatibility

constructed by applying $\sigma[\bar{H}, H] = \{h_0 \mapsto H_0, \ldots, h_n \mapsto H_n\}$ to the abducible concept K^h. The *approximated logical concept subsumption* $C \sqsubseteq_{AC} D$ is defined as follows: $C \sqsubseteq_{AC} D \Leftrightarrow C' \sqsubseteq D$ with $(G, K) = CCP(C, D)$, $H = SAP(K, D)$ and $C' = \sigma[\bar{H}, H](K^h)$. ◇

To avoid strict logical false negatives leading to lower average precision, iSeM assumes the user to be willing to give up those parts of logical signature concept definitions that cause strict logical subsumption failures and keeping the remaining parts instead. The latter are used to compute approximated concept subsumption relations and the respectively approximated signature matching. A tableau algorithm for computing near-optimal solutions to the problem is given by Di Noia et al. in [3]. Figure 5.2 provides a schematical overview of the approximation process: given the incompatible concept definitions C and D, the *contraction* is computed to establish compatibility in terms of a less specific definition K based on C (step 1). Based on this result, *structural abduction* is applied to construct the approximation C', for which concept subsumption $C' \sqsubseteq D$ holds (step 2).

Example 5.2. Consider Example 5.1. The approximated logical subsumption between strict logically disjoint siblings *DebitAccount, CreditCard* is computed as follows:
$(G, K) = CCP(DA, CC) = (\neg\exists allows.Credit^P, MOE \sqcap \exists issuedBy.Bank^P)$, i.e. the restriction of not allowing credit of the debit account is given up, which establishes compatibility with the *CreditCard* definition.
$K^h = h_0 \sqcap Object^P \sqcap \exists hasValue.(h_1 \sqcap Value^P) \sqcap \exists issuedBy.(h_2 \sqcap Bank^P)$. The abducible concept K^h determines the positions for concept refinement in the structure of the remaining concept definition K.
$\bar{H} = (h_0, h_1, h_2)$, $H = SAP(DA, CC) = (\exists allows.Credit^P, \top, Company^P)$ then is the solution computed according to [3].
The approximated concept *DebitAccount'* is then constructed using the following mapping function: $\sigma[\bar{H}, H] = \{h_0 \mapsto \exists allows.Credit^P, h_1 \mapsto \top, h_2 \mapsto Company^P\}$,
$DA' = \sigma[\bar{H}, H](K^h) = \exists allows.Credit \sqcap MOE \sqcap \exists issuedBy.(Bank \sqcap Company)$.
DA, CC and *MOF* are abbreviations for concept names *DebitAccount, CreditCard* and *MediumOfExchange* respectively. It holds that *DebitAccount'* $\sqsubseteq$ *CreditCard*, hence *DebitAccount* $\sqsubseteq_{AC}$ *CreditCard*. ○

It is worth mentioning that for the special case, where $C \sqsubseteq D$ initially holds, the algorithm presented in [3] that is used by iSeM yields a trivial solution, which later on causes the overall approximate logic-based matching filter to be redundant to strict logic-based matching in terms of (true or false) positive classification, i.e. it can only be used to remedy strict logical matching failures.

In order to rank the computed approximations, we valuate them by means of their informative quality. Roughly, the informative quality of approximated logical subsumption between signature concepts C, D is the difference between the information gain and loss induced by its construction. That is, the utility of the respectively approximated concept C' is the trade off between its information-theoretic similarity [14] with the original concept C and the targeted one D. The similarity is based on the probabilistic information content of concepts with respect to the frequency of their occurrence in semantic service signatures.

Definition 5.3.   Informative quality of approx. subsumption.
Let SR be the set of service offers registered at the matchmaker (service registry), S_{in}, S_{out} the multi-sets of concepts used for signature parameter annotation of service S, $SAC(SR)$ the set of all concepts used for annotating services in SR. We define the *informative quality v of approximated concept subsumption* $C \sqsubseteq_{AC} D$ (cf. Definition 5.2) as:

$$v(C, D) = sim_{inf}(C', D) - (1 - sim_{inf}(C', C))$$

with the information-theoretic similarity of concepts C and D proposed by Lin [14]:

$$sim_{inf}(C, D) = 2 \cdot IC(maxdcs(C, D))/(IC(C) + IC(D)),$$

where $maxdcs(C, D) = argmax_{c \in dcs(C,D)}\{IC(c)\}$ is the direct common subsumer (*dcs*) of C and D in ontology O with maximum information content $IC(c)$. The *information content* of concept $C \in SAC(SR)$ is $IC(C) = -\log P(C)$, else $IC(C) := max_{D \in SAC(SR)}\{IC(D)\}$. We define the *probability of concept C being used* for semantic service annotation as the frequency of its occurrence in semantic signatures of services in service registry SR:

$$P(C) = \frac{1}{|IO_{SR}|} \cdot \sum_{S \in SR} |\{D \in S_{in} \cup S_{out} : D \sqsubseteq C\}|,$$

where IO_{SR} is the multiset of all parameters used in SR. Please note that we adapted the original notion introduced by Resnik [15] for our approach based on description logics to account for implicit subsumption relationships.   ◇

Example 5.3.   The informative quality of *DebitAccount* $\sqsubseteq_{AC}$ *CreditCard* given in Example 5.2 is computed as follows:
$IC(DA) = -\log P(DA) = -\log 0.045 \approx 1.348$ is the information content of the original concept *DebitAccount* and $IC(CC) = -\log P(CC) = -\log 0.075 \approx 1.125$ the information content of target concept *CreditCard* accordingly. For the approximated concept *DebitAccount'*, it holds that $IC(DA') = -\log 0.035 \approx 1.456$, since $DA' \notin SAC(SR)$. $sim_{inf}(DA', CC) = \frac{2 \cdot 1.125}{1.456 + 1.125} \approx 0.872$ is the information gain from

using the approximated concept instead of the original one and $sim_{inf}(DA', DA) = \frac{2 \cdot 1.348}{1.456 + 1.348} \approx 0.962$ the information loss of the approximation. The valuation then is computed as follows: $v(DA, CC) = 0.872 - (1 - 0.962) = 0.834$.   ○

For each service pair, depending on the computed type of their approximated signature concept subsumption relations, one can determine two hypotheses of approximated logical service signature matching: approximated logical plug-in and approximated logical subsumed-by. For both, the maximal informative quality is computed using bipartite concept graph matching.

Definition 5.4. Approximated logical signature match.
Let S, R be semantic service offer and request, $S_{in}, S_{out}, R_{in}, R_{out}$ multisets of their signature concepts and $BPG_{\sqsubseteq_{AC}}(\bar{C}, \bar{D})$ the concept assignment via bipartite graph matching as in Definition 5.1 but with approximated subsumption $\sqsubseteq_{AC}$ and informative quality of edge weights $v(C, D)$ for $C \in \bar{C}, D \in \bar{D}$; $BPG_{\sqsupseteq_{AC}}(\bar{C}, \bar{D})$ analogously with edge weights $v(D, C)$.
Approximated logical plug-in matching hypothesis $H_1(R, S)$ holds iff:

$$\forall I_S \in S_{in} : \exists I_R \in R_{in} : (I_S, I_R) \in BPG_{\sqsupseteq_{AC}}(S_{in}, R_{in})$$
$$\wedge \forall O_R \in R_{out} : \exists O_S \in S_{out} : (O_S, O_R) \in BPG_{\sqsubseteq_{AC}}(S_{in}, R_{in}).$$

Approximated logical subsumed-by matching hypothesis $H_2(R, S)$ holds iff:

$$\forall I_S \in S_{in} : \exists I_R \in R_{in} : (I_S, I_R) \in BPG_{\sqsupseteq_{AC}}(S_{in}, R_{in})$$
$$\wedge \forall O_R \in R_{out} : \exists O_S \in S_{out} : (O_S, O_R) \in BPG_{\sqsupseteq_{AC}}(S_{in}, R_{in}).$$

Informative quality $val_{(S,R)} : \{H_1, H_2\} \to [-1, 1]$ of an approximated signature matching hypothesis is the average of informative qualities of its respective approximated concept subsumptions:

$$val_{(S,R)}(H_1) =$$

$$\frac{1}{2 \cdot |S_{in}|} \cdot \sum\nolimits_{(I_R, I_S) \in BPG_{\sqsupseteq_{AC}}(R_{in}, S_{in})} v(I_R, I_S)$$

$$+ \frac{1}{2 \cdot |R_{out}|} \cdot \sum\nolimits_{(O_S, O_R) \in BPG_{\sqsubseteq_{AC}}(S_{out}, R_{out})} v(O_S, O_R).$$

$$val_{(S,R)}(H_2) =$$

$$\frac{1}{2 \cdot |S_{in}|} \cdot \sum\nolimits_{(I_R, I_S) \in BPG_{\sqsupseteq_{AC}}(R_{in}, S_{in})} v(I_R, I_S)$$

$$+ \frac{1}{2 \cdot |R_{out}|} \cdot \sum\nolimits_{(O_S, O_R) \in BPG_{\sqsupseteq_{AC}}(S_{out}, R_{out})} v(O_S, O_R).$$

The *approximated logical signature matching degree* is the approximation hypothesis with maximum informative quality: $MatchIO_{ALogic}(S, R) := (H, v)$ with $H = arg\ max_{x \in \{H_1, H_2\}} val(x)$ and $v = val_{(S,R)}(H)$. Semantic relevance ranking of services S bases on $MatchIO_{ALogic}(S, R)[2] \in [-1, 1]$. *Binary relevance classification by approximated logical matching*: $MatchIO_{ALogic}(S, R) * = 1$ iff $MatchIO_{ALogic}(S, R)[2] \geq 0$, else $MatchIO_{ALogic}(R, S)^* = 0$. ◇

Example 5.4. Consider Examples 5.1–5.3. The approximated logical signature match of S, R is computed as follows:
$BPG_{\sqsupseteq_{AC}}(R_{in}, S_{in}) = \{(Book, Article), (DA, CC), (Person, Customer)\}$ is the assignment based on concept approximation and information-theoretic valuation for inputs and $BPG_{\sqsubseteq_{AC}}(S_{out}, R_{out}) = \{(Invoice, Ack)\}$ the assignment for outputs accordingly, both assuming approximated signature matching hypothesis H_1. The informative quality valuation for H_1 is $val_{(S,R)}(H_1) = \frac{1}{2 \cdot 3} \cdot (0.829 + 0.834 + 0.927) + \frac{1}{2 \cdot 1} \cdot 0.895 = 0.879$. In this example, the same valuation holds for H_2, which can be easily seen considering the fact that computation of $val_{S,R}(H_1)$ and $val_{S,R}(H_2)$ only differ regarding the outputs, for which only one assignment is possible and concepts already subsume. The overall matching result then is $MatchIO_{ALogic}(S, R) := (H_1, 0.851)$ ○

Obviously, the approximated logical matching relation $MatchIO_{ALogic}(R, S)$ always exists. Moreover, its binary decision variant $MatchIO_{ALogic}(R, S)^*$ is redundant to its logical counterpart $MatchIO_{Logic}(R, S)$ with respect to positive service classification. That is, their true and false positives are the same, but not vice versa. This can be easily seen by considering that strict logical positives already provide parameter assignments based on subsumption relations and approximation is trivial in those cases. This fact is used in iSeM to restrict its computation of approximated logical signature matches in the learning phase to cases of strict logical false negatives only and use the evidential coherence of the matching results to heuristically prune the feature space for precision (cf. Sect. 5.3.3).

Text and Structural Signature Matching

Non-logic-based approximated signature matching can be performed by means of text and structural similarity measurement. For iSeM, we adopted those of the matchmaker OWLS-MX3, since they have been experimentally shown to be most effective for this purpose [8]. For text matching of signature concepts in the classical vector space model, their unfoldings in the shared ontology are represented as weighted keyword vectors for token-based similarity measurement. Structural semantic similarity of concepts relies on their relative positioning in the subsumption graph, in particular on the shortest path via their direct common subsumer and its depth in the taxonomy [13].

Definition 5.5. Approx. non-logic-based signature matching
Let SR be the service registry of the matchmaker, I the text index of service
signature concepts, O the shared ontology and $\overrightarrow{S_{in}}$, $\overrightarrow{S_{out}}$, $\overrightarrow{R_{in}}$, $\overrightarrow{R_{out}}$ the TFIDF
weighted keyword vector of the conjunction of unfolded input or output concepts of
S and R respectively. *Text similarity-based signature matching* is the average of the
respective signature concept similarities:

$$\mathrm{MatchIO}_{Text}(S, R) = \tfrac{1}{2} \cdot (sim_{text}(\overrightarrow{S_{in}}, \overrightarrow{R_{in}}) + sim_{text}(\overrightarrow{S_{out}}, \overrightarrow{R_{out}}))$$

with Tanimoto coefficient (alternatively Cosine similarity) $sim_{text}(\overrightarrow{C}, \overrightarrow{D}) \in [0, 1]$.
Structural semantic signature matching is the averaged maximal structural similar-
ity of their signature concepts:

$$\mathrm{MatchIO}_{Struct}(S, R) = \frac{1}{2} \cdot (sim_{struct}(S_{in}, R_{in}) + sim_{struct}(S_{out}, R_{out}))$$

with

$$sim_{struct}(A, B) = \frac{1}{|A|} \sum_{a \in A} max\{sim_{csim}(a, b) : b \in B\} \in [0, 1],$$

and structural concept similarity adopted from [13]:

$$sim_{csim}(C, D) = \begin{cases} e^{-\alpha l} \cdot \frac{e^{\beta h} - e^{-\beta h}}{e^{\beta h} + e^{-\beta h}}, & C \neq D \\ 1, & C = D \end{cases},$$

with l shortest path via direct common subsumer between given concepts and h
its depth in O, $\alpha = 0.2$ and $\beta = 0.6$ weighting parameters manually adjusted to
structural features of ontology O based on results of [13].   ◇

Example 5.5. Applied to Example 5.1, we obtain a high score for text-based
signature matching $\mathrm{MatchIO}_{text}(S, R) = 0.71$ which correctly accounts for semantic
relevance of S to R, hence avoids the strict logical false negative. The same
holds for the structural semantic matching $\mathrm{MatchIO}_{struct}(S, R) = 0.69$. For
example, text and structural similarities of the strict logically disjoint input
concept siblings *DebitAccount* and *CreditCard* are high ($sim_{text}(DA, CC) = 0.94$,
$sim_{csim}(DA, CC) = 0.63$) which indicates their semantic proximity. Please note, that
we do not apply a threshold value do determine relevance but perform semantic
relevance learning (cf. Sect. 5.3.3). However, matching pairs tend to get higher
results for $\mathrm{MatchIO}_{text}$ and $\mathrm{MatchIO}_{struct}$ than irrelevant pairs.   ○

While text matching of signatures may avoid strict logical matching failures,
structural semantic matching may also compensate for text matching failures, in
particular when mere is-a ontologies with inclusion axioms only are used for
semantic annotation of service signatures. For reasons of space limitation, we refer
to [8] for more details and examples.

5.3.2 Stateless Logical Specification Matching

As mentioned above, semantic signatures of services do not cover functional service semantics usually encoded in terms of logical service preconditions and effects. This may cause signature matching only to fail, for example if signatures are equivalent for a book selling service offer and a book borrowing request. Though semantic service descriptions rarely contain such specifications in practice [10], we equipped the implemented iSeM matchmaker with the most prominent PE-matching filter adopted from software retrieval: logical specification plug-in matching.

Definition 5.6. Stateless, logical specification plug-in matching.
Let (S, R) be services with preconditions (P_R, P_S) and effects (E_R, E_S) defined in SWRL. Service S *logically specification-plugin matches* R:

$$\text{MatchPE}(S, R) \text{ iff } \models (P_R \Rightarrow P_S) \wedge (E_S \Rightarrow E_R).$$

Stateless checking of MatchPE(S, R) in iSeM 1.0 is adopted from LARKS [18]: Preconditions and effects specified as SWRL rules are translated into PROLOG as in [16] and then used to compute the required logical implications by means of θ-subsumption checking stateless, that is without any instances (ABox), as given in [17]:

$$(\forall p_S \in P_S : \exists p_R \in P_R : p_R \leq_\theta p_S) \Rightarrow (P_R \Rightarrow P_S)$$

$$(\forall e_R \in E_R : \exists e_S \in E_S : e_S \leq_\theta e_R) \Rightarrow (E_S \Rightarrow E_R).$$

A clause C θ-subsumes D, written $C \leq_\theta D$, iff there exists a substitution θ such that $C\theta \subseteq D$ holds; θ-subsumption is an incomplete, decidable consequence relation [5]. ◇

Example 5.6. If applied to Example 5.1, this PE-matching filter succeeds, hence avoids the respective false negative of strict logical signature matching only. Further, consider a service pair (S, R') having the identical or strict logically equivalent semantic signatures as (S, R) given in Example 5.1 – but with the requested effect of R' to only register a book at a given local index such that service S is irrelevant to R': The false positive S of (strict or approximated) logical signature matching only can be avoided by an additional specification plug-in matching filter, which, in this case, would correctly fail. ○

5.3.3 Off-Line Service Relevance Learning

In order to find the best combination of its different matching filters for most precise service selection, iSeM learns their optimal weighted aggregation by using a support vector machine (SVM) approach. In particular, the underlying feature space is pruned by evidential coherence-based weighting of approximated against strict logical signature matching results over the given training set to improve precision.

Overview: Learning and Selection

The training set TS is a subset (5%) drawn uniformly at random from the service test collection OWLS-TC4. It contains user-rated service pairs (S, R) each of which is equipped with a 10-dimensional matching feature vector x_i for positive and/or negative service relevance samples $(x_i, y_i) \in X \times \{1, -1\}$ in the possibly non-linearly separable[7] feature space X. The different matching results for (S, R) are encoded as follows: $x[1] \ldots x[5] \in \{0, 1\}^5$ for MatchIO$_{Logic}(R, S)$ in decreasing order; $x[6] = val_{(S,R)}(H_1)$ and $x[7] = val_{(S,R)}(H_2) \in [-1, 1]$ for MatchIO$_{ALogic}(R, S)$; $x[8] \in [0, 1]$ for MatchIO$_{Text}(R, S)$; $x[9] \in [0, 1]$ for MatchIO$_{Struct}(R, S)$; and $x[10] \in \{0, 1\}$ for MatchPE(R, S). For example: $x = (0, 0, 0, 0, 1, 0.85, 0, 0.4, 0.6, 1)$ encodes a strict logical fail but approximated logical plugin with informative quality of 0.85, text (structural) match of 0.4 (0.6) and plugin specification match.

The SVM-based classification learning problem of iSeM then is to find a separating hyperplane h in X such that for all samples $(x, y) \in TS$ for (S, R) with minimal distances to h these distances are maximal. This yields a binary relevance classifier $d(x)$ with respect to the position of feature vector x to the separating h. The ranking of S is performed according to the distance $dist(x)$ of x for (S, R) to h. Once that has been done, the learned classifier can be applied to any service pair (S, R) with potentially unknown request R and returns MatchIOPE$(S, R) = (d(x), dist(x))$. As kernel, we employed the *Radial Basis Function* (RBF). For more details of this learning process in general, we refer to [8, 12].

Evidential Coherence-Based Feature Space Pruning

To improve the performance of the binary SVM-based relevance classier to be learned, iSeM exploits information available from the given training set TS to prune the feature space X based on the classification results of strict vs. approximated logical signature matching. Due to redundancy of both logical matching types for (true and false) positive classification, it restricts the pruning of feature vectors $x \in X$ to cases of strict logical matching failures $(MatchIO_{ALogic}(R, S) = LFail)$. The respective set $Ev = \{(x, y) : x[5] = 1\}$ of classification events is partitioned with respect to binary classification results of approximated logical matching $(MatchIO_{ALogic}(R, S)^*)$: events correctly classified by $MatchIO_{ALogic}$ as (true) positives or (true) negatives are kept for the subsequent learning step, while wrong negative classifications of approximated matching are pruned due to the redundancy to strict logical matching.

---

[7]Example feature space for OWLS-TC4 is non-linearly separable.

Additionally, inspired by the work of Glass [4], the feature space X is pruned further by modification of logical matching entries in feature vectors $x \in X$ of remaining events based on evidential coherence-based weighting of approximated matching results. To accomplish this, the evidential coherence values of the following hypotheses (A1, A2) of relevance explanation are computed and used as weighting parameters: (A1) $MatchIO_{ALogic}$ is a correct explanation of semantic *relevance* (avoids logical false negatives), and (A2) $MatchIO_{ALogic}$ is a correct explanation for semantic *irrelevance* (avoids introduction of false positives). Following [4], iSeM determines their quality by measuring the impact of evidence on the probability of explanations A1 and A2 (with coherence or confirmation measures) rather than measuring its posterior probability with Bayes. In other words, it determines the most plausible explanation instead of the most probable over the given training set. The coherence overlap measure $Co(H, E) = \frac{P(H \cap E)}{P(H \cup E)}$ performed best in practice [4] and is therefore also used by iSeM. For more details on this, we refer the interested reader to [9].

5.4 Lessons Learned

The performance evaluation of the first version of iSeM (namely iSeM 1.0) has been conducted using the service retrieval test collection OWLS-TC4,[8] which consists of 1,083 service offers in OWL-S 1.1 and 42 queries including binary and graded relevance assignments from nine different application domains. Since version 4, it also includes definitions of preconditions and effects for a subset of services (180 offers, 18 queries) which enables us to apply the full-fledged iSeM including specification matching as presented above. However, since only a subset of definitions actually contain PE and therefore the used θ-subsumption algorithm trivially yields MatchPE(S, R) (because $\top \Rightarrow \top$) for a larger portion of the test collection, we added another binary dimension to feature space X of our learning algorithm that allows iSeM to identify those cases: $x[11] \in \{0, 1\}$ with $x[11] = 1$ iff request R contains a non-trivial precondition or effect ($P_R \neq \top \vee E_R \neq \top$). Moreover, service parameter annotations in OWLS-TC4 are not restricted to the DL subset SH, which is a requirement for the current version of the approximated logic-based signature matching algorithm used in iSeM 1.0. To overcome this, we implemented a trivial and non-optimal approximation for cases where the algorithm is not applicable: given concepts C and D with one of them not in SH, the result of concept contraction is $CCP(C, D) = \langle C, \top \rangle$ and concept abduction yields $C' = SAP(C, D) = D$, i.e. every aspect of the original definition of C is neglected to derive the most obvious solution such that $C' \sqsubseteq D$. However, even considering this weak approximation for those cases, we observed a significant improvement with respect to ranking precision as we will show in the following.

---

[8]Publicly available at http://www.semwebcentral.org/projects/owls-tc

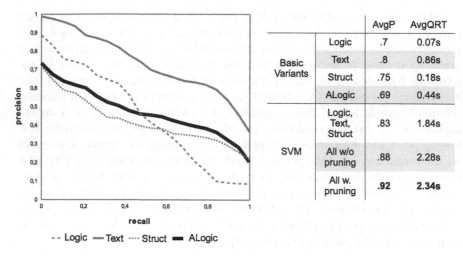

Fig. 5.3 Macro-averaged recall/precision (MARP), average precision (AvgP) and average query response time (AvgQRT) of basic and adaptive signature matching by iSeM 1.0

For evaluation, we used the public tool SME2 v2.1[9] on a WinXP SP3 32 bit machine with Intel Core2Duo T9600 (2.8 GHz) processor and 3 GB RAM. We measured macro-averaged precision at 20 equidistant recall levels (MARP graph), averaged *average precision* and average query response time. iSeM 1.0 is implemented in Java and publicly available at http://www.semwebcentral.org/projects/isem/.

5.4.1 Evaluation Results

In summary, the evaluation results shown in Fig. 5.3 reveal that (a) approximated logical matching via abduction and informative quality performs similarly to its strict logical counterpart with respect to average precision, but differs to a large extent at fixed recall levels, (b) this kind of matching performs close to but still worse than its non-logic-based approximated counterparts (text and structural matching), and (c) adaptive hybrid combination outperforms all other variants in terms of precision.

As expected, due to the redundancy of strict and approximated logical signature matching positives (cf. Theorem 1), approximated logic-based matching alone was not able to outperform its non-logic-based counterparts but performed close to strict logical matching. As already hinted in statement (a) before, the rankings of approximated logic-based and strict logic-based matching vary to a large extent, which provides evidence that both variants are mutually independent to a

---

[9]http://projects.semwebcentral.org/projects/sme2/

satisfactory degree. This fact has been validated using a Friedman test conducted on average precisions per query, which revealed that there is no significant difference at 5% level ($p \approx 0.088$), i.e. neither was able to outperform the other for a majority of queries. As has already been shown in context of OWLS-MX3 (cf. [8]), this also holds for the other basic matching variants leading to the conclusion that each of the basic signature matching filters of iSeM contributes to an overall increase of performance for some cases of strict logical false classification, i.e. none of the tested variants outperformed the others for almost all service requests in the test collection.

The adaptive hybrid aggregation of all matching filters as done by iSeM (cf. Sect. 5.3.3) significantly increases the retrieval performance compared to that of its individual matching filters. While the combination of strict logic-based, text similarity and structure matching already yields good results as expected from previous observations with OWLS-MX3, the additional consideration of approximated logical matching and stateless logical specification matching (in the learning process) performs best. Moreover, the comparative performance analysis conducted for the annual S3 contest in 2010[10] resulted in iSeM being among the top contestants regarding precision-based measures. In fact, it won the OWL-S track with the best average precision (0.92) ever measured in this contest so far. For our specific use case, the proposed feature space pruning for relevance learning performed best, but arguably not in general [1].

Regarding query response times, the adaptive hybrid aggregated variants performed significantly slower than the basic matching filters (cf. Fig. 5.3), which is not surprising considering the fact that each of the presented filters has to be evaluated per offer/query pair in case of hybrid matching. For the basic variants, it is worth mentioning that the approximated logic-based matching performs significantly slower than strict logic-based matching, but performance is still reasonable looking at the benefit with respect to ranking precision of the full-fledged iSeM system.

5.4.2 Advantages and Disadvantages

As the evaluation results show, hybrid matchmakers may benefit from integration of the presented approximated logic-based matching approach and thus increase ranking precision significantly. As motivated in Sect. 5.1.1, the reason for this is the improved *avoidance of strict logical false negatives* by additionally considering approximated logic-based matching, which shows sufficient mutual independence of all other approaches presented here.

The proposed feature space model as basis for the applied machine-leaning approach allows for easy integration of arbitrary matching filters and similarity

---

[10]S3 2010 summary report is available at http://www-ags.dfki.uni-sb.de/~klusch/s3/html/2010. html

functions and facilitates straightforward matchmaker tool configuration without manually setting up weights for a fixed result aggregation. This approach implicitly solves the question of how to find the *best combination of semantic matching filters* to achieve high precision on average. Moreover, the application of SVM using RBF-kernel nicely fits the non-linear separable nature of the feature space in context of semantic service retrieval on the Web as presented in this chapter. For example, in OWLS-TC4 it is not possible to strictly perform linearly-weighted separation based on the various features into matching true positives and true negatives.

Failure of signature matching only has been minimized satisfactorily using the presented stateless specification matching step whenever preconditions or effects were available. Besides the increased overall average precision achieved by the fully-fledged iSeM matchmaker, this has also been shown exemplarily in the S3 2010 summary report. However, as already stated before, OWLS-TC4 only consists of few services and request documents with full IOPE profile. A majority of examples does not provide preconditions and effects yet, which alleviates the overall benefit in precision for the experimental performance analysis to some degree.

On the other hand, as shown above, the presented approach results in a linear increase of query response times, because every filtering and similarity computation is performed for each service request and offer pair, even in cases where the adapted aggregation strategy gives very low weights on some features for certain circumstances. Moreover, the adaption is done such that precision is optimized on average for the whole training set and thus is rather coarse-grained. Even though this turned out not to be a problem for OWLS-TC4, there may be cases where some basic approaches (features) are better than others given certain contexts and vice versa. For example, the presented approximated logic-based matching may perform better in domains described in terms of rich-detailed ontologies like medical domains, where it may prove inferior for coarse-grained domain descriptions. Finally, the presented adaption strategy is strictly off-line with a distinct training and exploitation phase. Adapting iSeM over time, for example while collecting more and more user feedback, would require to drop the current aggregation function and train a new one from scratch after some period. This could be controlled by a threshold value for the resulting precision based on the retrieved user feedback, but training the SVM itself is a costly process.

5.4.3   Conclusions and Future Work

The presented approach for adaptive combination of matching variants based on a feature space representation provides a flexible basis for detailed experiments with different machine-learning approaches. Besides well-known off-line algorithms, we intend to also implement *on-line* approaches to add flexibility at runtime as described above. Moreover, the approximated logical matching results of iSeM can also be exploited for explanation-based interaction with the user during the selection process. Though in its initially implemented version iSeM is non-obtrusive in this respect, such interaction together with extending the abductive approximated reasoning to OWL2-DL annotations is subject to future work.

5.5 Summary

We presented the first adaptive, hybrid and full semantic service profile (IOPE) matchmaker that, in particular, performs approximated logical reasoning and respectively evidential coherence-based pruning of learning space to improve precision over strict logical matching. The evaluation results for iSeM revealed, among other things, that its adaptive hybrid combination with non-logic-based approximated signature matching improves on each of them individually. Moreover, it proved to be among the top contestants regarding precision-based measures and won the OWL-S track of the 2010 edition of the annual S3 contest.

References

1. A.L. Blum, P. Langley, Selection of relevant features and examples in machine learning. Artif. Intell. **97**, 245–271 (1997)
2. S. Colucci et al., Concept abduction and contraction for semantic-based discovery of matches and negotiation spaces in an e-marketplace. Electron. Commerce Res. Appl. **4**(4), 345–361 (2005)
3. T. Di Noia, E. Di Sciascio, F.M. Donini, A Tableaux-based calculus for abduction in expressive description logics: preliminary results, in *Proceedings of 22nd International Workshop on Description Logics (DL)*, Oxford, 2009
4. D. H. Glass, Inference to the best explanation: a comparison of approaches, in *Proceedings of the AISB 2009 Convention*, Edinburgh, 2009, www.aisb.org.uk/convention/aisb09/Proceedings/
5. P. Idestam-Almquist, Generalization of clauses under implication. Artif. Intell. Res. **3**, 467–489 (1995)
6. C. Kiefer, A. Bernstein, The creation and evaluation of iSPARQL strategies for matchmaking, in *Proceedings of the 5th European Semantic Web Conference (ESWC)*. (Springer, Berlin/New York, 2008)
7. M. Klusch, Semantic web service coordination, in *CASCOM – Intelligent Service Coordination in the Semantic Web*, Chapter 4, ed. by M. Schumacher, H. Helin, H. Schuldt (Birkhäuser Verlag/Springer, Basel, 2008)
8. M. Klusch, P. Kapahnke, OWLS-MX3: an adaptive hybrid semantic service atchmaker for OWL-S, in *Proceedings of 3rd International Workshop on Semantic Matchmaking and Resource Retrieval (SMR2), USA; CEUR*, vol. 525, Washington, 2009
9. M. Klusch, P. Kapahnke, iSeM: approximated reasoning for adaptive hybrid selection of semantic services, in *Proceedings of 4th IEEE International Conference on Semantic Computing (ICSC)*, Pittsburgh, 2010
10. M. Klusch, Z. Xing, Deployed semantic services for the common user of the web: a reality check, in *Proceedings of the 2nd IEEE International Conference on Semantic Computing (ICSC)*, (IEEE Press, Santa Clara, 2008)
11. M. Klusch, B. Fries, K. Sycara, OWLS-MX: A hybrid semantic web service matchmaker for OWL-S services. Web Semant. **7**(2),121–133 (2009), Elsevier

12. M. Klusch, P. Kapahnke, I. Zinnikus, Hybrid adaptive web service selection with SAWSDL-MX and WSDL analyzer, in *Proceedings of 6th European Semantic Web Conference (ESWC)* (IOS Press, Heraklion, 2009)
13. Y. Li, A. Bandar, D. McLean, An approach for measuring semantic similarity between words using multiple information sources. Trans. Knowl. Data Eng. **15**, 871–882 (2003)
14. D. Lin, An information-theoretic definition of similarity, in *Proceedings of the 15th International Conference on Machine Learning*, Madison, 1998
15. P. Resnik, Semantic similarity in a taxonomy: an information-based measure and its application to problems of ambiguity in natural language. J. Artif. Intell. Res. **11**, 95–130 (1999)
16. K. Samuel et al., Translating OWL and semantic web rules into prolog: Moving toward description logic programs. Theory Pract. Logic Program. **8**(3), 301–322 (2008)
17. T. Scheffer, R. Herbrich, F. Wysotzki, Efficient theta-Subsumption based on Graph Algorithms. *Lecture Notes In Computer Science*, vol. 1314 (Springer, Berlin/New York, 1996)
18. K. Sycara, S. Widoff, M. Klusch, J. Lu, LARKS: dynamic matchmaking among heterogeneous software agents in cyberspace. Auton. Agent Multi-Agent Syst. **5**, 173–203 (2002), Kluwer

Chapter 6
SPARQLent: A SPARQL Based Intelligent Agent Performing Service Matchmaking

Marco Luca Sbodio

Abstract This chapter describes the experimental results of SPARQLent, a SPARQL-based intelligent agent that performs exact and approximate service matchmaking. We give an introduction describing (1) how SPARQL can be used as expression language to describe the preconditions/effects of services, as well as the goals of agents, and (2) how SPARQL query evaluation supports computation of effects, and checking of preconditions/goal satisfiability. We describe experimental results in a real world application where our approach has been used to automate the selection of assistance services for citizens. We also present a comparative evaluation based on the standard test collection OWLS-TC. Finally, we conclude with some lessons learned, and some suggestions for future work.

6.1 Introduction

The Semantic Web vision proposed by Tim Berners-Lee in 1999 [2] almost immediately suggested the possibility of building Semantic Web services [18]. At the same time, the Semantic Web languages give information a well defined meaning, thus enabling the definition of machine processable world descriptions. These two trends combine in the idea of deploying Intelligent Agents in the Semantic Web [9], and to use them for service discovery and planning. These remain interesting and promising ideas, especially today when the Semantic Web vision has crystallized a set of standards and well supported languages (RDF, OWL, SPARQL) and related technologies.

In general, effective service matchmaking requires service descriptions that are adequately expressive, including not only the semantics of the inputs and outputs, but also the definitions of *preconditions* and *effects*. Preconditions are conditions

M.L. Sbodio (✉)
Smarter Cities Technology Centre, IBM Research, Dublin, Ireland
e-mail: marco.sbodio@ie.ibm.com

M.B. Blake et al. (eds.), *Semantic Web Services*, DOI 10.1007/978-3-642-28735-0_6,
© Springer-Verlag Berlin Heidelberg 2012

that must hold true before invoking a service, to ensure successful use of the service, and effects are conditions that will hold true after the successful use of a service.

There have been several proposals for the definition of Semantic Web services, the most well know being OWL-S [17], WSMO [3], and SAWSDL [5]. Remarkably, all these proposals are either underconstrained or based on non-standard formalisms. OWL-S uses standard Semantic Web languages (OWL) to provide an expressive and detailed vocabulary for describing services. Although it offers direct binding mechanisms to traditional Web services (WSDL), it is actually general enough to enable the description of any kind of service. Unfortunately, it is underconstrained and somewhat vague with respect to the definition of preconditions and effects, and it lacks the notion of goal. WSMO offers a very comprehensive framework for describing services in a planning domain, defining not only services preconditions and effects, but also agents goals. Unfortunately, WSMO relies on formalisms and languages falling outside the set of Semantic Web standards. Finally, the recently standardized SAWSDL takes a conservative approach by adding some semantics to existing services descriptions (WSDL). Although SAWSDL relies on standard technologies, it has at least two major limitations: (1) it addresses only WSDL-based services and (2) it define only the semantics of their input/output messages without taking into account preconditions and effects.

Our research [23] aims at filling in the gaps outlined above, thus showing (1) how standard Semantic Web languages can fully characterize services and agents goals, and (2) how Intelligent Agents can perform service matchmaking and planning over the Web. In the context of our work we consider an agent's goal as a state of affairs that the agent wants to bring about in the world; the goal can be formally characterized by a condition that expresses what the agent wants to be true. The specification of preconditions and effects, and the drawing of inferences based upon them, is a distinguishing feature of our work. We use SPARQL [21] as an expression language to describe the preconditions and effects of services, as well as the goals of a service-requesting agent. We describe the overall approach in Sect. 6.2, showing that SPARQL query evaluation can be used to check the truth of preconditions in a given context, construct the effects that will result from the execution of a service in a context, and determine whether a service execution with those results will satisfy the goal of an agent. We describe our implementation of a SPARQL based agent (*SPARQLent*) performing service matchmaking (and planning) in Sect. 6.3. Finally, we evaluate our implementation and discuss lessons learned and future work in Sect. 6.4.

6.2   Approach: SPARQL as an Expression Language

From an abstract point of view, a service can be seen as an action that causes a world state transition. A service description defines the semantics of input and output types, the preconditions and the effects. An agent can invoke the service if and only if its preconditions hold when evaluated against the current description of the world state. Assuming that the preconditions hold in the current world state, the service yields some effects, which express what will be true in the world state resulting from the service's execution.

We consider an *intelligent agent* [29] that wants to accomplish some task or to achieve some *goal*, and therefore looks for Web services that offer appropriate operations to achieve its intentions. The agent is situated in an environment, that is, it has a (possibly incomplete) consistent description of the current state of the world. This world state description is given in the agent's *knowledge base*, which, in our approach, is an RDF graph. The agent's goal and the services' preconditions and effects are modeled with SPARQL graph patterns, which are evaluated against the current world state as given by the agent's knowledge base. A detailed description of the approach is given in [24]; for an in depth and comprehensive discussion including also the theoretical foundations of the approach we refer to [23]. Section 6.2.1 gives a short introduction to SPARQL, and defines the terminology for the rest of the chapter; Sect. 6.2.2 give an overview of how SPARQL can be used to define services' preconditions and effects, and agents goals.

6.2.1 A Short Introduction to SPARQL

In this section we present an abstract view of SPARQL for clarity of the examples in the next sections. SPARQL is a standardized query language that allows to query RDF data sources as directed labeled graphs. It has capabilities for querying required and optional graph patterns and their conjunctions and/or disjunctions; it supports also value testing and filtering of results. For an in depth description of SPARQL we refer to [20, 21]; for a discussion on the expressive power of SPARQL we refer to [1].

SPARQL queries can yield either result sets or RDF graphs. A SPARQL graph pattern is made of triple patterns belonging to the set $(\mathcal{T} \cup \mathcal{V}) \times (\mathcal{I} \cup \mathcal{V}) \times (\mathcal{T} \cup \mathcal{V})$, where $\mathcal{T}$ is the set of RDF terms (namely IRIs, blank nodes and literals), $\mathcal{V}$ is a set of variable names, and $\mathcal{I}$ is the set of IRIs. Following [20], a SPARQL graph pattern Γ can be inductively defined as:

$$\Gamma ::= \{p_0, p_1, \ldots p_n\} \mid$$
$$\{\gamma_0, \gamma_1 \ldots \gamma_n\} \mid$$
$$\gamma_0 \text{ OPTIONAL } \gamma_1 \mid \qquad (6.1)$$
$$\gamma_0 \text{ UNION } \gamma_1 \text{ UNION } \ldots \gamma_n \mid$$
$$\gamma_0 \text{ FILTER } r$$

where $\gamma_0, \ldots \gamma_n \in \Gamma$, $p_0, p_1, \ldots p_n$ are triple patterns, and r is an expression that eliminates those solutions that, when substituted into r, either result in an effective boolean value of false or produce an error. A *basic graph pattern* $\{p_0, p_1, \ldots p_n\}$ is a set of triple patterns, where each query result must match all triple patterns. A *group graph pattern* $\{\gamma_0, \gamma_1 \ldots \gamma_n\}$ is a set of graph patterns, where each query result must match all graph patterns. An *optional graph pattern* γ_0 OPTIONAL γ_1 is made of a pair of graph patterns, where the second pattern extends the results of the first, but does not cause the overall graph pattern to fail. Finally, an *alternative graph pattern* γ_0 UNION γ_1 UNION $\ldots \gamma_n$ is the disjunction of two (or more) graph patterns, where any graph pattern can match. SPARQL has various *query forms*, among which are SELECT (returning the variable bindings that result from each match of the query graph pattern), ASK (returning a boolean that indicates whether the query graph pattern matches or not), and CONSTRUCT (returning an RDF graph specified by a graph template).

6.2.2 Describing Services and Goals with SPARQL Graph Patterns

We use the CONSTRUCT query form to give a compact representation of the preconditions and effects of a service. A CONSTRUCT query is made of a *template pattern* consisting of a basic graph pattern ε, and a WHERE clause consisting of a graph patter π. The CONSTRUCT query yields an RDF graph G_ε formed by taking each query solution, substituting for the variables into the graph template ε, and combining the triples into a single RDF graph by set union. We use the graph pattern π to represent the service's preconditions, and the template pattern ε to define its effects.

The semantics of input and output types of an atomic service can be included in the graph patterns π and ε, by adding triple patterns with the RDF property rdf:type. More precisely:

- The graph pattern π may contain triple patterns that constrain the semantics of the service's inputs;
- The template patterns ε may contain triple patterns that constrain the semantics of the service's output.

Figure 6.1 shows an example of a SPARQL graph pattern π and template pattern ε defining the preconditions and effects of a fictitious bookseller. We assume that the namespaces bookont and ecom refer to ontologies defining respectively the publishing domain and the e-commerce domain. The namespace readmore identifies a proprietary ontology of the bookseller.

Note that the graph patterns π and ε share some variables (thus constraining the definition of the effects to the context in which preconditions are evaluated), and that they define also the semantics of input and output types. The preconditions π shown in Fig. 6.1a requires that the book is identified by a bookont:ISBN (subgraph π_1), the customer is a registered user of the bookseller Web site (subgraph π_2), and the

a

```
{
    ?bookISBN a bookont:ISBN .                              (π₁)

    ?signInInfo a readmore:SignInData ;
        readmore:hasAcctID ?acctID .                        (π₂)
    ?acctID a readmore:AcctID .

    ?creditCard a ecom:CreditCard ;
        ecom:cardNumber ?creditCardNumber ;

        ecom:cardType [ a ecom:CreditCardType ] ;

        ecom:cardExpiration ?expirationDate ;

        ecom:validity ecom:Valid .                          (π₃)

    FILTER (
        dataType(?creditCardNumber) = xsd:string &&

        dataType(?expirationDate) = xsd:gYearMonth
    )
}
```

π

b

```
{
    _:book a readmore:InStockBook ;
        bookont:hasISBN ?bookISBN .                         (ε₁)

    _:output a readmore:OrderShippedAck .                    (ε₂)

    _:shipment a readmore:Shipment ;
        readmore:shippedTo ?acctID ;                        (ε₃)

        readmore:shippedBook _:book .

    ?creditCard ecom:charged _:purchaseAmount .

    _:purchaseAmount a ecom:Amount ;
        ecom:hasValue _:purchaseValue ;                     (ε₄)

        ecom:hasCurrency _:purchaseCurrency .
}
```

ε

Fig. 6.1 Preconditions and effects of a bookseller's atomic service (π, ε) expressed as SPARQL graph patterns. (**a**) Preconditions. (**b**) Effects

given credit card, whose number is a string, and whose expiration date is specified by a month and a year, is a valid credit card (subgraph π_3). The effects shown in Fig. 6.1b intuitively state that there exists a book with the specified ISBN and that it is in stock (subgraph ε_1), there is an acknowledgment of the shipped order (subgraph ε_2), there is a shipment including the required book and shipped to the specified account (subgraph ε_3), and finally the specified credit card is charged with an amount having a value and a currency (subgraph ε_4).

From an abstract point of view, given the agent's world state w_a, and an RDF graph G_{w_a} representing the (possibly incomplete) consistent view of w_a as known by the agent's knowledge base, the evaluation of the preconditions π, and the construction of the effects ε of the service is done by evaluating the SPARQL query CONSTRUCT ε WHERE π on G_{w_a}. The CONSTRUCT query form allows for the programmatic creation of the RDF graph that expresses the effects of the service; the construction of this graph is constrained by the template pattern ε. Note that if the graph pattern π has no solution over G_{w_a}, then the CONSTRUCT query yields an empty graph pattern. This represents the case where the service preconditions do not hold in the world state w_a, and therefore the service cannot be executed. Conversely, if the graph pattern π has solutions over G_{w_a}, the CONSTRUCT query yields an RDF graph G_e. By merging G_e with G_{w_a}, we compute the new RDF graph $G_{w_{a'}}$, that is the updated content of the agent knowledge base, corresponding to the partial description of the new world state $w_{a'}$ resulting from the execution of the service. We observe that the merging of RDF graphs is computed according to [8]. The description of strategies for ensuring consistency of the resulting RDF graph is beyond the scope of this chapter. We simply observe that the consistency of world descriptions is a well known problem that affects system reasoning about action and change (see [4, 7, 10, 11, 22, 26–28]); for a more in depth discussion on how this problem affects our approach we refer the reader to [23, 24].

Finally, we model the agent goal with a SPARQL graph pattern γ, which essentially characterizes the conditions expressing what the agent wants to be true in a world state. Note that the use of SPARQL allows us to include in the goal condition not only ontological concepts, but also values (individuals) and variables. We can check weather the goal would be achieved by using the SPARQL ASK query form. Given the RDF graph $G_{w_{a'}}$ describing the world state resulting from the execution of a service, we can evaluate the SPARQL query ASK γ on $G_{w_{a'}}$: if such a query returns true, then the goal represented by γ would satisfied.

6.3 Solution: Service Index and SPARQLent

The envisioned approach can be implemented using a distributed Web architecture. A *Services Index* (Sect. 6.3.1), inspired by traditional Web indexes, harvest services descriptions from the Web, builds internal data structures with service representation models, and answers agent queries. A *SPARQLent* (Sect. 6.3.2), a SPARQL based Intelligent Agent, performs exact or approximate service matchmaking (and planning) by querying a Services Index, and reasoning on services preconditions and effects.

6.3.1 Services Index

The Services Index exploits the SPARQL expressions defining the services' preconditions and effects to build an internal data structure that supports the construction of
answer sets corresponding to agents queries. For an in depth discussion on (1) how
to embed SPARQL expressions in various services descriptions (including OWL-S,
SAWSDL, and RESTful services), (2) how to build the Services Index internal data
structure, and (3) how to use it to answer agents queries we refer to [23].

In principle, the functioning of a Services Index is similar to that of a traditional
Web search engine. Background processes feed a Services Index with updated
information on services descriptions. On the other side, agents querying a Services
Index receive as a result a set of items describing services matching their queries.

An agent querying a Services Index is searching for services whose effects (fully
or partially) fulfill its goal. In our approach, an agent's goal is a SPARQL graph
pattern γ, and it is therefore desirable that a Services Index is able to accept γ as a
query. In order to answer this kind of query, a Services Index $\mathbb{X}$ should find the set of
services whose execution in an initial world state w_a can terminate in a world state
w_i such that the graph pattern γ (the agent's goal) has solutions when evaluated in a
description of w_i. The initial world state w_a should be the current world of the agent
making the query γ, and $\mathbb{X}$ would use w_a to check if services' preconditions are
satisfied. However, it is unlikely that a Services Index has any knowledge of w_a. It
is therefore necessary to find a way for a Services Index to answer queries without
having any description of the initial world w_a. To this purpose, a Service Index
builds a special representation of the effects of the indexed services, that we call
unconstrained effects. Intuitively, given the SPARQL template pattern ε defining the
effects of a service, we can instantiate it into an RDF graph by substituting every
variable in ε with an RDF blank node.[1]

The computation of the unconstrained effects of a service is done through a
skolemization function (which is similar to First Order Logic skolemization). Given
the SPARQL template pattern ε defining the effects of a service, its unconstrained
effects are given by an RDF graph G_ε computed by evaluating the SPARQL query
CONSTRUCT *skolemize* (ε) WHERE $\gamma_\emptyset$ on the empty RDF data set $D_\emptyset$ (also written
as $G_\varepsilon \leftarrow (\gamma_\emptyset, D_\emptyset, CONSTRUCT\ skolemize(\varepsilon))$). Figure 6.2 shows the
unconstrained effects G_ε corresponding to the effects ε of the bookseller service
shown in Fig. 6.1.

The Services Index stores the RDF graph representing the unconstrained effects
of indexed services in its internal data structure, which is essentially the RDF dataset
$DS_{\mathbb{X}} = \{G_{idx}, (u_0, G_{\varepsilon_0}), \ldots, (u_n, G_{\varepsilon_n})\}$. The named graph (u_i, G_{ε_i}) corresponds to
an *index entry*, and it gives the unconstrained effects G_{ε_i} of a service identified
by IRI u_i. The default graph G_{idx} is used as index for the whole dataset, and it

---

[1]A blank node is by definition equivalent to an existentially quantified variable, and in fact blank
nodes serve the purpose of representing resources that cannot be named at present.

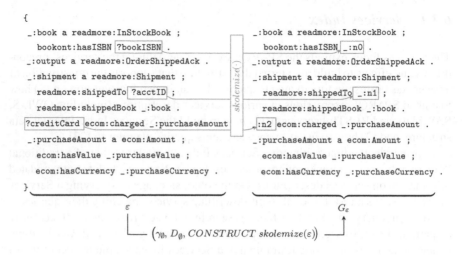

Fig. 6.2 Unconstrained effects G_ε of the bookseller service

contains relevant information about index entires, including the SPARQL graph pattern defining the preconditions and effects.

A SPARQLent agent can query the Services Index by passing the SPARQL graph pattern γ representing its goal. If the goal is too specific (its triple patterns refer to specific resources or individuals), then checking its satisfiability in the RDF graph representing the unconstrained effects of a service may be unfeasible. In fact, the unconstrained effects represent a kind of generalization of the actual effects, in which the *skolemize* function has introduced blank nodes in place of currently unknown resources. Therefore the Services Index *generalizes* the graph pattern γ. Intuitively, the function $\gamma_{gen} = generalize(\gamma)$ replaces named individuals in the triple patterns in γ with freshly created variables, and it is essentially the dual of the previously introduced *skolemize* function.

Finally, a Services Index can answer an agent query γ by (1) computing γ_{gen}, and then (2) evaluating the SPARQL query

$$\text{SELECT ?u WHERE GRAPH ?u} \left\{ \gamma \text{ UNION } \gamma_{gen} \right\}$$

against its dataset DS_X. Such a query returns the set of IRIs identifying services whose effects may satisfy the agent goal γ. Such an answer set is inherently imprecise (because its computation is based on unconstrained effects and generalized goals). However, its cardinality is is very likely to be smaller than that of the set of all possible services, and it is therefore useful to limit the number of candidate services that SPARQLent agent must check when performing service matchmaking.

6.3.2   SPARQLent

A SPARQLent is a goal-directed Intelligent Agent. Its goal is specified as a SPARQL graph pattern. It has a knowledge base, maintained by a reasoner, which can be serialized into an RDF graph. Its algorithms perform service matchmaking by reasoning on the SPARQL graph patterns defining the preconditions and effects of services. A SPARQLent can perform both exact and approximate matchmaking, and it can also perform regression planning to build service sequences satisfying its goal.

The basic discovery algorithm relies on the answer set returned by a Services Index. For each service identified by an entry u_i returned by the Service Index, the SPARQLent retrieves the graph patterns π and ε representing respectively the services preconditions and effects, and then it computes the the RDF graph G_e as described in Sect. 6.2.2. If G_e is not empty, then the SPARQLent updates its knowledge base by merging G_e into it (such a merging is temporary, and the SPARQLent will undo it when preparing for evaluating the next candidate service). Finally, it uses the updated knowledge base to check the satisfiability of its goal as described in Sect. 6.2.2. This allows the SPARQLent to filter the set of candidate services returned by the Services Index, and to select only those services whose preconditions are satisfiable, and whose effects causes a transition to a world state where the agent goal is satisfied.

An interesting feature of a SPARQLent is the ability of performing approximate matchmaking through *graph pattern relaxation.* Intuitively, the SPARQLent can progressively relax constraints represented by SPARQL triple patterns in the graph pattern π corresponding to a service's preconditions. This is done by identifying the minimal subgraph o of π of unsatisfiable constraints, and by replacing π with the SPARQL optional graph pattern μ $OPTIONAL$ o, where μ is, broadly speaking, the set complement of the triples of the subgraph o with respect to π. The relaxation of a generic graph pattern is defined by induction on its structure, using the basic graph pattern as base case (see [23]).

6.4   Lessons Learned

6.4.1   Evaluation Results

We present here the evaluation results of our approach in two domains: (1) automatic selection of assistance and welfare service for citizens, and (2) with respect to the standard test collection OWLS-TC. The first evaluation domain shows the flexibility of our approach, which can be used also for non-traditional Web services, and it describes the integration of our SPARQLent in a real-world application through which we collected feedbacks from real users. The second evaluation provides a quantitative evaluation of our approach with respect to a standard test collection (OWLS-TC), which allows for comparison with other approaches.

6.4.1.1 Automatic Selection of Services for Citizens

This section describes our experience in using SPARQLent agents to discover and compose e-Government services. This work has been conducted within the FP6 European funded project Terregov; for an in-depth description of Terregov results see also [25].

A very common process in the e-Government domain is the selection of assistance and welfare services that public administrations offer to citizens. Such services are usually associated with a set of eligibility criteria, which define the categories of citizens that may have access to (or may benefit from) a specific service. The eligibility criteria for a given service may vary from one local public administration to another (both country-specific and region-specific), and may also change over time reflecting modifications in potentially related laws. This makes the selection of appropriate services for a citizen a challenging and time/resource consuming process. Such a process, which we refer to as *e-Government services selection*, consists of the three major phases listed below.

- *Request* phase. The citizen makes a request, which can be either specific (the citizen would like to benefit from a specific service), or generic (the citizen would like to know which services she/he might be eligible for).
- *Profile building* phase. The public administration gathers general information about the citizen. Such information is often augmented with specific information provided by various specialists who assess the citizen's situation: the assessments may involve, for example, medical examinations, or interviews with the citizens. The overall information bundle is called the *citizen profile*.
- *Selection* phase. A group of domain experts, who know the details of the available services, examine the various citizen cases, evaluate the information of each citizen profile, and select the most appropriate service(s).

The citizen profile consists of a broad set of information items, some of which are directly provided by the citizen when making the request, while others are disseminated in various government agencies, or provided by the various specialists who assess the actual citizen's situation. Collecting and consolidating all these information items is often very difficult and time consuming. Moreover the third phase (selection) often requires physical meetings among domain experts. Such meetings are usually difficult to schedule, and thus the final phase becomes a bottleneck for the whole e-Government services selection process, further reducing its overall efficiency.

During the Terregov project we studied a real world use case which falls into the above general scenario. The use case is based on a large public authority in northern Italy (Regione Veneto[2]), which offers various social care services for elderly or physically/mentally impaired people. We have applied our approach both to traditional Web services and to general e-Government services (social services,

---

[2]http://www.regione.veneto.it/

health assistance, economic support services, etc.). In order to improve the overall efficiency of the e-Government service selection process we used SPARQLent to automate the final selection phase, during which the domain experts meet to identify the appropriate services for a citizen based on her/his profile.

Although e-Government services (such as health assistance, economic support, housing services, etc.) are not Web services, we used OWL-S to give their formal semantic descriptions. We chose OWL-S because its grounding part is optional, and so it is possible to describe services that are not tied to a particular interface: this is exactly the case of e-Government services. We encoded the eligibility criteria of the corresponding service as preconditions using SPARQL graph patterns. We extended the Terregov ontology with a hierarchy of classes defining the e-Government services identified in the Terregov use case. The root of this hierarchy is the concept Assistance. We used subclasses of Assistance to define the effects of the services.

Figure 6.3 shows two examples. The *CONSTRUCT* query shown in Fig. 6.3a defines a service providing economic assistance; its eligibility criteria require that either the citizen has a job with an income lower than 5,000, or the citizen is jobless and is classified as having "low" wealth. The *CONSTRUCT* query shown in Fig. 6.3b defines a service providing medical assistance at home; the associated eligibility criteria require that the citizen is alone (no cohabitants), has "low" social status, and she/he is older than 65.

The Terregov use case provided us with 20 different e-Government services that we formally described using OWL-S and SPARQL. We used a SPARQLent to discover which service a particular citizen was eligible for. The SPARQLent's beliefs base was initialized with a subset of the citizen's profile, and its goal simply consisted in the following graph pattern:

```
{?citizen tgv:hasSocialBenefit [ a tgv:Assistance ] .}
```

We integrated the SPARQLent in the back-end layer of a Web application supporting the e-Government selection process. When a citizen's profile was complete, the Web application used the SPARQLent to discover the services that the citizen was eligible for, and then sent an e-mail to the domain expert with the set of identified services. The e-mail contained also three links: the first link gave access to the complete citizen's profile; the other two links allowed the domain expert to either approve or reject the proposed set of services. If all domain experts approved such a set, then the process completed without any meeting among them. In the other case (one or more domain experts rejected the proposed set of services) the citizen's request was put on hold, and postponed until the next meeting among domain experts.

We conducted three trial sessions during the Terregov project. The trial sessions involved respectively 5, 7, and 10 domain experts, who processed various citizens requests using our Web application. We tested 40 different citizen profiles (cases). We performed the same test twice, using both exact and approximate capabilities of the SPARQLent. In the case of relaxed discovery the list of identified e-Government

a   **b**

```
CONSTRUCT {

  ?citizen tgv:hasSocialBenefit [

    a tgv:EconomicAssistance ;

    a tgv:Assistance

  ] .

}

WHERE {

  {

    ?citizen a tgv:Person ;

      tgv:hasJob ?job ;

      tgv:hasGainedIncome [

        tgv:hasAmount ?amount

      ] .

    FILTER (?amount <= 5000)

  }

  UNION

  {

    ?citizen a tgv:Person ;

      tgv:hasPersonalWealthIndicator ?w .

    OPTIONAL {

      ?citizen tgv:hasJob ?job .

    }

    FILTER (

      ! bound(?job) &&

      regex(?w, "low", "i")

    )

  }

}
```

```
CONSTRUCT {

  ?citizen tgv:hasSocialBenefit [

    a tgv:HomeMedicalAssistance ;

    a tgv:Assistance

  ] .

}

WHERE {

  {

    ?citizen a tgv:Person ;

      tgv:hasAge ?age ;

      tgv:hasSocialStatusIndicator ?status .

  OPTIONAL {

    ?citizen tgv:livesWith ?cohabitants .

  }

  FILTER (

    ! bound(?cohabitants) &&

    regex(?status, "low", "i") &&

    age >= 65

  )

  }

}
```

Fig. 6.3 Examples of e-Government service preconditions (eligibility criteria) and effects

services contained relaxed matches, where some eligibility criteria were not met by the subset of the citizen's profile available in the SPARQLent belief base.

Table 6.1 summarizes the result of the largest trial session (10 domain experts processing 40 citizen's cases): the table shows the number of cases for which SPARQLent was able to automatically suggest services (automated proposals), how many of these automated proposals were approved by all domain experts (approved proposals), and the number of cases for which the domain experts were not required to meet (avoided meetings).

We observe that the SPARQLent was not always able to identify services: the percentage of success ranges from 75% (with normal discovery) to 92.5% (with relaxed discovery). This was due to two reasons. Firstly, one of the 40

Table 6.1 Trial results: 10 domain experts reviewing SPARQLent selection on 40 citizen cases

		Exact matching		Relaxed matching
Automated proposals	30	75.00%	37	92.50%
Approved proposals	26	86.67%	30	81.08%
Avoided meetings	26	65.00%	30	75.00%

citizen profiles was actually designed to not satisfy any eligibility criteria for the available services. Secondly, some eligibility criteria involved information beyond the content of SPARQLent knowledge base, which was initialized with a subset of the citizen's profile. The second point explains also why the percentage of success was higher when using relaxed discovery. Note, however, that relaxed discovery still encountered a small percentage of cases for which it was not possible to find appropriate services. In fact, the graph pattern relaxation avoids the construction of entirely optional graph patterns (that would match on any knowledge base).

The domain experts accepted the proposed set of services in 65% of the cases when the SPARQLent was using normal discovery, and in 75% of the cases when using relaxed discovery. During post-trials interviews, some domain experts explained their rejection saying that, although the set of services was appropriate, the full information available in the citizen's profile suggested for a more in-depth analysis of the case. Noticeably, this happened more frequently when the SPARQLent was using relaxed discovery.

Overall, the domain experts were positively impressed by our results: we showed in fact that the SPARQLent helped to reduce the need for meetings among them in at least 65% of the cases, which was regarded as a considerable improvement in the efficiency of the e-Government services selection process.

6.4.1.2   Evaluation with Respect to OWLS-TC

A major issue in the area of Semantic Web services research has been the lack of reference test sets. Recently OWLS-TC[3] has filled in this gap. OWLS-TC is a test collection consisting of OWL-S services descriptions. Such a test collection aims at supporting the evaluation of the performance of OWL-S services matchmaking algorithms. We have used OWLS-TC version 3, which includes 1,007 Web services descriptions written in OWL-S 1.1, and 29 queries with corresponding relevance sets (true answers).

Unfortunately, the semantics of OWLS-TC services descriptions is only partially specified, because they give only the input/output types (by referring to concepts in various ontologies) without describing preconditions and effects. In order to use our Services Index and SPARQLent with OWLS-TC we developed a *Transformer*, which generates SPARQL graph patterns from OWLS-TC services and queries descriptions. More precisely:

---

[3]http://projects.semwebcentral.org/projects/owls-tc/

- OWLS-TC services descriptions essentially consists of OWL-S atomic processes giving the semantics of inputs and outputs by referring to concepts in various ontologies. Given the list of input concepts $\mathscr{S}_I = (I_1, I_2, \ldots, I_m)$, and the list of output concepts $\mathscr{S}_O = (O_1, O_2, \ldots, O_n)$ of an OWL-S atomic process, we build:

  - π, a Basic Graph Pattern containing a triple pattern for every input concept $I_i \in \mathscr{S}_I$; such triple patterns have the form `?x`$_i$ `rdf:type` I_i;
  - ε, a Template Pattern containing a triple pattern for every output concept $O_i \in \mathscr{S}_O$; such triple patterns have the form `_:output`$_i$ `rdf:type` O_i, where `_:output`$_i$ is a blank node.

  We essentially represent an OWL-S atomic process with the SPARQL graph pattern π giving the preconditions as constraints on the input types, and a SPARQL template pattern ε giving the effects as assertions on the output types.
- Similarly to services, OWLS-TC queries consists of OWL-S atomic processes giving the semantics of inputs and outputs by referring to concepts in various ontologies. Given the list of input concepts $\mathscr{Q}_I = (I_1, I_2, \ldots, I_m)$, and the list of output concepts $\mathscr{Q}_O = (O_1, O_2, \ldots, O_n)$ of a query, we interpret its description in the following way:

  - $\mathscr{Q}_O$ gives the list of required outputs, and therefore we use it to generate a Basic Graph Pattern γ representing the goal of our SPARQLent; γ contains a triple pattern for every output concept $O_i \in \mathscr{Q}_O$; such triple patterns have the form `_:output`$_i$ `rdf:type` O_i, where `_:output`$_i$ is a blank node;
  - We use $\mathscr{Q}_I$ to build the content of the SPARQLent knowledge base: for each $I_i \in \mathscr{Q}_I$ we create a blank node of type I_i.

  We essentially say that the SPARQLent goal corresponds to instances of all the output concepts specified in the query, and that its knowledge base contains instances of the input concepts specified in the query.

The transformations described above allow us to (1) index the OWLS-TC services descriptions in our services index, and (2) use our SPARQLent to answer OWLS-TC queries. We observe that the transformation outlined above can also take into account the subsumption hierarchies corresponding to the various input and output concepts.

We have implemented the `IMatchmakerPlugin` interface which allowed us to plug our code into the SME^2 test tool.[4] The Semantic Web Service Matchmaker Evaluation Environment (SME^2) is an open source tool for testing different semantic matchmakers in a consistent way. SME^2 uses OWLS-TC to provide the matchmakers with service descriptions, and to compare their answers to the relevance sets of the various queries.

---

[4]http://projects.semwebcentral.org/projects/sme2/

Table 6.2 Configurations of services index and SPARQLent tested with SME^2

Exact matchmaking		$\mathbb{X}AEe$	$\mathbb{X}_pA_pE_pe$	$\mathbb{X}_{pb}A_{pb}E_{pb}e$
Unconstrained effects in services	Infer super-concepts	n	y	y
index ($\mathbb{X}$)	Infer sub-concepts	n	n	y
SPARQLent knowledge base (A)	Infer super-concepts	n	y	y
	Infer sub-concepts	n	n	y
Computed effects in	Infer super-concepts	n	y	y
SPARQLent (E)	Infer sub-concepts	n	n	y
Relaxed matchmaking		$\mathbb{X}AEr$	$\mathbb{X}_pA_pE_pr$	$\mathbb{X}_{pb}A_{pb}E_{pb}r$
Unconstrained effects in services	Infer super-concepts	n	y	y
index ($\mathbb{X}$)	Infer sub-concepts	n	n	y
SPARQLent knowledge base (A)	Infer super-concepts	n	y	y
	Infer sub-concepts	n	n	y
Computed effects in	Infer super-concepts	n	y	y
SPARQLent (E)	Infer sub-concepts	n	n	y

SME^2 computes macro-averaged values of precision and fallout over all queries, thus giving equal weight to every query.[5] We observe that the computation of macro-averaged precision and recall requires ranking of the answer set: we adopted a subsumption-based ranking strategy as described in [19] to order the results returned by the SPARQLent discovery algorithm (more sophisticated ranking strategy may improve the test results).

We used SME^2 to test six configurations of our services index and SPARQLent, as summarized in Table 6.2.

The six configurations differ in the entailment regime supported by the services index and the SPARQLent, and in the ability of performing exact or relaxed matchmaking. The configurations $\mathbb{X}AEe$ and $\mathbb{X}AEr$ use RDF entailment regime. The configurations $\mathbb{X}_pA_pE_pe$ and $\mathbb{X}_pA_pE_pr$ use OWL-DL's entailment regime, but infer only super-concepts. Finally, the configurations $\mathbb{X}_{pb}A_{pb}E_{pb}e$ and $\mathbb{X}_{pb}A_{pb}E_{pb}r$ use OWL-DL entailment regime, and infer both super- and sub-concepts. The configurations $\mathbb{X}_{pb}A_{pb}E_{pb}e$ and $\mathbb{X}_{pb}A_{pb}E_{pb}r$ introduce an additional approximation: it is not necessarily correct to infer sub-concepts in the unconstrained effects in the services index ($\mathbb{X}$), and in the computed effects in the SPARQLent (E). For example, if the template pattern ε of an atomic service contains the triple pattern `_:w rdf:type wine:Wine`, then it is safe to assert `_:w rdf:type food:PotableLiquid`, but it is not necessarily correct to assert `_:w rdf:type wine:RedWine` (where the concepts `food:PotableLiquid` and `wine:RedWine` are respectively a super-concept and a sub-concept of `wine:Wine`).

---

[5]Precision, recall and fallout are standard measures for evaluating the performance of information retrieval systems. Intuitively, *precision* is the fraction of the answer set that is relevant to the query, whereas *recall* is the fraction of the set of relevant items for the query that has been retrieved. Finally, *fallout* represents the fraction of non-relevant items that are retrieved.

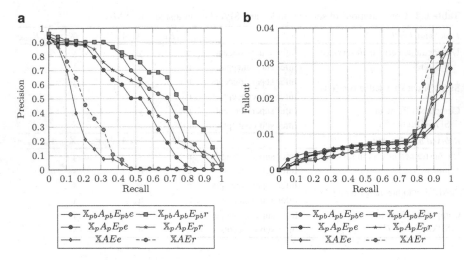

Fig. 6.4 Recall-Precision and Recall-Fallout curves for SPARQLent variants. (**a**) Recall-Precision of SPARQLent variants. (**b**) Recall-Fallout of SPARQLent variants

Figure 6.4a and b show the macro-averaged precision and recall of the various configurations of Table 6.2. Figure 6.4b shows that all configurations have a very small fallout, thus indicating that SPARQLent retrieves very small fractions of nonrelevant services. Figure 6.4a shows that given two configurations with the same entailment regime, the one using relaxed matchmaking has better performance than the one using exact matchmaking; this demonstrates that the graph pattern relaxation technique increases the fraction of the SPARQLent answer set that is relevant to the query. The configuration $\mathbb{X}_{pb}A_{pb}E_{pb}r$ gives the best performance with respect to the recall-precision curve.

Figure 6.5a and b compare our best configuration $\mathbb{X}_{pb}A_{pb}E_{pb}r$ with some variants of OWLS-MX, an hybrid Semantic Web services matchmaker providing both traditional input/output subsumption and approximate matching based on information retrieval techniques [15, 16]. We tested three variants of OWLS-MX:

- *OWLS-M0 (logic-based)* is a purely logic-based matchmaker that relies on subsumption reasoning.
- *OWLS-MX textSim only (Cos)* compares query descriptions and service descriptions based on text similarity. It performs text similarity matching on concept descriptions: it considers inputs and outputs separately (looking at concatenated concept description strings of either inputs or outputs as a plain text document), and then average the results to obtain an overall similarity value.
- *OWLS-M3 (MX2, hybrid, Cos)* is an hybrid matchmaker performing both logic-based subsumption reasoning and text similarity matching. It uses text similarity to avoid false positive arising, for example, from poor concepts definitions or incomplete services descriptions.

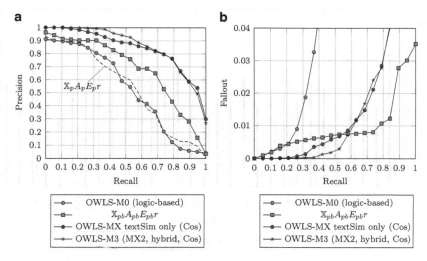

Fig. 6.5 Precision and Fallout for SPARQLent $\mathbb{X}_{pb}A_{pb}E_{pb}r$ and OWLS-MX variants (**a**) Recall-Precision of OWLS-MX variants versus SPARQLent $\mathbb{X}_{pb}A_{pb}E_{pb}r$. (**b**) Recall-Fallout of OWLS-MX variants versus SPARQLent $\mathbb{X}_{pb}A_{pb}E_{pb}r$

Technically, the only fair comparison is between *OWLS-M0* and $\mathbb{X}_{pb}A_{pb}E_{pb}r$, which are both purely logic-based matchmakers. The other OWLS-MX variants exploit also text similarities in the services and/or concepts descriptions, thus detecting also aspects that escape the formal descriptions. For example, OWLS-TC services and queries descriptions do not have any formal precondition, but some of them have text comments that informally state preconditions: while $\mathbb{X}_{pb}A_{pb}E_{pb}r$ and *OWLS-M0* cannot exploit such comments, the other variants of OWLS-MX can.

Nevertheless, the comparison among $\mathbb{X}_{pb}A_{pb}E_{pb}r$ and OWLS-MX variants highlights some interesting results. Firstly, Fig. 6.5a shows that $\mathbb{X}_{pb}A_{pb}E_{pb}r$ has generally the same or higher precision (with respect to recall) than *OWLS-M0*, which behaves approximately as $\mathbb{X}_{p}A_{p}E_{p}r$; the same figure shows also that the two OWLS-MX variants using text similarity outperform $\mathbb{X}_{pb}A_{pb}E_{pb}r$. Figure 6.5b highlights that the fallout is substantially smaller for $\mathbb{X}_{pb}A_{pb}E_{pb}r$ than for OWLS-MX variants: at the highest recall level (1), $\mathbb{X}_{pb}A_{pb}E_{pb}r$ fallout is 0.035, compared to 0.232 for *OWLS-M3 (MX2, hybrid, Cos)*, 0.240 for *OWLS-MX textSim only (Cos)*, and 0.931 for *OWLS-M0 (logic-based)*.

Figure 6.6 illustrates the response times for the three matchmakers $\mathbb{X}_{pb}A_{pb}E_{pb}r$, *OWLS-M0 (logic-based)*, and *OWLS-M3 (MX2, hybrid, Cos)* when answering the 29 queries (Q01 ... Q29) of OWLS-TC; the last column (Avg) gives the average response time for the three matchmakers.

The experimental results shows that $\mathbb{X}_{pb}A_{pb}E_{pb}r$ is considerably faster than the OWLS-MX variants. A remarkable exception is query Q26, where $\mathbb{X}_{pb}A_{pb}E_{pb}r$ is much slower than the others. This is due to the fact that query Q26 has no output (it searches for services that checks the credit card account of an authorized person, and add a given book to her/his shopping cart). The lack of outputs originates an

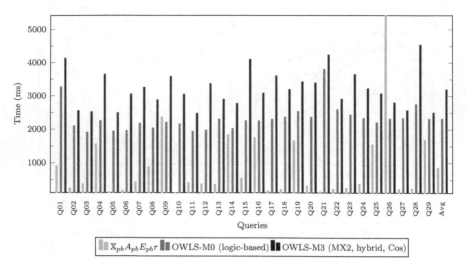

Fig. 6.6 Comparison of query response times for OWLS-TC

empty goal for our SPARQLent, thus all services in the services index are returned, and the amount of time to process all of them is high. The average values show that $\mathbb{X}_{pb}A_{pb}E_{pb}r$ is about 2.7 times faster than *OWLS-M0 (logic-based)* (860 ms vs. 2,321 ms), and about 3.7 times faster than *OWLS-M3 (MX2, hybrid, Cos)* (whose average query response time is 3,200 ms).

Finally, Fig. 6.7 illustrates the memory usage statistics for the three matchmakers $\mathbb{X}_{pb}A_{pb}E_{pb}r$, *OWLS-M0 (logic-based)*, and *OWLS-M3 (MX2, hybrid, Cos)*. The diagram clearly shows that $\mathbb{X}_{pb}A_{pb}E_{pb}r$ requires less memory than the OWLS-MX variants. The graph corresponding to $\mathbb{X}_{pb}A_{pb}E_{pb}r$ is more coarse grained than the others: this is due to the differences in the respective total execution times. Since $\mathbb{X}_{pb}A_{pb}E_{pb}r$ is almost 12 times faster than the OWLS-MX matchmakers, the SME^2 testing tool collects only 7 sample values during its execution (compared to about 80 sample values for the OWLS-MX matchmakers).

6.4.2 Advantages and Disadvantages

We summarize here some of the most important advantages and disadvantages of our approach, based on our experience, real-world trials and experiments.

- A distinguishing feature of our approach is the possibility of specifying services preconditions and effects using a standard and well know language (SPARQL). The use of standards may lower the adoption barrier of new technologies, often simplifying integration with existing software.

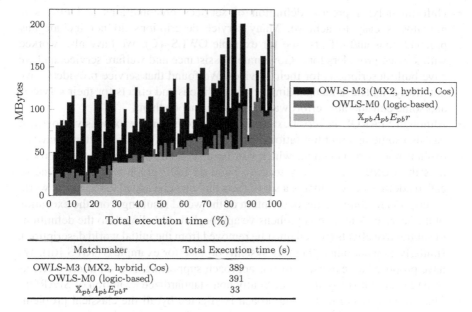

Matchmaker	Total Execution time (s)
OWLS-M3 (MX2, hybrid, Cos)	389
OWLS-M0 (logic-based)	391
$\mathbb{X}_{pb}A_{pb}E_{pb}r$	33

Fig. 6.7 Memory usage statistics

- Our usage of SPARQL graph patterns is compatible with various (Semantic) Web Service descriptions (including OWL-S, SAWSDL, and RESTful Web services), and it enriches such descriptions with formal definitions of preconditions and effects, that were previously left unspecified.
- We showed that SPARQL can also be used to define a goal of an Intelligent Agent that performs service matchmaking, thus filling in a gap in Semantic Web services formalisms such as OWL-S and SAWSDL.
- Our SPARQLent can reason on SPARQL expressions defining services preconditions and effects to perform both exact and approximate matchmaking. Our graph pattern relaxation technique is quite powerful. Comparison of precision curves (see Fig. 6.4) shows that SPARQLent variants exploiting graph pattern relaxation ($\mathbb{X}AEr$, $\mathbb{X}_pA_pE_pr$, and $\mathbb{X}_{pb}A_{pb}E_{pb}r$) perform better than their equivalent using only exact matchmaking ($\mathbb{X}AEe$, $\mathbb{X}_pA_pE_pe$, and $\mathbb{X}_{pb}A_{pb}E_{pb}e$).
- Since graph pattern relaxation is done by induction on the structure of the graph patterns, this technique remains in the logic-based domain. A SPARQLent can in fact isolate unsatisfiable triple patterns moving them into a SPARQL optional subgraph, which could become a sub-goal for the agent. This technique, although not discussed in this chapter, is used to build sequences of services by regression planning (see [23]).
- Test results show that our SPARQLent has good performance both in terms of precision, execution/response time, and memory usage. Additionally, the use of SPARQL and RDF dataset on the Services Index should support good scalability of server side processes answering agent queries.

- Unfortunately, a precise definition of services preconditions and effects is not always easy to achieve. Many service descriptions do not include any preconditions and effects (see for example OWLS-TC). We have also worked with service providers for e-Government assistance and welfare service, and we have built descriptions for their services. We found that service providers have not always a clear understanding of preconditions and effects for their services, and some considerable effort was required to encode them.
- Although SPARQL is very flexible and has a considerable expressive power, it has also some inherent limitations. Noticeably, SPARQL graph patterns have no explicit notion of negation, which can be a problem. Moreover, our approach uses the CONSTRUCT query form to build an RDF graph representing the so called additive effects, that is a set of facts that must be added to the initial world description to compute the description of the world resulting from the execution of the service. A more comprehensive approach would allow also the definitions of subtractive effects (which must be removed from the initial world description), similarly to what other planning systems do (see for example STRIPS [6]). We have proposed an extension of our approach supporting also subtractive effects (see [23]), but it is based on a currently non-standardized evolution of SPARQL.
- Finally, we observe that our approach is affected by all the classical problems related to systems aiming at reasoning about action and change:
    - Maintaining the consistency of the world description when incorporating into it the description of the effects of a service (*beliefs revision problem*);
    - Identifying the things that do not change when executing a service (*frame problem*);
    - Recording all the possible consequences of a service (*ramification problem*);
    - Listing all the possible preconditions of a service (*qualification problem*).

For an in depth discussion of these problems we refer the reader to [23].

6.4.3 Conclusions and Future Work

Our approach uses SPARQL as an expression language for characterizing services preconditions and effects. More precisely, the CONSTRUCT query form offers a natural way to (1) assert services preconditions, (2) check their satisfiability in a given context, (3) define (parametric) services effects, and (4) compute the actual effects in a context where the preconditions are satisfied. Additionally, we have also used SPARQL to define goals of matchmaking agents, that perform the service discovery task by interacting with a Services Index.

An interesting research direction for future work is related to the computation of service ranking within the Services Index. For example, providers may advertise their service in an HTML page that contains both a human readable description of the service functionalities, and a link to its formal service description. In this case the Services Index could combine the ranking computed by formal reasoning on input/output types (subsumption) and preconditions/effects with the ranking of the

HTML page referring to the service. Another approach is what we call *collaborative service ranking*: agents that have successfully discovered and used a service to achieve a goal can further interact with the Services Index, and tag the service, or vote for it. If we imagine that this collaborative services tagging/voting happens on a sufficiently large scale, then the Services Index will end up having a good set of information to apply classical data analysis and data mining algorithms for computing refined service ranking.

Finally, it is possible to extend our approach by combining our logic-based reasoning with non-deductive reasoning and information retrieval techniques (an area already explored for example in [13, 15]). The recently proposed iSPARQL [12, 14] extends SPARQL with a set of similarity functions, and thus it represents a very promising direction for extending our approach with non-deductive reasoning. More precisely, iSPARQL supports similarity reasoning, that is the definition of new (virtual) triples from a set of asserted triples based on the similarity among resources. The similarity is computed by using various strategies or measures originating from the area of information retrieval. By using iSPARQL a service provider could allow for a certain degree of "imprecision" in the matching of services preconditions, and (possibly) in the definition of services effects. On the other side, an agent could exploit iSPARQL to define less restrictive goals. We regard the combination of these features with our logic-based graph pattern relaxation as a very promising direction for future research in services matchmaking.

6.5 Summary

In this chapter we have described how to use SPARQL as an expression language for the definition of (1) services preconditions/effects, and (2) agent goals. Our approach, which is entirely based on the SPARQL computational model, can effectively evaluate a service's preconditions in a given context (the agent's knowledge base), compute the actual effects of a service being executed in that context, and check the satisfiability of the agent goal in the resulting world description.

The implementation of our approach relies on a distributed architecture where intelligent agents (SPARQLent) perform service matchmaking by querying a Services Index, and by reasoning not only on services' input/output types, but also on SPARQL graph patterns defining their preconditions/effects. Our SPARQLent can also perform logic-based approximate matchmaking.

We have described experimental results of a real-world application in the e-Government domain, where domain experts have validated the automated selection of services performed by our solution. We have also validated our approach with the standard OWLS-TC test collection.

To summarize, experimental results demonstrate that our approach has very good performance in terms of query response time and memory occupation, and that our graph pattern relaxation technique consistently improves the precision of the matchmaking operation. We consider the combination of our approach with non-deductive reasoning and information retrieval techniques as a very promising direction for future work.

References

1. R. Angles, C. Gutierrez, The expressive power of SPARQL. Technical Report TR/ DCC-2008-5, Department of Computer Science, Universidad de Chile (2008)
2. T. Berners-Lee, M. Fischetti, *Weaving the Web: The Original Design and Ultimate Destiny of the World Wide Web by its Inventor* (Harper San Francisco, San Francisco, 1999)
3. J. de Bruijn, C. Bussler, J. Domingue, D. Fensel, M. Hepp, U. Keller, M. Kifer, B. König-Ries, J. Kopecky, R. Lara, H. Lausen, E. Oren, A. Polleres, D. Roman, J. Scicluna, M. Stollberg, Web service modeling ontology (WSMO). W3C member submission (2005), http://www.w3. org/Submission/WSMO/
4. R. Fagin, J.D. Ullman, M.Y. Vardi, On the semantics of updates in databases, in *PODS '83: Proceedings of the 2nd ACM SIGACT-SIGMOD Symposium on Principles of Database Systems* (ACM, New York, 1983), pp. 352–365
5. J. Farrell, H. Lausen, Semantic annotations for WSDL and XML schema. W3C recommendation (2007), http://www.w3.org/TR/sawsdl/
6. R.E. Fikes, N.J. Nilsson, STRIPS: a new approach to the application of theorem proving to problem solving. Artif. Intell. **2**(3–4), 189–208 (1971)
7. M.L. Ginsberg, Counterfactuals. Artif. Intell. **30**(1), 35–80 (1986)
8. P. Hayes, RDF semantics. W3C recommendation (2004), http://www.w3.org/TR/rdf-mt/
9. J. Hendler, Agents and the semantic web. IEEE Intell. Syst. **16**(2), 30–37 (2001)
10. A. Herzig, O. Rifi, Propositional belief base update and minimal change. Artif. Intell. **115**, 107–138 (1999)
11. H. Katsuno, A.O. Mendelzon, On the difference between updating a knowledge base and revising it, in *KR*, IEEE (1991), pp. 387–394
12. C. Kiefer, *Non-deductive Reasoning for the Semantic Web and Software Analysis*. PhD thesis, University of Zurich, Department of Informatics, Zürich, January 2009
13. C. Kiefer, A. Bernstein, The creation and evaluation of iSPARQL strategies for matchmaking, in *Proceedings of the 5th European Semantic Web Conference (ESWC)*, Lecture Notes in Computer Science, Tenerife. Springer, February 2008 (to appear)
14. C. Kiefer, A. Bernstein, M. Stocker, *The Fundamentals of iSPARQL: A Virtual Triple Approach for Similarity-Based Semantic Web Tasks* (Springer, Berlin/New York, 2008), pp. 295–309
15. M. Klusch, B. Fries, K. Sycara, Automated semantic web service discovery with OWLS-MX, in *AAMAS '06: Proceedings of the Fifth International Joint Conference on Autonomous Agents and Multiagent Systems* (ACM, New York, 2006), pp. 915–922
16. M. Klusch, B. Fries, K.P. Sycara, OWLS-MX: a hybrid Semantic Web service matchmaker for OWL-S services. J. Web Semant. **7**(2), 121–133 (2009)
17. D. Martin, M. Burstein, E. Hobbs, O. Lassila, D. McDermott, S. Mcilraith, S. Narayanan, B. Parsia, T. Payne, E. Sirin, N. Srinivasan, K. Sycara, OWL-S: semantic markup for web services. W3C member submission (2004), http://www.w3.org/Submission/OWL-S/
18. S.A. McIlraith, T. Cao Son, H. Zeng, Semantic web services. IEEE Intell. Syst. **16**(2), 46–53 (2001)
19. M. Paolucci, T. Kawamura, T.R. Payne, K.P. Sycara, Semantic matching of web services capabilities, in *ISWC '02: Proceedings of the First International Semantic Web Conference on The Semantic Web*, London. Springer (2002), pp. 333–347
20. J. Pérez, M. Arenas, C. Gutierrez, *Semantics and Complexity of SPARQL* (Springer-Verlag, Berlin/New York, 2006), pp. 30–43

21. E. Prud'hommeaux, A. Seaborne, SPARQL query language for RDF. W3C recommendation (2008), http://www.w3.org/TR/rdf-sparql-query/
22. R. Reiter, On specifying database updates. J. Logic Progr. **25**(1), 53–91 (1995)
23. M.L. Sbodio, *Planning Web Agents – Combining Intelligent Agents and Semantic Web Languages for Service Planning*. PhD thesis, Université de Technologie de Compiègne (France), Politecnico di Torino (Italy), October 2009
24. M.L. Sbodio, D. Martin, C. Moulin, Discovering semantic web services using SPARQL and intelligent agents. Web Semant. **8**(4), 310–328 (2010) Semantic Web Challenge 2009; User Interaction in Semantic Web research
25. M.L. Sbodio, C. Moulin, N. Benamou, J.-P. Barthès, *Toward an e-Government Semantic Platform* (Springer, Berlin/Heidelberg, 2010), pp. 209–234
26. M. Winslett, Reasong about action using a possible models approach, in *Proceedings of AAAI-88*. St. Paul (1988), pp. 89–93
27. M. Winslett, Sometimes updates are circumscription, in *International Joint Conference on Artificial Intelligence*, Detroit (Morgan Kaufmann, San Francisco, 1989), pp. 859–863
28. M. Winslett, *Updating Logical Databases* (Cambridge University Press, New York, 1990)
29. M. Wooldridge, *Introduction to MultiAgent Systems* (Wiley, New York, 2002)

Chapter 7
Semantic Annotations and Web Service Retrieval: The URBE Approach

Pierluigi Plebani and Barbara Pernici

Abstract The goal of this chapter is to discuss how annotating the Web service interfaces can improve the precision of a Web service matchmaking algorithm. To this aim, we adopt URBE (UDDI Registry By Example) as a matchmaking algorithm for calculating the similarities between two Web service interfaces described using the SAWSDL or WSDL. The approach adopted in URBE takes into account both the structural and semantic analysis of the interfaces: the former takes into account the number of operations, inputs, and outputs as well as the data types involved; the latter considers the concepts related to the names given to the service, the operations, and the parameters. In case the Web services are described with WSDL, WordNet is used to find the relationships between names. In case of SAWSDL-based descriptions, the analysis is based on the ontologies referred by the annotations.

7.1 Introduction

In the area of Autonomic Computing [8] methods and tools are required for making the execution of business processes as reliable as possible. When considering service-based processes, the reliability of a process strongly depends on the reliability of the composing services. As a consequence, in case of a service failure, it is fundamental to figure out how to find an alternative solution, i.e., a similar service. According to this scenario, inside the PAWS (Processes with Adaptive Web Services) framework [2], we have developed URBE (Uddi Registry By Example) a UDDI compliant service registry that also performs content-based retrieval. Generally speaking, URBE is a tool for supporting process design. For specifying a

P. Plebani (✉) · B. Pernici
Dipartimento di Elettronica ed Informazione – Politecnico di Milano, Via Ponzio 34/5 – 20133 Milan, Italy
e-mail: plebani@elet.polimi.it; pernici@elet.polimi.it

M.B. Blake et al. (eds.), *Semantic Web Services*, DOI 10.1007/978-3-642-28735-0_7,   107
© Springer-Verlag Berlin Heidelberg 2012

process definition or for substitution purposes, given a service interface description, with URBE a designer, following a *query by example* approach, can find the services published in a repository that expose the interfaces as similar as possible to the requested one.

The goal of this chapter is to give an overview of the matchmaker which URBE is based on. A detailed discussion of this matchmaker is given in [13]. In particular, since URBE can analyze both WSDL and SAWSDL Web service interface descriptions, in this chapter we focus on how the annotations defined in a SAWSDL file can be useful to improve the accuracy of the matchmaking algorithm in terms of precision and recall.

The chapter is structured as follows. Section 7.2 introduces the ideas underlying the URBE approach. Section 7.3 enters into the details of the algorithm that calculates the similarity between two Web service description interfaces. Section 7.4 analyzes the matchmaking results, especially considering the influences on the annotations included in SAWSDL documents. A summary of the content of this chapter is given in Sect. 7.5.

7.2 Approach: Web Service Substitution

As discussed in the introduction, Web service substitution might be required when the execution of a service-based business process fails due to a failure of one of the composing services. Regardless of when the selection of the substituting Web service occurs (i.e., at design or run-time), one of the main goals is to minimize the engineering effort for the Web service substitution required on the client-side to re-implement the Web service functionalities invocations. URBE aims at supporting this situation by providing a similarity function:

$$f\,Sim(ws_a, ws_b) \rightarrow [0..1] \tag{7.1}$$

where ws_a and ws_b are two Web service interfaces described with WSDL (or SAWSDL). The higher the result of $f\,Sim$, the higher the similarity between the two interfaces is. Since our goal is the Web service substitution, a higher value of $f\,Sim$ also means less burden with the Web service substitution. So, we assume that:

Definition 7.1. Given two Web service interfaces ws_a and ws_b, then $f\,Sim(ws_a, ws_b) = 1$ if the two Web services expose the same interface, whereas $f\,Sim(ws_a, ws_b) = 0$ in case the interfaces are completely different.

Figure 7.1 shows the interfaces of two similar Web services. In this case, even if they fulfill the same goal, i.e., currency exchange, the number of available operations, as well as the way in which the input and output parameters are named, is different. Since one of our goals is to evaluate the similarity for substitutability, we need to consider that substituting `CurrencyWS` with `CurrencyExchangeService` is different to the opposite activity. Thus:

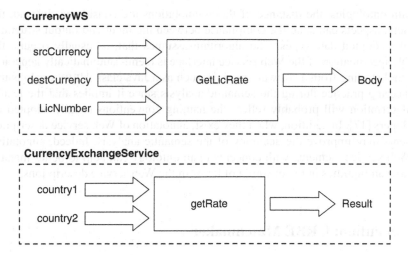

Fig. 7.1 Example of similar web services

Definition 7.2. The function f *Sim* is not reflective. So, f *Sim*(ws_a, ws_b) could differ from f *Sim*(ws_b, ws_a) as the similarity depends on which Web service holds the role of substituting and which the role of substituted.

Indeed, if we usually invoke the CurrencyWS, in case of a failure we can start invoking the corresponding operation of the CurrencyExchangeService after implementing a mediator able to transform the messages: skipping the value of the license number, i.e. LicNumber, obtaining the country name from the related currency symbol, and modifying the name of the invoked operation and the parameters. On the contrary, if we are using CurrencyExchangeService and we have to switch to CurrencyWS, the new Web service needs an additional parameter that could be obtained by payment of registration fees, i.e., LicNumber.

Generally speaking, URBE relies on the assumption that two Web services could be defined as functionally equivalent, and thus f *Sim* returns 1, if their interfaces expose the same operations with the same inputs and outputs. Thus, the two interfaces must use the same names to define the operations and the parameters and, with respect to the latter, the same data types are used. In case URBE realizes that these constraints are only partially satisfied, then the value returned by f *Sim* decreases accordingly. This results in a pair-wise comparison of the elements composing the service description. This approach has been inspired by the literature on reusable software components [20] and by work done in the Web service community [7]. With respect to the existing approaches, our algorithm combines both semantic and syntactic aspects of the Web service that can be derived from a WSDL description. The semantic aspects derives from the analysis of the relation between the names used for the whole service, the operations and the parameters and the concepts stored in WordNet. In particular, we are not interested on the meaning of the names, but on their distance. In case, the service description includes explicit references to domain ontologies, the distance of these annotations are considered. Instead, the syntactic aspects can state the compliance between the input and output structures and the adopted data types. The algorithm assumes that, as usually occurs, the WSDL specification of the Web service interface is (semi-)automatically generated by a tool starting from a software module, such as a Java class. URBE exploits this engineering practice during the semantic analysis since it implies that the resulting description will probably reflect the naming conventions usually adopted by developers [17]. In addition, when they exist, annotation of Web service description elements may improve the accuracy of the semantic analysis. Indeed, annotating the Web service elements with concepts in an ontology can help to better manage possible ambiguities in the meaning of terms in the Web service descriptions.

7.3 Solution: URBE Matchmaker

The URBE matchmaker implements the algorithm that computes the similarity function $f\ Sim$. Generally speaking, the hierarchical structure of a WSDL/SAWSDL description affects the structure of $f\ Sim$. For this reason, $f\ Sim$ is defined in terms of $opSim$, which in turn, is defined in terms of $inParSim$ and $outParSim$ (see Fig. 7.2). This approach results in the algorithm shown in Listing 7.1.

Regardless of the function considered, it is worth noting that at each level the algorithm is based on a function $maxSim$ that implements the maximum weighted assignment in a bipartite graph problem [3]. Given a graph $G = (V, E)$, a *matching* is defined as $M \subseteq E$ so that no two edges in M share a common end vertex. If the edges of the graph have an associated weight, then a *maximum weighted assignment* is a matching such that the sum of the weights of the edges is maximum. Let us suppose that the set of vertices is partitioned in two sets Q and P, each edge of the graph connects a vertex from Q with a vertex from P, and that the edges of the graph have an associated weight given by a function $f : (Q, P) \rightarrow [0..1]$. The function $maxSim : (f, Q, P) \rightarrow [0..1]$ returns the maximum weighted assignment.

Applying the assignment in bipartite graphs problem to our context, the set Q represents a query, whereas P is what we compare with the query to evaluate the similarity. Let us assume, for instance, that Q and P are composed of the operations in ws_a and ws_b. $|Q| < |P|$ means that the number of operations in Q is lower than the number of operations available in P; so, for each operation in Q we may find a corresponding operation in P. On the contrary, $|Q| > |P|$ means that we are asking for more operations than are actually available. Since our approach aims to state if ws_a can be replaced with ws_b, then the situation in which $|Q| \leq |P|$ is, in general, better than the case $|Q| > |P|$. For this reason, we divide the result of the maximization by the cardinality of $|Q|$. So, if $|Q| \leq |P|$ then $maxSim : (f, Q, P) \rightarrow [0..1]$, whereas if $|Q| > |P|$ then $maxSim : (f, Q, P) \rightarrow [0..\frac{|P|}{|Q|}]$. In this way, the function $maxSim$ is asymmetric, i.e., $maxSim(f, Q, P) \neq maxSim(f, P, Q)$, and this justifies the property of $f\ Sim$ introduced the Definition 7.2.

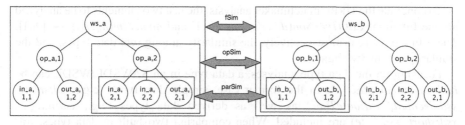

Fig. 7.2 Structure of the service similarity function *f Sim* [13]

```
function parSim(par_a, par_b) : double

   parSim = wParNameSim * nameSim(par_a.name, par_b.name);
   parSim = parSim + (1-wParNameSim) *
                     dataTypeSim(par_a.type, par_b.type);

end function

function opSim(op_a, op_b) : double

   opSim = wOpNameSim * nameSim(op_a.name, op_b.name);
   opSim = opSim + (1-wOpNameSim) *
           (0.5 * maxSim(parSim, op_a.inputs, op_b.inputs)  +
            0.5 * maxSim(parSim, op_b.outputs, op_a.outputs));

end function

function fSim(ws_a, ws_b) : double

   fSim = nameSim(ws_a.portType_name, ws_b.portType_name);
   fSim = fSim + maxSim(opSim, ws_a.operations, ws_b.operations)

end function
```

Listing 7.1 URBE algorithm

The URBE matchmaker also includes a set of weights to assign the relevance of the similarity at the different levels during the computation of the overall similarity value. More specifically, the weight *wPTNameSim* $\in$ [0..1] defines how much the similarity of the names of the portTypes has more importance than the similarity between the operations that these portTypes contain in computing the overall similarity. In the same way, at operation level, the weight *wOpNameSim* weights the importance between the similarity of the operation names and the similarity of the related parameters in computing the operation similarity. Finally, *wParNameSim* weights the importance between the similarity of the parameter names and the similarity of the data types.

To conclude the URBE matchmaker analysis, the last two elements to be analyzed are the functions $dataTypeSim(dt_a, dt_b) \rightarrow [0..1]$ and $nameSim(n_a, n_b) \rightarrow [0..1]$. These functions return, respectively, the similarity among two data types, and the similarity among two names.

Focusing on the data type analyses, a data type in an SAWSDL/WSDL can be *built-in* or *complex* [5]. In the former case, simple data types (e.g., *xsd:string*, *xsd:decimal*, *xsd:dateTime*) as well as derived data types (e.g., *xsd:integer*, *xsd:short*, *xsd:byte*) are included. When comparing two built-in data types, following the approach defined in [16], their similarity is inversely proportional to the information loss that will occur if we apply a casting from dt_a to dt_b. For instance, if we move from an integer to a real, we do not have any information loss since all the integers can be represented with a real variable, i.e., $dataTypeSim(integer, real) = 1$. On the other way round, when casting a real to an integer, we lost the decimal part so we assume that $dataTypeSim(integer, real) = 0.5$. In the case of complex data types, data type is expressed according to an XSD schema which is included, or imported, in the WSDL specification as a *complexType*: a data type which includes other data types (either built-in or complex). To reduce the complexity of the overall algorithm, the URBE matchmaker only considers the name of the data types. The analysis of the data type structure is now under investigation by considering work on service compatibility based on subtyping theory [1]. As a consequence, in case of comparison of complex data types, $dataTypeSim(dt_a, dt_b) = nameSim(dt_a.name, dt_b.name)$. Due to its importance, in the next section we discuss in detail the *nameSim* function and the effects of its parametrization for the evaluation of the Web service interfaces similarity.

7.4 Lessons Learned

7.4.1 Evaluation Results

Generally speaking, in URBE the similarity among two names relies on a *domain specific knowledge base* and a *general purpose ontology*. The *domain specific knowledge base* includes terms related to a given application domain. We assume that this ontology can be built by a domain expert also analyzing the terms included in the Web services published in the registry. The *general purpose knowledge base* includes all the possible terms.

The effect of considering these two different ontologies is emphasized when using the SAWSDL Test Collection[1] as the benchmark for evaluating the accuracy of the matchmaker. The Web services in this collection include annotations only for some of the elements composing the interfaces. Indeed, in such a benchmark

---

[1]The test collection is available at http://projects.semwebcentral.org/projects/sawsdl-tc/

the operation names are usually not annotated, whereas the data types of the input and output parameters are annotated. Moreover, the annotations refer to concepts stored in a set of ontologies that, in some cases, are related each other. This scenario affects the way in which $f\,Sim$ is computed: the function *nameSim* compares the names used to define the elements of the Web service description if the annotation is not available, and WordNet[2] is adopted as general purpose knowledge base. Otherwise, *nameSim* will invoke the function $annSim(a_q, a_p) \rightarrow [0..1]$ to compare the annotations of these elements, if they exist. In this case, the ontologies specified in the annotations hold the role of domain specific knowledge bases. For instance, giving the example in Listing 7.2, at operation level, URBE has to consider the name get_PRICE since no annotation is available. On the contrary, at the parameter level, the *parSim* function can exploit the annotations for the data types PriceType and BookType: namely, concept.owl#Price and books.owl#Book.

The *nameSim* function, due to the nature of the names normally included in an automatically generated WSDL, can be applied only after a tokenization process which produces the set of terms to be actually compared. Considering our example, terms like get_PRICE are difficult to find in WordNet or in any other ontologies. On the contrary, the resulting tokens can be found. Thus, giving $n_a = \{t_{a,i}\}$ and $n_b = \{t_{b,j}\}$ as the set of tokens composing n_a and n_b:

$$nameSim(n_a, n_b) = maxSim(termSim, \{t_{a,i}\}, \{t_{b,j}\}) \qquad (7.2)$$

where *termSim* $:(t_a, t_b) \rightarrow [0..1]$ is the function that computes the similarity between two tokens. In the literature, several approaches are available to state the similarity and the relatedness among terms [12]. These algorithms usually calculate the similarity based on the relationships among terms defined in a reference ontology (e.g., *is-a*, *part-of*, *attribute-of*). In our approach, to compute the similarity among terms we adopt the approach proposed by Seco et al. [15] where the authors adapt existing approaches relying on the assumption that concepts with many hyponyms[3] convey less information than concepts that have less hyponyms or any at all (i.e, they are leaves in the ontology).

About the annotation similarity, *annSim* $:(a_q, a_p) \rightarrow [0..1]$ receives as input two annotations and returns their similarity according to the way in which they are related in the reference ontology. In the current implementation, we assume that a_q and a_p are included in the same ontology, otherwise *annSim* returns 0. In future work will calculate the similarity of annotations referring to different ontologies. Since the annotations can be classes or properties, as shown in the Listing 7.3, the *annSim* has different behaviors.

In case both annotations are classes or both annotations are properties, to compute the similarity between the two annotations we take into account the

---

[2]http://wordnet.princeton.edu/

[3]A hyponym is a word of more specific meaning than a general term applicable to it, i.e., spoon is a hyponym of cutlery.

```
<wsdl:definitions ...>
 <wsdl:types>
     <xsd:element name="Book" type="BookType" .../>
     <xsd:element name="Price" type="PriceType" .../>
     <xsd:complexType name="PriceType"
                      sawsdl:modelReference="concept.owl#Price">
        ...
     </xsd:complexType>
     <xsd:complexType name="BookType"
                      sawsdl:modelReference="books.owl#Book">
        ...
     </xsd:complexType>
     <xsd:simpleType name="Currency"
               sawsdl:modelReference="currency.owl#Currency"/>
     <xsd:simpleType name="Author"
               sawsdl:modelReference="books.owl#Author"/>
     <xsd:simpleType name="Title"
               sawsdl:modelReference="books.owl#Title"/>
     <xsd:simpleType name="Book-Type"
               sawsdl:modelReference="books.owl#Book-Type"/>
   </xsd:schema>
 </wsdl:types>
 <wsdl:message name="get_PRICEResponse">
   <wsdl:part name="_PRICE" type="tns:PriceType" />
 </wsdl:message>
 <wsdl:message name="get_PRICERequest">
   <wsdl:part name="_BOOK" type="tns:BookType" />
 </wsdl:message>
 <wsdl:portType name="BookPriceSoap">
   <wsdl:operation name="get_PRICE">
     <wsdl:input message="tns:get_PRICERequest" />
     <wsdl:output message="tns:get_PRICEResponse" />
   </wsdl:operation>
 </wsdl:portType>
...
</wsdl:definitions>
```

Listing 7.2 Sample annotated file

subsumption path which connects them in the knowledge base. If there is no paths connecting the classes, or properties, the similarity is 0. In case a_q is a class and a_p a property, it is required that the domain of the property corresponds to the class. If so, it means that (1) the annotation in the query, i.e., a_q, refers to a class with all its properties, and (2) the annotation in the published service, a_p, refers only to one of those properties. Finally, in the opposite case, i.e., a_q is a property and a_p is a class, if a_p corresponds to the domain of the property a_q, the similarity between annotations is 1; otherwise, it is 0. Indeed, now (1) the annotation in the query refers to a specific property, and (2) the annotation in the published service certainly includes such a property since it refers to the whole set of properties for the defined class.

```
function annSim(a_q, a_p) : double
  if ((a_q is class) and (a_p is class)) or
     ((a_q is property) and (a_p is property))
    annSim = 1/(pathlength(a_q, a_p)+1)
  elseif (a_q is class) and (a_p is property) and
         (a_q = domain(a_p))
       annSim = 1/#properties in a_q
  elseif (a_q is property) and (a_p is class) and
         (a_p = domain(a_q))
       annSim = 1
end function
```

Listing 7.3 Annotation similarity function

According to this scenario, URBE is based on both knowledge bases: the domain specific knowledge base offers more accuracy in the relationships of the terms and is mainly used in *annSim*; the general purpose one offers wider coverage and it is mainly used by *nameSim*. This happens because in a general purpose knowledge base a word may have more that one synonym set (a.k.a. *synset*): a set of one or more synonyms that are interchangeable in some context. On the contrary, we assume that in a domain specific ontology each word has a unique sense with respect to the domain itself. For instance, if we consider the noun *currency*, in WordNet it has two synsets. The first one is about the financial domain, i.e., the metal or paper medium of exchange currently being used; the second one is about a generic meaning, i.e., general acceptance or use. Comparing the term *currency* with the term *money*[4] we can realize that they are strictly related only if we consider the financial domain. On the other hand, if we consider the other synset the relationship is looser. Therefore, in case of general purpose ontologies, since it is hard to figure out which is the correct domain to consider, we employ the average similarity for each synset.

The approach presented in this chapter has been implemented in a prototype. The source code of URBE is freely downloadable from SourceForge.[5] In the current implementation, WordNet is available as a general purpose ontology and the Java WordNet similarity library[6] developed by Seco et al. [15] is used to compute similarity between terms in WordNet. SAWSDL4J is used to parse the SAWSDL and WSDL files. An open-source implementation of a Mixed Integer Linear Programming solver, i.e., LpSolve,[7] is used to solve the linear programming model on which *f Sim* relies. Finally, the Jena library is used for accessing OWL-based domain-specific ontologies.

---

[4]http://marimba.d.umn.edu/cgi-bin/similarity.cgi

[5]http://sourceforge.net/projects/urbe/

[6]http://eden.dei.uc.pt/~nseco/javasimlib.tar.gz

[7]http://sourceforge.net/projects/lpsolve

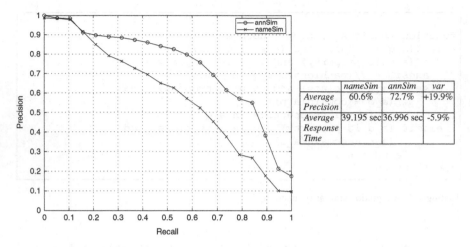

	nameSim	annSim	var
Average Precision	60.6%	72.7%	+19.9%
Average Response Time	39.195 sec	36.996 sec	-5.9%

Fig. 7.3 Annotation similarity and name similarity comparison

To evaluate how this approach affects the accuracy of the matchmaker, Fig. 7.3 shows how the precision-recall trend changes if the annotations are considered or not, i.e., if only WordNet or also the domain specific knowledge bases are taken into account. For this experiment, we ran URBE twice: one time ignoring the annotations and comparing only the names (*nameSim* curve) and the other considering the annotation similarity (*annSim* curve), too.[8]

As shown in the table of the Fig. 7.3, the existence of annotation improves not only the average precision (AP) by almost 20%, but also the response time by about 6%. This difference about the response time depends on the lower time required to compare the annotations in the ontology with respect to the time required to compare the names in the WordNet. Indeed, the annotation analysis does not need to tokenize the terms and, as a consequence, it does not result in more than one comparison.

Regardless of the existence of the annotations, it is also interesting to analyse how the accuracy of the URBE matchmaker varies with respect to a variation of the weights *wPTNameSim*, *wOpNameSim*, and *wParNameSim*. The results discussed above are obtained with the following configuration: *wPTNameSim* = 0.1, *wOpNameSim* = 0.1, and *wParNameSim* = 0.7. This means that to obtain the best results, the influence of the comparison at the different levels is the one shown in Fig. 7.4. It is worth noting that these values for the weights are valid for the adopted benchmark but, considering the different types of services included in it, generally speaking we can say that the analysis of parameter names has more than half of

---

[8]All the experiments discussed in this chapter have been done on an Windows XP Pro installed on a Virtual Machine configured with Intel Core 2 Due 2.33 GHz and 512 MB of RAM. The test collection is SAWSDL-TC v.1 (26 queries and 895 services). The average precision and the response time are obtained using the Semantic Web Service Matchmaker Evaluation Environment (SME2) available at: http://projects.semwebcentral.org/projects/sme2/

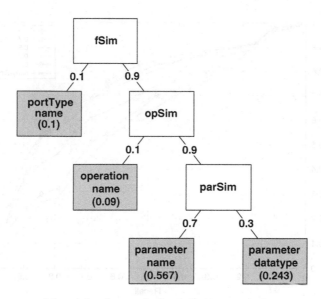

Fig. 7.4 Importance of the service elements in the similarity computation

Table 7.1 AP for different values of wParNameSim (considering nameSim)

wParNameSim	AP(%)
0.9	58.0
0.7	60.6
0.5	58.5
0.3	58.4
0.1	57.5

Table 7.2 AP for different values of wParNameSim (considering annSim)

wParNameSim	AP(%)
0.9	71.3
0.7	72.7
0.5	72.0
0.3	66.4
0.1	60.9

the overall importance, i.e., $56.7\%(= 0.9 \cdot 0.9 \cdot 0.7)$, whereas the `portType` and `operation` names comparisons have a lower influence.

Varying these weights, it is interesting to see how the accuracy varies in a different way with respect to existence or absence of annotations. Now, for the sake of clarity, we decide to vary only *wParNameSim* due to its importance in the overall computation as discussed above. Tables 7.1 and 7.2 report the average precision of the URBE matchmaker for different values of *wParNameSim*. It is worth noting how the accuracy is much more sensitive to the variation of the weight in case the annotations are considered. This because the annotations are more meaningful than the names. As a consequence, if two annotations are related *annSim* returns

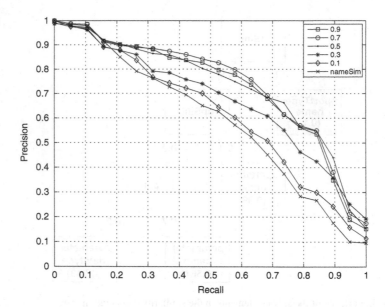

Fig. 7.5 Precision/recall chart with different values of *wParNameSim*

a value that is close to 1. Thus, even lowering the weight, the contribution of this comparison remains quite significant. On the other side, when the names are considered, even if they are strictly related, a significant difference in a token makes the result of *nameSim* lower. Thus, with lower values of the weight, the impact of this contribution is more reduced. As shown in the tables, the gap between the best and worst cases is 11.8%, whereas in case the annotations are not considered this gap is only 1.16%. Figure 7.5 shows the precision and recall curves for each of the five different values assigned to *wParNameSim* that correspond to the average precisions reported in Table 7.2 plus the best curve for the *nameSim* (i.e., when no annotations are available and *wParNameSim* = 0.7).

It is worth noting that, even in the worst case, i.e., *wParNameSim* = 0.1, the similarity computed considering the annotations is better than the best case when considering only the names, i.e., *nameSim* curve.

Focusing on the other weights, i.e., *wPTNameSim* and *wOpNameSim*, Figs. 7.6 and 7.7 show how the best trends are obtained for lower values of these weights. It is worth noting that it does not mean that name analysis should be skipped. Indeed, the 'off' curves, that represent a null value of these two weights, are under the optimal behavior, obtained with *wPTNameSim* = 0.1 and *wOpNameSim* = 0.1.

7.4.2 Advantages and Disadvantages

In URBE the similarity computation takes into account all the aspects that define a Web service interface: the number of elements, the data types, the names,

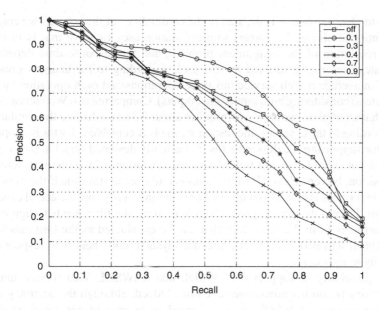

Fig. 7.6 Precision/recall chart with different values of *wPTNameSim*

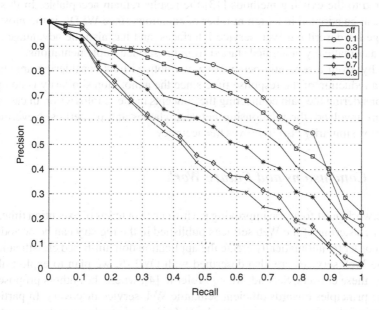

Fig. 7.7 Precision/recall chart with different values of *wOpNameSim*

and the annotations. Although, the Precision/Recall trends is comparable to other approaches [10, 11], the response time is the main drawback. Indeed, the execution-time of *f Sim* is directly affected by the exponential complexity to solve the assignment in bipartite graphs problems [19]. Some heuristics [18] reduce the complexity to $O(n^2)$, where n is the sum of the cardinalities of the two sets we consider. As mentioned above, the current implementation uses LpSolve that is in charge of the resolution of the assignment problem, and the response time depends on the strategy internally adopted by this tool. According to the analysis presented in [9], on average a Web service has three operations and each operation has four parameters (considering both inputs and outputs). Comparing two Web services with these characteristics, our approach requires about 0.3 s to calculate the similarity.

According to these values, the response time is acceptable if URBE is adopted as a tool for supporting the designers (as it is actually designed for). On the contrary, URBE is not suitable for run-time discovery, for instance in support of automatic composition. Nevertheless, URBE remains useful even at run-time if the number of available services is low. This requires a pre-filtering step before the actual execution of URBE. During this phase, given the initial query, the filter needs to figure out a set of services from the repository that can be considered as the best candidates. Next, URBE will perform a finer-grained analysis to rank them with respect to the similarity to the query.

The possibility to support both WSDL and SAWSDL Web service interface descriptions is another advantage of URBE. Indeed, although the accuracy of the algorithm in case of WSDL is not as good as in case of annotated interfaces, compared to the existing methods [13] the results remain acceptable. In this way, URBE can be adopted in a high number of situations since WSDL is the most used language for describing Web service interfaces, and has also the advantage that it can be automatically generated started from the service implementations.

Finally, from a semantic perspective, we noticed how considering annotations brings a reduction of the response time since the annotation similarity is computed only considering the path connecting the concepts in the ontologies or, in case properties are involved, the relationship between classes and properties. Nevertheless, annotation similarity also improves the accuracy.

7.4.3 Conclusions and Future Work

Further work must focus on improving performance in terms of execution time. First of all, a clustering of the Web services published in the registry can be periodically done in order to automatically create the application domain-based classification. In case the Web services are also described with OWL-S, we plan to exploit also in creating these clusters. Second, we will refer to [4], where the authors propose a set of basic principles towards efficient semantic Web service discovery. In particular, these principles focus on: semantic level (reducing ontology management) and matching level (reducing the number of comparisons).

Moreover, the semantic analysis of a WSDL specification can consider differently the comparison between method names and parameter names. About the former, the verb is more important since a method name should define an action. About the latter, the parameter name similarity should mainly consider the noun, i.e., the meaning of data on which the action is performed or its output.

Considering the SAWSDL analysis, the next steps aim to consider in a single step the annotations at different levels in the structure. For instance, if the required operation is called *formatDocument*, whereas the offered operation has the operation and input parameter annotated with the ontology concepts *format* and *document*, then we should realize that they are strictly related.

So far, URBE has been designed to support the service substitution from the perspective of a client that is looking for a service providing an interface similar to one previously invoked. Changing the standpoint to the provider perspective, we can assume that the user request is mandatory and the provider must evolve its service to satisfy the user requirements. Inside the research area of Service Evolution [1], which also deals with this scenario, URBE can be adopted as a metric for estimating the effort needed to evolve a service to another one by analyzing the initial and the final interfaces.

Finally, we are now also investigating the possibility of translating the idea underlying the URBE matchmaker to a Constraint Logic Programming (CLP) problem [14]. In this case, from the query the matchmaker can define a set of constraints that the service to be analyzed needs to deal with. If all the constraints are satisfied then the similarity will be the maximum. On the other side a null similarity would indicate that none of the constraints are satisfied. In particular, the work needs to be based on an extension of CLP, i.e., Semiring-based Constraint Logic Programming [6], which also allows for ranking the solutions obtained by the constraint analysis process.

7.5 Summary

In this paper we have presented URBE, an approach for evaluating the similarity between Web service interfaces for substitution purposes. The Web service requestor, after submitting the interface of the desired Web service, can obtain a list of similar Web services. The evaluation of the similarity between Web services considers both the semantics and the structure of a WSDL description. The semantic analysis takes into account the names adopted to describe the elements composing a Web service (operations and parameters), whereas the structure analysis takes into account the number of operations as well as the number and data types of the parameters. In addition, our approach also supports SAWSDL as a description model. In this case, the semantic analysis takes advantage of the semantic relationships between annotations in SAWSDL, as demonstrated in the Semantic Service Selection (S3) Contest [10, 11].

A prototype of URBE has been developed as a UDDI-compliant registry that supports our retrieval model and has been used to validate of our approach. Based on this implementation, in this chapter we have shown how the annotations included in a SAWSDL file can influence the accuracy of the matchmaking algorithm in terms of precision and recall and how this accuracy is also affected by the different elements composing a Web service interface description: portType, operation, and parameters.

References

1. V. Andrikopoulos, S. Benbernou, M.P. Papazoglou, Managing the evolution of service specifications, in *Proceedings of the 20th International Conference on Advanced Information Systems Engineering*, CAiSE '08 (Springer, Berlin/Heidelberg, 2008), pp. 359–374
2. D. Ardagna, M. Comuzzi, E. Mussi, B. Pernici, P. Plebani, PAWS: a framework for executing adaptive web-service processes. IEEE Softw. **24**, 39–46, (2007)
3. A. Asratian, T. Denley, R. Häggqvist, *Bipartite Graphs and Their Applications* (Cambridge University Press, Cambridge/New York, 1998)
4. S. Ben Mokhtar, A. Kaul, N. Georgantas, V. Issarny, Towards efficient matching of semantic web service capabilities, in *Proceedings of International Workshop on Web Services Modeling and Testing (WS-MaTe2006)*, Palermo, 9 June 2006, pp. 137–152, ed. by A. Bertolino, A. Polini
5. P.V. Biron, A. Malhotra, XML schema Part 2: datatypes second edition (W3C recommendation) (Oct 2004), http://www.w3.org/TR/xmlschema-2/. Accessed 04 Mar 2011
6. S. Bistarelli, U. Montanari, F. Rossi, Semiring-based constraint logic programming: syntax and semantics. ACM Trans. Program. Lang. Syst. **23**, 1–29 (2001)
7. J. Garofalakis, Y. Panagis, E. Sakkopoulos, A. Tsakalidis, Contemporary web service discovery mechanisms. J. Web Eng. **5**(3), 265–290 (2006)
8. J.O. Kephart, D.M. Chess, The vision of autonomic computing, IEEE Comput. **36**(1), 41–50 (2003)
9. H. Kil, S-C. Oh, D. Lee, On the topological landscape of web services matchmaking, in *Proceedings of International Workshop on Semantic Matchmaking and Resource Retrieval (VLDB-SMR'06)*, CEUR, vol. 178 (2006), http://ceur-ws.org/Vol-178/proceedings_SMR_06.pdf
10. M. Klusch, OWL-S and SAWSDL service matchmakers. S3 contest 2008 summary report (Oct 2008), http://www-ags.dfki.uni-sb.de/~klusch/s3/s3c-2008.pdf. Accessed 04 Mar 2011
11. M. Klusch, OWL-S and SAWSDL service matchmakers. S3 contest 2010 summary report (Oct 2010), http://www-ags.dfki.uni-sb.de/~klusch/s3/s3c-2010-summary-report-v2.pdf. Accessed 04 Mar 2011
12. T. Pedersen, S. Patwardhan, J. Michelizzi, WordNet::Similarity – measuring the relatedness of concepts, in *Proceedings of National Conference on Artificial Intelligence*, San Jose, 25–29 July, 2004, pp. 1024–1025
13. P. Plebani, B. Pernici, URBE: web service retrieval based on similarity evaluation. IEEE Trans. Knowl. Data Eng. **21**(11), 1629–1642 (2009)
14. F. Rossi, P. van Beek, T. Walsh, *Handbook of Constraint Programming (Foundations of Artificial Intelligence)* (Elsevier Science Inc., New York, 2006)
15. N. Seco, T. Veale, J. Hayes, An intrinsic information content metric for semantic similarity in wordnet, in *Proceedings of Eureopean Conference on Artificial Intelligence (ECAI'04)*, Valencia, Aug 22–27, (IOS Press, Amsterdam, 2004), pp. 1089–1090
16. E. Stroulia, Y. Wang, Structural and semantic matching for assessing web-service similarity. Int. J. Coop. Inf. Syst. **14**(4), 407–438 (2005)
17. Sun Microsystems, Code conventions for the Java programming language (Apr 1999), http://java.sun.com/docs/codeconv/html/CodeConvTOC.doc.html. Accessed 04 Mar 2011
18. J. Wang, J. Xiao, C.P. Lam, H. Li, A bipartite graph approach to generate optimal test sequences for protocol conformance testing using the Wp-method, in *Proceedings of Asia-Pacific Software Engineering Conference (APSEC'05)*, Taipei, 2005, pp. 307–316
19. L. Wolsey, *Integer Programming* (Wiley, New York, 1998)
20. A.M. Zaremski, J.M. Wing, Signature matching: a tool for using software libraries. ACM Trans. Softw. Eng. Methodol. **4**(2), 146–170 (1995)

Chapter 8
SAWSDL Services Matchmaking Using SAWSDL-iMatcher

Dengping Wei and Abraham Bernstein

Abstract This chapter presents a SAWSDL service matchmaker, called SAWSDL-iMatcher. It supports a matchmaking mechanism, named *iXQuery*, which extends XQuery with various similarity joins for SAWSDL service discovery. SAWSDL-iMatcher currently supports several matching strategies, including syntactic and semantic matching strategies. Meanwhile, we employ several statistical model based matching strategies to effectively aggregate similarity values from matching on various types of service description information such as service name, description text and semantic annotation. These matching strategies have been evaluated in SAWSDL-iMatcher on SAWSDL-TC2 and Jena Geography Dataset (JGD). The evaluation shows that different matching strategies fit for different tasks and contexts. We discuss this and other lessons learned from the evaluation.

8.1 Introduction

Matching strategy is considered as the core of a service matchmaker, which defines how to measure the similarity between the query and the service to return the most similar services to the user. There are many types of functional and nonfunctional service description information that can be used for matchmaking. Moreover, there are many similarity measures for information retrieval (IR) available for each type of the description information. However, how to select the suitable similarity measures for the compared contents is very important for a service matchmaker. Different

D. Wei (✉)
National University of Defense Technology, Changsha, China

University of Zürich, Zürich, Switzerland
e-mail: dpwei@nudt.edu.cn

A. Bernstein
University of Zürich, Zürich, Switzerland
e-mail: bernstein@ifi.uzh.ch

M.B. Blake et al. (eds.), *Semantic Web Services*, DOI 10.1007/978-3-642-28735-0_8,
© Springer-Verlag Berlin Heidelberg 2012

kinds of descriptions represent different facets over Web service. It is considered that the more comprehensive service description information compared the much fairer matching results obtained. This is exactly why most current matchmakers compare different types of description information at the same time and integrate them into an overall similarity value for ranking. There are several aggregation schemata like weighting schemes, statistical model based schemes, etc. However, how to select the suitable aggregation schema that can better aggregate the matching values from different compared information still deserves to investigation.

This chapter introduces a customizable SAWSDL service matchmaker, named SAWSDL-iMatcher, which supports several kinds of matching strategies. In SAWSDL-iMatcher, users can customize their preferred matching strategies for the evaluation of their requests, and developers can easily deploy their new-designed matching strategies and compare them with existing matching strategies. To query SAWSDL services, SAWSDL-iMatcher exploits the so-called iXQuery mechanism that extends XQuery with similarity joins for query evaluation.

In addition, this chapter presents the evaluations of various matching strategies in SAWSDL-iMatcher, and aims to reveal some empirical evidence for customizing matching strategies by analyzing evaluation results. Several matching strategies have been evaluated on two datasets SAWSDL-TC2 [1] and Jena Geography Dataset (JGD),[2] including the syntactic and semantic matching strategies as well as statistical model based matching strategies that use statistical models to aggregate different matching values that are obtained by comparing various types of description information. From the evaluations, some observations can be made for Web service discovery. For example, aggregating the results of single matching strategies on service name and interface annotations can often get better results than that returned by each single matching strategy. Such evidence would be useful for users to guide them to customize their matching strategies when they are confused on selecting suitable matching strategies.

8.2 Approach: Aggregating Multiple Matching Strategies

SAWSDL-iMatcher supports several matching strategies, including single matching strategies and aggregated matching strategies. Each single matching strategy exploits a certain kind of description component in SAWSDL service description. For each kind of service description, SAWDSL-iMatcher uses different logic-based or IR-based techniques to search for suitable services. SAWSDL-iMatcher also supports several good-performing aggregation schemata like weighting schemes, statistical model based schemes, etc. These aggregation schemata can integrate the matching results that come from different kinds of matched service description

---

[1] http://projects.semwebcentral.org/projects/sawsdl-tc

[2] http://fusion.cs.uni-jena.de/professur/jgdeval

into an overall similarity value. When the user's request involves several kinds of description information of Web service, such aggregation schemata can be used to construct a combined matching strategy.

8.2.1 Single Matching Strategies

- **Name based Matching Strategies**. The services' names are usually given by programmers who usually follow some coding conventions. A good service name can briefly summarize the capability and meaning of the service. Therefore, the matching strategies that compare service names would be useful if the service names contain either the function that the service (e.g., BookingFlightService) can do or the input/output parameters that the service involves (e.g., BookPrice-Service).
- **Description Text based Matching Strategies**. Description texts usually consist of comments written in natural language by service developers to make the codes more understandable. These description texts [14] have two advantages. First, description texts usually use simple sentences rather than complicated phrases and thus are easily processed. Second, these texts use natural language in a specific way. The description texts of services in a specific domain may have similar characteristics such as using domain specific terminology, abbreviations and phrases. Therefore, description text are considered important for service matchmaking.
- **Semantic Annotations based Matching Strategies.** Semantic annotations usually are considered as the most important information for automated discovery due to the formal semantic representation. The similarity between semantic annotations can be measured by either syntactically comparing the sets of semantic concepts, or logic reasoning. In this paper, the former are called syntactic matching strategies on semantic annotations, and the latter are called semantic matching strategies. In semantic matching strategies, the degrees of semantic matching are determined by the subsumption relationships in domain ontologies and often categorized into several grades such as *exact*, *plugin*, etc. [10].

8.2.2 Aggregated Matching Strategies

Different components in SAWSDL describe different facets of Web services. To discover Web services effectively, all these facets need to be considered together. When the user's query is comprehensive, aggregating all the matching values on different parts of description is an intuitive way to get the overall similarity score between the query and the service. Many matchmakers use empirical values as the weights for different types of description [11] to aggregate various matching values linearly. However, due to different quality or characteristics of services collections, it is difficult to fix the weights in practice. In other words, in service matchmaking, it is difficult to say how one type of information is much more important than another type of information.

In SAWSDL-iMatcher, these weights are learned from the known pairs of query and service, for which the relevance is known in advance by inspection. Each pair of query and service is represented by a vector space model, in which all the selected matching strategies and the relevance information are considered as the dimensions of the vector space. Especially, each matching strategy represents one dimension of the feature vector, and the value in each vector is given by the corresponding matching strategy. A pair of query and service is represented as a vector: $Pair(r_i, s_j) = \langle ms_1(r_i, s_j), ms_2(r_i, s_j), \ldots, ms_N(r_i, s_j), relevant(r_i, s_j) \rangle$, where r_i is the query and s_j is the service, $ms_k(r_i, s_j)$ represents the similarity value between r_i and s_j according to the k-th matching strategy ms_k ($k = 1, \ldots, N$), N is the number of matching strategies used and $relevant(r_i, s_j)$ specifies whether s_j is a relevant service to the request r_i. All the vectors $\{\langle r_i, s_j \rangle\}$ are considered as the training set. The statistical model learned is used to predict the probability that the new pair of query and service is relevant. The matchmaker then ranks the services for a request according to these probabilities.

8.3 Solution: SAWSDL-iMatcher

8.3.1 Architecture of SAWSDL-iMatcher

The three-level architecture of SAWSDL-iMatcher is sketched in Fig. 8.1. It contains a user interface, iXQuery framework and data model. In Fig. 8.1, rectangles represent components in SAWSDL-iMatcher and the arcs represent data flow. The user interface level consists of one main component called *query generator* which helps users to generate requests in terms of iXQuery expression. The data model level contains several knowledge bases that SAWSDL-iMatcher will use. The collection of SAWSDL/WSDL documents is the source for retrieval; The document *alignment* stores all the alignment results of heterogeneous domain ontologies, which are helpful to measure the similarity between heterogeneous concepts. Since Web services are usually annotated with heterogeneous ontologies by different people, the similar interface annotated with heterogeneous concepts may fail to match by using the logic-based reasoning. The ontology database manages all the domain ontologies related to Web services; The classification cache is used to reduce the computational complexity by caching the ancestor classes of some annotated classes.

The iXQuery framework is the core of SAWSDL-iMatcher, which has three main components: *XQuery engine, similarity engine* and *description extractor*. SAWSDL-iMatcher employs Saxon[3] as its XQuery engine. It passes parameters

---

[3]http://saxon.sourceforge.net/

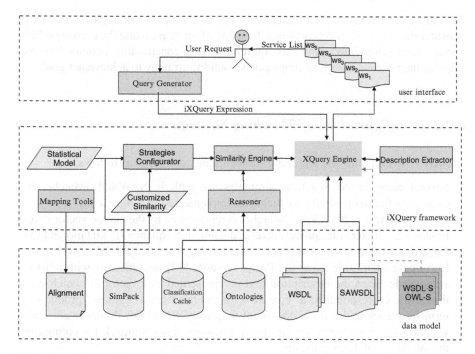

Fig. 8.1 System architecture of SAWSDL-iMatcher

to *similarity engine*, receives the results from *similarity engine* and binds the similarity scores to variables in XQuery expressions. *Similarity engine* embeds the similarity strategies by configuring the parameters received from *XQuery engine* and returning similarity scores to *XQuery engine*. *Description extractor* is used to extract different types of Web service description, like service name, description text, input parameters, and output parameters, etc. When a query expression is evaluated, *XQuery engine* will invoke the specified *description extractor* to get the corresponding Web service description.

An ontology reasoner is used to classify ontologies, and the resulting sub-sumption hierarchy is used by the semantic matchmaking strategies to define the semantic relationships between concepts. SAWSDL-iMatcher employs Pellet[4] as its semantic reasoner and OWL API[5] as the interface for accessing OWL-based domain-specific ontologies.

SAWSDL-iMatcher provides a flexible interface for users to customize match-making strategies according to different requirements and application domains. For example, two users *A* and *B* want to find a weather forecast service. Supposing *A* does not want to get into the precise details of how the required services should be

---

[4]http://clarkparsia.com/pellet/

[5]http://owlapi.sourceforge.net/

defined, then she may exploit the name or text matchmaking strategies which only consider the syntactic match between the string of the request and the corresponding service description. Supposing *B* is comfortable with constructing a comprehensive request, then she can adopt an aggregated matching strategy to achieve her goal.

8.3.2   Configurations of Matching Strategies

In SAWSDL-iMatcher, the matching strategies are configured as follows.

- Several name based matching strategies are built in SAWSDL-iMatcher by exploiting the string similarity measures implemented in Simpack [3].
- Description text in SAWSDL-iMatcher is represented by the classic vector space model, i.e., the term frequency-inverse document frequency (tf-idf) model [15]. First, description texts were preprocessed, using a text tokenizer, converting to lower case, stemming using the Porter stemmer [12], and filtering with a list of stop-words. Then the description text is represented as a vector, in which each dimension corresponds to a separate term and the term weights are products of term frequency and inverse document frequency. SAWSDL-iMatcher currently supports seven vector based similarity measures from Simpack for comparing the similarity of description text.
- Semantic annotations can be compared in two different ways in SAWSDL-iMatcher, using syntactic and semantic matching strategies. In syntactic matching, the input/output parameters of an operation are represented by the unfolded concept expressions (as in OWLS-MX [6]). The unfolded concept expression of a concept *C* includes all the ancestor concepts of *C* (including *C*) except the root concept *Thing*. Each unfolded concept expression is represented as a vector with boolean weight. That is to say, if a term is in the vector, then the term weight is 1, otherwise 0. All the vector similarity measures implemented in Simpack have been implemented in SAWSDL-iMatcher for measuring the similarity between two unfolded concept expressions.

  In semantic matching, the similarity between concept r' and s' is computed via Algorithm 2, in which $Ancestor(x)$ represents all the ancestor classes of class x, $Descendants(x)$ represents all the descendant classes of class x, and $sim_{syntactic}(r', s')$ represents a certain syntactic similarity measure which can estimate the semantic similarity between r' and s'. In this algorithm, we exploit the set similarity measures *jaccard coefficient* [16] to measure the syntactic similarity between two concepts. $AlignmentValue(r', s')$ represents the alignment value between r' and s' given by the ontology alignment tool Lily [18].

- SAWSDL-iMatcher supports several aggregated matching strategies using several different statistical models learned by the algorithms from Weka [4], such as simple linear regression, J48 decision tree [13, 20], logistic regression [7], support vector regression (ε-SVR) [5], etc.

Algorithm 2 *SemanticMatching*(r', s'): returns the degree between s' and r'.

Input:r' is the request concept
  s' is the serve concept
Output: *similarity* $\in [0, 1]$
$sim_{semantic} = 0$, $sim_{alignment} = 0$, *similarity* $= 0$.
if $r' \in Ancestor(s')$ *or* $s' \in Descendants(r')$ **then**
  $sim_{semantic} = 1$
else
  $sim_{semantic} = sim_{syntactic}(r', s')$
end if
if alignment and r', s' belong to two different ontologies **then**
  $Sim_{alignment}(r', s') = AlignmentValue(r', s')$
end if
similarity $= Max(Sim_{alignment}, sim_{semantic})$

For the evaluation in the S3 contest, we chose the best-performing similarity measure for each type of description to avoid the negative influence of noisy data, and then integrated the matching values into an overall similarity. To sum up, the matching strategies used in SAWSDL-iMatcher included the service name based matching strategy *Dice coefficient*, the description text based matching strategy *pearson*, the syntactic matching strategy on semantic annotations *euclidean*, and the semantic matching strategy described above.

8.4   Lessons Learned

8.4.1   Evaluation Results

8.4.1.1   Service Name Based Matching Strategies

Figure 8.2a shows the performance comparison of service name based matching strategies on SAWSDL-TC2. It depicts that *Dice's coefficient* [17] matching strategy clearly outperforms all other matching strategies in terms of precision and recall, such as *Levenshtein edit distance* [8], *Jaro coefficient* [19], TF-IDF [1] and *average string* [9]. Figure 8.2b shows the performance comparison of the above matchmaking strategies on Jena Geography Dataset (JGD). Here, *Dice's coefficient* based strategy also clearly outperforms all the other matchmaking strategies until about one-quarter of the relevant services have been retrieved. In addition, it has the highest mean average precision (MAP) of 0.4469 in this comparison.

The results of Fig. 8.2 also show that the performance of service name based matching strategies on SAWSDL-TC2 is better than that on JGD, since the naming convention for services and queries in SAWSDL-TC2 is much more consistent than that in JGD. The names in SAWSDL-TC2 are concatenated strings in which each word corresponds to one parameter name, while names in JGD do not have this characteristic.

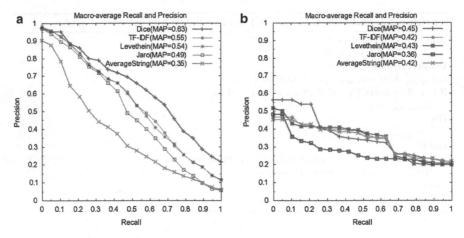

Fig. 8.2 The performance comparison of service name based matching strategies. (**a**) SAWSDL-TC2 (**b**) JGD

We can also analyze the average precision of each query for each service name based matching strategy. On SAWSDL-TC2, there are over 70.4% queries with average precision (AP) over 0.5% and 14.8% queries with AP less than 0.3. On JGD, there are 50% queries with AP over 0.5% and 20% queries with AP below 0.1. To illustrate this, consider the worst query "Altitude Request" in JGD as an example. It has two relevant services whose names are "GeoNames_SRTM3" and "EarthTools_Elevation_Height_Above_Sea_Level", which do not have common strings. These results show that the performance of service name based matching strategies depends on the characteristics of names in different datasets.

To demonstrate the characteristics of the names of real world services, we have investigated the data set of real world services QWS-wsdls.[6] After eliminating the services that are repetitive or no longer exist in the Internet, there are 1,598 services left. All the services' names are ranked by initials. The conventions for naming services can be categorized into six classes. Table 8.1 shows the categories and the corresponding examples with initial letter 'a'. These services' names show that most services' names are meaningful except those services whose names are numbers or acronym in capitals. A service name in the form of a concatenated strings such as "AddressDistanceCalculator", gives an explicit indication of the functionality of the corresponding service.

Although services are often generated automatically, names or naming rules are also given by people who write the codes of services or generate WSDL documents. The programmer usually follows certain coding conventions, and the names of variables as well as methods often have some meaning. Therefore, we believe that names of service are indeed useful for discovery. A good service name can briefly

---

[6]http://www.uoguelph.ca/~qmahmoud/qws/index.html

Table 8.1 Conventions for naming services in QWS-wsdls

Conventions	Examples
Concatenated string with initial capital letters	AccountingService, AdaptiveInterfaceService, AddressDistanceCalculator, AddNumbersService, AddressImageWSService, AddressLookup, AddressManager
Concatenated string with initial lowercase letters	acdtableService, acdtraceService, acdvalidService
Strings concatenated by underline	alignment_wu_blastn_rawService, alignment_wu_blastn_xmlService, alignment_consensus_consService, alignment_consensus_megamergerService, alignment_consensus_mergerService
Acronym in capitals	ABA, ARSA, ATTSMS
Numbers or letters with numbers	2004, A7Postal, acq2xx
Company name	AmazonBox, AmazonEC2

show the general description of the capability of services, like the title in a news report. Usually, the service name contains information about the function that the service provides (e.g., BookFlight) or the input/output parameters that the service involves (e.g., BookPriceService).

The reason for this may be that, unfortunately, there is no standard convention for naming Web services. Some people prefer to use "verb noun" phrases to name services, e.g., "FindBookPriceService", while others may specify the composition of the interface elements to name services, e.g., "BookPriceService". Therefore, the names of web services lack consistency, and seem to rely on the whim of the creator. As the simplest way for retrieving web services, service name based matching strategies would be much more effective if the names of services follow a standard convention and describe the capabilities of the services as much as possible. In this chapter, we suggest the following conventions for naming services, which can improve the quality of service matchmaking:

- Use "verb noun" phrases to name services. The verb specifies the utility of the service, i.e., what kind of operation this service can provide. The noun specifies the entities that the service handles and returns. For example, in a service name "BookFlight", the word "Book" specifies the utility of the service and "Flight" specifies the entities that the service mainly handles.
- Use CAMEL case: capitalize each word in service name. This would make the tokenization easier and more precise.
- Avoid implementation and protocol information, like words "soap", "http", "java", etc., since this kind of information is not important to describe the capability of services.

Table 8.2 Examples of description text in JGD dataset

Services	wsdl:definitions/ws:documentation	wsdl:operation/wsdl:documentation
5704_6846_ GeoNames_ FindNearby Postal- Codes1.wsdl	This is a WSDL 1.1 description that has been created for a RESTful service for evaluation and testing purposes. It is not guaranteed to be correct or appropriate.	Find postal codes close to the given location.
5808_6791_ AddressLookup_ CalculateDistance InMiles by cdyne.com.wsdl	This service corrects U.S. addresses, provides geocoding (U.S. down to address level and Canadian to Postal Code Level), and allows you to convert zip codes (and Canadian Postal Codes) to city and state names. We also offer PMSA, CMSA, and various other codes. <b>BE SURE TO USE A LICENSE KEY OF 0 FOR TESTING.	Calculates the distance between two areas using longitude and latitude. This is calculated using spherical geometry. This is a free function. You can get the calculations behind this function via support@cdyne. com.

- Avoid the word "service" in service names. Currently, many service names contain the word "service", which is not important to describe the capability of service. If two names both have the word "service" at the end, it is possible to bring inappropriate results when they are compared by a string similarity measure. For example, there are two services named "BookService" and "CarService", which are totally different. If we use a string similarity measure, e.g., Dice's coefficient, to compute the similarity between them, we will get a similarity value 0.62 because of the common substring "Service".

8.4.1.2 Description Text Based Matching Strategies

In a WSDL document, there are several components that description texts can be in. Example, the description text for the whole service is written under the element "wsdl:definitions/ws:documentation", and the description text for a certain operation is written under the element "wsdl:definitions/wsdl:portType/wsdl:operation/ wsdl:documentation". Two examples of description texts in JGD dataset is shown in Table 8.2.

Figure 8.3 only the results of description text based matching strategies on the JGD dataset, since services in SAWSDL-TC2 do not have any description text. Specifically, Fig. 8.3a shows the macro average recall versus precision curves of the matching strategies on the description text within the corresponding *operation*. The results show that the *overlap* [7] outperforms all other vector similarity measures

---

[7]http://staffwww.dcs.shef.ac.uk/people/S.Chapman/stringmetrics.html

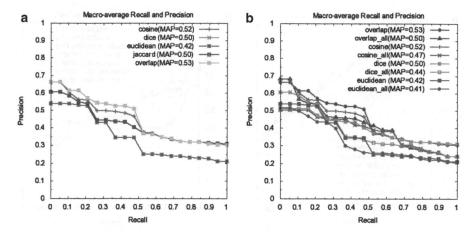

Fig. 8.3 The performance comparison of description text-based matching strategies on JGD. (**a**) Description text within *operation*. (**b**) All the description texts

Table 8.3 Percentages of services without description text

Datasets	Components that have no description text				
	Definition	Operation	Service	Message	Types
JGD-50(50)	19(38%)	**7(14%)**	33(66%)	28(56%)	29(58%)
JGDFull(203)	91(44.8%)	**28(13.8%)**	144(70.9%)	125(61.6%)	122(60.0%)
QWS-wsdls(1977)	1,779 (90.0%)	**1,204(60.9%)**	1,508(76.3%)	1,940(98.1%)	1,823(92.2%)

(with MAP of 0.53). Figure 8.3b additionally shows the macro average recall vs. precision curves of the matching strategies on all the description texts within the service (including all the documentation in each WSDL language element). The curves show that the matching strategies based on description text within *operation* component have much higher precisions that on all the description texts. That is, description text within *operation* is more suitable for service discovery than other description texts. From the analysis of existing datasets (see the examples in Table 8.2), the main reason for this maybe that description texts within elements other than *operation* often describe something else that is not related to the functionality of the service, and thus bring noise to the functionality description. Description text within *operation* on the other hand, actually describes what the operation can do.

Furthermore, we have compiled statistics on the existence of description texts in several different real service collections shown in Table 8.3, where the number of each cell (r, c) represents the number of services in collection r (row) which do not have any description text within the component c (column). These statistics show that the services that do not have documentation within *operation* have the lowest percentage in each dataset, compared with other components. In other words, description text appears in service operation with much higher probability than it appears in other service components. In real dataset QWS-wsdls, the services

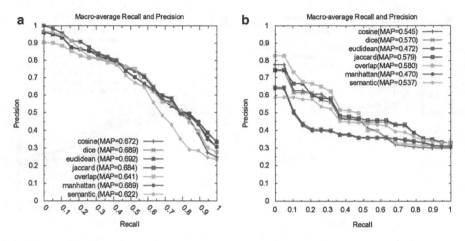

Fig. 8.4 The performance comparison on semantic annotations. (a) SAWSDL-TC2 (b) JGD

without description text in *operation* has percentage of 60.9%, since many WSDL documents in this dataset are automatically generated without any configuration of documentation for operations. However, the fact that the description text is useful for Web service discovery can not be easily dismissed.

8.4.1.3 Semantic Annotation Based Matching Strategies

Figure 8.4 shows the performance comparison of matching strategies on semantic annotations, including syntactic and semantic strategies. On SAWSDL-TC2, Fig. 8.4a illustrates that *euclidean distance* based matchmaker slightly outperforms other matchmakers with MAP of 0.692. Generally, there is no distinct difference between our semantic matching strategy and most syntactic matching strategies on both datasets. The semantic matching strategy slightly outperforms several syntactic matching strategies such as *jaccard*, *cosine*, and *overlap* based matching strategies until about 45% of the relevant services have been retrieved, after which the average precision of semantic matching strategy drops rapidly.

Figure 8.4b shows that the *overlap coefficient* based matching strategy outperforms other matching strategies with MAP of 0.5798 on JGD dataset. The *jaccard coefficient* based matching strategy is the second best one on this dataset, with MAP of 0.5795. It outperforms *overlap coefficient* based matchmaker after half of the relevant Web services are retrieved. Semantic matching strategy has the lowest average precision at the beginning, but outperforms *overlap*, *cosine*, *euclidean*, and *manhattan* based matching strategies after half of the relevant services have been retrieved.

The results of Fig. 8.4 also show that semantic annotation based matching strategies perform better on SAWSDL-TC2 than on JGD. This may be because of the different quality of annotations between the two datasets. In dataset JGD, there are some semantic annotations that do not exist in the domain ontologies.

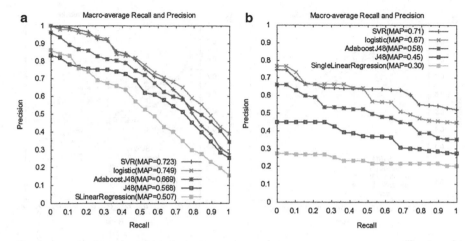

Fig. 8.5 The performance comparison of statistical model based strategies. (**a**) SAWSDL-TC2 (**b**) JGD

For example, the output concept "protont.owl#AltitudeAboveSeaLevel" of query "5914_6770_Altitude Request.wsdl" in JDG does not exist in the ontology "protont.owl". Such error-prone annotations fail to match with other semantic annotations, and thus some relevant services can not be returned.

Furthermore, we also compared the semantic matching strategy with and without ontology alignment. Experimental results show that using alignment does not improve the results in this dataset. This is because there are no test cases such that the request and service descriptions which have heterogeneous semantic annotations are actually similar or related.

8.4.1.4 Aggregated Matching Strategies

In this evaluation, the aggregated matching strategies combine service name based matching strategy, description text based matching strategy, the syntactic matching strategies on semantic annotations and semantic matching strategies. We do not consider the matching strategies on XML schema due to the high computational complexity. Description text based matching strategies are only used for JGD, since there is no description text in the service information of the test collection SAWSDL-TC2.

Figure 8.5 shows the performance comparison of statistical model based matchmakers. On SAWSDL-TC2 (shown in Fig. 8.5a), the *logistic regression* based matchmaker performs better than other statistical model based matchmakers with MAP of 0.749, although it is slightly outperformed by ε-SVR based matchmaker at the beginning. The second best statistical model based matchmaker is ε-SVR with MAP of 0.723.

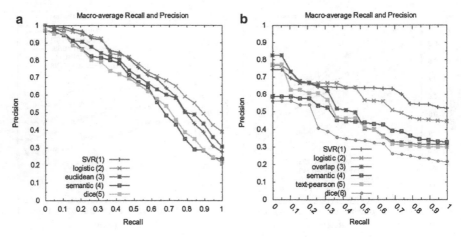

Fig. 8.6 The performance comparison between statistical model based strategies and single strategies. (**a**) SAWSDL-TC2 (**b**) JGD

On JGD, ε-SVR based matchmaker performs best with MAP of 0.71. The second one is the logistic based matchmaker with MAP of 0.67. Simple linear regression performs worst on both datasets. AdaBoosting algorithm on the weak learner J48 outperforms J48 decision tree itself on both datasets, but it is still outperformed by logistic and ε-SVR based matchmaker on both datasets.

Figure 8.6a indicates that, on SAWSDL-TC2, logistic based matchmaker and ε−SVR based matchmaker perform better than each of the single strategies which are used to learn the model. On JGD (shown in Fig. 8.6b), the same conclusion can also be drawn, although at the very beginning they are outperformed by single matching strategies such as semantic annotation based *overlap* strategy and description text based *pearson* strategy. These results validate that each type of information contributes differently in service matchmaking. Combining matching strategies on different types of description information can improve the effectiveness of matching by learning a selection of strategies with complementary strengths and weaknesses.

8.4.2 Advantages and Disadvantages

We show above that several kinds of matching strategies in SAWSDL-iMatcher have been evaluated, from service name based matching strategies, description text based matching strategies, semantic annotations based syntactic/semantic matching strategies, to statistical model based matching strategies. It is difficult to determine a clear "winner" for Semantic Web service matchmaking because all the matching strategies have their strengths and weaknesses. Nevertheless, we can make the following important observations when looking at the results as well as the

Table 8.4 Characteristics comparison between SAWSDL-TC2 and JGD

Component	Characteristics	SAWSDL-TC2	JGD
Name	Concatenated string	$+++^b$	$+++^b$
	Consistency of queries and services	$+++^b$	$++^b$
Description text	Service description text	$-^a$	$+^b$
	Operation description text	$-^a$	$+++^b$
Semantic annotation	Quality of annotations	$+++^b$	$++^b$
	Annotating style	Top level	Top and bottom level
	Heterogeneous annotations	$-^a$	$-^a$

[a]Represents there is no such element or situation
[b]Represents the degree of minimal, middle, and maximum respectively

characteristics comparison of each description component in the SAWSDL-TC2 and JGD datasets (shown in Table 8.4).

- The service name based matching strategies are the worst, compared to description text based matching strategies and semantic annotation based matching strategies. As the simplest matching method, there is a need for service offers to name their services with as much information as possible. In general, *Dice's coefficient* based matching strategy is a good choice when the user's request contains service name.
- For semantic annotations, the semantic matching strategy is slightly worse than syntactic matching strategies, although they perform very close on the whole.
- Semantic annotations can describe service capabilities very well in most cases. Single matching strategies on semantic annotations can obtain better results than on service name and description text.
- Statistical model based matching strategies are good at aggregating the matching values on simple service description components, such as service name, description text and interface annotations. However, the performance depends on the statistical model that is used. Usually, non-linear statistical models outperform linear statistical models. In other words, it is not a good idea to aggregate the matching values from different matching strategies in a linear way.
- Logistic regression and ε-SVR on service name and semantic annotations of the operation element can get better results than single matching strategies and also other statistical model based matching strategies on the same service descriptions.

8.4.3 Conclusions and Future Work

Above, we have evaluated the matching strategies supported in SAWSDL-iMatcher. From the evaluation, we find that the best performing similarity strategy seems to be domain dependent, echoing the results of [2]. Also, we should enable users to easily adopt matching strategies to their own domains, which is one of the main goals of SAWSDL-iMatcher. To further extend the lessons learned above, we plan to investigate more effective matching strategies and analyze their performance on more datasets.

- We will investigate the semantic annotation methods and contribute semantically annotated Web services to help alleviate the shortage of Semantic Web service descriptions.
- We plan to investigate effective structure matching strategies for the structure of semantic annotations rather than the structural definition of the XML Schema elements. In SAWSDL specifications, several components in WSDL can be optionally annotated with semantics via the extension attribute *modelReference* using two principal techniques to annotate complex types, i.e., bottom level and top level annotation. Different publishers or annotators of Semantic Web services may annotate the same Web services in different ways. Meanwhile, the *modelReference* properties can be propagated from a type definition component to all element declaration components that are defined with that type. In other words, the *modelReference* property of an element/attribute declaration also contains the values of the *modelReference* property from the type definition component referenced by this element/attribute declaration. Therefore, the semantic annotations of a parameter in an operation would contain not only the semantic annotations annotated on the parameter element itself but also the semantic annotations propagated up to it. That is to say, the semantic annotations of a parameter may be organized as a tree. This thus brings challenges to the semantic matchmaking of services.
- We also plan to investigate the matchmaking of Web services in specific domains. From our observation, different domains have different characteristics in describing the services. The matching strategies could be adapted and improved by considering these specific characteristics.

8.5 Summary

In this chapter, a SAWSDL service matchmaker, SAWSDL-iMatcher, is introduced, which is based on iXQuery that extends XQuery with similarity joins. We have shown how iXQuery combines structured query with similarity joins to perform SAWSDL service matchmaking and how users can easily customize their preferred matching strategies in SAWSDL-iMatcher. Various single matching strategies and statistical model based matching strategies have been evaluated on two datasets. The evaluation has shown that it is difficult to determine a "winner" for SWS matchmaking, since different matching strategies have their own strengths and weaknesses and are thus suitable for different tasks and contexts. Nevertheless, several empirical observations can be made from experimental results and the characteristics comparison of test datasets, which will be helpful for users to customize their requests. We observe that the semantic annotations of Web service operations are sufficient to describe the semantics of Web services, and syntactic matching strategies like *Euclidean distance* are suitable for measuring the similarity of semantic annotations effectively. Statistical model based matching strategies are good at aggregating the matching values on simple service description components, such as service name, description text and semantic annotations. Nevertheless, not all the statistical models are good for such tasks, and non-linear statistical models such as logistic and ε-SVR seem to be better than linear statistical models for aggregating results from different single matching strategies.

References

1. R. Baeza-Yates, B. Ribeiro-Neto, *Modern Information Retrieval*, 1st edn. (Addison–Wesley, Harlow, 1999)
2. A. Bernstein, E. Kaufmann, C. Buerki, M. Klein, How similar is it? Towards personalized similarity measures in ontologies, in *Wirtschaftsinformatik* (Lucius & Lucius, Stuttgart, 2005), pp. 1347–1366
3. A. Bernstein, E. Kaufmann, C. Kiefer, C. Bürki, SimPack: a generic Java library for similiarity measures in ontologies. Technical report, Department of Informatics, University of Zurich, 2005
4. M. Hall, E. Frank, G. Holmes, B. Pfahringer, The weka data mining software: an update. SIGKDD Explor. **11**(1), 10–18 (2009)
5. C.-W. Hsu, C.-C. Chang, C.-J. Lin, A practical guide to support vector classification. Technical report, Taipei, 2003
6. M. Klusch, B. Fries, K.P. Sycara, Owls-mx: a hybrid semantic web service matchmaker for owl-s services. J. Web Semant. **7**(2), 121–133 (2009)
7. S. le Cessie, J.C. van Houwelingen, Ridge estimators in logistic regression. Appl. Stat. **41**(1), 191–201 (1992)
8. V.I. Levenshtein, Binary codes capable of correcting deletions, insertions, and reversals. Technical Report 8, Soviet Physics Doklady, 1966
9. Er. Maedche, S. Staab, Measuring similarity between ontologies, in *Proceedings of the European Conference on Knowledge Acquisition and Management (EKAW)* (Springer, Berlin/New York, 2002), pp. 251–263
10. M. Paolucci, T. Kawamura, T.R. Payne, K. Sycara, Semantic matching of web services capabilities, in *First International Semantic Web Conference*, Sardinia, vol. 2342, 2002, pp. 333–347
11. P. Plebani, B. Pernici, Urbe: Web service retrieval based on similarity evaluation. IEEE Trans. Knowl. Data Eng. **21**(11), 1629–1642 (2009)
12. M.F. Porter, An algorithm for suffix stripping. Program **14**(3), 130–137 (1980)
13. R. Quinlan, *C4.5: Programs for Machine Learning* (Morgan Kaufmann Publishers, San Mateo, 1993)
14. M. Sabou, C. Wroe, C.A. Goble, H. Stuckenschmidt, Learning domain ontologies for semantic web service descriptions. J. Web Semant. Sci. Serv. Agent World Wide Web **3**(4), 340–365 (2005)
15. G. Salton, A. Wong, C.S. Yang, A vector space model for automatic indexing. Commun. ACM. **18**(11), 613–620 (1975)
16. P.-N. Tan, M. Steinbach, V. Kumar, *Introduction to Data Mining* (Addison–Wesley, Boston, 2006)
17. C.J. van Rijsbergen, *Information Retrieval* (Butterworths, London/Boston, 1979)
18. P. Wang, B. Xu, Lily: ontology alignment results for oaei 2008, in *OM*, Karlsruhe (2008)

19. W.E. Winkler, Y. Thibaudeau, An application of the fellegi-sunter model of record linkage to the 1990 U.S. decennial census, in *U.S. Decennial Census*. Technical report, U.S. Bureau of the Census, 1987
20. I.H. Witten, E. Frank, *Data Mining: Practical Machine Learning Tools and Techniques*, 2nd edn. (Morgan Kaufmann, Amsterdam/Boston, 2005)

Chapter 9
Self-Adaptive Semantic Matchmaking Using COV4SWS.KOM and LOG4SWS.KOM

Ulrich Lampe and Stefan Schulte

Abstract This chapter presents the methodological and technical approach, as well as evaluation results, for two semantic matchmakers, COV4SWS.KOM and LOG4SWS.KOM. Both matchmakers operate on WSDL-based service description with SAWSDL annotations. COV4SWS.KOM applies similarity measures from the field of semantic relatedness, namely the metrics by Lin and Resnik. It automatically adapts to varying expressiveness of a service description on different abstraction levels through the utilization of an Ordinary Least Squares (OLS) estimator. LOG4SWS.KOM employs traditional subsumption reasoning, but maps the resulting discrete Degrees of Match (DoMs) to numerical equivalents to allow for the integration with additional similarity measures. As proof of concept, a path length-based measure is applied. The DoM mapping process may either be conducted manually or using an OLS estimator. Both matchmakers participated in the Semantic Service Selection (S3) Contest in 2010, providing very competitive evaluation results across all regarded performance metrics.

9.1 Introduction

In the envisioned *Internet of Services*, (Web) services will be commodities that are traded via public marketplaces. One important prerequisite to realizing this vision consists in effective and efficient service discovery, i.e., the ability to find (functionally) matching services based on a given query. In current research, this discovery process is commonly not only based on syntactical, but also on semantic information, as provided by *Semantic Web Services* (SWS) [17].

U. Lampe (✉) · S. Schulte
Technische Universität Darmstadt, Darmstadt, Germany
e-mail: ulrich.lampe@kom.tu-darmstadt.de; stefan.schulte@kom.tu-darmstadt.de

M.B. Blake et al. (eds.), *Semantic Web Services*, DOI 10.1007/978-3-642-28735-0_9,   141
© Springer-Verlag Berlin Heidelberg 2012

In the chapter at hand, we introduce COV4SWS.KOM and LOG4SWS.KOM,[1] two semantic matchmakers for WSDL-based service descriptions with SAWSDL annotations.[2] Both matchmakers participated in the *Semantic Service Selection* (S3) Contest in 2010, achieving very favorable results in terms of the regarded Information Retrieval (IR) metrics [10].

COV4SWS.KOM and LOG4SWS.KOM are based on a common framework, named XAM4SWS ("Cross-Architectural Matchmaker for Semantic Web Services"). However, in the treatment of semantic annotations and the implementation of self-adaptiveness, we pursue different approaches in both matchmakers.

COV4SWS.KOM applies similarity measures from the field of semantic relatedness, namely the metrics by Lin [14] and Resnik [25]. It automatically adapts to varying expressiveness of a service description on different abstraction levels through the utilization of an Ordinary Least Squares (OLS) estimator [30].

LOG4SWS.KOM employs traditional subsumption reasoning, but maps the resulting discrete *Degrees of Match* (DoMs) to numerical equivalents. This allows for the direct integration with additional (numerical) similarity measures. As proof of concept, a path length-based measure is applied. The DoM mapping process may either be conducted manually or using an OLS estimator.

Common features of both matchmakers include the use of a rudimentary fallback strategy, based on the WordNet English language ontology [18]. Also, the principal methodology of determining service similarities is identical. Namely, this concerns the use of bipartite graph matching and the aggregation of similarity values from different service abstraction levels.

9.2 Approach: COV4SWS.KOM and LOG4SWS.KOM

9.2.1 Common Characteristics

While COV4SWS.KOM and LOG4SWS.KOM differ in their treatment of semantic annotations, they are based on the identical matchmaker framework. As a result, they share a significant number of characteristics.

Most importantly, both matchmakers employ the notion of *operations-focused matching*. An overview of the process is depicted in Fig. 9.1. In detail, individual

---

[1]The names of our matchmakers have historical roots: COV was traditionally based on the determination of the degree of coverage between semantic concepts; LOG refers to logic subsumption matching. The common name component 4SWS means "for Semantic Web Services", KOM refers to the abbreviated name of our institute at Technische Universität Darmstadt.

[2]As a matter of fact, both matchmakers are also applicable to service description formalisms that exhibit a structure similar to (SA)WSDL. An application of LOG4SWS.KOM to hRESTS with MicroWSMO annotations – service description formalisms for RESTful services – has been presented by Lampe et al. [12].

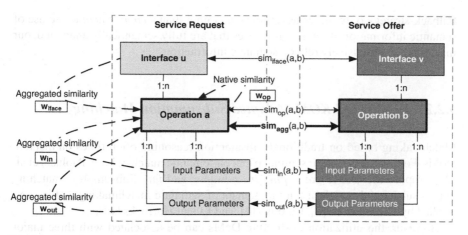

Fig. 9.1 Overview of the matchmaking process

similarity values are computed for the components on all levels of abstraction in a service, i.e., interfaces, operations, inputs, and outputs (yielding sim_{iface}, sim_{op}, sim_{in}, and sim_{out} respectively). Subsequently, these similarity values are aggregated using a linear function on the level of operations, resulting in sim_{agg}. For this aggregation process, the respective weights may be freely chosen (w_{iface}, w_{op}, w_{in}, w_{out}). The weights thus account for varying expressiveness of (semantic) descriptions on the different service abstraction levels.

Subsequently, the objective of the matching process consists in the determination of an optimal pairing between operations in a service request and service offer. This procedure is based on the notion that operations constitute *the* essential unit of functionality in a service. Based on the similarities of the paired operations, the *average similarity* of both services is determined.

The similar notion of average similarity is, for instance, applied by Plebani and Percini in the *URBE* matchmaker [22]. This differs from the concept of *global DoMs*, as initially defined by Paolucci et al. [21], further elaborated by Bellur and Kulkarni [1], and, for instance, applied by Klusch et al. in the *SAWSDL-MX* matchmaker [7]. A global DoM can be interpreted as minimal lower bound of similarity a service offer guarantees with respect to a given query. In contrast, the average similarity can be interpreted as the amount of effort that is required to adapt a service offer to the requirements of the service consumer. Both approaches have their pros and cons; a more extensive discussion can be found in our previous work on LOG4SWS.KOM [27].

Another common aspect in both matchmakers is the utilization of a fallback strategy based on the WordNet ontology [18]. It comes into effect if semantic annotations are unavailable or cannot be processed for a certain service component. In this case, the similarity value is determined based on the inverse distance between the individual English words in a component name. It is important to note that the fallback-strategy only serves as a *substitute*, rather than a *complement* to the use of semantic information. That is, for services that are fully semantically annotated, our matchmakers exclusively rely on semantic information.

9.2.2   LOG4SWS.KOM: Adapted Subsumption Matching

Matchmaking based on traditional subsumption reasoning often relies on *discrete* DoMs. For instance, in their seminal paper on semantic matchmaking, Paolucci et al. [21] propose the DoMs *exact, plug in, subsume*, and *fail*. Subsumption matching enjoys substantial popularity in the domain of semantic matchmaking and is, e.g., applied by Klusch et al. [7], Cardoso [4], and Li and Horrocks [13].

However, the utilization of discrete DoMs can be associated with three major disadvantages. First, it results in a relatively coarse-grained ranking of services; a subsequent, more fine-grained ranking requires the inclusion of additional (generally non-logic) similarity assessments. Second, the approach complicates or inhibits the combination with additional similarity measures, such as word similarity, if a hybrid matching methodology is applied. Third, the approach makes basic assumptions regarding the generalization and specialization of semantic concepts in ontologies which are not necessarily met. A more elaborate discussion of this issue can be found in our previous work [27].

LOG4SWS.KOM addresses these shortcomings by mapping discrete DoMs onto a continuous numerical scale. Such mapping procedure has been proposed in the past [5, 15]. However, the determination of correspondences between DoMs and numerical equivalents is fairly arbitrary in nature. LOG4SWS.KOM avoids this problem by using an *Ordinary Least Squares* (OLS) estimator. The estimator automatically determines numerical equivalents for each DoM for each service abstraction level and thus self-adapts to a given training data set. As a more fine-grained complement to the subsumption DoM, the inverse minimal path length between semantic concepts is additionally taken into consideration. The principal concept of such measure can be traced back to the *edge counting* approaches that were first introduced by Rada et al. [24].

For detailed information on all aspects of LOG4SWS.KOM, please refer to our previous publication [27].

9.2.3   COV4SWS.KOM: Semantic Relatedness

Through its mapping mechanism, LOG4SWS.KOM alleviates the problem of a coarse-grained ranking of service. However, the similarity assessment is ultimately still based on logic subsumption matching with discrete DoMs. Thus, in COV4SWS.KOM, we follow an alternative approach. Namely, we apply similarity measures from the field of semantic relatedness.

The assignment of semantic relatedness of concepts in an ontology or taxonomy is a well-known problem from computational linguistics and artificial intelligence. Research in this domain has resulted in a variety of different similarity measures; for additional details, we refer to a survey by Budanitsky and Hirst [3].

For COV4SWS.KOM, we have selected the measures by Lin [14] and Resnik [25]. Both approaches require the assignment of probabilities of occurrence to all semantic concepts in the utilized ontologies. Due to the lack of a standard corpus, we exploit the set of registered services in our matchmaker as training corpus.

COV4SWS.KOM self-adapts to a given set of training data through the automatic determination of service level weights. For that purpose, an OLS estimator is used. Thus, COV4SWS.KOM can automatically account for fluctuating richness and expressiveness of semantic and syntactic information on different abstraction levels of a service.

9.3 Solution

COV4SWS.KOM and LOG4SWS.KOM have been implemented in Java based on the identical technical foundation. We apply Pellet as reasoner[3] and Java WordNet Library (JWNL)[4] as interface to WordNet. We further utilize a proprietary parser, based on the Java Document Object Model (JDOM) framework,[5] in order to process (SA)WSDL files.

A number of restrictions apply for both matchmakers: In the parsing process, we solely regard the topmost level of parameters, i.e., only those XML Schema *types* or *elements* that are directly referred to by a WSDL message. With respect to semantic annotations, we make exclusive use of *modelReference* attributes (i.e., *schemaMappings* are not taken into account). As an additional restriction, only the first semantic concept (i.e., the first value of modelReference) for each component is utilized in the matchmaking process. In our experience, aforementioned restrictions are common in the semantic matchmaking domain.

In order to compute an optimal matching of components (specifically, inputs, outputs, and operations), bipartite graphs are employed, as initially suggested by Guo et al. [6]. For this purpose, an implementation of the *Hungarian algorithm* by Nedas is applied [20]. This implementation also supports bipartite graphs with differing cardinalities in the two partitions. The principal extension of the Hungarian algorithm for this purpose has been suggested by Bourgeois and Lassalle [2].

For the OLS estimator, input data is acquired by matching a given set of example service requests against a given set of example offers. In case of LOG4SWS.KOM, the so-called design matrix [23] – commonly abbreviated X – is given by the

---

[3]http://clarkparsia.com/pellet/

[4]http://jwordnet.sourceforge.net/

[5]http://www.jdom.org/

relative frequency of the four DoMs (weighted using the inverse path length) on all levels of abstraction in a service. In case of COV4SWS.KOM, the design matrix is inferred from the similarity values on all service levels. For both matchmakers, the vector of predictors – commonly abbreviated y – is inferred from a given binary or graded relevance rating. Each pair of service request and offer yields one row in the design matrix and vector of predictors respectively. For further details, we refer the interested reader to our previous work [27].

In order to speed up the matching process, we utilize various caching mechanisms. In detail, this includes a cache for splitting component names into individual English words, a cache for word distances in WordNet, and a cache of subsumption relations and path lengths between semantic concepts. Caches may be populated at both registration- and query-time. We additionally map all service descriptions into a lightweight internal model. This model essentially only holds the names and semantic concepts for all service components, as well as their parent-child relations.

9.4 Lessons Learned

9.4.1 Evaluation Results

For both matchmakers we have evaluated multiple configurations, i.e., variants and corresponding versions.

For COV4SWS.KOM, the variation concerns the level weights (variants) and the applied similarity metrics (versions). Variant 1 is signature-based, i.e., we assign a level weight of 0.5 to both inputs and outputs and a level weight of 0 to operations and interfaces. Furthermore, the fallback-strategy is disabled in this variant. In Variant 2, we utilize weights of 0.4 for inputs and outputs and 0.1 for operations and interfaces. This weighting accounts for the fact that only the parameter level is annotated in our utilized test collections. In Variant 3, we follow a naive approach and assign equal weights of 0.25 to all service abstraction levels. In Variant 4, we utilize OLS for the determination of optimal weights. Version A makes use of Lin's similarity measure, whereas Version 2 applies Resnik's measure.

For LOG4SWS.KOM, the variation concerns the level weights (variants) and the numerical DoM mappings (versions). We only evaluate Variants 1–3, with the identical definition as for COV4SWS.KOM. For Version A, the numerical equivalents have been set to 1 for exact matches and 0 for fail matches. Plug-in and subsume matches are assigned an numerical equivalent of 0.5. This reflects their intermediate positions between exact and fail matches. The same idea is followed by Syeda-Mahmood [28]. In Version B, we apply OLS for the determination of numerical DoM equivalents.

An overview of all configurations of COV4SWS.KOM and LOG4SWS.KOM is provided in Tables 9.1 and 9.2 respectively. Level weights are given in the order interface, operation, input, output; numerical DoM equivalents are in the

Table 9.1 Evaluated configurations of COV4SWS.KOM

Config.	Level weights	Sim. Measure
1A	0, 0, 0.5, 0.5	Lin
1B	0, 0, 0.5, 0.5	Resnik
2A	0.1, 0.1, 0.4, 0.4	Lin
2B	0.1, 0.1, 0.4, 0.4	Resnik
3A	0.25, 0.25, 0.25, 0.25	Lin
3B	0.25, 0.25, 0.25, 0.25	Resnik
4A	From OLS	Lin
4B (S3)	From OLS	Resnik

Table 9.2 Evaluated configurations of LOG4SWS.KOM

Config.	Level weights	Num. DOM equivalents
1A	0, 0, 0.5, 0.5	1, 0.5, 0.5, 0
1B	0, 0, 0.5, 0.5	From OLS
2A	0.1, 0.1, 0.4, 0.4	1, 0.5, 0.5, 0
2B (S3)	0.1, 0.1, 0.4, 0.4	From OLS
3A	0.25, 0.25, 0.25, 0.25	1, 0.5, 0.5, 0
3B	0.25, 0.25, 0.25, 0.25	From OLS

order exact, plug-in, subsume, and fail.[6] Configuration 4B of COV4SWS.KOM and configuration 2B of LOG4SWS.KOM are marked with "S3" because they participated in the S3 Contest in 2010 [10].

For all aforementioned configurations, we conducted separate evaluation runs using SAWSDL-TC1 (which constituted the basis for the SAWSDL track of the S3 Contest in 2009) and SAWSDL-TC3 (S3 Contest in 2010).[7]

For the configurations where OLS was applied, the full test collections served as training data. In the evaluation, we apply k-fold cross-validation [19]. In the example at hand, k corresponds to the number of queries in the utilized test collection (i.e., 26 for SAWSDL-TC1 and 42 for SAWSDL-TC3), because every query and corresponding relevance set from SAWSDL-TC1 and TC3 respectively serves as a partition from the service set. That is, in the evaluation, for each individual query, all data sets that refer to this query are eliminated from OLS training data.

Even though SAWSDL-TC3 contains an additional graded relevance rating, we made exclusive use of the binary relevance rating for training purposes. This procedure allows for a better comparison of results. For the actual evaluation process, the *Semantic Matchmaker Evaluation Environment* (SME2) was applied.[8]

---

[6]In fact, we utilize generic definitions of DoMs in LOG4SWS.KOM that slightly deviates from the ones introduced by Paolucci et al. [21]. However, this does not have any practical implications for the evaluated configurations. For additional details, please refer to our previous work [27].

[7]Both test collections are available at http://projects.semwebcentral.org/projects/sawsdl-tc/

[8]http://projects.semwebcentral.org/projects/sme2/

Table 9.3 Evaluation results for COV4SWS.KOM and SAWSDL-TC1

Config.	AP	AP'	Q	Q'	nDCG	nDCG'	P5	P10	RP
1A	0.644	0.644	–	–	–	–	0.731	0.727	0.603
1B	0.665	0.665	–	–	–	–	0.723	0.742	0.605
2A	0.737	0.737	–	–	–	–	0.915	0.835	0.672
2B	0.752	0.752	–	–	–	–	0.885	0.819	0.693
3A	0.743	0.743	–	–	–	–	**0.954**	0.846	0.684
3B	**0.778**	**0.778**	–	–	–	–	0.931	0.827	**0.707**
4A	0.722	0.722	–	–	–	–	0.892	0.831	0.669
4B	0.755	0.755	–	–	–	–	0.908	**0.850**	0.681

Table 9.4 Evaluation results for COV4SWS.KOM and SAWSDL-TC3

Config.	AP	AP'	Q	Q'	nDCG	nDCG'	P5	P10	RP
1A	0.617	0.710	0.616	0.725	0.692	0.787	0.724	0.681	0.599
1B	0.635	0.734	0.598	0.708	0.662	0.760	0.686	0.674	0.615
2A	0.706	0.784	0.728	0.806	0.809	0.873	0.795	0.738	0.655
2B	0.710	0.796	0.706	0.791	0.780	0.851	0.776	0.712	0.658
3A	0.710	0.796	0.729	0.812	0.803	0.867	**0.800**	0.733	0.661
3B	0.726	0.808	0.727	0.808	0.803	0.869	0.790	0.726	0.683
4A	0.680	0.802	0.701	0.813	0.791	0.877	0.795	0.733	0.624
4B	**0.736**	**0.823**	**0.741**	**0.825**	**0.818**	**0.884**	0.790	**0.755**	**0.686**

Table 9.5 Evaluation results for LOG4SWS.KOM and SAWSDL-TC1

Config.	AP	AP'	Q	Q'	nDCG	nDCG'	P5	P10	RP
1A	0.718	0.718	–	–	–	–	0.869	0.792	0.647
1B	0.742	0.742	–	–	–	–	0.846	0.827	0.678
2A	0.747	0.747	–	–	–	–	0.931	0.842	0.685
2B	**0.808**	**0.808**	–	–	–	–	**0.962**	**0.885**	**0.735**
3A	0.725	0.725	–	–	–	–	0.931	0.842	0.661
3B	0.758	0.758	–	–	–	–	0.954	0.835	0.699

Table 9.6 Evaluation results for LOG4SWS.KOM and SAWSDL-TC3

Config.	AP	AP'	Q	Q'	nDCG	nDCG'	P5	P10	RP
1A	0.666	0.750	0.667	0.768	0.741	0.824	0.757	0.721	0.617
1B	0.690	0.785	0.692	0.795	0.757	0.846	0.743	0.710	0.648
2A	0.720	0.797	0.744	0.820	0.815	0.877	0.795	**0.764**	0.651
2B	**0.763**	**0.837**	**0.778**	**0.851**	**0.836**	**0.896**	**0.800**	0.755	**0.709**
3A	0.696	0.792	0.725	0.813	0.797	0.875	0.795	**0.764**	0.623
3B	0.721	0.814	0.745	0.831	0.810	0.882	0.795	**0.764**	0.653

A summary of evaluation results is provided in Tables 9.3–9.6. For each configuration, we include the *Information Retrieval* (IR) metrics that SME2 automatically computes, namely *Average Precision* (AP), *Q-measure* (Q), and *normalized Discounted Cumulative Gain* (nDCG). Apostrophes (') denote the adapted metrics for incomplete relevance sets. Furthermore, *Precision at 5* (P5), *Precision at 10* (P10), and *r-Precision* (RP) are provided in the result overview. The best respective value for each metric is highlighted in boldface.

In the case of SAWSDL-TC1, the metrics based on graded relevance (Q, Q', $nDCG$, and $nDCG$) have been omitted because they cannot be computed due to the lack of predefined ratings. For an overview and formal definition of aforementioned metrics, we refer to Sakai and Kando [26] and Manning et al. [16].

We refrain from the inclusion of *Query Response Time* (QRT) results. In our opinion, the characteristics of the machine that is used for evaluation and the utilization of caches renders concrete QRT figures largely incomparable. The interested reader is, however, referred to the results of the 2010 S3 Contest for QRT rankings [10]. We further provide a qualitative discussion of the matter in Sect. 9.4.2.

9.4.2 Advantages and Disadvantages

As can be seen from the evaluation results, both matchmakers generally perform worse for SAWSDL-TC3 in comparison to SAWSDL-TC1 with respect to *AP*. The difference amounts to roughly 0.05 points across all versions and variants. In the following, if not noted differently, our discussion will concern the evaluation results for SAWSDL-TC3. However, the findings are also valid for SAWSDL-TC1.

In general, with the results of the S3 Contest in 2010 serving as a basis, both matchmakers deliver a very competitive matchmaking performance for most configurations. LOG4SWS.KOM performs slightly better than COV4SWS.KOM with respect to all considered metrics.[9] In the following, we will discuss both match-makers separately. Subsequently, we provide a discussion of common observations and additional findings from the development process.

The results for COV4SWS.KOM indicate that metrics from the field of semantic relatedness are well applicable to the problem of matchmaking. Variants B, which utilize Resnik's similarity measure outperform Variants A, which are based on Lin's metric, at all level weights in terms of *AP*, *P5*, *P10*, and *RP*. Interestingly, for the evaluation metrics that are based on graded relevance (namely, Q, Q', $nDCG$, and $nDCG'$), the picture is more or less reversed.

A potential explanation may lie in the elementary difference between Lin's and Resnik's measure. Whereas Lin's measure is normalized to a value range of [0, 1], Resnik's measure may correspond to [0, ∞]. This has two implications: First, because the WordNet-based fallback strategy also provides value in the range [0, 1], Resnik's measure (and thus, the semantic information) is potentially overweighted in the aggregation process. Second, the relative difference between similarity values

---

[9]Using the mean average of each metric across the comparable Variants 1A–3B as a basis for comparison.

for similar and non-similar semantic concepts may be larger with Resnik's measure, due to the unbounded value range. A speculation is that this leads to two "clusters" of rather small and rather large similarity values. These value partitions may be very good determinants of binary relevance (which corresponds to two clusters of *relevant* and *non-relevant* services).

As the comparison of Version 1 with Versions 2 and 3 shows, the matchmaking performance of COV4SWS.KOM notably profits from the inclusion of service abstraction levels beyond the service signature (i.e., inputs and outputs). In fact, there also is a small improvement in all metrics observable between Version 2 and Version 3. This indicates that syntactic information (i.e., the names of interface and operation components) can be of similar importance as semantic information in the determination of service similarity, at least as far as SAWSDL-TC1 and -TC3 are concerned.

This assumption is supported by a manual examination of relevance sets in the SAWSDL-TC3. For most services within each relevance set, the names of both interface and operation components are either very similar or identical. In this case, our rather rudimentary fallback-strategy correctly determines very high similarity values. However, the approach is vulnerable to false positives in cases where the lexical similarity between two distinct relevance sets is high. An example are the *bookpersoncreditcardaccount_service.wsdl* and *bookperson-creditcardaccount_price_service.wsdl* queries and corresponding relevance sets in the SAWSDL-TC3. In these specific cases of high lexical service similarity, the semantic concepts associated with inputs and outputs can provide significantly more discriminative power.

With respect to Version 4, where OLS is applied, we observe a diametric effect on Variants A and B. For Variant A, i.e., the variant based on Lin's measure, the utilization of OLS results in a deterioration of matchmaking performance in terms of most metrics, as compared to the manual level weights in Versions 2 and 3. It is worthy to note that Klusch et al. [7] have made a similar observation – namely, the degradation of matchmaking performance due to the use of machine-learning techniques – in their SAWSDL-MX2 matchmaker.

In contrast, for Variant B (based on Resnik's measure), we observe a notable increase in most metrics with OLS, as compared to the manually configured variants. In fact, configuration 4B delivers the best overall matchmaking performance of all configurations of COV4SWS.KOM. Again, this may potentially be attributed to the characteristics of Resnik's measure, which have been previously discussed.

As the evaluation results for LOG4SWS.KOM show, our adapted variant of subsumption reasoning provides very promising matchmaking results. In fact, configuration 2B of LOG4SWS.KOM achieved the first place in the S3 Contest in 2010 concerning the Q and $nDCG$ metrics. It only trailed *iSEM*, a matchmaker by Klusch et al. [9], by a small margin regarding AP. This indicates that improvements in semantic matchmaking performance do not necessarily require revolutionary changes; in fact, our extension of traditional and well-proven subsumption matching with an OLS estimator is rather evolutionary in nature.

In line with our observations for COV4SWS.KOM, the hybrid Versions 2 and 3 of LOG4SWS.KOM perform significantly better than the signature-based Version 1. The improvement is observable for all regarded evaluation metrics. However, with respect to most evaluation metrics (i.e, AP, Q, and $nDCG$), Version 3 – which puts higher weight on the not semantically annotated interface and operations levels – performs worse in comparison to Version 2. This implies that the determination of semantic similarity works very well in LOG4SWS.KOM with respect to the overall task of determining service similarity. Accordingly, the semantically annotated input and output levels should be assigned greater weight.

In this context, the utilization of path length as a complimentary measure of similarity appears to be a good choice for the SAWSDL-TC1 and -TC3. In fact, URBE – the matchmaker which achieved the highest AP in the 2009 S3 Contest's SAWSDL track [8] – uses the path length as the exclusive measure of semantic similarity [22]. The methodology we apply in LOG4SWS.KOM can be interpreted as a weighted path length measure, with the weights depending on the basic subsumption type.

Across all versions, Variants B, which utilize OLS, deliver an improved matchmaking performance compared to the manually configured Variants A. The effect is most notable for the AP and AP' metrics in terms of absolute gain. This comes as little surprise, because the training data is based on the binary relevance rating of services. Accordingly, the improvement should be the highest for those metrics that are computed based on binary relevance, namely AP and AP'. In practice, however, the use of the more fine-grained graded relevance is preferable for the training process, because it likely leads to a better overall fit of the OLS estimation.

A common disadvantage of COV4SWS.KOM and LOG4SWS.KOM is the need for suitable training data if the self-adaptation mechanisms are to be exploited. Suitability, in this context, refers to the following minimal requirements: The training data has to comprise a set of service queries and a set of service offers, and at least a part of the resulting query/offer-pairs has to be associated with some form of numerical relevance ranking. As the example of the SAWSDL-TC1 and -TC3 demonstrates, the process of assigning rankings commonly requires significant human effort. Additionally, the training data should be representative of the services that are generally processed by the matchmaker. If the latter condition is not met, the matchmaker performance may strongly deteriorate. This regard, it should be noted that the utilization of the whole test collection in our evaluation constitutes an ideal scenario that will commonly not occur in practice.

A similar problem is the need for a representative corpus of semantic concepts. As outlined in Sect. 9.2.3, the application of Lin's and Resnik's measure requires the assignment of probabilities of occurrence to all referenced semantic concepts. In case of the English language, for instance, the so-called *Brown Corpus* [11] provides a well-established source of information for this purpose; a likewise corpus for SWS would be desirable. Again, the utilization of all registered services in our matchmaker can only be considered a temporary solution. Specifically, in practical application, the registration of new service offers and the processing of queries will occur intermittently. Thus, following each registration of a service that contains previously unknown semantic concepts, all probabilities would have to be reassigned.

An additional drawback consists in the computational effort of the training phase. In detail, each service query in the training set has to be matched against each offer. In the case of SAWSDL-TC3 with its 42 queries and 1,080 offers, for example, this results in a total of 45,360 matchmaking operations. Even under the assumption that each matchmaking operation solely requires 100 ms, the training phase would take approximately 75 min. Whether this is problematic in practice largely depends on size of the training data and the frequency at which the training phase is repeated.

On the positive side, the computational effort for the OLS estimator is relatively low. In fact, for the utilized test collections with approximately 1,000 service offers, the determination of level weights (in COV4SWS.KOM) or numerical DoM equivalents (LOG4SWS.KOM) takes less than 100 ms per query. This figure includes the required time for the preliminary filtering and partitioning of the input data, which is triggered by the application of cross-validation, cf. Sect. 9.4.1.

In this context, it is interesting to note that the fallback strategy-related operations require the most computational effort in our matchmakers. URBE, for instance, implements a rather simple strategy for splitting component names into words, based on common separators, such as dash (-) or underscore (_). Such a strategy can very efficiently be implemented using a string tokenizer. However, it fails for names such as *Academic-degreegovernmentorganizationFundingSoap*, which occur in the SAWSDL-TC1 and -TC3. In our matchmakers, we employ a strategy that recursively extracts substrings from component names and checks for the existence of these substrings in the WordNet ontology. For the given example name, this results in dozens of lookup operations. In contrast, the comparison of two semantic concepts via subsumption reasoning is far less "costly" in terms of required computational effort.

Generally, the matchmaking process significantly profits from the utilization of caches. In fact, query response times of a few hundred milliseconds can only be realized through efficient caching mechanisms. In the optimal case where all required similarity assessments are cached, only the computation of component assignments is required. Using the Hungarian algorithm, this process can be conducted in a few milliseconds for each pair of services. In this respect, both COV4SWS.KOM and LOG4SWS.KOM profit from their preliminary training phase, because it leads to an optimal population of caches for the already processed pairs of queries and offers.

Lastly, we would like to discuss an useful observation that is not evident from the presented evaluation results, but was made throughout the development process of our matchmakers. As discussed in Sect. 1.3, our approach considers only the topmost level of XML schema declarations in the matchmaking process. We consider this approach valid, because the underlying parameter structure seems to have been introduced through the semi-automatic conversion process from OWLS-TC[10] to SAWSDL-TC. Thus, according to our experience, the XSD structure beneath the

---

[10]http://www.semwebcentral.org/projects/owls-tc/

topmost types does not have any informational value as far as the SAWSDL-TC is concerned. In fact, as the evaluation results for an initial implementation of the WSDL parser showed, the matchmaking performance degraded if the structure of each *complexType* was parsed. This degradation concerned both the runtime as well as the precision of the matchmaking process.

9.4.3 Conclusions and Future Work

From the evaluation results presented in this chapter, a wide range of conclusions can be drawn.

As the results for COV4SWS.KOM indicate, similarity metrics from the field of semantic relatedness can be applied to the problem of service matchmaking with promising results. These metrics also have one significant advantage over traditional subsumption matching: They natively provide a numerical similarity assessment on a continuous scale. Thus, metrics of semantic relatedness can immediately be integrated with other similarity measures. This is specifically helpful in a (hybrid) matchmaking process with weighted similarity aggregation, such as implemented in our matchmakers. A possible future extension concerns the integration of additional similarity measures; for that matter, a survey by Budanitsky and Hirst [3] may provide a good starting point.

The results of LOG4SWS.KOM show that an extension of classical subsumption matching through a numerical mapping process may also yield very competitive matchmaking performance. In this case, the arbitrary nature of such a mapping process can be addressed through the inclusion of a self-adaptation mechanism; in our case, an OLS estimator. A possible future revision of LOG4SWS.KOM concerns the extension of the OLS estimator to the determination of level weights, as it is applied in COV4SWS.KOM. However, this would also require a more extensive two-phase training process, because the determination of optimal level weights depends on a prior determination of numerical DoM equivalents.

In general, the application of self-adaptation mechanisms provides improved results compared to a manual configuration. This is true for both matchmakers, COV4SWS.KOM and LOG4SWS.KOM. However, in line with previous findings by Klusch et al. [7], we also observed a deterioration in matchmaking performance for selected variants. A straightforward extension in future work concerns the integration of additional adaptation mechanisms. In fact, the domain of machine learning provides a rich source of applicable techniques for that matter, cf. Witten and Frank [29].

An observation for both matchmakers is that hybrid matchmaking and the inclusion of additional service abstraction levels has a positive impact on matchmaking performance. Unfortunately, the effects cannot be quantified for both features individually, because neither SAWSDL-TC1 nor -TC3 provides semantic annotations on the interface or operation level. Thus, the syntax-based fallback strategy (and only the fallback strategy) comes into effect on these abstraction levels.

However, it is interesting to observe the increase in matchmaking performance despite the fact that a rather rudimentary matchmaking strategy – namely, inverse WordNet distance – is applied in our matchmakers. A potential future extension consists in the integration of more sophisticated fallback strategies. In fact, the same methods from the field of semantic relatedness that we already apply in COV4SWS.KOM are candidates of interest in this respect, because they originate in the area of language processing.

9.5 Summary

In the chapter at hand, we presented COV4SWS.KOM and LOG4SWS.KOM, two self-adaptive matchmakers for semantic Web services that operate on the WSDL description format with SAWSDL annotations. Both matchmakers are based on the identical platform, XAM4SWS, and thus share a large amount of common features.

Most notably, this includes an operations-focused matchmaking approach that aggregates similarities of different service abstraction levels on the level of operations. Additional common aspects are the determination of average service similarity, reflecting the required effort for adaption to service consumer demands. Lastly, a WordNet-based fallback strategy is employed in both matchmakers.

COV4SWS.KOM uses methods from the field of semantic relatedness – namely the metrics by Lin and Resnik – for the computation of similarity between semantic concepts. The matchmaker further utilizes an OLS estimator to determine optimal weights for the aggregation of similarity values from different abstraction levels.

LOG4SWS.KOM makes use of traditional subsumption matching, but maps the resulting discrete DoMs to numerical equivalents. For this mapping process, an OLS estimator may be utilized. The inverse path length serves as complementary similarity measure.

As our evaluation on the basis of SAWSDL-TC1 and -TC3 shows, both matchmakers provide very competitive results in terms of common IR metrics. Specifically, the results for COV4SWS.KOM indicate the principal applicability of metrics from the field of semantic relatedness to the problem of SWS matchmaking. At the same time, the evaluation LOG4SWS.KOM leads us to conclude that the combination of two rather "traditional" matchmaking approaches (namely, subsumption reasoning and path length measure) may also be very efficient.

While LOG4SWS.KOM significantly profits from its self-adaptation mechanism, we obtain mixed results for COV4SWS.KOM. In fact, for selected variants, a notable deterioration in matchmaking performance can be observed. Further, the selection of a representative service set for training may constitute a challenge in practical application.

Both matchmakers heavily profit from the inclusion of (not semantically annotated) service abstraction levels beyond the service signature in the matchmaking process. This is true in spite of the rather rudimentary nature of our implemented fallback strategy, which is based on the inverse WordNet distance.

In our future work, we will primarily focus on two points. The first concerns the inclusion of additional similarity metrics from the field of semantic relatedness in COV4SWS.KOM. In fact, this domain offers a wide range of well-explored methodologies that could be adapted to the problem of semantic matchmaking with comparatively little effort. The previously mentioned survey paper by Budanitsky and Hirst [3], for instance, includes a comparative assessment of five similarity measures (including those by Lin and Resnik), both information- and path-length-based. In addition, these measures may also act as a substitute or extension to the rather rudimentary, WordNet-based fallback strategy that we have implemented so far.

The second point concerns the implementation of additional self-adaptation mechanisms. In this area, research in IR and data mining provides a rich set of options. In fact, the popular Weka toolkit by Witten and Frank [29] implements a multitude of different machine learning techniques that are potentially suited for the purpose of semantic matchmaking, such as decision trees or support vector machines.

Final Note

In order to permit an independent assessment and verification of the evaluation results for COV4SWS.KOM and LOG4SWS.KOM through the SWS research community, the complete XAM4SWS matchmaker framework is available via SemWebCentral at http://projects.semwebcentral.org/projects/xam4sws.

References

1. U. Bellur, R. Kulkarni, Improved matchmaking algorithm for semantic web services based on bipartite graph matching, in *2007 IEEE International Conference on Web Services*, Hong Kong, 2007, pp. 86–93
2. F. Bourgeois, J.-C. Lassalle, An extension of the Munkres algorithm for the assignment problem to rectangular matrices. Commun. ACM **14**(12), 802–804 (1971)
3. A. Budanitsky, G. Hirst, Evaluating wordNet-based measures of lexical semantic relatedness. Comput. Linguist. **32**(1), 13–47 (2006)
4. J. Cardoso, Discovering semantic web services with and without a common ontology commitment, in *Third International Semantic and Dynamic Web Processes Workshop*, Chicago, 2006, pp. 183–190
5. A. Fernández, A. Polleres, S. Ossowski, Towards fine-grained service matchmaking by using concept similarity, in *First International Joint Workshop SMR² 2007 on Service Matchmaking and Resource Retrieval in the Semantic Web at the 6th International Semantic Web Conference*, vol. 243, Busan, 2007, pp. 31–46
6. R. Guo, D. Chen, J. Le, Matching semantic web services across hetero-geneous ontologies, in *Fifth International Conference on Computer and Information Technology*, Shanghai, 2005, pp. 264–268
7. M. Klusch, P. Kapahnke, I. Zinnikus, Hybrid daptive web service selection with SAWSDL-MX and WSDL-Analyzer, in *The Semantic Web: Research and Applications*, ed. by L. Aroyo,

P. Traverso, F. Ciravegna, P. Cimiano, T. Heath, E. Hyvönen, R. Mizoguchi, E. Oren, M. Sabou, E. Simperl. Lecture Notes in Computer Science, vol. 5554 (Springer, Berlin/New York, 2009), pp. 550–564

8. M. Klusch, A. Leger, D. Martin, M. Paolucci, A. Bernstein, U. Kuster, 3rd international semantic service selection contest – retrieval performance evaluation of matchmakers for semantic web services (S3 contest), in *Third International Workshop SMR² 2009 on Service Matchmaking and Resource Retrieval in the Semantic Web at the 8th International Semantic Web Conference*, Busan, 2009

9. M. Klusch, P. Kapahnke, iSeM: approximated reasoning for adaptive hybrid selection of semantic services, in *The Semantic Web: Research and Applications*, vol. 6089 (Springer, Berlin, 2010), pp. 30–44

10. M. Klusch, A. Leger, D. Martin, M. Paolucci, A. Bernstein, U. Küster, 4rd international semantic service selection contest – retrieval performance evaluation of matchmakers for semantic web services (S3 contest), in *Fourth International Workshop SMR² 2009 on Service Matchmaking and Resource Retrieval in the Semantic Web at the 9th International Semantic Web Conference*, Busan, 2010

11. H. Kucera, W.N. Francis, *Computational Analysis of Present-Day American English* (Brown University Press, Providence, 1967)

12. U. Lampe, S. Schulte, M. Siebenhaar, D. Schuller, R. Steinmetz, Adaptive matchmaking for RESTful services based on hRESTS and MicroWSMO, in *5th Workshop on Enhanced Web Service Technologies*, Ayia Napa, 2010, pp. 10–17

13. L. Li, I. Horrocks, A software framework for matchmaking based on semantic web technology. Int. J. Electron. Commer. **8**(4), 39–60 (2004)

14. D. Lin, An information-theoretic definition of similarity, in *Fifteenth International Conference on Machine Learning*, Madison, 1998, pp. 296–304

15. C. Liu, Y. Peng, J. Chen, Web services escription ontology-based service discovery model, in *2006 IEEE/ WIC/ ACM International Conference on Web Intelligence*, Hong Kong, 2006, pp. 633–636

16. D.C. Manning, P. Raghavan, H. Schütze. *Introduction to Information Retrieval* (Cambridge University Press, New York, 2008)

17. S.A. McIlraith, T.C. Son, H. Zeng. Semantic Web Services. IEEE Intell. Syst. **16**(2), 46-53 (2001)

18. G.A. Miller, WordNet: a lexical database for English. Commun. ACM **38**(11), 39–41 (1995)

19. T.M. Mitchell, *Machine Learning* (McGraw-Hill, New York, 1997)

20. K.A. Nedas, Munkres' (Hungarian) Algorithm (2005), Available online at http://konstantinosnedas.com/dev/soft/munkres.htm. Accessed 21 Feb 2011

21. M. Paolucci, T. Kawamura, T.R. Payne, K.P. Sycara, Importing the semantic web in UDDI, in *International Workshop on Web Services, E-Business, and the Semantic Web in Connection with the 14th Conference on Advanced Information Systems Engineering*, Toronto, 2002, pp. 225–236

22. P. Plebani, B. Pernici, URBE: web service retrieval based on similarity evaluation. IEEE Trans. Knowl. Data Eng. **21**(11), 1629–1642 (2009)

23. S.T. Rachev, S. Mittnik, F.J. Fabozzi, M. Focardi, T. Jasic, *Financial Econometrics: From Basics to Advanced Modeling Techniques* (Wiley, Hoboken, 2007)

24. R. Rada, H. Mili, E. Bicknell, M. Blettner, Development and application of a metric on semantic nets. IIEEE Trans. Syst. Man Cybern. **19**(1), 17–30 (1989)

25. P. Resnik, Using information content to evaluate semantic similarity in a taxonomy, in *Fourteenth International Joint Conference on Artificial Intelligence*, Montréal, 1995, pp. 448–453

26. T. Sakai, N. Kando, On information retrieval metrics designed for evaluation with incomplete relevance assessments. Inf. Retr. **11**(5), 447-470 (2008)

27. S. Schulte, U. Lampe, J. Eckert, R. Steinmetz, LOG4SWS.KOM: self-adapting semantic web service discovery for SAWSDL, in *Fourth International Workshop of Software Engineering for Adaptive Service-Oriented Systems*, Washington, 2010

28. T. Syeda-Mahmood, G. Shah, R. Akkiraju, A.-A. Ivan, R. Goodwin, Searching service repositories by combining semantic and ontological matching, in *2005 IEEE International Conference on Web Services*, Orlando, 2005, pp. 13–20
29. I.H. Witten, E. Frank, *Data Mining: Practical Machine Learning Tools and Techniques*, 2nd edn. (Morgan Kaufmann, San Francisco, 2005)
30. J. Wooldridge, *Introductory Econometrics: A Modern Approach*, 4th edn. (South-Western Cengage Learning, Mason, 2008)

Part II
Results from the S3 Contest:
Cross Evaluation Track

Chapter 10
Overview of the Jena Geography Dataset Cross Evaluation

Ulrich Küster and Birgitta König-Ries

Abstract This chapter informs about the Jena Geography Dataset Evaluation which has been implemented as a third complementary track of the S3 Contest initiative starting in 2009. The main objective that distinguishes this track from Tracks I and II is to cross-evaluate approaches based on different formalisms. The chapter motivates the track's evaluation goals and explains the evaluation setup, test data, procedures and measures. An overview of the participating systems and the evaluation results will be given, including insights about the measurement reliability that can be derived from the evaluation results. Finally, an outlook on future work will be provided.

10.1 Introduction

The traditional tracks of the S3 Contest described in the preceding part of this book follow the evaluation approach of the Text REtrieval Conferences (TREC) from Information Retrieval (IR). This approach is based on test collections which contain a set of services, a set of sample requests and relevance judgments that state which of the services are relevant for which request. Matchmakers are then required to process the test collection and rank the available services by decreasing estimated relevance to each request. The ranking created by the matchmakers is then compared with the ranking induced by the reference judgments to assess the quality of the service retrieval. Furthermore, the time required to process the test collection is measured to assess the runtime performance of the evaluated systems.

U. Küster · B. König-Ries (✉)
Department of Computer Science, University Jena, Jena, Germany
e-mail: Ulrich.Kuester@uni-jena.de; Birgitta.Koenig-Ries@uni-jena.de

M.B. Blake et al. (eds.), *Semantic Web Services*, DOI 10.1007/978-3-642-28735-0_10,   161
© Springer-Verlag Berlin Heidelberg 2012

The traditional tracks of the S3 Contest provided two readily annotated test collections using the OWL-S [6] and SAWSDL [1] formalisms respectively. The main advantage of this approach is that comparatively little effort is required by participants in the evaluation. The main drawback is that an evaluation across different description formalisms and a direct comparison of semantic and traditional retrieval approaches is not possible. Furthermore, using readily provided semantic descriptions, it is difficult to analyze whether retrieval errors are caused by (a) insufficient expressivity of the used formalism, (b) incorrect semantic annotations of the services or requests, (c) shortcomings of the algorithm used to compare the service and request descriptions, or (d) problems in the alignment of the descriptions and the algorithm that processes them.

To extend the coverage of the S3 Contest in the directions indicated above, a new complementary evaluation track, the Jena Geography Dataset Cross Evaluation (JGDEval), was added to the S3 Contest in 2009. The setup and overall results of this track are presented in this chapter. The following chapters will complement this chapter by presenting the evaluation results and lessons learned by the evaluation from the viewpoints of selected participants.

The rest of this chapter is organized as follows. Section 10.2 describes the evaluation goals and approach of the JGDEval in detail. Subsequently, Sect. 10.3 will provide an overview of the participants in the evaluation and the evaluation results. Section 10.4 will discuss lessons learned and give an outlook on future work. A short summary is given in Sect. 10.5.

10.2 Evaluation Setup

The evaluation setup was devised to complement the existing S3 Contest tracks by an evaluation across formalisms. In the following, we will describe the goals and assumptions of the track, the employed evaluation methodology and the test data and evaluation measures being used.

10.2.1 Evaluation Goals

JGDEval targets the use case of a human developer who is searching for a Web service that provides functionality needed in some application being developed. Currently, a developer will query and browse a Web service registry to identify promising candidate services. Semantic descriptions are expected to make such manual discovery more efficient by improving the filtering and ranking of the services in the registries. It is the aim of JGDEval to test this hypothesis and investigate the strengths and weaknesses of current approaches by comparing the performance of different semantic and non-semantic service retrieval technologies.

Among the primary questions being investigated are:

- How precise, complete and efficient are current technologies for service retrieval?
- How much information needs to be shared between providers of the service descriptions and developers posing service queries to allow for efficient retrieval?
- What is the right level of detail to describe services for the given task of retrieval from a registry?
- How is the trade-off between description effort and retrieval precision?
- What is the best pattern and formalism to describe services?
- Which retrieval techniques are good for which retrieval problems?
- What are the properties that make a specific retrieval problem difficult for some or all techniques?

10.2.2   Evaluation Methodology

The setup of JGDEval was designed to help answering these questions. Like the other tracks of the S3 Contest, this one also provides a test collection of services, queries and relevance judgments. However, unlike the other two tracks, it is the task of the technology developers participating in the evaluation to provide the semantic annotations of the services and queries. Thus, the evaluation is open to all kind of technologies regardless of the formalism which is employed.

The semantic annotations of the services, of course, have to be developed independently of those of the queries and in particular without knowledge of the reference judgments. Thus, each participating group had to staff different roles with different people. First, each group was provided with the *natural language descriptions and WSDLs of the services* used for the evaluation. The *service annotators* had to annotate these services using the formalism of their choice. During this step, they were supposed to create the necessary *domain ontologies* and, if required, *annotation documentation* which was made available to the *request annotators*. After the *service annotations* were collected, the *natural language descriptions and WSDLs of the sample requests* were released to the request annotators. They created the annotations of the requests using the previously created domain ontologies and annotation documentation. After the *request annotations* were collected, the participants had to provide the binaries of their matchmaking systems which were made pluggable into the SME2 evaluation environment[1] by means of a public interface. SME2 was then used to execute the matchmaking systems and collect runtime measurements as well as the resulting service rankings which formed the base for the further retrieval performance analysis.

---

[1] http://projects.semwebcentral.org/projects/sme2/

10.2.3   Test Data

To support the evaluation, a special dataset, the Jena Geography Dataset (JGD) was created. One of the difficulties when building a test collection for service retrieval is to ensure for a sufficient variety of services and, at the same time, make sure that the contained services are still somewhat related and similar. We therefore examined public Web service repositories to identify a domain with many public services that meet this requirement. The geography domain was chosen since it appears to be the domain with the most publicly accessible Web services available.

We analyzed and collected over 200 service operations within this domain from sources like seekda.com, xmethods.com, webservicelist.com, programmable-web. com, or geonames.org. The services were collected with complete information, including natural language documentation of what the service delivers and pointers to the implementation of the services. In some cases the available information was manually enhanced with information obtained from calling the services and inspecting the results. Additionally, WSDL descriptions were created for the REST-based services that did not have original WSDL descriptions already. Finally, SOAP-based services that offered several independent service operations within one WSDL file were split such that each service in the dataset offered exactly one operation and was described by exactly one WSDL file. Further information on the Jena Geography Dataset is available in [3, Chap. 5.4].

In order to reduce the entry barrier to the participation, the dataset was divided into inclusive smaller datasets of 200 (full dataset), 150 (JGD150), 100 (JGD100), respectively 50 (JGD50) services. It turned out that except for one, all participants chose to participate on JGD50, i.e., the smallest dataset. To further reduce the necessary effort of participants, an OWL geography domain ontology[2] based upon the PROTON ontologies[3] was created. Usage of this ontology was entirely optional but most participants based their ontologies on this provided one.

Finally, ten sample queries were devised. The queries ranged from rather simple and very specific queries (like a query for a service that delivers the altitude above sea level for a given location) to rather complex and vague ones (like a query for a service that provides as much information about a given city as possible). For the ten queries, graded relevance judgments according to a multidimensional relevance scale were created. The used relevance scale and the process of creating the judgments (and ensuring their reliability) is described in detail in [4]. Since one of the requests did not have matching services within JGD50, it was later removed, leaving nine service queries as the base of the evaluation.

---

[2]http://fusion.cs.uni-jena.de/professur/jgd
[3]http://proton.semanticweb.org/

10.2.4 Measures

To assess the runtime performance, the average query response time and the time required to process the whole test collection (including the time required to load, parse and register the services) was measured. Measurements were performed and provided by Patrick Kapahnke, DFKI Saarbrücken, on an Intel Core2 Duo T9600 (2.8 GHz) machine with 4 GB RAM running Windows XP 32 bit. No measures of the memory consumption were taken, since the memory consumed by the matchmakers outside of the SME2 environment was not traced.

Various retrieval correctness measures were used to evaluate the retrieval performance of the returned service rankings. A complete coverage is beyond the scope of this chapter, but available in [5]. Here, we restrict the coverage to *binary average precision* and *normalized discounted cumulated gain* which are introduced in the following.

Binary *Recall* and *Precision* are set-based measures using binary relevance, i.e., a service is considered relevant or irrelevant to a query but no further distinction is made. Let L be the set of services which are returned in response to a query. Let R be the set of services which are relevant for a given query. Then, recall is defined as the proportion of relevant services which are retrieved and precision as the proportion of retrieved services which are relevant:

$$Recall = \frac{L \cap R}{R}, \ Precision = \frac{L \cap R}{L}.$$

If a system's performance needs to be captured in a single measure, the most often used one is *Average Precision* over relevant items (AveP). This measure is not set-based but based upon rankings, i.e. ordered lists of services. Let $isrel(i)$ be a binary function that is 1, iff the service at rank i of a given ranking is relevant to a given query and 0 otherwise. Let $count(i)$ be a function that returns the number of relevant services among the services at ranks 1 through i, i.e., $count(i) = \sum_{j=1}^{i} isrel(j)$. Then AveP is defined as:

$$AveP = \frac{1}{|R|} \sum_{i=1}^{|L|} isrel(i) \frac{count(i)}{i}.$$

If one uses graded instead of binary relevance, i.e., if multiple levels of relevance of a service with respect to a query are distinguished, the most commonly used measure is *Cumulated Gain*. Intuitively, Cumulated Gain at rank i measures the gain that a user receives by scanning the top i items in a ranked output list. Let $g(i) \geq 0$ denote the gain (or relevance) of the service at rank i with respect to a given query. Then *Cumulated Gain* at rank i is defined as:

$$CG(i) = \sum_{j=1}^{i} g(j).$$

Since $CG(i)$ can take arbitrarily large values for queries with many relevant items it has to be normalized to average or compare results across queries. Therefore, consider an ideal ranking, i.e., a ranking, where $g(i) \geq g(i + 1)$. The *Ideal Cumulated Gain* at rank i, $ICG(i)$, refers to the cumulated gain with respect to such an ideal ranking (i.e., it measures the optimal performance). *Normalized Cumulated Gain* at rank i is defined as the retrieval performance relative to the optimal retrieval behavior, i.e.:

$$NCG(i) = \frac{CG(i)}{ICG(i)}.$$

In order to account for the fact that the retrieval performance at the top positions of a ranking is typically more important than that at the bottom positions of a ranking (users may not scan a ranking to the very end), a discounting factor is introduced. This factor reduces the gain of items at the bottom positions of a ranking. *Discounted Cumulated Gain* at rank i is then defined as $DCG(i) = \sum_{j=1}^{i} \frac{g(j)}{disc(j)}$ with $disc(j) >= 1$ being an appropriate discount function, i.e., $\log_2(j + 1)$. An according definition of the *Ideal Discounted Cumulated Gain IDCG(i)* leads to the definition of *Normalized Discounted Cumulated Gain*:

$$NDCG(i) = \frac{DCG(i)}{IDCG(i)}.$$

Evaluation results in the following section will be reported with respect to Recall, Precision, *AveP* and *NDCG* using discounting $\log_2(i + 1)$. Note that the graded relevance judgments of the JGD have to be reduced to binary ones if binary measures are used. This can be done in different ways (e.g., using more strict or more relaxed definitions of binary relevance). Eight different settings were used, but a detailed treatment of this issue and the used relevance levels in general is beyond the scope of this chapter, but available in [3, Chap. 7.8].

10.3   Participants and Results

Six systems participated in the evaluation in 2009. Themis-S is an IR-style service discovery engine, which can be regarded as a meet-in-the-middle approach between heavyweight Semantic Web technologies and easy-to-use syntactic information retrieval models [2]. It operated on English natural language descriptions that were generated automatically from the service documentation available in the test collection.

WSColab is a service retrieval engine based upon the folksonomy approach of collaborative tagging. The tags which were used to facilitate the service discovery were collected from a community of users via a web portal developed for this task. WSColab is described in detail in Chap. 11.

SAWSDL-MX1 and SAWSDL-MX2 combine logic-based and syntactic (text similarity-based) matching to perform hybrid semantic matching of I/O parameters defined for potentially multiple operations of a Web service interface. The descriptions were developed by manually linking IO types from the WSDL descriptions of the JGD to concepts from an OWL domain ontology based upon the one provided as part of JGD. References to both matchmakers can be found in Chap. 3.

SAWSDL iMatcher is also a hybrid matchmaker based on I/O concepts and service names. It exploits a learned linear regression function to predict the similarity between a query and a service. For participation in JGDEval, SAWSDL iMatcher trained on the SAWSDL-TC used in Track 2 of the S3 Contest (see Chap. 3) was used on the descriptions created for SAWSDL-MX1 and SAWSDL-MX2. SAWSDL iMatcher is described in detail in Chap. 8.

Finally, IRS-III is an ontology-based reasoning and SWS broker environment based on OCML and LISP. It uses a SWS model compliant with the Web Service Modeling Ontology WSMO. For participation in the evaluation, a preliminary implementation of a new discovery algorithm was used instead of IRS-III's typical goal invocation mechanism (which solves a goal by invoking a suitable Web service instead of returning a ranked list of candidate services). The descriptions used by IRS-III were created by manually linking I/O types from automatically generated description templates to concepts from a domain ontology. IRS-III is described in detail in Chap. 12.

One additional remark concerning the participating matchmakers need to be made. While Themis-S, SAWSDL-MX1/2 and SAWSDL-iMatcher internally determine the relevance of a service to a query on a continuous scale, WSColab and IRS-III deploy a multi-valued respectively binary relevance scale. Natively, WSColab and IRS-III return only matching services. In order to be comparable to the other matchmakers and the evaluation task, both were changed to return a ranked list of all services with services deemed irrelevant following the relevant ones in arbitrary order. This has to be considered when interpreting the following evaluation results.

Performance measurements averaged over all queries are displayed in Table 10.1. With respect to the runtime performance both, the query response time as well as the total execution time varies widely with WSColab being the fastest system and Themis-S and IRS-III being the more computationally intensive systems. This results from the matchmaking technique being employed and will be discussed in the following chapters.

The retrieval performance in terms of AveP and NDCG also varies notably, albeit not as significantly as the runtime performance. Figure 10.1 provides a more detailed account of the retrieval performance by showing the macro averaged binary precision for standard recall levels. An ideal retrieval system would yield a precision value of 1.0 for all recall levels. However, the worst case performance is dependent from the number of relevant services within the test collection. To indicate a value for the performance bottom line, we added the performance of a random matchmaker which was estimated by averaging the performance values of 50 random rankings. Overall, WSColab delivers the best results, even though the

Table 10.1 Performance results of the JGD evaluation

Matchmaker	Total execution time (s)	Average query time (ms)	AveP	NDCG(50)
WSColab	0.125	0	0.54	0.8
SAWSDL iMatcher	1.66	177	0.53	0.75
SAWSDL-MX1	4.41	162	0.41	0.67
SAWSDL-MX2	11.05	785	0.45	0.74
IRS-III	25.5	2,826	0.41	0.69
Themis-S	99.97	2,043	0.48	0.71

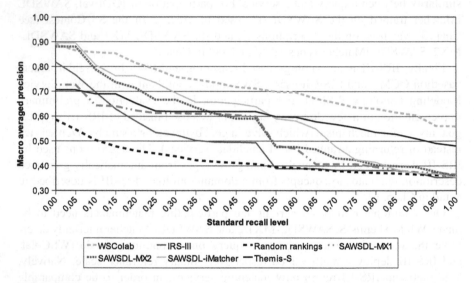

Fig. 10.1 Macro averaged binary precision

precise interpretation of the results depends on the evaluation use case at hand and the concrete measure being used. Themis-S, for instance, performs comparatively poor at low recall levels but comparatively good at high recall levels. Compared to the other systems, it is more recall than precision oriented. A further discussion of these issues from the point of view of the individual systems will be provided in the following chapters.

Figure 10.2 shows the normalized discounted cumulated gain (NDCG) measure for the 50 ranks in the JGD50 test collection. Again, an ideal retrieval system would yield a normalized gain of 1.0 over all ranks and the bottom line performance is indicated by an average over 50 random rankings. Compared to the binary AveP, NDCG provides a more fine-grained evaluation and emphasizes the performance at the top positions of the ranking compared to the performance at the bottom ones. This explains that the overall performance difference between the evaluated real systems and the random rankings is higher than if measured with binary precision. Otherwise, results show a similar tendency with WSColab performing best. Again, the different retrieval characteristic of Themis-S can be observed by the different nature of its chart compared to those of the other systems.

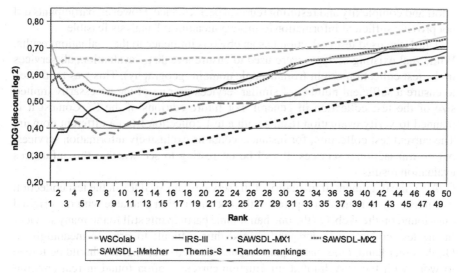

Fig. 10.2 Normalized discounted cumulated gain

10.4   Lessons Learned and Outlook

Overall, the evaluation setup has worked very well and was commented very positively by participants. People especially appreciated that description templates were individually generated such that they did not have to create their semantic annotations from scratch. There was no critique to the general setup of the benchmark by the participants. To the best of our knowledge, this was the first attempt ever to compare the retrieval performance of different semantic matchmakers across formalisms and very successful as such. However, there are a few caveats.

First, due to limitations of the resources available on side of the participants, the evaluation had to be performed on a significantly downsized version of the test collection (50 instead of 200 services). This obviously reduces the significance and reliability of the evaluation results. It is thus planned to repeat the evaluation based on an extended dataset in the future editions of the S3 Contest.

Second, the number of participants was encouraging, but not really sufficient to perform a true cross evaluation to isolate the different factors (formalism complexity, description quality, algorithm efficiency, description and algorithm alignment) that influence the evaluation results. The problem was aggravated by the fact that three matchmakers (SAWSDL-MX1, SAWSDL-MX2 and SAWSDL iMatcher) used the same set of descriptions. Had they created and used different descriptions, a better cross evaluation would have become feasible. Furthermore, it was planned to also gather data from participants about the effort involved in creating their semantic annotations. This would have allowed to investigate the tradeoff between description effort and complexity and resulting retrieval performance. However, participants did not provide sufficient information to make a meaningful analysis feasible.

Third, the used test collection has an obvious influence to the evaluation results. While real existing services were used to ensure a realistic evaluation, all services in the test collection origin from a single domain (geography). This was motivated to ensure a sufficient number of similar services despite of the necessarily limited size of the test collection in general. For future editions of the S3 Contest it is planned to verify evaluation results with a test collection from a different domain. The current test collection, for instance, contains exclusively information services, but no transactional services. It will be interesting to see whether this influences evaluation results.

Also, the documentation quality of the services and WSDLs in the test collection was manually enhanced compared to the documentation available with the original ones found on the Web. On the one hand, some participants still found many services in the test collection underspecified and thus difficult to process meaningfully. On the other hand, other participants argued that retrieval engines should be forced to work with the very limited information currently often found in real environments. This highlights another controversy about the desirable characteristics of test collections and its influence on the evaluations. Again, we will continue to investigate this in future editions.

Apart from lessons learned regarding the general evaluation methodology, the data gathered during the evaluation allowed to perform a meta evaluation of the retrieval effectiveness performance measures being used as well as the effects of using different relevance settings and judgment scales. A comprehensive discussion is beyond the scope of this chapter and available in [4, 5]. Here, we just report the main findings:

- Binary AveP is highly sensitive towards changes in the definition of relevance and should be used with corresponding caution.
- In contrast, graded relevance is extremely stable against moderate changes in the underlying definition of relevance.
- Inconsistency in reference judgments influences evaluation results, but only moderately.
- The choice of evaluation measure influences the evaluation results. One should not choose a particular measure without reflecting why this measure is chosen. In case of doubt, it seems wise to analyze with different measures and report correspondingly.
- NDCG charts are probably the most informative way of presenting evaluation results, since they provide an indication of the performance of matchmakers over ranks and still provide a summary measure by the value at the bottom rank ($NDCG_{50}$ in our case).

10.5   Summary

This chapter introduced to the Jena Geography Dataset Cross Evaluation Track
of the S3 Contest. The track was motivated by the need for an evaluation of
the retrieval performance of service matchmakers across different semantic and
traditional approaches. The evaluation goals, methodology, the test data as well
as the measures being used were presented. Afterwards, a brief introduction to
the participants in the evaluation and the evaluation results was provided. Finally,
lessons learned during the organization and execution of the evaluation including
some insights regarding the reliability of the evaluation were discussed. An outlook
on future improvements was also given. The introduction provided by this chapter
will be complemented by the following chapters that describe the participant's
results and lessons learned in detail.

References

1. J. Farrell, H. Lausen (ed.), *Semantic Annotations for WSDL and XML Schema*. W3C Recommendation (2007), http://www.w3.org/TR/sawsdl/, last accessed May 2012
2. R. Knackstedt, D. Kuropka, O. Polyvyanyy, An ontology-based service discovery approach for
   the provisioning of product-service bundles, in *Proceedings of the 16th European Conference
   on Information Systems (ECIS08)*, Galway, 2008
3. U. Küster, *An Evaluation Methodology and Framework for Semantic Web Services Technologies*.
   PhD thesis, Friedrich-Schiller-University Jena, Jena, 2010
4. U. Küster, B. König-Ries, Relevance judgments for web services retrieval – a methodology
   and test collection for sws discovery evaluation, in *Proceedings of the 7th IEEE European
   Conference on Web Services (ECOWS09)*, Eindhoven, 2009
5. U. Küster, B. König-Ries, Measures for benchmarking semantic web service matchmaking
   correctness, in *Proceedings of the 7th Extended Semantic Web Conference (ESWC2010)*,
   Heraklion, 2010
6. D. Martin (ed.), *OWL-S: Semantic Markup for Web Services*, W3C Member Submission (2004),
   http://www.w3.org/Submission/OWL-S/, last accessed May 2012

Chapter 11
Evaluation of Structured Collaborative Tagging for Web Service Matchmaking

Maciej Gawinecki, Giacomo Cabri, Marcin Paprzycki, and Maria Ganzha

Abstract Turning Web services into Semantic Web Services (SWS) can be prohibitively expensive for large repositories. In such cases collecting community descriptions in forms of structured tags can be a more affordable approach to describe Web services. However, little is understood about how tagging impacts performance of retrieval. There are neither real structured tagging systems for Web services, nor real corpora of structured tags. To start addressing these issues, in our approach, we motivated taggers to tag services in a partially controlled environment. Specifically, taggers were given application requirements and asked to find and tag services that match the requirements. Tags collected in this way were used for Web service matchmaking and evaluated within the framework of the Cross-Evaluation Track of the Third Semantic Service Selection 2009 contest. As part of the lessons learned, we explain relations between description schema (SWS, tags, flat document) and matchmaking heuristics, and performance of retrieval in different search scenarios. We also analyze reliability of tagging system performance as related to taggers'/searchers' autonomy. Finally, we identify threats to results' credibility stemming from partial control of the tags collection process.

M. Gawinecki (✉) · G. Cabri
Department of Information Engineering, University of Modena and Reggio Emilia, Modena, Italy
e-mail: maciej.gawinecki@unimore.it; giacomo.cabri@unimore.it

M. Paprzycki
Warsaw School of Management, Warsaw, Poland

Systems Research Institute, Polish Academy of Sciences, Warsaw, Poland
e-mail: marcin.paprzycki@ibspan.pl

M. Ganzha
Institute of Informatics, University of Gdańsk, Gdańsk, Poland

Systems Research Institute, Polish Academy of Sciences, Warsaw, Poland
e-mail: maria.ganzha@ibspan.pl

M.B. Blake et al. (eds.), *Semantic Web Services*, DOI 10.1007/978-3-642-28735-0_11,
© Springer-Verlag Berlin Heidelberg 2012

11.1 Introduction

To build reliable applications in a short time, and for little money, a software engineer should reuse existing artifacts: functionalities, data and resources. Access to such artifacts is often provided through Web services. However, if services are not described with proper metadata, software developers cannot find them. Here, Semantic Web Services (SWS) are to provide service metadata and, thus, make retrieval effective. However, most of SWS research is devoted to effective matchmaking, neglecting costs of turning traditional services into semantic ones. The main obstacles are investment and operating costs, stemming from: (1) complex formalisms requiring skilled experts to annotate, (2) ontologies that are expensive to develop and maintain [7, 20], and (3) the lack of motivating scenarios for the community to participate in the description process [25]. Without eliminating these obstacles SWS may remain unused on large scale, similarly to many formal approaches for traditional software components repositories [14, 15].

Discovery based on community tags for Web services supports software developers, but has only modest requirements [2,4,5,13,23,27]. Software developer without background in SWS can provide metadata. She decides which aspects to capture, in which vocabulary without the need for a predefined ontology. Participation in tagging is embedded in the service search process: by tagging, the programmer organizes her collections of bookmarked services to ease further (re)discovery of services.

Given the promising low costs of implementation and maintenance of tagging (as an approach to getting service metadata), our goal is to try to understand whether it can be competitive when compared to the SWS. In particular, we are interested in answers to the following questions:

- In collaborative tagging users have much autonomy. For instance, taggers decide which service to tag. Can a tagging system provide satisfying retrieval performance for Web services? How much the autonomy impacts performance?
- Search scenarios differ in goals and constraints. For instance, one programmer may search for a very specific functionality, e.g., geocoding; while another may search for services providing *any* information about a given input, e.g., a geographic region. For which search scenario structured tags work better? Why?

Obviously, answering these questions is hard for one major reason. There are neither real structured tagging systems for Web services, nor real corpora of structured tags.

To start addressing these issues, in our approach, users worked in a partially controlled environment. Specifically, taggers were given application requirements and asked to find and tag services that match the requirements. Tags collected in this way were used in the WSColab [5], our Web service matchmaker for structured tags. Performance evaluation was completed within the framework of the Cross-Evaluation Track of the Third Semantic Service Selection 2009 contest [19]. Our approach was compared to SWS matchmakers (using experts annotations), and a matchmaker using automatically generated descriptions.

Given that the tags collection process was partially controlled, our results may *not* be useful for predicting performance of an uncontrolled tagging system. Nevertheless, our results can yield insights into *ideal* performance of tagging approaches and threats to this performance.

In summary, the contributions of this chapter are:

- Identification of factors that need to be controlled during tag and query collection processes (Sect. 11.3).
- Insight into relation between descriptions schema (SWS, tags, flat document) and matchmaking heuristics, and performance of retrieval in different search scenarios (Sect. 11.4.2).
- Analysis of reliability of tagging system performance as related to tag-gers'/searchers' autonomy (Sect. 11.4.3).
- Identification of threats to results credibility (Sect. 11.4.4). Particularly we compare tagging dynamics between our and real systems (from better studied domains [6, 18]).

11.2   Approach: WSColab

Originally, tagging was used in Web service and software component repositories as a classification schema *complementary* to traditional ones (e.g., faceted-based search) [4, 13, 23, 27].[1] In such form it is useful only to minimize the distance between how a service is described in the repository and how a user describes it [27].

In our approach, WSColab [5], structured tagging *replaces* existing classification schema. In this way it captures primary aspects, important for most of searchers but still allows inclusion of complementary aspects, relevant for individual users. For instance, taggers are encouraged to describe service input, output and behavior (e.g., `distance`), but can also add detailed information, e.g., `miles` as a length unit of the distance. Example of a tagged service is shown in Fig. 11.1.

Our matchmaker for tag descriptions of services supports:

- *Interface/Behavior Matchmaking*: To facilitate matching of services that act similarly but have different interfaces it returns services that are interface compatible, i.e., service input/output tags match at least one input query keyword and one output query keyword (interface matching heuristics) or behavior compatible, i.e., there is a match with a behavior tag (behavior matching heuristics).
- *Approximate search*: Matches are ranked to help a user to assess their relevance. Ranking is generated by combining rankings for each service part (input, output, behavior) that are created using traditional information retrieval techniques adopted for folksonomies.

---

[1]See also online registries, e.g., SeekDa.com, ProgrammableWeb.com

distance   distance_calculator   location_distance   geographic   geography   location   length   distance_between_two_places   county   get_distance   geocoding   points_distance   geographical   worldwide   information   coordinates   real_services   global_distance_calculator   find_distance

license_key   location   licence   two_locations   latitude   longitude   geographical_point   target_location   second_location   permit   coordinates   source_coordinates   start_location   target_coordinates   first_location   geographic_point   license   country_names   licence_key   locations   two_places   source_location   stop_location

distance   map   distance_in_feet   distance_in_miles   length   points_distance   distance_in_km

Fig. 11.1 Tag clouds for behavior, input and output of the DOTSGeoCoder_GetDistance service. The bigger the tag the more actors have used it to annotate the service

- *Primary/complementary aspects search*: It scores higher services with matching primary aspects than those with only complementary ones.
- *Incomplete information search*: A user with unclear goal in mind can formulate incomplete queries. Incompletely annotated services can still be matched.
- *Interactive search*: Fast query evaluation algorithm based on (in-memory) inverted indexes [29] enables a system to return services in short time.

11.3 Solution: Using WSColab for Annotation and Retrieval

11.3.1 Matchmaker Alterations

For participation in the contest, an altered version of the matchmaker was used – it returns the ranked matched services, followed by all non-matched services in a random order. This procedure allows results of the proposed matchmaker to be compared to the results of other matchmakers in the competition.

11.3.2 Configuration of Tag Collection Process

Collaborative tagging is a complex dynamic system where users interact with each other *indirectly* by sharing tags about common resources, e.g., a user X tags a service, while a user Y uses the same tags to pre-filter services for her. Next, when Y finds the relevant service, she tags it with her tags, probably based on the tags of X. This is a fragment of a *feedback cycle* [18] that allows semantics of a service to emerge from annotations of different users. The following factors affect the results of this process (we do not claim the list to be complete):

- *Tagging context*. Why a user decides to tag impacts *which services* get tagged and *what aspects* the tags cover [6, 12].
- *Participants*. Motivations to participate vary across different users [12].

- *Tagging system architecture.* What is the user's task that a system aims to support? Who has the right to tag? Which tags are visible? How tagging activity is supported? Are initial tags bootstrapped? [12, 18, 21].
- *Service types.* Different functionalities and data provided by services may be differently described by taggers.
- *Available information.* What does a user know about a service to tag? For instance, users tend not to tag Web services if they do not have any comprehension of them, for instance they have not tried them [3].

The two last factors were constrained by the Jena Geography Dataset [10] provided by the contest organizers. The dataset provides a collection of data-centric services from geography and geocoding domains. The information available about services includes WSDL definitions and initial categories/tags assigned by authors of the test collection (see Fig. 11.2). The authors had also saved the taggers' cognition effort by documenting all missing but relevant information in original WSDL definitions. To ease the process of service understanding we used: (1) names and natural language documentation of service, an operation and its parameters extracted from WSDL, (2) other users' understanding documented in form of tags (see tagging system architecture). The remaining factors have been controlled in the following way.

Tagging context. We have simulated the situation in which users take part in an early phase of software development with services [26]. Each incoming user was given a random use case scenario, describing a particular *applications goal* (why to search and to tag) and *search indications* (what to search for). We assumed that people would tag only services relevant to their specifications and thus we prepared ten different use cases to capture functionalities of all services in the test collection. We have performed tag collection in an open (non-laboratory) environment. We motivated people to tag by providing a form of a *social bookmarking* portal[2] that supports them in browsing and tagging. We encouraged users to focus on specific aspects by highlighting sections from documentation about input, output and behavior and prompting for tags those aspects explicitly in separate fields. The portal was opened for 12 days between September 16 and 27, 2009.

Tagging system architecture. The portal was sceded with automatically generated tags to avoid the *cold-start problem* [16]. *System annotations* were bootstrapped automatically from the service offers included in the JGD dataset. Furthermore, the interaction between taggers was based on tag sharing in two forms. By tag clouds a tagger could see the vocabulary that others used to tag services she or he classified as relevant, irrelevant or left to be yet classified. With tag suggestions a tagger could see the top five tags for a given service (provided by at least two actors, including also the system), i.e., *recommended tags*, and also her/his her *own most popular tags*. By the latter we tried to help a user to utilize the same, consistent vocabulary. Tags bootstrapping and recommendation have been shown in Fig. 11.2.

---

[2]http://mars.ing.unimo.it/wscolab/new.php

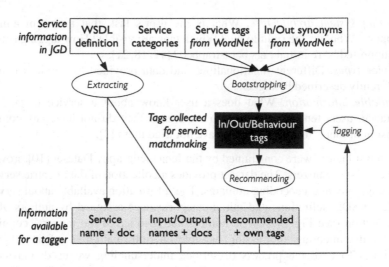

Fig. 11.2 Information flow in tag collection process

Participants. Our user base (27 users) consisted of two groups. A group of our 17 colleagues, with either industrial or academic experience in Web services, SOA or at least some experience in software engineering; and a group of 10 users from the open community, invited through several public forums and Usenet groups concerned with related topics.

11.3.3 Configuration of Query Collection Process

User comprehension in formulating queries, for a specific matchmaker, may cause a bias in performance towards this specific matchmaker. To avoid the bias, queries for the SWS-based solutions have to be formulated by experts in a given query language, while for the collaborative tagging solutions – by a "typical" software developer. Still, the bias towards a particular query formulating strategy may appear, because the query language for structured collaborative tagging is little constrained, and hence, the same service request can be formulated differently depending on a searcher. We addressed this problem on two levels. First, to obtain desirably diverse collection of strategies, we have asked as many users as possible to formulate queries for a given service request. Hence, the performance of our matchmaker could have been averaged over all query formulations. Second, to have control over the vocabulary used, we provided *query formulation assistance*. We have extended our annotation portal with a functionality of presenting service requests and collecting system queries from users. A user could not see any services in the registry nor results of her queries. Only the vocabulary, used during tagging phase to describe services, was shared. It was presented as: (1) query suggestions (through query autocompletion, showing maximally the top 15 commonly used tags for a given service part), and (2) three tag clouds, one for each service part of the annotation.

To assure that searchers were persons that had not tagged service offers previously, the process of query formulation was done in a controlled environment.

11.4   Lessons Learned

11.4.1   Evaluation Results

11.4.1.1   Statistics of Tags and Query Collection Processes

Our tags corpus contains 4,007 annotations for 50 services from the smallest subset of the Jena Geography Dataset (JGD50). Community annotations are 68% (2,716) of all annotations. System annotations (boostrapped automatically, see tagging system architecture in Sect. 11.3.2) are 32% (1,291) of all annotations. Our colleagues (17) have tagged all 50 services, providing 94% (2,541) of community annotations, while the remaining 10 users came from the open community and have tagged only 10 services, providing only 6% (175) of community annotations. The new tags were added by taggers continuously during the collection process (Fig. 11.3a). Taggers were selective which service to tag and to what degree (Fig. 11.3b).

Our corpus contains 45 query formulations for 9 services requests from the JGD50 test collection. Query formulations were provided by five volunteers with background in software engineering or programming. Fortunately, with respect to service requests encodings our corpus has no bias towards a particular query formulation strategy: query formulations differed much in their verbosity and vocabulary. The length of a formulation (averaged over service requests) ranges from 4.2 to 11.2 words depending on the user. Formulations for a single service request shared 50–100% words. System tags, were found somewhat useful by users during the query formulation, but there was no strong bias towards reusing them in the queries. Majority of words used in queries were non-system tags (78%, 74%, 66% for a behaviour, input, output service part, respectively).

11.4.1.2   Contest Evaluation Results

We report effectiveness of Web service retrieval measured as the *normalized Discounted Cumulative Gain* (nDCG) for a result rank i ($nDCG_i$) [8] with respect to the graded relevance judgments [11]. Figure 11.4 shows the nDCG curves for the participating matchmakers. WSColab has a relative performance of 65–80% over most of the ranks (except for the first two ranks) while the remaining systems have

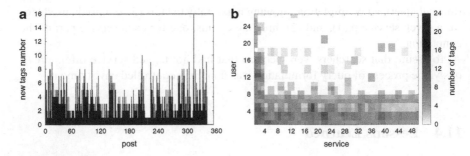

Fig. 11.3 Analysis of service annotation process and its outcome: (**a**) posts differs in the number of new tags added, (**b**) user contributions in tagging the same services (*darker* area represents more tags provided by a given user for a given service)

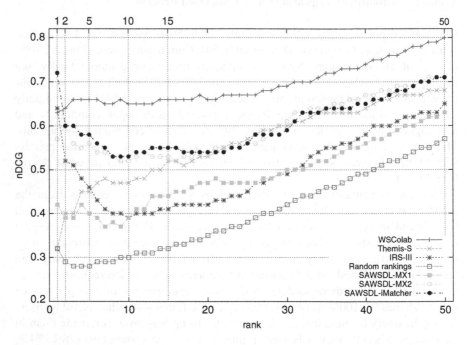

Fig. 11.4 The normalized Discounted Cumulative Gain (nDCG) curves of six different match-makers for graded relevance judgments with all relevance criteria equally important

a relative performance less than 55–70%. Here, the intuition is that a user needs to spend less effort to find relevant services with WSColab than with other approaches. Figure 11.6 shows the changing effectiveness of retrieval for different searchers formulating queries. Labels U131, U142, ... are used to denote IDs of subsequent searchers. Labels Q5914, Q5835, ... are used to denote IDs of service requests from the JGD test collection. Figure 11.5 reports the effectiveness for different class of approaches: Semantic Web Services (excluding adaptive approaches),

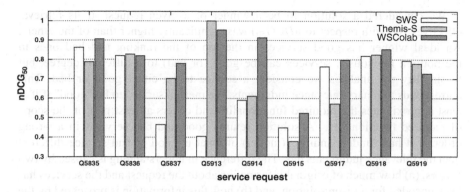

Fig. 11.5 Retrieval effectiveness of three different class of approaches for different service requests. Effectiveness of SWS has been averaged over only non-adaptive matchmakers: SAWSDL-MX1 and IRS-III. Measured with respect to graded relevance judgments with equal dimension settings

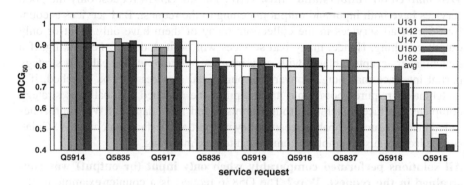

Fig. 11.6 Retrieval effectiveness of five searchers for nine different service requests. Effectiveness averaged over four settings for graded relevance judgments

based on monolithic/flat service descriptions (Themis-S), and collaborative tagging (WSColab) across different requests.

11.4.2   When and Why the Solution Fails and Succeeds?

The retrieval effectiveness of WSColab, on average, is the closest to the effectiveness of an ideal matchmaker (Fig. 11.4) but it varies across particular service requests (Fig. 11.5). For instance, for the Q5914 request the non-adaptive SWS approaches and Themis-S performed significantly worse than WSColab. In this subsection we asked what characteristics WSColab shares with losers and what – with winners, in particular queries.

We considered a solution to be a winner of a given request, if its retrieval effectiveness (with respect to $nDCG_{50}$) was significantly higher than of the others. An ideal winner has good services in the top of the ranking and bad ones in the bottom. Obviously, services can be good (or bad) to a different degree, but to simplify the analysis we consider a service to be either good or bad. This corresponds to binary relevance judgments. We mean a service to be "good" if it at least approximates the required functionality and covers at least part of the scope of required functionality.[3] A solution returns good and bad services in a wrong order, if it has "understanding" (model) of what is good or bad service different than the relevance judgments has. The difference in understanding is caused by two factors: (a) how much of original information about the request and the services has been encoded for a given solution, and (b) how this information is processed by the solution matchmaker. We analyzed both elements for the four requests that differ in losers and winners.

Services with only input or only output matching a request can be bad. Only WSColab could "understand" this. Why? For the Q5914 request only the good services have both input and output matching to the request. Bad services account for 96% of all services in the collection; many of them have only input or only output matching. Hence, many bad services will be included in the ranking, if a matchmaker accepts a match with only input or only output. We call this strategy partial interface matching. Conversely, only good services will be matched, if a matchmaker requires both input and output to be matched. We call this strategy complete interface matching. Both Themis-S and non-adaptive SWS approaches failed in this request probably because they use partial interface matching. WSColab succeeded, because it employs complete interface matching.

All solutions performed comparably when only input (or output) was constrained in the request. Why? The Q5836 request is a counter-example to the previous one. The expected functionality is very generic: it constrains mainly the input, and leaves a wide range of possible values for the expected output. Thereby, the request captures 76% of the services in the collection. Partial interface matching works in this case well, because there is little probability (24%) that a service, that has a similar input, is bad. Hence, Themis-S and non-adaptive SWS approaches performed pretty well (about 80% of the ideal matchmaker performance). Complete interface matching cannot match any service if only input (or only output) is constrained by the request. Therefore, in WSColab, complete interface matching rejected many good candidates.

Even a service having input like the required output can be (approximately) good. Only non-adaptive SWS approaches could not "understand" this. Why? For the Q5837 request some good services only approximates the required functionality. For instance, about 20% of good services do not provide a distance between

---

[3]It does not need to have interface compatible to the requested one. This corresponds to the binary relevance setting number seven in the contest [19].

two places, but return a list of locations within the specified range. Those services have a required output parameter (distance) as part of the input and one of required input parameter (location) as the output. Hence, those good services will be included in the results, if a matchmaker ignores the difference between input and output. We call this input/output indifferent strategy. Conversely, the same services will be excluded, if a matchmaker differentiates between input and output. We call this input/output aware strategy. The poor performance of SWS approaches can be explained by the use of input/output aware strategy. On the other hand, Themis-S operates on flat documents, i.e., is not aware of interface structure. Similarly, behavior matching heuristics in WSColab does not differentiate between input and output information.

A service having input like the required output can be bad. Only monolithic approaches (Themis-S) could not "understand" this. Why? The Q5918 request is a counter-example to the previous one. The bad services account for 66% of all services in the collection; many of them have output the same as the requested input, e.g., one of them provides a city for a given zip code, not the opposite. Hence, input/output indifference strategy will include many bad services in the results. Themis-S performed worse than other solutions because it implements only this strategy.

Overall, there is no winning strategy for all requests. Rather, the choice of a strategy depends on how strict and specific a searcher's expectation (a request) is, i.e., whether it also accepts approximate services or whether she has no constrains on expected service input (or output). A combination of partial interface matching and input/output indifference can provide more complete results for such relaxed constrains. We call this combined strategy relaxed matching, in opposition to strict matching: complete interface matching with input/output awareness. One must, however, accept, that completeness of relaxed matching is done for the price of precision: also more bad services can be included in the results.

Furthermore, there may be no winning strategy for a given request as summarized in Table 11.1. It shows that winning strategy might be very specific for a given collection of service/request pairs. For instance, having an input similar to the output of required functionality (or vice versa) is not a definite feature of being a good or bad service. Therefore, the winning strategy predicted only on such a test collection-specific feature will work for this collection, but *may* not work for another.[4] For a human searcher, this simply means that she must be more flexible and assess the relevance of returned results herself, and, if she is not satisfied, submit the same query with an alternative matching strategy.

Despite the lack of one universal strategy, WSColab performed relatively stable across different requests. Why? This can be explained by two facts. First, it combines strict matching with relaxed matching. The strict strategy is

---

[4]This motivated us to exclude adaptive approaches, which learn from relation between such feature and relevance judgments, from this analysis.

Table 11.1 Summary of identified winning strategies

Strategy		Winning strategy when	Used by
Interface matching	Partial	(a) A request constrains only input (or output), and (b) bad services do not have input similar (or output, respectively) to the request.	Themis-S, IRS-III, SAWSDL-MX1, WSColab
	Complete	Good services have both input and output similar, while bad ones – only one of them	WSColab
Input/output	Awareness	Many bad services have some input parameters like some requires output parameters	IRS-III, SAWSDL-MX1, WSColab
	Indifference	Many good services have some input parameters like some required output parameters	Themis-S, WSColab

implemented by the interface matching heuristics. The relaxed strategy – by behavior matching heuristics, because, behavior tags and behavior query keywords were used to describe interface. These heuristics were combined together using a logical alternative, i.e., a service is matched if it satisfies at least one of them. WSColab ranks results of the less precise heuristics lower and thus limits impact of errors on the *nDCG*.

Surprisingly, behavior tags played a different role in matchmaking than we expected. We introduced behavior tags to name service behavior and thus enable matching services acting similar, but having incompatible interfaces. However, users used behavior field to describe service input or output. Only a small fraction of behavior tags describe the behavior as expected,[5] e.g., converter, get_location_info, geocode, geocoding, find, location_finder, compute_distance, find_zip_code. Since these tags were yet less common in query formulations, many good services were ranked low.

11.4.3 How Reliable Is Structured Collaborative Tagging?

In traditional matchmakers the retrieval effectiveness is the function of test collection (services and requests) and a matchmaker algorithm. Adding human factor to the system makes it more realistic but also makes the function more complex, especially because both taggers and searchers in the system have much autonomy. In this subsection we consider retrieval errors caused by autonomy.

We analyzed in details results for two requests that had the highest standard deviation over all users in the $nDCG_{50}$: Q5914 (19%) and Q5837 (15%), both shown

---

[5]However, this phenomenon might be characteristic for data-centric services, for which behavior is often identified with the data it consumes and returns.

in Fig. 11.6. We also analyzed in detail the results of query Q5915; most difficult for all matchmakers (see Fig. 11.5).

We found that retrieval errors can be attributed to causes typical for tagging systems [9, 17]: *spam tags*, when a service has been tagged by irrelevant tags (either on purpose or accidentally by a "bad tagger"), and a *vocabulary gap* between the service encoding and the query formulation. Additionally, we have identified problems characteristic for structured tagging [1]: a *structure gap*, when a tagger describes a certain service aspect in a different part of a structure than the searcher does, and an *invalid usage of structure*, when a tagger/searcher use input to describe output or behavior, or output to describe input or behavior. The difference between the last two issues is that the structure gap is caused by vagueness of structure semantics: tags can be assigned to more than one part of a structure. Each tagger has his/her own point of view and it is his/her decision where to assign a tag. Finally, we found that some errors can be attributed to matching only *complementary tags*, which capture detailed information about a service.

Let us now see what retrieval errors those issues caused. In the case of considered data-centric services the community often identifies the behavior of a service with the data it returns. For instance, the searcher U142 could not find service described with a behavior tag `distance_in_miles` because he required this tag to be in the output of a service (structure gap). The same searcher also achieved the worst effectiveness on average ($nDCG_{50}$) for all queries, because he was constantly putting keywords related to the output as the input query keywords (invalid use of a structure), e.g., his formulation for the query Q5837 contained: `input:city_name1 input:distance behavior:distance`. The matchmaker was not able to compute the interface compatibility (both input and output are required); thus, it computed relevance of a service candidate based only on the behavior compatibility. The effectiveness of the U142 was also affected by the vocabulary gap. He looked for a service with the `sea_level_high` behavior, while the `altitude` and the `height`, as semantically related, were very common tags among service encodings. Complementary tags were not a problem themselves: if there was no vocabulary nor structure gap, complementary tags could help a ranking function to discriminate between services that act very similarly. However, in many cases, WSColab ranked bad service highly, because a complementary tags (e.g., `worldwide`) was the only one shared with the query.

We also asked, how significant was the autonomy impact on the effectiveness of retrieval. The impact of vocabulary and structure gap depends on how much similar taggers and searchers describe the same types of services [22]. On average the WSColab solution handled surprisingly well with provided service requests. Figure 11.6 shows that the standard deviation of the retrieval effectiveness among searchers for the same service request was on average only at 4%. Quantifying impact of spam is more difficult. However, the case of the Q5915 shows it can be a serious problem for our matchmaking heuristics. The request asked for services returning map and many bad services have been matched and ranked highly because their behavior or output have been tagged been with the wrong map tag. Consequently, effectiveness of all users was affected significantly by the spam.

11.4.4 Can We Trust Evaluation Results?

Threats from partial control of collection process. In real collaborative tagging systems distribution of tags over objects converge to a stable point over time. Thereby, the community achieves consensus on how objects should be described [18]. If such consensus has not been achieved yet, then the description can still change and so the reported retrieval effectiveness is not stable over time. Therefore, we asked whether the community in our simulated scenario achieved such consensus. Figure 11.3a shows it was not the case: new tags were continuously posted by users during the whole collection period. This, as we believe, was for the two reasons. First, the duration of tags collection process was too short; we stopped it after an arbitrary period of time. Second, taggers could not validate discriminatory power of assigned tags, because the feedback cycle (see Sect. 11.3.2) was incomplete. Particularly, the users could not search using provided tags, they could only iterate through services listed in the portal. In real collaborative tagging systems users often minimize the number of tags used to describe an object and they add new tags incrementally – only when existing tags do not allow to differentiate the object from similar ones [18]. Conversely, Fig. 11.3a shows that taggers in the WSColab have been providing large quantities of tags at once.

Threats from matchmaker non-determinism. Both the WSColab and the IRS-III are binary matchmakers, originally returning only a subset of matching services. To be able to compare them with other matchmakers, they were forced to return matching services followed by a randomly ordered "tail" of non-matching services (see Sect. 11.3.1). The random tail introduced non-determinism to their behavior, i.e., the order of services in the tail was determined by the factor external to a matchmaking algorithm. For instance, for WSColab this order was determined by the sequence in which services were indexed. This limited repetitiveness of the evaluation. We asked to what degree this non-determinism affected the reported results of retrieval effectiveness for the WSColab matchmaker. For each configuration (a service request and its formulation) we generated 50 random permutations of services to index. For each configuration we executed the matchmaker and calculated the $nDCG_{50}$. The retrieval effectiveness differed between two different permutations for up to 24%. However, on average (over all configurations) the span of changes to retrieval effectiveness was of 4% with standard deviation of 5%.

11.5 Summary

In this chapter we investigated whether collaborative structured tagging can be a reliable and competitive method to describe Web services (as compared to SWS-based approaches). Understanding pros and cons of this approach may be of great value to find a low cost method to provide metadata in classic Web service repositories. This can be also important for the SWS research, searching for incentives to attract the community to annotate services in their approach [25]. Analysis of both the contest results and the tagging process has shown that increased autonomy in tagging, and formulating queries, was often the major reason of decreased performance for some users, or for all users for a specific request. Retrieval errors were often caused by: spam, vocabulary and structure gaps. Those issues are typical in open systems and thus well-known instruments exist to resolve them. One must, however, accept that some services will never be described by the community due to the lack of interest in their specific functionalities. In this sense, this makes collaborative tagging different from other annotation approaches that rely on voluntary participation of online users. Unlike tagging, they provide appropriate instruments to control labor distribution [24,28] and thus grant that objects that need to be annotated will be annotated.

Despite those challenges matchmaking based on structured tagging provided very encouraging results. First, retrieval effectiveness of matchmaking was competitive to other approaches, including adaptive ones (like SAWSDL-MX2) that were tuned toward this specific test collection with machine learning. Second, across different scenarios, retrieval performance based on tagged data was more stable than that of other non-adaptive approaches. This, was the effect of combining two strategies: strict matching and relaxed matching. The first differentiates between input and output and accepts only complete interface matching. However, it does not handle well less constrained requests and search for approximate services. Relaxed matching address those limitations, but is also more sensitive to errors. WSColab ranks results of relaxed matching strategies lower. Overall, returned results are more complete, while possibly bad services have smaller impact on effectiveness.

Nevertheless, continued research on tagging-based methods needs a more credible evaluation methodology. For instance, we observed that tagging behavior was not completely realistic and thus its output could not be. This was because a tagger could not verify the "search power" of her and other taggers' tags. To address this issue we plan to allow taggers to be also searchers during the tag collection process. Enabling a user to play a role of both a searcher and a tagger can be also a good instrument to eliminate retrieval problems caused by autonomy. Here, a user will be able to immediately notice the retrieval problems, and fix them with more and better tags. Finally, it will give users an instrument to control the sufficient level of details by which a service has been described.

There is still much to be concluded from the experimental results. We would like to understand whether our approach implements the graded functional relevance criterion correctly. For instance, whether a searcher can find more exact services ranked higher than services that only approximate the required functionality.

Acknowledgements We would like to thank to: Ulrich Küster (for the organization of the Cross-Evaluation track and discussion), Patrick Kapahnke and Matthias Klusch (for their general support and organization of the S3 contest), and to Elton Domnori and anonymous reviewers for valuable comments. Finally, we would like to thank voluntary taggers and searchers for their time.

References

1. J. Bar-Ilan, S. Shoham, A. Idan, Y. Miller, A. Shachak, Structured versus unstructured tagging: a case study. Online Inf. Rev. **32**(5), 635–647 (2008)
2. E. Bouillet, M. Feblowitz, H. Feng, Z. Liu, A. Ranganathan, A. Riabov, A folksonomy-based model of web services for discovery and automatic composition, in *IEE SCC*, Honolulu, 2008, pp. 389–396
3. R. Cuel, O. Morozova, M. Rohde, E. Simperl, K. Siorpaes, O. Tokarchuk, T. Wiedenhöfer, F. Yetim, M. Zamarian, Motivation mechanisms for participation in human-driven semantic content creation. Int. J. Knowl. Eng. Data Min. **1**(4) 331–349 (2011)
4. A. Fernández, C. Hayes, N. Loutas, V. Peristeras, A. Polleres, K.A. Tarabanis, Closing the service discovery gap by collaborative tagging and clustering techniques, in *SMRR*, Karlsruhe, 2008
5. M. Gawinecki, G. Cabri, M. Paprzycki, M. Ganzha, Structured collaborative tagging: is it practical for web service discovery? in *WEBIST*, Valencia, 2010
6. S.A. Golder, B.A. Huberman, Usage patterns of collaborative tagging systems. J. Inf. Sci. **32**(2), 198–208 (2006)
7. A. Heß, N. Kushmerick, Learning to attach semantic metadata to web services, in *ISWC*, Sanibel, 2003, pp. 258–273
8. K. Järvelin, J. Kekäläinen, Cumulated gain-based evaluation of IR techniques. ACM Trans. Inf. Syst. **20**(4), 422–446 (2002)
9. G. Koutrika, E. Frans, Z. Gyongyi, P. Heymann, H. Garcia-Molina, Combating spam in tagging systems: an evaluation. ACM Trans. Web (TWEB) **2**(4), 1–34 (2007)
10. U. Küster, Jena Geography Dataset (2009), http://fusion.cs.uni-jena.de/professur/jgd, last accessed May 2012
11. U. Küster, B. König-Ries, Relevance judgments for web services retrieval – a methodology and test collection for SWS discovery evaluation, in *ECOWS*, Eindhoven, 2009
12. C. Marlow, M. Naaman, D. Boyd, M. Davis, HT06, tagging paper, taxonomy, Flickr, academic article, to read, in *HYPERTEXT*, Odense, Denmark, 2006, pp. 31–40
13. H. Meyer, M. Weske, Light-weight semantic service annotations through tagging, in *ICSOC*. LNCS, vol. 4294, Chicago, 2006, pp. 465–470
14. H. Mili, F. Mili, A. Mili, Reusing software: issues and research directions. IEEE Trans. Softw. Eng. **21**(6), 528–562 (1995)
15. A. Mili, R. Mili, R.T. Mittermeir, A survey of software reuse libraries. Ann. Softw. Eng. **5**, 349–414 (1998)
16. M. Montaner, B. López, J. De La Rosa, A taxonomy of recommender agents on the internet. Artif. Intell. Rev. **19**(4), 285–330 (2003)
17. I. Peters, K. Weller, Tag gardening for folksonomy enrichment and maintenance. *Webology* **5**(3), 1–18 (2008)
18. V. Robu, H. Halpin, H. Shepherd, Emergence of consensus and shared vocabularies in collaborative tagging systems. ACM Trans. Web **3**(4), 1–34 (2009)
19. Semantic Service Selection Contest (2009), http://www-ags.dfki.uni-sb.de/~klusch/s3/index.html, last accessed May 2012
20. M. Sabou, C. Wroe, C.A. Goble, G. Mishne, Learning domain ontologies for web service descriptions: an experiment in bioinformatics, in *WWW*, Chiba, Japan, 2005, pp. 190–198
21. S. Sen, S.K. Lam, Al.M. Rashid, D. Cosley, D. Frankowski, J. Osterhouse, F.M. Harper, J. Riedl, Tagging, communities, vocabulary, evolution, in *CSCW*, Banff, 2006, pp. 181–190
22. C. Shirky, Ontology is overrated: categories, links, and tags (2005), http://www.shirky.com/writings/ontology_overrated.html, last accessed May 2012
23. I. Silva-Lepe, R. Subramanian, I. Rouvellou, T. Mikalsen, J. Diament, A. Iyengar, SOAlive service catalog: a simplified approach to describing, discovering and composing situational enterprise services, in *ICSOC*, Sydney, 2008

24. K. Siorpaes, M. Hepp, Games with a purpose for the semantic web. IEEE Intell. Syst. **23**, 50–60 (2008)
25. K. Siorpaes, E. Simperl, Human intelligence in the process of semantic content creation. World Wide Web **13**(1–2), 33–59 (2010)
26. I. Sommerville, *Software Engineering*. International Computer Science Series, 8th edn. (Addison–Wesley, Harlow, 2007)
27. T.A. Vanderlei, F.A. Durão, A.C. Martins, V.C. Garcia, E.S. Almeida, S.R. de L. Meira, A cooperative classification mechanism for search and retrieval software components, in *ACM SAC*, Seoul, 2007, pp. 866–871
28. L. von Ahn, L. Dabbish, Designing games with a purpose. Commun. ACM **51**, 58–67 (2008)
29. J. Zobel, A. Moffat, Inverted files for text search engines. ACM Comput. Surv. **38**(2), 6 (2006)

Chapter 12
Ontology Based Discovery of Semantic Web Services with IRS-III

Liliana Cabral and John Domingue

Abstract We present the IRS-III approach to Semantic Web Service (SWS) discovery and the evaluation results obtained in the cross-evaluation track of the S3 contest 2009. IRS-III is a SWS broker suited for goal-based invocation of services semantically described using the WSMO conceptual model. The discovery component of the IRS-III broker can match ontological descriptions of Goals, i.e. service requests, against ontological descriptions of service capabilities. The matchmaking algorithm of IRS-III uses the underlying OCML interpreter for reasoning over input and output types and also exploits the meta-level definitions of the service models. As shown in our evaluation results, IRS-III tends to favor precision over recall as expected of most logic-based systems. The results are encouraging considering that IRS-III has been designed within the context of business applications.

12.1 Introduction

The Semantic Web Service (SWS) discovery activity consists of finding Web Services based on their semantic descriptions. Tools for SWS discovery or matchmaking can be evaluated on retrieval performance, where for a given goal, i.e. a semantic description of a service request, and a given set of service descriptions, i.e. semantic descriptions of service offers, the matchmaking tool returns a list of ranked services, expressing the match degree between the goal and each service, and the evaluation platform measures the rate of matching correctness based on a number of metrics.

In this chapter we present the IRS-III [1] approach to Semantic Web Service discovery and the evaluation results obtained in the cross-evaluation track (JGDEval)

L. Cabral (✉) · J. Domingue
KMi, The Open University, Milton Keynes, UK
e-mail: l.s.cabral@open.ac.uk; j.b.domingue@open.ac.uk

M.B. Blake et al. (eds.), *Semantic Web Services*, DOI 10.1007/978-3-642-28735-0_12,   191
© Springer-Verlag Berlin Heidelberg 2012

of the S3 contest 2009.[1] The discovery component of the IRS-III broker can match ontological descriptions of Goals, i.e. service requests, against ontological descriptions of service capabilities. The matchmaking algorithm of IRS-III uses the underlying OCML interpreter for reasoning over input and output types and also exploits the meta-level definitions of the service models. As shown in our evaluation results, IRS-III tends to favor precision over recall as expected of most logic-based systems. However, it is possible to improve recall by exploiting more relaxed matching criteria and syntactic similarity checking.

In Sect. 12.2 we present a brief overview of the IRS-III approach, including the SWS knowledge components and the underlying reasoning and execution environment. In Sect. 12.3 we describe the SWS descriptions and the matchmaking algorithm used for our SWSdiscovery solution. In Sect. 12.4 we provide an analysis of our evaluation results, including our conclusions and future work.

12.2 Approach: The IRS-III SWS Modeling and Execution Environment

IRS-III[2] [1] is a SWS broker suited for goal-based invocation of services semantically described using the WSMO[3] [2] conceptual model. IRS-III provides an ontology-based reasoning system and execution environment based on OCML and LISP (explained below). IRS-III implements the WSMO conceptual model using the following top-level knowledge-based models:

- **Domain ontologies** – Provide the foundation for semantically describing domain data in order to achieve semantic interoperability. Thus, the concepts involved in application scenarios that are used to describe service requests and capabilities are provided in domain ontologies.
- **Goal** – Describes the task that a service requester expects a web service to fulfill. The request for a service is expressed from a consumer viewpoint and represented as a goal.
- **Web service** – Describes the capability of an existing deployed Web Service. The capability includes the types of inputs and outputs, and logical expressions for provider restrictions. The description also outlines how Web Services communicate (choreography) and how they are composed (orchestration).
- **Mediator** – Describes connections between the components above and represent the type of conceptual mismatches that can occur. Mediator descriptions can be used to declare a mediation service or mapping rules that will be used to provide alignment between goals, web services and domain ontologies.

---

[1]http://www-ags.dfki.uni-sb.de/~klusch/s3/html/2009.html

[2]http://kmi.open.ac.uk/technologies/irs/

[3]http://www.wsmo.org/TR/d2/v1.3/

OCML (Operational Conceptual Modelling Language) [5] is a language and operational environment for ontology and knowledge modeling. That is, the language is integrated with an interpreter and a proof system (reasoner engine) on top of a Lisp-based environment. OCML combines a frame system with an integrated forward and backward chaining rule system. OCML constituent constructs include classes, instances, relations, functions, procedures and rules, following on the Ontolingua formalism [4]. In OCML, procedures and functions can be attached to Lisp code. Classes are unary relations and class attributes are binary relations. The operational semantics of the forward chaining system are equivalent to OPS5 [3] and the backward chaining rule system has equivalent operational semantics to Prolog.

OCML has been used in a wide variety of projects covering knowledge management and it is also the core component of IRS-III. All the SWS components are defined in OCML and use the OCML reasoner. Below we present the main elements of a Knowledge Model or ontology in OCML, reproduced from [5] (see examples in the next section):

- **Classes** – Classes are defined by means of a Lisp macro, *def-class*, which takes as arguments the name of the class, a list (possibly empty) of superclasses, optional documentation, and a list of slot (attribute) specifications. The semantics of class is the same as unary relations. The semantics of slots are the same as binary relations with respect to the class.
- **Class instances** – Class instances are simply members of a class. An instance is defined by means of *def-instance*, which takes as arguments the name of the instance, the parent of the instance (i.e. the most specific class the instance belongs to), optional documentation and a number of slot-value pairs.
- **Relations** – Relations allow the OCML user to define labeled n-ary relationships between OCML entities. Relations are defined by means of a Lisp macro, *def-relation*, which takes as arguments the name of a relation, its argument schema (a list of variables), optional documentation and a number of relation options. Relation options provide formal specifications with different semantics, which are used to find out whether or not a relation holds for some arguments. Relations also have an operational role in OCML. Some of the available relation options are *:iff-def, :sufficient, :constraint, :prove-by* and *:lisp-fun*.
- **Rules** – These are backward rules and forward rules, defined by means of *def-rule*. Backward rules play a specification role and provide a dynamic mechanism to associate values between relations.They have the same semantics as relations with options :iff-def. When carrying out a proof by means of a backward rule, the OCML interpreter will try to prove whether some tuple is an instance of the relevant relation by firing the clauses in the order in which these are listed in the rule definition. As in Prolog, depth-first search with chronological backtracking is used to control the proof process. Forward rules provide a mechanism for changing the state of the running system (e.g. asserting or deleting facts); or causing external actions (e.g. printing information).
- **Functions** – Functions are defined by means of a Lisp macro, *def-function*. This takes as argument the name of a function, its argument list, an optional

variable indicating the output argument, optional documentation and zero or
more function specification options. The :body option for instance allows the
attachment of a functional term which is evaluated in OCML's environment.

* **Procedures** – Procedures define actions or sequences of actions which cannot be
  characterized as functions between input and output arguments.
* **Logical expressions** – The simplest kind of logical expression is a relation
  expression, which has the form *(rel fun-term*)*, where *rel* is the name of a relation
  and *fun-term* is a functional term. More complex expressions can be constructed
  by using the logical operators (*and*, *or*, *not*) and quantifiers operators (*forall* and
  exists).

12.3   Solution: IRS-III SWS Matchmaking

For our solution, basically, we created semantic descriptions for the services in the
test suite according to the IRS-III framework and provided a tailored matchmaking
algorithm for IRS-III discovery, as described in the next sections.

12.3.1   Semantic Descriptions

We created the semantic descriptions for the services in the JGD50[4] collection,
as required for participation in the cross-evaluation track (JGDEval) of the S3
contest. First, we had the natural language descriptions of the services translated
to our service models in a semi-automated way by the organizers, according to our
provided templates in OCML, as shown in the sample in Listing 12.1. Similarly, we
also had the service requests translated to our Goal models (see e.g. Listing 12.2).
We used the WordNet definitions available in the database to create the types
(concepts) for inputs and outputs as part of the semantic descriptions. Second, we
translated the *Geography Domain Ontology* from OWL to OCML, which was used
as the main domain ontology. We added the types for inputs and outputs to this
ontology, either by creating new classes, subclasses or mappings (via rules), as can
be seen partially in Listing 12.3. Third, we created http URLs for each request in the
test suite that mapped to our corresponding Goal descriptions. The URLs were used
to invoke the matchmaking component for a specific Goal over the defined service
descriptions.

```
(in-package ''OCML'')
(in-ontology geography-dataset-ou)
(DEF-CLASS 5717_GeoNames_PostalCodeSearch (WEB-SERVICE) ?WEB-SERVICE

''Source: http://www.geonames.org/export/web-services.html#postalCodeSearch
```

[4]http://fusion.cs.uni-jena.de/professur/jgd

```
Comment:Returns a list of postal codes and places for the placename/postalcode
query as xml document. For the US the first returned zip code is determined
using zip code area shapes, the following zip codes are based on the centroid.
For all other supported countries all returned postal codes are based on
centroids.''
((HAS-INPUT-ROLE
      :VALUE has-postal_code
      :VALUE has-country
      :VALUE has-placename-in
      :VALUE has-style
      :VALUE has-mayRows )
  (HAS-OUTPUT-ROLE
      :VALUE has-placename-out
      :VALUE has-postalcode
      :VALUE has-countryCode
      :VALUE has-lat
      :VALUE has-lng )
  (has-postal_code :TYPE postal_code)
  (has-country :TYPE country)
  (has-placename-in :TYPE name)
  (has-style :TYPE comprehensiveness)
  (has-mayRows :TYPE amount)
  (has-placename-out :TYPE geographic_area)
  (has-postalcode :TYPE postal_code)
  (has-countryCode :TYPE country)
  (has-lat :TYPE latitude)
  (has-lng :TYPE longitude)
  (HAS-CAPABILITY :VALUE 5717_GeoNames_PostalCodeSearch-CAPABILITY)
  (HAS-INTERFACE :VALUE 5717_GeoNames_PostalCodeSearch-INTERFACE)
  (HAS-NON-FUNCTIONAL-PROPERTIES :VALUE 5717_GeoNames_PostalCodeSearch-NFP)
))
```

Listing 12.1 Sample service description in IRS-III

In Listing 12.1 we show the semantic description for service *5717_GeoNames_Postal CodeSearch*, taken from the testsuite. The text between double quotes, describing the service, was provided by the database and translated as a comment in the class definition. The slots *HAS-INPUT-ROLE* and *HAS-OUTPUT-ROLE* are meta definitions for inputs and outputs respectively. *:VALUE* provides the name of the input/output and *:TYPE* provides the type accordingly. For example, this service has one input named *has-postal-code* of type *postal_code*. All the slots are attributes (relations) of the *web-service* class. The same syntax is used for Goal definitions, as can be seen in Listing 12.2.

```
(in-package ''OCML'')
(in-ontology geography-dataset-goals-ou)
(DEF-CLASS 5835_US_Geocoding_Request (GOAL) ?GOAL

''Source: Comment: The client is looking for a service to geocode US addresses
(e.g. lookup the geographic location of a postal addresses). The license status
of services should be ignored for the search.''

((HAS-INPUT-ROLE
      :VALUE has-US_postal_address)
  (HAS-OUTPUT-ROLE
      :VALUE has-geographic_location )
  (has-US_postal_address :TYPE address)
  (has-geographic_location :TYPE geographic_point)
  (HAS-CAPABILITY :VALUE 5835_US_Geocoding_Request-CAPABILITY)
  (HAS-INTERFACE :VALUE 5835_US_Geocoding_Request-INTERFACE)
  (HAS-NON-FUNCTIONAL-PROPERTIES :VALUE 5835_US_Geocoding_Request-NFP)
))
```

Listing 12.2 Sample goal description in IRS-III

In Listing 12.3 we partially show the domain ontology with some class definitions for the types from the services and goals descriptions. In addition, we show a couple of rules, which provide relation mappings to be applied during reasoning. For example, we define the class *geographic_point*, which is a subclass of *Geographic_Coordinate*, which in turn is a subclass of *Location*. In addition, the rule *locatedIn-belongsToTimeZone* maps the relation *belongsToTimeZone*(attribute in class *Location*) to relation *locatedIn*.

```
(def-class Location () (
(belongsToTimeZone :type Time_Zone)
(hasClimate :type ClimateData)
(hasAverageTemperature :type TemperatureMeasure)
(localTime :type datetime)
(daylightSavingTime :type boolean)
(hasArea :type AreaMeasure)
(adjacentTo :type Location) (hasAltitude :type LengthMeasure)
(hasPopulation :type Population) ) )

(def-class Geographic_Area (Location)
''An area that has an extent on the surface of the globe (or some other
planet).
It is defined by some shape and a set of coordinates. In the simplest case a
rectangle identified by two locations (northwest and southeast corner).''
((northwestCorner :type Location)
(southeastCorner :type Location) ) )

(def-class Geographic_Coordinate (Location )
''A geographic coordinate identifying a point in space according to some
reference system (e.g. wgs84). Note that the same coordinate specified with
respect to the same reference system may have different representations, i.e.
decimal or degree-based.'')

(def-class geographic_point (Geographic_Coordinate))

(def-class latitude (Coordinate))

(def-class longitude (Coordinate))

(def-class amount (UnitMeasure))

(def-class distance (LengthMeasure))

(def-class elevation (distance))

(def-class city (Geographic_Area))

(def-class Country (Geographic_Area))

(def-rule locatedIn-isMidPointOf
  ((locatedIn ?x ?y) if (isMidPointOf ?x ?y)))

(def-rule locatedIn-belongsToTimeZone
  ((locatedIn ?x ?y) if (belongsToTimeZone ?x ?y)))
```

Listing 12.3 Partial content of the domain ontology

12.3.2 Matchmaking Algorithm

We have implemented a matchmaking algorithm within IRS-III, which returns a list of matched services for a given query (service request), as required for evaluation in the SME2[5] environment. This algorithm was tailored for this evaluation, but can be also used internally by IRS-III as one of the steps for goal-based invocation.

As can be seen partially in Listing 12.4, the outermost part of the algorithm is implemented as an OCML relation. The relation *match-services* holds true for every *goal* and *web-service* in the (loaded) knowledge base that complies with the restrictions (defined by *:constraint* and *:sufficient*) given by the logical clauses. As explained in Sect. 12.2, relations are powerful constructs in OCML, allowing for example function execution within the clauses. The *match-services* relation has access to the input/output names (function named *all-class-slot-local-values*), and types (function named *input-roles-with-types*), within goals and web services descriptions.

With respect to names (in the meta definitions), the matching algorithm checks for equivalence between goal input/output names and service input/output names. At least one input and one output must match. Regarding types, the matching algorithm will match the goal input type against a service input type by verifying if it is equivalent to it via inheritance or any mappings (axiom or rule) available. The same is done between output types.

In summary, IRS-III enables three techniques: (a) separating input definitions from output definitions; (b) reasoning over type definitions (class inheritance) and ontology mappings (rules); (c) performing (lexical) similarity checking over input and output names.

```
(def-relation match-services (?goal ?ws)
''Matches services against a goal
according to input/output names and types''
 :constraint (and (subclass-of ?goal goal)(class ?goal))
 :sufficient
  (and
   (subclass-of ?ws web-service)(class ?ws)
   ;;input names
   (= ?inwsroles (all-class-slot-local-values ?ws has-input-role))
   (= ?ingoalroles (all-class-slot-local-values ?goal has-input-role))
   ;;output names
   (= ?outwsroles (all-class-slot-local-values ?ws has-output-role))
   (= ?outgoalroles (all-class-slot-local-values ?goal has-output-role))
   ;; input types
   (= ?instypes (map 'first
                (map 'second (input-roles-with-types ?ws ?inwsroles))))
   (= ?ingtypes (map 'first
                (map 'second (input-roles-with-types ?goal ?ingoalroles))))
   ;; output types
   (= ?outstypes (map 'first
                (map 'second (output-roles-with-types ?ws ?outwsroles))))
   (= ?outgtypes (map 'first
                (map 'second (output-roles-with-types ?goal ?outgoalroles))))
   ...
)
```

Listing 12.4 Partial definition of the match-services relation in IRS-III

───────────────

[5]http://www.semwebcentral.org/projects/sme2

In addition, the results are binary and there is no score associated with the matched services, thus the order of the relevant services can be random. In fact, the ranking of the results is a consequence of the order in which the algorithm first checks for name similarity and then performs type matching.

12.4 Lessons Learned

12.4.1 Evaluation Results

The overall results for the six participating tools can be found in the introductory chapter (Table 10.1) and in the JGDEval website.[6]

As mentioned in a note in the website, "IRS-III and WSColab were originally designed to return only matching services, sorted by decreasing relevance. They were forced to return full rankings of all services to allow for meaningful comparison of results. Thus, both matchmakers had to return (attach) services they deemed irrelevant in random order. IRS-III performs a rather strict high precision, low recall matchmaking. Therefore, it returned many services in random order. This explains the decline in performance after the top ranks".

In summary, IRS-III tends to favor precision over recall as expected of most logic-based systems. By the same token, the reasoning over the models on top of a LISP system tends to be time inefficient. It is worth noting that our implementation had no caching or optimization techniques applied to it. In addition, our matchmaking algorithm was strict in matching services that had at least one input and one output in common with ones in the request.

In the following we show the result for one random query and explain the typical behavior of IRS-III matchmaking. Table 12.1 shows the list of returned services for the given query (also in Listing 12.2). As pointed out before, IRS-III is very selective, and for this query in particular only returned (found relevant) 5 services out of 50 (the remaining 45 were randomly attached to the results list). The five returned services were judged relevant (true positive). Generalizing, IRS-III typically performed very high precision for all goals in this evaluation.

By observing the names and the types of inputs and outputs of the relevant returned services (taken from the respective semantic descriptions), as shown in Table 12.2, we point out that type relationship had a stronger influence in the matching results than name similarity. In fact, service 5857 was correctly found, even though the names of input and outputs in the service have no correlation with the ones in the goal. By contrast, the service shown in Listing 12.1 that was judged relevant, could not be retrieved by IRS-III (thus, not in Table 12.1). This is

---

[6]http://fusion.cs.uni-jena.de/professur/jgdeval/jgdeval-at-s3-contest-2009-results

Table 12.1 Results for one sample request (query)

Query Id
5835_US_Geocoding_Request
Services
5738_DOTSGEOCODER_GETGEOLOCATION_BY_SERVICEOBJECTS.NET.lisp
5768_GEOCODESERVICE_GEOCODE_ADDRESS_BY_GEOCODER.US.lisp
5815_YAHOO_MAPS_WEB_SERVICES_-_GEOCODING_API.lisp
5857_GOOGLE_GEOCODING_API.lisp
5903_WHERE2GETIT_GEOSPATIAL_API_GEOCODE.lisp

Table 12.2 Input and output definitions for sample results

Query Id	In names	In types	Out names	Out types
5835	Has-US-postal-address	Address	Has-geographic-location	Geographic_point
Service Id	In names	In types	Out names	Out types
5738	Has-US-address	Address	Has-location	Geographic_point
	Has-License-key	Licence		
5768	Has-US-address	Address	Has-geographic-point	Geographic_point
5815	Has-address-in	Address	Has-address-out	Address
			Has-geographic-location	Geographic_location
			Has-level	Preciseness
5857	Has-key	Licence	Has-address	Address
	Has-q	Address	Has-coordinates	Geographic_point
	Has-output	Data_format	Has-accuracy	Accuracy
	Has-ll	Geographic_point		
	Has-spn	Geographic_area		
	Has-gl	Country		
	Has-sensor	Electric_switch		
5903	Has-addresses-in	Address	Has-addresses-out	Address
			Has-locations	Geographic_point

because IRS-III could find no name or type correlation between this service and the goal above. For example, IRS-III could not find a relation between the input types *postal-code* and *country* of the service and the input type *address* of the goal. This mapping could have been manually provided in the domain ontology, but it was overlooked for this evaluation. In conclusion, IRS-III performance is dependent on the completeness of the mappings and relations available.

12.4.2   Advantages and Disadvantages

Among the advantages of the IRS-III approach is that semantics for the services are explicit and reusable. In addition, the matching takes advantage of both the logical reasoning over the types and the meta definitions in the service and goal descriptions (knowledge models), which allows for distinguishing between inputs and outputs.

On the other hand, IRS-III requires that the provided semantics are as accurate and complete as possible, since missing classes, subclass definitions or mappings will result in poor matching results. The models in IRS-III have also some requirements: input names have to be different from output names in the same service description (this is not required for types).

The high precision of the IRS-III results suggests that our matchmaking algorithm is suitable for use in business applications, in which matched services are later used for composition or invocation. As IRS-III considers semantic interoperability, mediators can easily be applied to bridge between services and goals using the mappings available.

12.4.3   Conclusions and Future Work

Since IRS-III is a SWS broker aiming at the automated execution of services in the context of business applications, we consider that high precision is more important than high recall during discovery. Thus, with respect to precision, the results of IRS-III were very encouraging. This would have been more noticeable if PR@n (for n equals to a rank of 10 or 15) was shown in the comparison, due to IRS-III being very selective. We believe that high precision is justifiable for the purpose of automated business interaction, since only the top ranked services would be of interest. However, high precision is achieved at the cost of low recall.

IRS-III provides an operational environment, which is very efficient for building executable model based applications. More precisely, OCML combines logical specification constructs (relations) with operational constructs (e.g. functions) within knowledge models (ontologies), which alleviates the problem of using semantics for decision (e.g. selection of services) while allowing for the execution of component models (e.g. Goal achievement).

This implementation, being mainly logic-based, only allows binary results (match or no-match). However, by using the meta-definitions, we allow flexibility in the way we apply the matching criteria. Currently we check for strict equivalence between input/output names of service and goals, but in the future we could easily check for lexical proximity or synonyms between these names. We could also relax the requirement of having both inputs and outputs to match. These changes would improve recall.

Beyond the algorithm used in this evaluation, IRS-III also allows the definition of preconditions and post-conditions (within service capabilities), which can can be logically analysed, provided that the values (instances) for the inputs and outputs are available. This capability was not explored during the evaluation, as the queries (service requests) in the test suite contained no values or restrictions for inputs and outputs. However, this could be exploited in future evaluations with test suites that include such capability.

As mentioned previously, IRS-III had the disadvantage of not providing the matching results (ranked services) in the format required by the evaluation tool (SME2), thus affecting its evaluation results. SME2 requires that all services in the test dataset are returned and that the order reflects the matching rank. This is an issue for evaluating IRS-III using SME2 because the OCML engine will only return services that match and it will be random with the ranking. In order to follow the format of results required by SME2, we had to include the non-matching services in random order in the result set. Thus, this affected how IRS-III was measured by SME2.

Although it was important for us to participate in the evaluation, we considered the level of effort as fairly high. As explained in Sect. 12.3, the test suite and ontologies had to be translated in a semi-automated way to our language (OCML). As our algorithm greatly depended on the quality of these ontologies, we believe that our performance was penalized for having overlooked some concepts or precise mappings (relations) during this translation.

12.5   Summary

The Semantic Web Services vision exploits the idea of using ontologies for semantically describing services in order to enable their automated discovery, composition and execution. In particular, our framework, IRS-III, uses ontology-based models to describe goals, service capabilities as well as domain knowledge.

The matchmaking algorithm of IRS-III is essentially based on reasoning. Both, service offers and service requests are modeled as knowledge components. The models allow inputs and outputs to have names in addition to types (ontology classes). The algorithm also includes a simple name equivalence checking. Matching results are binary. The services are ordered/ranked according to the matching from the names and types.

Domain ontologies were used to define service input/output types, or any mappings. In this case we translated the provided Geography Dataset ontology from OWL to our language (OCML). The Web Service descriptions were generated semi-automatically from the test collection using the provided WordNet vocabulary as types. These types were mapped to concepts in the domain ontology. Queries were translated to Goal descriptions and matched against Service descriptions.

References

1. L. Cabral, J. Domingue, S. Galizia, A. Gugliotta, B. Norton, V. Tanasescu, C. Pedrinaci, IRS-III: A broker for semantic web services based applications, in *Proceedings of the 5th International Semantic Web Conference (ISWC2006)*, Athens, 2006
2. D. Fensel, H. Lausen, A. Polleres, J. Bruijn, M. Stollberg, D. Roman, J. Domingue, *Enabling Semantic Web Services: the Web Service Modelling Ontology (WSMO)* (Springer, Berlin, 2006)
3. C. Forgy, OPS5 User's Manual, Technical report CMU-CS-81–135, Carnegie Mellon University, 1981
4. T. Gruber, A translation approach to portable ontology specifications. Knowl. Acquis. **5**(2), 199–220 (1993).
5. E. Motta, *Reusable Components for Knowledge Modelling: Case Studies in Parametric Design Problem Solving* (IOS Press, Amsterdam, 1999)

Part III
Results from the Semantic Web Service Challenge

Chapter 13
Overview of the Semantic Web Service Challenge

Liliana Cabral

Abstract This chapter provides an overview of the Semantic Web Service Challenge evaluation initiative. We provide an overview and update of the methodology and evaluation scenarios. In addition we present and analyse the accumulated results from the past workshops.

13.1 Introduction

The SWS Challenge[1] is an online evaluation initiative on the mediation, discovery and composition of Semantic Web Services. The SWS Challenge was first set up by members of STI Innsbruck[2] in 2006, and has since been organized by appointed members of the SWS community, who contributed with the specification of evaluation scenarios. Members of the organizing committee are responsible for organizing workshops in which they manually evaluate the solutions provided by the participants according to a set of criteria.

The goal of the SWS Challenge is to provide a forum for discussion of Semantic Web Service approaches based on a common application base. The evaluation approach consists of providing a number of problems within specific SWS scenarios that participants can solve and present in a workshop. The scenarios are described in English and supported with the provision of service specifications (WSDL) and data specifications (XML Schema).

---

[1]http://sws-challenge.org

[2]http://www.sti-innsbruck.at/

L. Cabral (✉)
KMi, The Open University, Milton Keynes, UK
e-mail: l.s.cabral@open.ac.uk

M.B. Blake et al. (eds.), *Semantic Web Services*, DOI 10.1007/978-3-642-28735-0_13,
© Springer-Verlag Berlin Heidelberg 2012

The evaluation methodology is based on the level of effort of the software engineering technique. That is, given that a certain tool can solve correctly a problem scenario, the tool is certified on the basis of being able to solve different levels of the problem space. In each level, different inputs are given that requires a change in the provided semantics.

Results from the first year have been published in [4]. So far, the solution approaches have ranged from conventional programming techniques with purely implicit semantics, to software engineering techniques for modeling the domain in order to more easily develop applications, to partial use of restricted logic, to full semantics annotation of the web services.

In the following sections we provide an overview of the methodology and scenarios (see also [4]), including updates and new scenarios since 2008. Finally, we present and analyse the accumulated results from the workshops.

The following five chapters, contained in this part of the book, provide an updated description of the approaches from participants in the latest SWS Challenge workshops organized in 2008 [3,4] and 2009. [5]

13.2   Evaluation Methodology

A report [3] on the methodology of the SWS Challenge has been published as part of the W3C SWS Challenge Testbed Incubator.[6] In the following we quote the methodology, extracted from the best practice recommendations in the report:

> We evaluate the software engineering advantages of the technologies of the participants. The approach emphasizes making minimal changes to a particular programming solution in a very limited time. We could measure the time participant teams take to make a change but this might focus more on programming skills than on technologies.
>
> Participants can attempt to solve any of the "ground" problems; the details of which are publicly available on the SWS Challenge Wiki. If the solution is verified, the participating team gets a check-mark by this problem. Problems for which surprise variations are available are noted on the Wiki problem description.
>
> The verification is performed by the SWS Challenge committee by examining the message exchanges in order to see if they are correct.
>
> A short time before each workshop, participants who request to do so, may receive the details of surprise variations. This length of time needs to be more precisely determined, but will typically be no longer than 2 days. In order to get a plus mark in each problem variation, participant teams must be able to solve the variations at the time of the workshop. We require that the solutions be reversible to the original problem. This is not only verified by testing at the workshop, but also by consensus inspection of the code.

---

[3]http://sws-challenge.org/wiki/index.php/EON-SWSC2008

[4]http://sws-challenge.org/wiki/index.php/Workshop_Karlsruhe

[5]http://sws-challenge.org/wiki/index.php/Workshop_ECOWS_2009

[6]http://www.w3.org/2005/Incubator/swsc/XGR-SWSC-20080331

The general procedure is: (a) ground problem solution is verified prior to the workshop, and if feasible, we may require uploading the current code and/or problem representation; (b) surprise variation is verified during the workshop; (c) participant demonstrates what changes are required to revert to a solution of the ground problem; (d) ground solution is re-verified and the code is inspected by the workshop participants.

This ground and surprise problem solution procedure requirement lessens the importance of consensus code inspection, and it emphasizes the value of software that works based upon high-level specification of the goals and constraints associated with the problem description. It is the job of the scenario variance specifier to ensure that problem reversibility is indeed possible.

Any participating team may submit new problems and variations. However, their evaluations will receive only check marks rather than plus marks, indicating that they were the authors of the problems.

13.3 Evaluation Scenarios

The SWS Challenge benchmark (as of 2009) includes six scenarios, which are thoroughly described in the Wiki[7] (and the original first five in [4]). They are divided into three mediation scenarios and three discovery scenarios, as below:

- Mediation Scenarios

  - Purchase Order Mediation
  - Purchase Order Mediation v2
  - Payment Problem

- Discovery Scenarios

  - Shipment Discovery
  - Hardware Purchasing (Discovery II and Simple Composition)
  - Logistics Management

The mediation scenarios involve process and data alignment as well as service composition, whereas the discovery scenarios involve service matching and selection, and may include simple composition or mediation.

The mediation scenarios have been developed by staff from STI Innsbruck and Stanford University. The *Shipment Discovery* scenario has originally been developed by STI Innsbruck and then refined by Ulrich Küster at University of Jena. The *Hardware Purchasing* scenario has been developed by Ulrich Küster at University of Jena. The *Logistics Management* scenario has been developed by CEFRIEL, Milano, and the University of Bicocca, Milano in cooperation with Ulrich Küster at University of Jena.

---

[7]http://sws-challenge.org/wiki/index.php/Scenarios

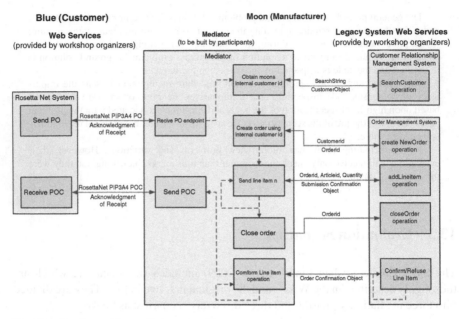

Fig. 13.1 Purchase order mediation scenario

Problems are typically layered into levels of sub-problems, which focus on different aspects of the overall scenario. This allows a fine-grained evaluation. Usually, problem levels are organized such that the first problem is very basic and subsequent problems add additional complexity on top of the previous problems or focus on complementary but more advanced problem aspects [2].

13.3.1 Mediation Scenarios

The mediation scenarios focus on interoperability problems of software systems. The aim is to show how semantic technologies can help to overcome the need for manual development of mediation processes. The scenario description provides relevant information about the systems involved by providing process diagrams, Web Service implementations (WSDL and SOAP), and data specifications (XML Schema).

The three mediation scenarios (listed above) are in fact three variants of the same *Purchase Order Mediation* problem (see Fig. 13.1), which consists of the *Mediator* process and two partner processes: the service requester (customer), company **Blue**, which order products; and the service provider, company **Moon**, which sells products. The mediator process must be implemented by the participants to mediate between Blue and Moon. The goal of the mediator is to map the incoming and outgoing messages between Blue and Moon and also invoke required services so that the interactions necessary to buy a product is complete. Company Blue sends a purchase order and receives an acknowledgment via the mediator.

The correct behavior of the Mediator Process can be verified by checking that messages exchanged (sent and received) between services are correct. The mediation requirements derive from the fact that (a) messages sent by Blue do not correspond to the messages expected by Moon; and (b) Blue's messages have a different data format than the one ones required by Moon. The message format from the Blue context is specified in (RosettaNet) XML Schema. The message enables Blue (as a buyer) to issue a purchase order and to obtain from Moon (as a seller) a response that acknowledges which of the purchase order product line items are accepted, rejected or pending.

Using current state-of-the-art technologies the participants have to interpret the information given and to code (and compose) components that overcome the heterogeneity between the different processes. The participants are asked to extend the syntactic descriptions in a way that their algorithms/systems can perform the necessary translation tasks in a semi or fully automatic manner. The mediator system should: (a) adequately invoke the requisite Web Services, whereby success is measured by the legality of the messages exchanged, and can include error handling; (b) adapt to a new problem (changes in the messages or conditions), whereby success is measured by checking whether code, data or neither has to be changed.

13.3.2 Discovery Scenarios

The scenarios for evaluating SWS discovery or matchmaking approaches focus on the problem of comparing semantic goal descriptions with semantic offer descriptions to determine services relevant to a given task. The benchmark is primarily concerned with evaluating the retrieval correctness of SWS matchmakers, but also covers runtime performance, usability and coupling characteristics to some extent.

As an overview of the problem levels within the discovery scenarios, related to the matchmaking capabilities of approaches, we present below a summary of functional challenges as in [2]:

Basic discrete matchmaking These include matching *discrete conditions*, such as a conjunctive list of requirements (e.g. color and price) as well as *hierarchical concept inclusion*, as for example in classes and subclasses.

Matchmaking with numbers Refers to the ability of processing numbers with respect to relations like *equal, smaller, greater* as well the ability to perform arithmetic calculations (e.g. a price formula).

Matchmaking with temporal reasoning Refers to the ability to compare time and date instances as well as ability to process time notions like *now, today, tomorrow, this week*, and calendar related aspects like holidays and business days, time zones etc.

Rules Ability to express rules beyond basic discrete matchmaking, such as conditional expressions (e.g. time between pickup and delivery must not exceed 24 h)
and matchmaking rules (e.g. If paid then deliver)
Preferences, ranking and selection Preferences are used to rank a list of matches in
order to select the best one. This either refers to a situation with approximation,
i.e., imperfect matches, or to a setting where a request explicitly distinguishes
between hard constraints that must be fulfilled by any candidate service and
soft constraints (often called non-functional properties or preferences) that are
desirable but not mandatory and can thus be used to order the list of candidate
services that match the hard constraints of the requestor.
Composition Service composition might be contemplated during service discovery
if no single service is able to fulfill a request, but multiple services are able to
deliver the required functionality when properly combined. For example, some
goals may require the purchase of multiple products from the same or different
vendors without linking the different products to each other using some global
requirements.
Mediation Service mediation might be contemplated during service discovery if
heterogeneities, incompatibilities or grounding is necessary.
Advanced matchmaking aspects Covers aspects not falling in any of the previous
categories. These include matchmaking under uncertainty, performing and evaluating service calls, retrieving and leveraging dynamic information as well as
representing domain functions or relations.

As mentioned before, the discovery scenarios are described in detail in the Wiki.
As an example, we include in this section a description of the Logistic Management
Scenario, which was the last scenario to be designed, but not included in [4].

13.3.2.1 Logistics Management Scenario

The Logistics Management scenario,[8] as described in [2] and [1], extends and
complements the other discovery scenarios and is also the most complex one.
The evaluation goal is two-fold: ranking discovered services on the basis of a
set of soft constraints, and resolving heterogeneity between the provider and the
requester perspectives and terminologies. With respect to ranking and selection, the
Logistics Management Scenario complements the Hardware Purchasing Scenario
by introducing further problems which require dealing with customer preferences
to suitably rank a set of services that all meet the hard constraints of the requester.
User preferences need to be expressed in the requests and matched against the given
service descriptions. This problem is far from trivial when it comes to expressing
priorities among different preferences or choosing optimal compromises in cases
of contradicting preferences, for instance, considering price versus quality aspects.

---

[8]http://sws-challenge.org/wiki/index.php/Scenario:_Logistics_Management

With respect to mediating terminologies, providers and customers in the scenario use different terminologies, because they have different points of view. Hiding this heterogeneity in a mediation system and allowing each of the partners to use the terminology he is familiar with is particularly desirable, if the rules that allow linking a term of one terminology to a term (or structure of terms) of another terminology are very complex. This is the case in the logistics domain covered by this scenario. Complex legal regulations need to be considered that a customer may not know of and does not want to deal with.

During the transport of perishable goods certain temperature ranges need to be maintained at all time. The classes of perishable goods, the temperature ranges to maintain for such goods and various types of vehicles able to maintain certain temperature ranges are specified in the international Accord Transport Perishable (A.T.P.) normative.[9] Dangerous goods, on the other hand, include gases, flammable or explosive products, toxic substances, radioactive materials and such. The Accord européen relatif au transport international des marchandises Dangereuses par Route (A.D.R.)[10] regulates the transportation of dangerous goods. It defines nine classes of peril and specifies the constraints that a truck has to meet in order to be admissible for transporting dangerous goods of the different types.

In this scenario, logistics operators offer transportation of freight between locations and storage capabilities in warehouses. They specify their storage and transport capabilities in terms of the A.T.P. and A.D.R. classes that their vehicles and warehouses support whereas the clients specify the concrete goods to be transported. It is the responsibility of the mediation system to connect these perspectives by reasoning about the applicable A.T.P. and A.D.R. regulations to determine whether a logistics operator is suitable for a given transportation request. The seven logistics operators that the scenario defines are further characterized via the following properties:

- Geographic scope: They provide transportation within a specified list of countries and continents.
- Operating hours: They offer pickup and delivery of goods within specified daily operating hours.
- Order management Speed: They require a certain time for order handling and management. The time necessary for a transport is the combination of the time necessary for order management and the mere driving time.
- Prices and payment: The cost of a transportation is given as a function of a base price and a weight and distance dependent price. Some operators offer discounts if several shipments are ordered. Furthermore, logistics operators offer different payment methods where either the sender ("carriage paid") or the recipient ("carriage forward") pays the freight. Furthermore, payments need to be made within a specified payment deadline.

---

[9]http://www.unece.org/trans/main/wp11/wp11fdoc/ATP-2007e.pdf

[10]http://www.unece.org/trans/danger/publi/adr/adr2007/07ContentsE.html

- Insurance: The operators also offer different insurance models where the freight is insured against loss ("refund for loss") or damage ("refund for damage") or both.
- Fleet: Each operator specifies the list of vehicle types they possess. Vehicles are characterized by the A.T.P. and A.D.R. classes they support as well as their average speed.
- Warehouses: Operators may provide storage capabilities in warehouses. Warehouses are characterized by their locations and the A.T.P. and A.D.R. classes they support. Temporary storage in a warehouse either in the pickup or delivery city is necessary if the interval between requested pickup and delivery time exceeds the necessary transportation time by more than 24 h.

To further illustrate the scenario, an exemplary provider and an exemplary goal are provided.

Fresh And Fast Service

The *Fresh And Fast* service operates in Spain, France, Italy and Germany. Its operating hours are from 4:00 a.m. till 7:00 p.m. and it requires 8 h for order management. The base price is EUR 120, additionally EUR 15 per kg and EUR 0.20 per km are billed. The payment deadline is 60 days from ordering. The only supported billing model is "carriage paid". The only available insurance policy is "refund for loss". *Fresh and Fast* operates warehouses in Cannes (A.T.P. class "FNB" and Paris) (A.T.P. classes "FNC" and "RRC"). It operates with a fleet of pickup trucks (47.5 km/h, A.T.P. class "RRA"), refrigerator trucks (42.0 km/h, A.T.P. class "RNA") and big trucks (35.0 km/h, A.D.R. class 1).

Goal E1

Shipping of fruit ice cream to be picked up in Milano, Italy on 11/09/2008 10:00 (GMT + 1) and delivered in Paris, France on 27/09/2008 14:30 (GMT + 1). A total of seven shipments is requested. Ideally, the base price of the shipment should be less than EUR 250. The payment deadline should be between 45 and 60 days. Insurance, both for loss and damage is preferred.

As can be seen, goal E1 requires temporary storage in a warehouse because the pickup and delivery date are far apart. Furthermore, A.D.R. normatives need to be checked for both the vehicle and the warehouse since ice cream requires cooling. The goal specifies three distinct preferences on price, payment deadline and insurance. This does not establish a total ordering among the alternative services. The goal does not specify clear criteria how to deal with this situation, thus, different rankings are equally acceptable.

13.4   Evaluation Results

The tables in Figs. 13.2–13.4 present the aggregated certification results of all workshops until and including the ECOWS 2009 workshop (Eindhoven, November 2009). The results and presentations of the solutions are available in the wiki.[11]

The results show the extent to which participating solutions were able to solve particular problem levels of the mediation and discovery scenarios. The next chapters in this part of the book, contain the updated description of solutions from five participants (taking into account teams of institutions) from the latest workshops, including Fokus (Chap. 14), University of Dortmund & University of Potsdam (Chap. 15), DERI-IE & DERI-AT (Chap. 16), University of Milano-Bicocca & CEFRIEL (Chap. 17), and University of Twente & Novay (Chap. 18).

From the solution perspective, as reported in [2], "the execution of the benchmark within the SWS Challenge showed that different problem aspects are challenging for different approaches. However, it also turned out that approaches often face difficulties that are not anticipated, neither by the scenario designers nor the participants. This reflects the relatively low level of scientific experience and

Problem Level	PoliMi & - Cefriel &	DERI AT & & DERI IE &	FSU Jena &	University of Dortmund & & University of Potsdam & (jABC)	University of Dortmund & & University of Potsdam & (LTL)	University of Dortmund & & University of Potsdam & & SAP Research &	Fraunhofer FOKUS &	LSDIS Labs &	IBM - Max Maximilien &	Novay (formerly, Telematica Instituut) & & University of Twente &
0: Static mediation	√	√	√	√	√	√	√	√		√
1a: Changes data mediation	√	√[1]	√	√		√		√		√
1b: Changes process mediation	√[4]	√[2]	√	√		√		√		√
1c: Mediation/ Integration for payment authorization	√+	√	√+	√		√				√[5]
1d: Mediation Surprise			√+	√+		√+				√+

[1]Only adapters changed

[2]Different addresses on line item level have not been addressed correctly

[4]Abstract code model change

[5]Mediator runs in simulation environment only. It is accessible from the testbed and properly interacts with Moon and Blue, but it has not been transformed to BPEL and been made available as a web service.

+ Successfully implemented "Surprise Problem Changes" (see Surprise Problem Methodology)

Fig. 13.2 Aggregated evaluation results for the mediation scenarios

[11]http://sws-challenge.org/wiki/index.php/Solutions

	Problem Level	PoliMi ⌂ - Cefriel ⌂	University Milano-Bicocca ⌂ - Cefriel ⌂	DERI AT ⌂ & DERI IE ⌂	FSU Jena ⌂	University of Dortmund ⌂ & University of Potsdam ⌂
Shipping Discovery Scenario	2a: Discovery based on Destination	√		√	√	√[a]
	2b: Discovery based on Destination and Weight	√		√	√[2]	√[a]
	2c: Discovery based on Destination, Weight and Price	√		√	√	√[a]
	2d: Discovery involving simple composition	√			√	
	2e: Discovery including temporal reasoning	√			√[a]	
Hardware Purchasing Scenario	3a: Discovery based on clear defined product specifications - Goal A1	√		√	√	
	3a: Discovery based on clear defined product specifications - Goal A2	√		√	√	
	3b: Discovery 3B - Additionally specify preferences - Goal B1	√		√	√	
	3b: Discovery 3B - Additionally specify preferences - Goal B2				√	
	3c: Discovery with composition - Goal C1 (unrelated composition)	√		√	√	
	3c: Discovery with composition - Goal C2 (correlated composition)			√		
	3c: Discovery with composition - Goal C3 (unrelated but global condition)			√	√	
	3c: Discovery with composition - Goal C4 (unrelated with global condition and preferences)			√	√	

[1]No automated invocation

[2]Arithmetic calculation performed by external Web services (which is absolutely good)

[3]Algorithm is correct, but not complete

Fig. 13.3 Aggregated evaluation results for the shipping discovery and hardware purchasing scenarios

engineering knowledge about the whole problem space and further motivates this particular evaluation approach. The critical point of the evaluation is how a certain completeness and relevance of the employed problem scenarios can be promoted and how the certification by means of concrete use cases can be abstracted to more generally valid principles. The approach to the first issue is a contribution process that leverages the wisdom of the community in assembling a complete and relevant

	Problem Level	PoliMi ᵣ₂ - Cefriel ᵣ₂	University Milano-Biococca ᵣ₂ - Cefriel ᵣ₂	DERI AT ᵣ₃ & DERI IE ᵣ₃	FSU Jena ᵣ₃	University of Dortmund ᵣ₃ & University of Potsdam ᵣ₃
Logistics Management Scenario	A1: Standard single order		◢			
	A2: A.D.R. rules		◢			
	A3: A.T.P. truck		◢			
	B1: A2 + simple soft constraints		◢			
	C1: A3 + soft constraints with preferences		◢			
	D1: warehouse		◢*			
	E1: A.T.P. truck + warehouse		◢*			

*The representation and execution of the A.T.P. and A.D.R. regulations as well as the preference policies were solved correctly, but there were bugs in the underlying functional discovery with respect to the computation of shipping times and the corresponding filtering of providers.

Fig. 13.4 Aggregated evaluation results for the logistics management discovery scenario

set of problems. The approach to the second issue is to examine and compare the various solutions to the concrete scenarios. Such critical examination allows abstracting a list of functional challenges, such as the ones presented in Sect. 13.3.2, which are valid and interesting beyond the concrete scenarios or solutions. This way, the benchmark methodology allows exploring and delimiting the underlying problem space of interest. Obviously, this is an incremental process as the problem scenarios, the technologies used to solve them and the understanding of the problem space as such co-evolve".

13.5   Lessons Learned

The major benefit of the SWS Challenge to the SWS community is that it offers a rich testbed in terms of complexity and coverage of problems in the SWS area. However, many of the issues derive from difficulties related to the very objective of the SWS Challenge, which aims at not restricting the types of technologies used to solve a problem. The goal of being open, also makes it difficult to compare on what basis some approaches are better than others. Several evaluation techniques have been tried, including a surprise scenario, and finally a consensus has been reached to simply check-mark the levels of problems that the participants can solve. From the participation side, incentives for participants to participate regularly (across workshops) are low, since there is no performance evaluation in which to improve the same system. Other staff issue relates to having enough experts in the committee that can understand specific solutions as well as keeping the testbed server online and free of bugs, while the participants test their solutions. Discussion of the lessons learned from the methodology viewpoint has been reported in [3].

We believe, that part of the solution to make the SWS Challenge easier to execute for the organizers is to automate some of the evaluation steps. From the viewpoint of the participants, the SWS Challenge could provide test data in various standard semantic formats, and for those, provide also performance measurements.

Acknowledgements The author is grateful to the members of the SWS Challenge organizing committee, and in particular to Ulrich Küster, whose work has been used in this chapter, including the content from the SWS Challenge Wiki and W3C Incubator.

References

1. A. Carenini, D. Cerizza, M. Comerio, E. Della Valle, F. De Paoli, A. Maurino, M. Palmonari, M. Sassi, A. Turati, Semantic web service discovery and selection: a test bed scenario, in *6th International Workshop on Evaluation of Ontology-based Tools and the Semantic Web Service Challenge (EON-SWSC08)*, Tenerife, 2008
2. U. Küster, *An Evaluation Methodology and Framework for Semantic Web Services Technology*, PhD thesis, Friedrich-Schiller-Universität Jena, 2010
3. C. Petrie, U. Küster, T. Margaria-Steffen, W3C SWS challenge testbed incubator methodology report, http://www.w3.org/2005/Incubator/swsc/XGR-SWSC/ (2008)
4. C. Petrie, T. Margaria, H. Lausen, M. Zaremba (eds.), *Semantic Web Service Challenge: Results from the First Year* (Springer, New York, 2008)

Chapter 14
Loosely Coupled Information Models for Business Process Integration: Incorporating Rule-Based Semantic Bridges into BPEL

Nils Barnickel and Matthias Fluegge

Abstract This chapter discusses an approach that aims at transferring the principle of loose coupling to the semantic interoperability problem given in cross-organizational business process integration. It describes how semantic bridges realized by means of rule-based ontology mappings can be incorporated into BPEL processes which span heterogeneous services using different conceptualized information models. The approach is explained based on a semantic system integration scenario in the eBusiness domain defined as the "purchase order mediation" scenario in the context of the Semantic Web Service Challenge and discusses experiences and lessons learned. The presented approach strongly relies on existing Web standards and is based on widely adopted open source software components.

14.1 Introduction

The advent of the service-oriented architecture (SOA) model and its implementation in the form of Web services has contributed significantly to facilitate the technical integration of information systems. However, semantic interoperability, i.e. the semantically sound exchange of data between heterogeneous systems, still represents a challenging task. The main reason is that domain- and application-specific requirements have produced and will always produce different information models for one and the same problem.

The alignment of heterogeneous information models is impeded by the fact that they are often represented in a semantically poor manner, focusing only on structural specifications for data exchange. This makes system integration mainly a manual effort and it requires considerable technical skills to define appropriate

N. Barnickel (✉) · M. Fluegge
Fraunhofer Institute for Open Communication Systems, Kaiserin-Augusta-Allee 31, 10589,
Berlin, Germany
e-mail: nils.barnickel@fokus.fraunhofer.de; matthias.fluegge@fokus.fraunhofer.de

M.B. Blake et al. (eds.), *Semantic Web Services*, DOI 10.1007/978-3-642-28735-0_14,
© Springer-Verlag Berlin Heidelberg 2012

syntactical transformations. The application of Semantic Web technologies to system integration problems promises to mitigate this problem since the formal definition of semantics paves the way for (semi-)automated data and process mediation. Moreover, shifting information integration from the structural to the conceptual level represents a further step towards the ultimate goal of SOA, namely to align business and IT.

14.2 Approach: Incorporating Rule-Based Semantic Bridges into BPEL

A light-weight and effective semantic system integration approach is the use of semantic bridges as we have described in [2]. The basic idea is to wrap existing information resources with semantically described Web services and to leverage rule-based ontology mappings in order to achieve interoperability and to reduce manual efforts in the composition and execution of heterogeneous Web services. This chapter briefly presents how this approach can be applied to implement the "purchase order mediation" scenario as defined in the context of the Semantic Web Service Challenge (SWSC).

The interacting systems of the SWSC mediation scenario mainly differ with regard to the following aspects:

1. *Data formats* (i.e. granularity and denotation of data elements) and
2. *Interaction patterns* (order and granularity of operations)

The approach presented in this chapter will address the first issue by applying semantic bridges to mediate between different information models and representations. The second issue will be addressed by using the *Business Process Execution Language* (BPEL) [9] and an appropriate BPEL-compliant execution engine to orchestrate the services provided by both parties. The approach does not cover goal-oriented plan creation (compared to other approaches such as WSMO [17] or SWSF [14]) and leaves the planning task (i.e. which services to include at which part into the composition) to the business domain process expert. Thus, this chapter presents a lightweight approach to reduce manual semantic mediation efforts by integrating semantic bridges into BPEL.

Semantic bridges describe the relations between entities in business information models that are defined in different ontologies but have a similar meaning. A semantic bridge is defined on the conceptual level between concepts in terms of an appropriate mapping and then can be applied to translate instances of such entities or concepts. Furthermore, semantic bridges can be also applied purely on the conceptual level, e.g. during design time in service composition. Ideally such a mapping can be included directly and transparently in the reasoning processes, which allows for drawing conclusions and thus provides the foundation for tool-supported semi-automatic semantic mediation. An example for such reasoning processes is the semantics-sensitive recommendation of service parameter assignments in cross-organizational Web service compositions as we have described in [2].

The core concept of semantic bridges, more specifically the use of rule-based semantic mappings, lies in the shift of semantic mediation from the structural to the conceptual abstraction level in order to reduce efforts for achieving semantic interoperability. Moreover, semantic bridges cannot just be applied in the execution phase but also in the design phase of a business process. A matching engine transparently applies semantic bridges and performs the reasoning over semantically described relationships (such as inheritance or equality between concepts), thus enabling a composition tool to semi-automatically support the design of interaction patterns by issuing recommendations for suitable assignments between output and input parameters of different Web services. Consequently, achieving semantic interoperability requires less manual integration efforts.

A promising approach to meet the described requirements is the use of expressive rule languages to capture mappings and to enable the direct application of the specified mappings for corresponding instance transformations. Logic-based rules are computationally complete. Hence, by defining semantic bridges in terms of logic-based rules, any kind of mapping relation (one-to-one, one-to-many, many-to-many) can be described. In case of missing data or considerable differences in information granularity between different representations, external information has to be considered. Therefore, rule-based semantic bridges can be extended to incorporate external Semantic Web Service calls that process information on the same abstraction level as used within the description logic based rules, which then provide access to any kind of external functionality or information. The absence of technical transformation code increases ease and maintainability of the semantic bridges. Furthermore and most importantly, an inference service can directly apply the rules as part of its reasoning process, i.e. the transformation of concept instances and their correct classification as well as potential further conclusions are handled in a well-integrated manner.

When applying the approach in combination with existing ontology mapping tools [6, 10, 15] which allow to semi-automatically define the mappings as semantic bridge rules, manual integration efforts can be reduced substantially.

It has been recognized that the success of Semantic Web technologies relies on the reuse and integration of existing Web standards. The most widely-used standard for the composition of Web services is BPEL. A considerable number of mature BPEL-compliant process execution engines testify the broad industrial support for this standard which provides a rich set of control and data flow constructs for defining and aligning the interactions between the participating actors in a business process. The solution outlined in this chapter raises the claim of being not only of theoretical but also of practical relevance. Consequently, the approach described in [2] was extended towards semi-automated data mediation in Web service processes that are formalized in terms of the BPEL standard.

The main challenge in this regard is to find a suitable mapping between different abstraction levels: On the one hand, at design time ontologies and rules are used for data representation, data flow and mediation. However, on the other hand, BPEL execution engines make use of hierarchically structured XML Schema types, XPath and XSLT transformations. In order to face this challenge, the starting point is to exploit the RDF/XML serialization of ontologies for data representation on the BPEL level.

The application of rule-based semantic bridges and their integration into BPEL for semantic mediation in the context of the "purchase order mediation" scenario will be described and illustrated in the following section.

14.3   Solution: Mapping the Approach to the "Purchase Order Mediation" Scenario

In order to be able to apply our mediation approach to the "purchase order mediation" scenario provided by the SWSC workshop we have to introduce several conceptual components which are numbered from one to five in Fig. 14.1.

In the scenario solution we have two heterogeneous information models (1) representing the concepts that Blue and Moon want to exchange. Figure 14.2 shows an outline of these models which are formalized in the OWL [16] ontology language using defined classes.

The Web services are annotated (2) with these ontology concepts using OWL-S annotations [11]. The Semantic Web service descriptions also include lifting and lowering definitions for converting the incoming and outgoing XSD instances to OWL instances and vice versa.

Obviously the Buyer and Customer concepts presented above are not exchangeable by default, although they represent the same idea. The information models differ in their semantic sub-graph. As the concept *Partner* in the RosettaNet ontology is defined in terms of three object properties a semantically corresponding concept *Customer* in the Moon ontology just features two object properties containing the same information, however defined at a lower level at granularity.

In order to mediate between these concepts we define a semantic bridge (3) using rules specified in terms of the *Semantic Web Rule Language* (SWRL) [12] as illustrated in Fig. 14.3.

By applying the semantic bridge rules, an instance of type *Partner* is furnished with additional properties e.g. with *hasCustomerInfo* combining the values of the *BusinessDescription* and the *ContactInformation* properties *hasBusinessName* and *hasEmailaddress* as illustrated in Fig. 14.3. Having the class definitions on hand, a reasoner is now able to classify the instance as a member of the defined class *Customer*, since all required properties (including *hasCustomerInfo*) are present. Thus, within the scope of the mediation process any service, independently to which domain it belongs, can now make use of this instance as it is polymorph of type *Partner* and *Customer*, i.e. semantic interoperability has been established.

Using traditional XML-based Web services without semantic annotations, such an approach would not be feasible. As it has been argued in [8], the static

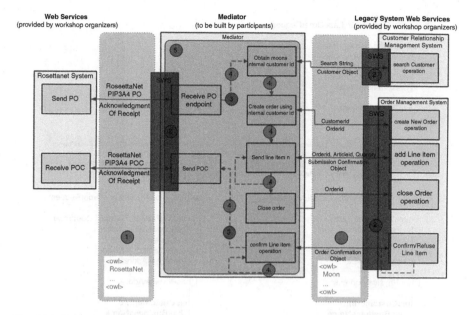

Fig. 14.1 Scenario with highlighted conceptual components for semantic mediation (*1*)–(*5*)

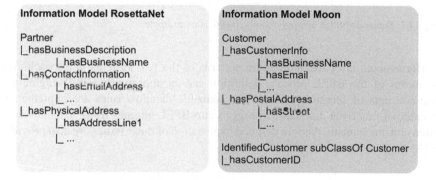

Fig. 14.2 Heterogeneous ontology-based information models of the *Blue* and the Moon system

type bindings do not allow for polymorphism; in particular XML Schema lacks inheritance relations to be exploitable for matching.

The usage of SWRL rules to mediate between heterogeneous concepts is similarly applied to express the dataflow (4) within the BPEL process. We distinguish between rules defining a semantic bridge and rules defining dataflow within the process. Semantic bridges are developed on an ontology level independently of actual application scenarios. Hence, they can be reused for various integration scenarios between the involved parties. Rules defining the data flow are, however, included into the BPEL process at design time of the integration scenario. The concept of rule-based dataflow is described in detail in [3].

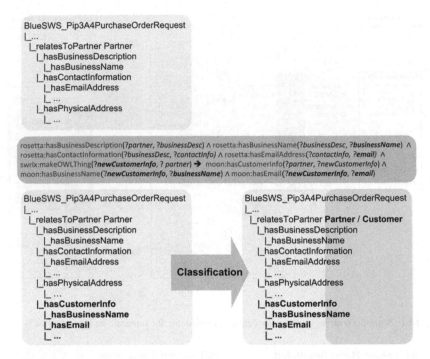

Fig. 14.3 Semantic bridge and polymorph classification example

Harmonization of the interaction patterns of the two systems is also achieved by means of the BPEL process definition and an appropriate BPEL engine (5). The concepts of semantic bridges and semantic dataflow rules are implemented as external functions that can be plugged into BPEL engines using a standardized extension mechanism. A more detailed explanation of these issues are also provided in [3].

14.4 Lessons Learned

14.4.1 Evaluation Criteria

The overall goal was to show how description logic based semantic technologies can be exploited to improve the task of semantic system integration in cross-organizational environments (cf. Sect. 14.1). To assess this goal the Semantic Web Service Challenge offers a suitable environment as it provides in many aspects a realistic business scenario addressing semantic interoperability problems in a cross-organizational context. The approach presented in this chapter considers some of the author's point of view, relevant assumptions and targets goals, which underpin its practical suitability. In the following, these goals are refined to be used as evaluation criteria for the developed approach. Furthermore, it is discussed how and to which extent these goals and underlying assumptions are already covered in the scenario setting provided by the SWSC.

- In a concrete semantic integration scenario, e.g. for the realization of a cross-organizational business process, the status quo of complicated and highly technical transformation coding (syntactical XML message transformations) for bridging heterogeneous information representations should be overcome. Furthermore, recurring manual efforts for integrating these transformations in the specific application or process context should be consolidated and automation for these tasks should be improved.

    This goal is well addressed in the SWSC scenario setting as it requires the use of semantic technologies to reduce technical and manual integration efforts.
- Heterogeneity and differences in business requirements and organizational boundaries should be respected. In particular, it should be anticipated that conceptualization and information modeling is strongly bound to organizational structures including the scope of influence and the feasibility of agreement and standardization of information models. Therefore, organizational independence should be reflected in an information architecture for large-scale SOA landscapes.

    This goal is not directly covered in the SWSC scenario setting. The scenario allows to define a homogeneous ontology on top of the two heterogeneous data schemas used in Blue and Moon system. However, this assumes that a standardized conceptualization can be agreed between the involved partners. Taking into account large-scale SOA landscapes with various independent organizations this assumption can be considered unrealistic. To reflect this challenge in future versions of the SWSC, additional information models on the conceptual level e.g. in UML could be provided as test data, which have to be respected for ontology design. This implies that a multiple ontology approach would be required from the challenge participants including measures for ontology mapping.
- As differences in information model representations can be complex, the mediation mechanism should be able to cover that complexity in terms of completeness and should as well remain easy to maintain by domain experts.

    This goal is addressed in the SWSC scenario setting as the additional surprise scenario, which also includes changes to information models, allows to test how easy adaptation to changes in terms of maintainability can be realized.
- The developed approach should remain consistent to well established good practice SOA methodologies. According to this, it should be based on process orientation starting with business analysis leading to process models, followed by deconstruction into building blocks in terms of services, which then can be independently realized and maintained based on standardized interfaces and service integration infrastructures. In particular, this implies that no opposing approaches are followed such as artificial intelligence motivated attempts that try to substitute the human business analyst and process modeler in terms of automating the design of processes with planning algorithms.

This goal is not targeted in the SWSC. The scenario is mainly designed to evaluate planning or goal-oriented Semantic Web Service approaches, which can be also seen by the number of solutions following this paradigm. However, well established good practice SOA methodologies start from modeled business processes and do not derive the process flow from automated planning algorithms. Planning or goal-oriented approaches are not able to cover organizational, cultural or political constraints, which nevertheless are determinant factors for business process design. This aspect should be further discussed in the SWSC community, in order to better bridge the gap between academic research and industry application of Semantic Web Service technologies.

- The approach should rely on existing concepts and standards of the World Wide Web, as it constitutes the dominant IT infrastructure for cross-organizational interaction. Accordingly, technological path dependency should be considered and thus it has to be ensured that any proposed solution can be based upon existing technology.

This goal could be also added to the evaluation criteria of the SWSC to increase industry suitability.

In the following, based on the proof-of-concept implementation and its application to the concrete "Purchase Order Mediation" scenario, the results can be assessed with regard to the evaluation criteria identified above.

14.4.2 Evaluation Results

The first criteria or sub-goal has been the reflection of limited feasibility of semantic standards in cross-organizational environments caused by differences in business requirements and organizational boundaries. The chosen approach based on the concept of loosely coupled information models which does not require one commonly shared ontology but accepts heterogeneity directly addresses this goal. In particular, autonomy and independent evolution of heterogeneous information models is anticipated and well reflected in the developed mediation mechanism based on semantic bridges.

The second sub-goal has been to overcome the status quo of complicated and highly technical transformation coding for bridging heterogeneous information representations in semantic integration scenarios. As demonstrated with the proof-of-concept implementation, the description logic rule-based semantic bridges enable to express the required semantic mediation declaratively on the conceptual level instead of coding highly technical transformations on the structural level. During rule-based semantic mediation, heterogeneous service parameter descriptions are transformed and expressed as polymorph representations which correspond to the conceptualizations of different domains. Furthermore, as the semantic bridges are defined between different domain ontologies, the semantic integration is shifted on the domain level, instead of implementing it recurrently within each service composition realizing a concrete business process.

Moreover, the transparent incorporation of declarative semantic bridges enables process experts to concentrate on the cross-organizational business logic without restrictions caused by heterogeneous information representations. As domain experts provide the semantic bridges between different domains from an overall domain perspective, the individual process expert is not required to have in parallel detailed insight into information models from other domains but can focus on the domain perspective he is familiar with.

Another criteria has targeted the expressiveness of the semantic mediation mechanism. As differences in information model representations can be complex, semantic bridges should be able to cover that complexity in terms of completeness but should as well remain easy to maintain by domain experts. With regard to this sub-goal it can be stated that the implementation of the semantic bridges, which is based on description logic rules, provides a computational complete solution. Any semantic mappings including one-to-one, one-to-many or many-to-many between corresponding concepts can be covered as well as any transformation of underlying semantic sub-graphs.

Furthermore, granularity differences (e.g. *Street* and *StreetNumber* as separate fields or in contrast *StreetAddress* containing the two values in a combined field) can be mapped. This is enabled by integrating so called built-in functions which provide procedures such as string concatenation or unit transformation, etc. within the declarative rules.

However, this completeness only covers mappings and transformations which are based on information contained explicitly or implicitly within the concepts to be mapped or static information such as unit transformations which can be embedded in built-ins. Other mappings which require external information such as the translation of zip codes to location names or representing a person with more or less detailed information about e.g. *name* and *place of birth* etc., which can also cause semantic integration problems, are not yet covered by the developed semantic mediation mechanism. These differences cannot be semantically bridged without considering further external information.

A starting point for this advancement is to extend the rule-based semantic bridges with function calls, which then provide access to the required external information or functionality. The built-in functions already applied to provide procedures within the declarative rules such as string concatenation to overcome certain granularity differences could be reused as an entry point for external function calls. The generic extension then would consider the incorporation of Semantic Web service calls that process information on the same abstraction level as used within the description logic based rules and which then provide access to any kind of external functionality or information.

The final two criteria have focused on industry suitability and technological path dependency. The conceptual approach should remain consistent to best practice SOA methodologies. As described in [4] the rule-based semantic mediation approach can be also incorporated into business process modeling, followed by service composition as discussed in [2] and process execution as shown in the proof-of-concept addressing the "Purchase Order Mediation" scenario [3]. Thus, it can be stated that the developed approach is fully compliant to the common SOA life cycle.

A further criteria in this regard has been the restriction to build upon existing concepts and standards of the World Wide Web and thus respect technological path dependency, especially with regard to Web service technologies which are the dominant instantiation of SOA. As described in Sect. 14.2 the semantic mediation toolkit provides its mediation functionality by means of an additional semantic layer (domain ontologies and semantic bridges) on top of existing XML-based Web service technology. Lifting and lowering mechanisms of Semantic Web service technology are used to connect the different abstraction layers between the semantics-based mediation layer and the existing traditional Web service technology. As opposed to other integration approaches which rely on proprietary service composition descriptions and process models, the presented approach relies on the BPEL standard. Tremendous efforts have been made to develop BPEL-compliant process engines that are suitable to be used in business-critical scenarios. Hence, the financial investments made by vendors and users of BPEL-compliant process engines are preserved and consequently it can be stated that technological path dependency has been respected.

According to the analysis above, it can be stated that the originally set conceptual goals could be almost completely covered. However, a proper evaluation should also mention difficulties and experienced problems, which are addressed in the following section.

14.4.3 Experienced Difficulties and Open Issues

The elaborated concept and the implemented prototypes are based on the Semantic Web service specification OWL-S [11]. However, originally the plan was to use the W3C SAWSDL [15] standard for semantic service descriptions. SAWSDL directly integrates semantic annotations into WSDL-based Web services descriptions – a light-weight approach which fits well to our solution described above. Unfortunately, solid tool support was still missing at the time of the prototype development and thus the older and more mature W3C specification OWL-S has been favored. Hence, it would be desirable that the Open Source and Semantic Web community launches a project for the development of an API for the execution of SAWSDL-compliant Semantic Web services.

The Mindswap OWL-S API has been applied to get programmatic access to read, execute and write OWL-S service descriptions [13]. However, support and maintenance for this Open Source component are not strong and thus several bugs and conceptual problems had to be tackled in the implementation phase. The two main problems and resulting modifications are briefly explained below.

The first problem results from the fact that the developed approach for rule-based semantic bridges is based on the concept of polymorphism (cf. Sect. 14.2). However, the original OWL-S API implementation does not allow for exploiting the full potential of polymorphism. When a polymorph individual is serialized using the RDF/XMLABBREV format, which is applied in the OWL-S API implementation, one of the types it holds is non-deterministically selected and the last fragment of the types URI is taken for the opening tag for this individual's XML serialization. The other types are expressed by separate *rdf:type* sub elements. This varying structure complicates the development of XSLT code dramatically. Secondly, the OWL-S API is not capable of handling WSDL-based Web services that require document-literal based SOAP communication and whose input or output is described via more than one OWL concept. However, such features were necessary in order to solve the Purchase Order Mediation scenario provided by the Semantic Web Service Challenge organizers. To overcome these weaknesses, the OWL-S API, has been adjusted accordingly. Now internally the basic RDF/XML serialization is applied. This means that all types are represented equally as sub elements, which allows defining straighter XSL transformations. Hence, the mapping from polymorph OWL serializations to single typed XML Schema instances can be achieved in terms of XSLT rules that match exactly the type which has been defined in the OWL-S input description. The other type tags resulting from the polymorphism are ignored as well as additional properties which the OWL individual might feature. The processing of the Web service results is less complicated as the received message parts correspond to the data model XSLT was designed for. XSLT rules can easily match the XML Schema instances and fill predefined skeletons of serializations of OWL individuals.

Another issue is related to the characteristics of the utilised ontology definition language OWL. First, the Web Ontology Language makes the Open World Assumption and second, OWL stays monotonic. The Open World Assumption implies that facts which are not explicitly stated in a knowledge base are not false but supposed to be currently "unknown" as opposed to the Closed-World Assumption. Monotony means that facts cannot be removed from a knowledge base or replaced with new facts. However, in most business use cases facts are subject to change and unknown facts are regarded as false [5].

For example if a class C is defined as the set of individuals having exactly one certain property p in terms of *minCardinality = 1* and *maxCardinality = 1* then due to open-world semantics an individual featuring this certain property p can not be classified to class C. The reasoner does not know if there maybe exists a second occurrence of p for this individual, so that the restriction would become unsatisfied. This behavior was not expected but has been detected during the implementation phase of the prototype. In order to overcome this problem and express exact cardinality constraints on service parameter properties which correspond to the constraints of type definitions in XML Schema domain standards required for the underlying traditional Web services, the feature of functional properties within OWL-DL is exploited. By declaring the property p as *functional* the reasoner knows that p exists exactly once. Thus, even with open-world semantics the individual (service parameter) can be classified to class C. Hence, basic cardinality restrictions are supported and the second part of the semantic bridges operation mode, the facet analysis classification, could be realized.

In order to use the most recent SWRL reasoning features including built-in function support etc., the latest (at that time) built of Protege 3.4 was used. However this version revealed several bugs regarding serialization of the inferred model as well as importing several models into one model, performing reasoning and serializing the resulting individuals in a clean model. Finding these bugs, reporting them to the Protege developers and finding alternative solutions was quite time consuming.

However, it can be stated that most of the problems and open issues discussed above are of technical nature while at the end (including the discussed technical workarounds) the conceptual approach has been implemented and demonstrated successfully as a proof of concept.

14.4.4 Conclusions and Future Work

Starting from the presented approach, additional questions arise. For example, it has to be ensured that all stakeholders in cross-organizational business processes covering multiple domains have access to the required assets, including process models, information models and particularly the corresponding semantic bridges. The adoption of the concept of loose coupling on the semantic level prevents from the limitations of cross-domain commitment to an overall ontology and thus minimizes less practical central structures. However, it still requires a certain central organizational framework or kind of central clearinghouse to support the stakeholders in the process of providing and sharing the semantic assets. Such a clearinghouse should include a repository to publish the various business process models, domain information models and semantic bridges. It should provide means to categorize them with retrievable and thus expressive semantics and provide methods for versioning and quality assurance to ensure their sound evolution.

Another organizational perspective includes the question regarding the scope of domains. The developed concept addresses semantic mediation on domain level but it leaves it open to the specific integration scenarios which coverage the domain ontologies should have. Generally, it can been argued that the scope of a domain ontology and the respective feasible semantic standardization is limited and depends on certain organizational structures such as the existence of an umbrella association etc. However, to derive concrete lower and upper bounds for adequate domain ontology coverage and to identify the relevant factors for it requires dedicated empirical studies in different organizational scenarios. From a macro-perspective this includes the question about the adequate granularity of a network of loosely coupled domain ontologies in an IT ecosystem of multiple organizations. Future research should address these issues with the goal to develop a certain heuristic on how to map the structure of relations between organizations or organizational entities to an adequate set of domain ontologies.

Besides these organizational issues, further functional advancements should be addressed in future work. One point has already been discussed within the evaluation and concerns the integration of external information into the semantic mediation mechanism (cf. Sect. 14.4.2).

Regarding the general range of functionality of the semantic mediation toolkit, it has to be stated that it just provides the basic functions to demonstrate how the approach can be incorporated into the SOA life-cycle as a proof-of-concept. Thus, in order to evolve towards mature industry products, the prototypes have to be extended substantially or integrated into existing products to provide the required comprehensive functionality.

When discussing the general readiness of the approach for wide industry adoption, it has to be taken into account that Semantic Web technologies are still an emerging technology. Most provided frameworks and APIs are still academic-driven and at so called beta stage and thus cannot yet be considered as technically stable and mature. In fact, during development and testing of the semantic mediation toolkit several problems and bugs occurred (cf. Sect. 14.4.3). To minimize these drawbacks and due to the raised claim of being not only of theoretical but also of practical relevance, the presented approach relies strongly on existing Web standards. This includes both: On the one hand, state-of-the-art XML-based technologies such as BPEL, XSLT, XPath and XML Schema. And on the one hand, Semantic Web technologies such as OWL, OWL-S and SWRL rules. The frameworks and APIs supporting these existing standards can be regarded as the most mature including available tool support and stability compared to others. Nevertheless, the evolution of these standards and tools is still in progress and future versions of the semantic mediation toolkit should consider this evolution.

In this process, the future will show to which extent the Semantic Web technologies exploited for the additional semantic layer on top of traditional Web service technology will emerge to mature industry standards. An alternative path could be as well a kind of convergence. In this perspective, the identified benefits of the underlying language concepts of Semantic Web technologies such as polymorphism or facet analysis classification will have an impact in terms of an infusion into the evolution of the XML-based standards itself. For instance, in [7], it is discussed how XML languages can be extended to support a polymorphic type system such as subtyping, inference of types, etc. However, irrespective of which path will be adopted, the gap between the two technology layers will be at the focus of further evolution. For example the already discussed recommendation for Semantic Web service descriptions SAWSDL seems to be promising and suitable to foster industry adoption. Another candidate for observation is XSPARQL [1], which promises to improve the translation between the traditional XML and the semantics-oriented RDF world. This is particularly relevant for grounding of Semantic Web services to existing traditional Web services. Currently, the required lifting and lowering translations have to be expressed as XSL transformations, which process the ontology annotations on the level of their XML serialization. XSPARQL promises a more adequate way as it is designed to understand both meta-models and to provide powerful means for transformation between the two in any direction. Consequently, the evolution of the prototype should consider these advancements to further ease the provision of the additional semantic layer and thus facilitate industry adoption.

14.5 Summary

The approach presented in this chapter aims at reducing the complexity of semantic mediation in order to facilitate system integration in a service-oriented architecture landscape. Semantic Web technologies have been used as an additional layer on top of existing WSDL-based Web services and XML Schema based message formats. With reference to the problem scenario provided by the Semantic Web Service Challenge, the heterogeneous information models of the Blue system (RosettaNet) and the Moon system have been additionally expressed in terms of two autonomously developed domain ontologies. These domain ontologies have been combined with specific upper ontologies for Web services (OWL-S) in order to realize the Semantic Web services.

The approach of multiple independent ontologies on the domain level takes into account the realistic point of view that in a system integration scenario the availability of a single global ontology covering the needs of all autonomous actors and organizations across various domains cannot be assumed. The well established paradigm of loose coupling is reflected on the semantic level by using independently evolving information models (ontologies) that are loosely coupled through semantic bridges.

While on the one hand semantic bridges target the semantic mediation challenge of heterogeneous data formats, the semantic mediation challenge of heterogeneous interaction patterns has been addressed by using a BPEL engine as the coordinating entity. The integration of Semantic Web services, semantic bridges and rule-based dataflow into BPEL processes thus provides the foundation for powerful tool support in semantic system integration scenarios. The data model based on description logic as provided by ontologies in conjunction with semantic bridges allows for applying automatic semantic matching mechanisms based on polymorph representations of service parameters. In [11] this approach has been demonstrated in order to provide semantics-based tool support for Web service orchestration: Semantically matching service parameter parts are presented as assignment recommendations to the process expert, thus facilitating the data flow design. Based on the selection of the involved Web services and of the assignment recommendations an execution plan for the Semantic Web service composition can be constructed in a semi-automated manner. By applying the mechanisms described in this paper the generated process can be expressed in BPEL and executed by appropriate industrial mature workflow engines.

The presented approach relies strongly on the existing Web standards BPEL and OWL and thus raises the claim of being not only of theoretical but also of practical relevance. In the long run these activities should contribute to the vision of performing cross-organizational process integration purely on the conceptual business level by exploiting powerful tool support based on established SOA concepts and standards combined and advanced with emerging Semantic Web technologies.

References

1. W. Akhtar, J. Kopeck, T. Krennwallner, A. Polleres, Xsparql: traveling between the xml and rdf worlds and avoiding the xslt pilgrimage, in *The Semantic Web: Research and Applications*, ed. by S. Bechhofer, M. Hauswirth, J. Hoffmann, M. Koubarakis. Lecture Notes in Computer Science, vol. 5021 (Springer, Berlin/Heidelberg, 2008), pp. 432–447
2. N. Barnickel, M. Fluegge, K.-U. Schmidt, Interoperability in e-government through cross-ontology semantic web service composition, in *Proceedings of the Workshop Semantic Web for eGovernment of the 3rd European Semantic Web Conference 2006*, Budva, 2006
3. N. Barnickel, R. Weinand, M. Fluegge, Semantic system integration – incorporating rule-based semantic bridges into bpel processes, in *Proceedings of the 6th International Workshop on Evaluation of Ontology-Based Tools and the Semantic Web Service Challenge*, CEUR-WS, vol. 359, Tenerife, 2008
4. N. Barnickel, J. Böttcher, A. Paschke, Incorporating semantic bridges into information flow of cross-organizational business process models, in *I-SEMANTICS '10: Proceedings of the 6th International Conference on Semantic Systems* (ACM, New York, 2010), pp. 1–9
5. N. Drummond, R. Shearer, The open world assumption. Technical report, University of Manchester, 2006
6. M. Ehrig, S. Staab, *Qom – Quick Ontology Mapping* (Springer, Berlin/New York, 2004), pp. 683–697
7. H. Hosoya, A. Frisch, G. Castagna, Parametric polymorphism for xml. SIGPLAN Not. **40**(1), 50–62 (2005)
8. M. Klein, D. Fensel, F. van Harmelen, I. Horrocks, The relation between ontologies and schema-languages: translating oil-specifications in xml-schema. In *Proceedings of the ECAI'00 workshop on applications of ontologies and problem-solving methods*, Berlin, August 2000.
9. OASIS WSBPEL TC: web services business process execution language version 2.0 (BPEL), (2007), OASIS committee specification, http://docs.oasis-open.org/wsbpel/2.0/wsbpel-v2.0.pdf
10. J. Ressler, M. Dean, E. Benson, E. Dorner, C. Morris, Application of ontology translation, in *ISWC'07/ASWC'07: Proceedings of the 6th International The Semantic Web and 2nd Asian Conference on Asian Semantic Web Conference* (Springer, Berlin/Heidelberg, 2007), pp. 830–842
11. Semantic Markup for Web Services (OWL-S), W3C member submission (2004), http://www.w3.org/Submission/OWL-S/
12. Semantic Web Rule Language (SWRL), W3C member submission (2004), http://www.w3.org/Submission/SWRL/
13. E. Sirin, B. Parsia, The owl-s java api, in *Proceedings of the 3rd International Semantic Web Conference*, Hiroshima, 2004
14. Semantic Web Service Framework (SWSF), W3C member submission (2005), http://www.w3.org/Submission/SWSF/
15. Semantic Annotations for WSDL and XML Schema (SAWSDL), W3C recommendation (2007), http://www.w3.org/2002/ws/sawsdl/
16. Web Ontology Language (OWL), W3C recommendation (2004), http://www.w3.org/2004/OWL/
17. Web Service Modeling Ontology (WSMO), Submission request to W3C (2005), http://www.w3.org/Submission/WSMO/

Chapter 15
The XMDD Approach to the Semantic Web Services Challenge

Tiziana Margaria, Christian Kubczak, and Bernhard Steffen

Abstract The Semantic Web Services Challenge addresses since 2006 the issue of finding adequate domain modeling formalisms that help taming the complexity of service orchestration and service discovery. In this chapter we sketch briefly our XMDD (eXtreme Model Driven Design) approach to the development of large service-oriented applications and describe how it was used to address the Challenge. Our approach gave rise so far to a collection of six solutions with different engines, methods, and profiles. We examine in this technological landscape the concrete settings, the dimensions of complexity that appear in the Challenge, and reflect on the essence of the evaluations and observations so far.

15.1 Introduction

Service-Oriented Computing is one of the most promising software engineering trends for mastering the complexity of distributed systems. Pushed by major industry players and supported by many standardization efforts, Web services and internet services in general are a prominent implementation of the service-oriented paradigm. They promise to foster reuse and to ease the implementation of loosely coupled distributed applications [15].

Though Web services are appealing especially in the area of enterprise application integration, the idea of service-oriented computing and the envisioned availability of thousands of services can not be fully leveraged as long as service-oriented applications are described merely in terms of the service's signatures, as

T. Margaria (✉)
Universität Potsdam, Chair Service and Software Engineering, Potsdam, Germany
e-mail: margaria@cs.uni-potsdam.de

C. Kubczak · B. Steffen
TU Dortmund, Chair Programming Systems, Dortmund, Germany
e-mail: christian.kubczak@cs.tu-dortmund.de; steffen@cs.tu-dortmund.de

M.B. Blake et al. (eds.), *Semantic Web Services*, DOI 10.1007/978-3-642-28735-0_15,
© Springer-Verlag Berlin Heidelberg 2012

in current WSDL. The lack of rich information on the kind of service offered, and under which circumstances it is applicable and/or adequate is largely responsible for the fact that composite services and applications that use services are created and maintained manually. It is a minimum requirement to use semantic technology, of the kind that enhances the service descriptions by annotations that precise its behavior beyond the signature information, for a certain application domain. Semantics is understood in this context as extended descriptions by means e.g. of ontologies, or pre- and postconditions. If this kind of semantics were carefully designed and automatically supported by tools, the tasks of service discovery, selection, negotiation, and binding could be automated, lifting service-oriented applications to a new level of adaptability and robustness. There, semantic issues play a central role in two directions:

- Expressing the purpose of the compound service, i.e. **What** should the service achieve?
- Expressing the suitability of the single services that appear in the service composition, i.e. *Once it is clear* **how** *to orchestrate single service functionalities to achieve that purpose,* **what** *(available) services are adequate to provide the functionalities required in the orchestration?*

This reminds strongly of the question *From the How to the What* we addressed at VSTTE 2005 in Zürich [17], where we considered the VSTTE Grand Challenge under a very specific (and Service-Orientation friendly) perspective: the enabling of application experts without programming knowledge to reliably model their processes/applications in a fashion that allows for a subsequent automatic realization on a given platform. This goal, which aims at simplifying the tasks of the many at the cost of ambitious and laborious tasks for the few, adds a new dimension to the techniques and concepts aimed at by the Grand Challenge: the application-specific design of platforms tailored for the intended goal. We were convinced already then that the outlined perspective provides a realistic and economically important milestone for the Grand Challenge.

The SWS Challenge addresses exactly this goal, albeit in a Web Service context instead of general programming:

- How can one specify, as clearly and declaratively as possible, the *What's* in the previous two questions, and
- How can one achieve as automatically, adaptably, and robustly as possible the implied *How's*, concerning the *composition* (orchestration) of composite services, and the *matchmaking* supporting the discovery of adequate implementations for the individual services (or components).

Other approaches followed in the SWS have different focus: WSMO/WSMX-based techniques [36] use more complete semantic descriptions and are more geared towards substituting rather than enhancing current practices of software engineering as XMDD proposes. Among the techniques used in the SWS Challenge so far, the SA-WSDL based approach of [4] is in this sense the closest to ours.

After briefly sketching our approach, its underlying technology, and the corresponding solutions we will focus on the discussion of the lessons learned and the potential for future research.

15.2   The XMDD Approach

During the last decade, we developed an extreme version of model-driven development (XMDD) [17], which is designed to continuously involve the customer/application expert throughout the whole system's life cycle. Technically, this is achieved following our 'One-Thing Approach' [22, 32], which works by enriching and refining one single artifact: user-level models are successively refined from the user perspective until a sufficient level of detail is reached, where elementary services can be implemented solving application-level tasks. Thus, in essence, system development becomes user-centric orchestration of intuitive service functionality. The realization of the individual services should typically be simple, often based on functionality provided by third-party and standard software systems.

XMDD differs radically from classical software development, which is in our opinion in fact no longer adequate for the bulk of application programming. This holds in particular when it comes to heterogeneous, cross organizational systems which must adapt to rapidly changing market requirements. The central technical hurdles we tackle in XMDD are *compatibility* and *interoperability*, which we successfully address by moving it to a *higher level of abstraction* (models, rather than code) and going towards more homogeneous final artifacts, that also increase interoperability. Accordingly, this model-driven, lightweight, and cooperative development paradigm puts the *user process* in the center of the development and the *application expert* in control of the process evolution. In the rest of this section we will address how to place XMDD in practice by addressing the key guiding questions and sketching our corresponding modeling framework, the jABC [7].

How to Address an New Application Scenario

In [20] we addressed cornerstones of the method while reflecting on our experience with XMDD in several industrial projects and in years of teaching. This concerns in particular the following six points:

- How to structure solutions from the application perspective (user-centric modeling) [8],
- How to validate the application logic (animation-based requirement validation and model checking),
- How to find an adequate level, where application modeling is handed over to the implementation of (elementary) services. Essentially this can be seen as an identification of the domain language,

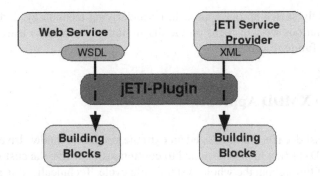

Fig. 15.1 Service integration via the jETI technology

- How to deploy their complex aggregations and compositions,
- How to monitor solutions at run time,
- How to adapt existing solutions according to new requirements.

Overview of the jABC/jETI Technology

For the process definition and management we use a multi-purpose domain-independent modeling framework, the *Java Application Building Center (jABC)* [7], complemented by the *Java Electronic Tool Integration* framework (*jETI*) [9, 23] for dealing with integration and execution of remote services. Both are based on well established software technology and have been used successfully in different application domains [18], most recently targeting bioinformatics processes [12,23].

jABC is a control-flow oriented environment for service design and analysis. It enforces a *one-thing-approach* [22,32] to eXtreme Model Driven Design [17,20], thus avoiding the typical discontinuity in modeling style and technologies between the business and the IT aspects of a running process [15,18].

Business processes become increasingly networked, parallel, conditional, event-driven, recursive, and asynchronous: this are the kinds of sources of complexity whose control is at the core of jABC's strengths. Additionally, clear formal semantics is the precondition for a formal analysis and verification of properties of the designed workflows based on automatic mathematical proofs. jABC is built with this formal verification capability in the focus, which scales for large business models. jETI is the technology that allows us to deal with remote and external services and functionalities in a homogeneous way, as shown in Fig. 15.1 for the specific SWS Mediation example.

In the following section we briefly summarize the successive campaigns that led us to increasingly automated and profile-oriented solutions of the Mediation scenario.

15.3   Solutions: Using XMDD Support

So far, we provided a number of solutions to the Mediation scenario problem with increasing level of automation and dynamism. They are all model-driven and service-oriented, use the jABC framework [7, 32] for design, composition, and execution of the mediator and the jETI [9, 23] technology for the integration and enactment of a) remote planners/model generation tools and b) remote heterogeneous services [10, 11, 24–26]. All of them follow the same generic pattern:

- Extract the *relevant* information from the *PurchaseOrderRequest*
- Call Moon's Customer Relation Management (CRM) to find the customer data inside the database, if she already has an account.
- Use the *CustomerID* to create an order using Moon's Order Management System (OMS).
- Add *LineItems* as needed and then
- Close the order.
- Finally the middle layer receives an *OrderConfirmationObject* and
- Sends a *PurchaseOrderConfirmation* back to Blue.

In the following we briefly discuss the two families of solutions we provide, *manual model development* and *synthesis from user-level specifications*, a well as our way to deal with change at the modeling level.

Manual Model-Driven Development

In [9, 11] we showed how to use the business and technical knowledge about the scenario setting in order to semi-automatically extract service and business object representations from the scenario description and the provided WSDLs. The representations are automatically sorted in a simple taxonomy that can be used as a guidance in composing the solution workflow at the business logic level. This is done graphically. The service representations in the jABC are automatically Java classes, thus they are executable and internally grounded to real executable code. Using these services within the jABC becomes very easy, so that in principle engaged (non-IT) professionals and even end users are able to compose new composite applications (that are service orchestrations) and to modify existing applications.

Automatic Synthesis from User-Level Specifications

In [10, 24, 31] and more recently in [25] we showed how to organize the business and technical knowledge already present in the just described MDD approach into taxonomies and semantically enhanced service descriptions, and how to use this knowledge to generate automatically the solution's workflow. To this aim,

- The taxonomies are internally represented as relations, in a notation close to Prolog facts or RDF triples, visualized in the jABC;
- The service descriptions corresponding to the information that is contained in the replacement types are formulated analogously.
- Constraints are formulated in SLTL[19], a semantically enriched linear time logic that allows expressing constraints over processes, using constructs like before/after.
- Business objectives are also formulated in SLTL.

Business designers can incrementally express their business knowledge as additional information/constraints, and use an automatic synthesis algorithm to obtain the collection of feasible service compositions that satisfy that objective and are consistent with the given constraints.

This way, business process composition elegantly arises without any need of programming, as a consequence of the enterprise knowledge and of the expressed business goals. Changes in the goal, in the situation, or in the objectives are automatically reflected in the new computed solution space. Thanks to the jABC framework, these solutions are immediately executable.

In particular, we showed in [24] how a naive formulation of the goals leads to solutions that processes empty orders, and how easy it is to add business-level knowledge to automatically obtain solution that are not only technically correct, but also useful and sensible from the business point of view.

Having the entire solution space available is a great help for managers: ensuring that further global properties – typically linked to business conduct rules, or to regulations, or to security/authorization – are always satisfied is then made possible (by automatic proof on the graph of the solution space). Examples of such business-level properties are

- P1: *No item can be billed multiple times, even in split billing scenarios,* or
- P2: *Operations in the Order Management System and in the corresponding ERP system should always be kept consistent.*

Dealing with Change in Heterogeneous Landscapes

The enhancement we proposed in [26] profits of the jABC/jETI technology, with a focus on the viewpoint of the Change Management Manager and Engineer: we assumed that the previous Mediator solutions are already available to them, and they now wished to enhance them by adding a SAP backend to the scenario.

Our approach provides automatic or semi-automatic support for evolution and change management in heterogeneous legacy landscapes where

1. Legacy heterogeneous, possibly distributed platforms are integrated in a service-oriented fashion,
2. The functionality is coordinated at the service level, through orchestration,
3. Compliance and correctness are provided through policies and business rules,

4. Evolution and correctness-by-design are supported by the eXtreme Model Driven Development paradigm (XMDD) offered by the jABC [20]. We use here for integration, design, evolution, and governance.

The artifacts (services or components) are semantically enriched, so that automatic synthesis plugins can provide knowledge driven business process development for the end user.

We enhanced the Mediation Scenario of the Semantic Web Service Challenge along the two central evolution paradigms that occur in practice: (a) Platform migration: platform substitution of a legacy system by an ERP system and (b) Backend extension: extension of the legacy Customer Relationship Management (CRM) and Order Management System (OMS) backends via an additional ERP layer.

15.4 Lessons Learned

In [16] we examined preliminarily the concrete settings, the dimensions of complexity that appear in the Challenge, and reflected on the essence of the observations so far. More detailed information on the activity and results so far can be found in [33], the book collecting the revised results from the first period of the Challenge.

15.4.1 Evaluation Results

Most of the solutions we provided do not appear in the official SWS charts because the criteria and methodology of the evaluation did not really fit with the structure of the approach taken by our group. This observation gave rise to a series of discussions in the various committees about the principle of evaluation, which in the end led to only three columns summarizing our work in the results table. The remainder of this subsection is meant to complement this very partial account of our achievements and the value of the solutions.

The central reason for the mismatch lies in our use of the XMDD approach, which moved both the effort and the challenges from the code level to the abstract level of models. Our first solution used jABC's Service Logic Graphs for the manual orchestration of the mediator and was for us just the basic starting point for the research we were interested in. However, already this approach exhibited traits that exceeded the expectations and thus the measurement criteria of the Challenge.

The central issue was here that a simple and intuitive graphical notation for the orchestration, coupled to automatic code generation and deployment, decouples the intellectual effort of finding a solution at the application level from the effort of producing running implementations. With such an approach, criteria that measure the additional coding effort (e.g. to modify or extend a scenario) and code changes in the running solution lose their meaning: small changes in the model can be easy to do, elegantly and intuitively solve the problem, yet disrupt completely the resulting deployable code. In the optic of a code review, the changes are massive, equivalent to extensive re-programming, but from a designer's perspective a simple modification of the model and a click for code generation sufficed to produce the new code.

Largely because the different groups used different means of expression for their designs and solution, we ended up not finding an adequate characterization of effort (creative or implementation related) in the design space, and therefore the evaluation rested with an inspection of the code basis that actually runs.

The several solutions we later produced abandoned the level of manual creation of the orchestrations for our true research interest: the automatic composition of service orchestrations. In fact we were interested primarily in the tradeoff between different algorithms, different implementations, and in the comparison between a number of generation techniques, both those we developed in house and related solutions using techniques by other groups.

We ended up over the 3 years of our participation in the Challenge to produce a total of six solution types, of which four use different in-house algorithms (the Yoo [24], LTL [19], Prophets [14], and jMosel techniques and tools [25]), and others use variants of Golog [25] and SAP's GEM [10], and a platform for their comparison, Plan-jETI [25, 34].

Only our very first solution was accepted as such and is listed, and only after a long series of reviews and discussions that aimed at assessing the running code. The running code is the same for all the solutions, including the manual one. In the automated approaches we have in fact a number of different ways of generating the same result, i.e. we produce with different methods the same SLG in the jABC, which then of course compiles to the same running code. The central debate concerned here whether the same solution achieved in a different way is a different solution, and thus deserves a distinct evaluation and an own column in the summary table. Again, this discussion is reconducible to the code-oriented perspective taken in the evaluation, which in our case clashed with our process-oriented approach of solution creation.

After it became clear that contributions like comparing the impact and profile of different methodologies like of Golog or Monadic second order logic on automated synthesis of orchestrations are out of scope of the SWS challenge, we started to publish these results independently, e.g. in [25].

Our understanding of the merit of this research was the creativity, experimentation, and comparisons in the design space. Especially the aspiration to make use of more declarative forms of knowledge seemed to us to be aligned with the Challenge objectives.[1]

---

[1]From the SWSC Wiki page: *The goal of the SWS Challenge is to develop a common understanding of various technologies intended to facilitate the automation of mediation, choreography and discovery for Web Services using semantic annotations. The intent of this challenge is to explore the trade-offs among existing approaches. Additionally we would like to figure out which parts of problem space may not yet be covered.*

15.4.2 Advantages and Disadvantages: Different Complexities

Examining the complexity issues in the SWS Challenge, we can distinguish three major sources of complexity: *data*, *control*, and *domain modeling*.

Data Issues

The Mediation scenario includes data mediation aspects, concerning how to deal with different granularities in provided and requested data (e.g. an entire address as a type vs. single parameters for single fields, like name, street, etc.) and with a type mismatch requiring type conversion, casting, embedding.

We expected here to have to deal with ontology mapping issues, assuming that data types and their compatibility relations would be expressed by relations stored in ontologies. Handling heterogeneous data types is a well known problem in software engineering and programming, and the solutions known there are applicable also in this case. However, we found out that in practice there are new aspects that hamper scalability, for example impede general approaches to type conversion of service's parameters to make them accessible inside usual programming environments. This is due for example to the fact that Web services exchange *complex documents*, rather than programming-style parameters. A typical RosettaNet data parameter is a Purchase order, or a Purchase offer: imagine having to deal with a document that has an internal structure as complex as the XML source of this book, and that this structure is completely exposed as a structured data type at the interface of the service! We attempted an automatic mapping of service interfaces provided as WSDL files to Java classes, with little success: as detailed in [9], several attempts to full automation failed. The central issue appears to be the complex structure of the Java classes that are automatically generated from the RosettaNet messages: a complete translation of the document structure yields very large, structured objects, much more involved than the objects customarily found in manually programmed Java.

As a consequence, we do not think that even leading-edge development environments like Java6 are ready (yet) for a generic automation of Web service import and export. Although each single type is by itself simple, the new phenomenon is just the fact that objects carry hundreds of them, nested recursively and organized in very complicated structures. Currently, we support fully automatically only the standard types, while custom types (like the specific structure of these proceedings) require a varying degree of manual intervention.

Indeed, similar automation problems have been recently reported by other researchers, who tried a similar approach for handling complex, automatically generated telecommunications messages inside a Java environment. Our first investigation of complex telecommunication services libraries offered as Web Services, like e.g. the Parlay-X collection for IMS (IP Multimedia Subsystem) in Next-Generation Networks [27], however, shows that even the complex telecommunication data types found there are much simpler than those used in an e-business service domain like RosettaNet. A possible reason is that established engineering fields like telecommunications successfully introduced layering and delegation to hide the internal complexity of messages. As an example, in telecommunication protocol services, one level interprets only the header of the large complex message, which contains only the metadata necessary for the processing of that level, and passes the bulk of the message as uninterpreted "payload" to the next-lower layer.

In the Challenge context, we observed that the solutions that resort to pure Web service environments do not face this translation issue, since they stay within the XML environment: the solutions just parse those documents but don't import them into a programming environment. This is simpler, and adequate for the Challenge, which involves only Web services, but limits the applicability of these approaches to handling pure XML documents.

We, however, are convinced that the strength of the service concept is in its capability to tame the complexity that arises from heterogeneity of the target environments, in particular in the presence of legacy systems. Mixing Web services with CORBA components, REST services, and programs in some language requires the capability to translate between these technologies, and leads to the discovery of mismatches that would not be detected in homogeneous environments.

Control Issues

The issue of control in the SWS Challenge concerns the orchestration itself, following the principle *Easy for the many, difficult for the few* that advocates ease of composition for non-IT experts. This issue is directly addressed by the Mediation scenario.

While the original quest was for a possibly declarative problem description followed by automated composition, we found out that all the first generation solutions proposed some form of handmade orchestration: directly programmed (in Java or Ruby on Rail) or achieved by graphical composition at the level of executable models, at different levels of abstractions. Our initial approach fell in this second group: it is based on the jABC/jETI environment [7], it is service-oriented and model driven, and it offers editing and composition facilities based on taxonomies of services, supporting hierarchy and service execution. In additions it offers advanced features like verification of the orchestrations by means of model checking as well as automatic code generation and deployment, which the other comparable solutions do not provide.

Concerning the semantic aspects, the approaches mentioned above do not require ontologies or semantic descriptions: manual programming and manual module definition and composition do not strictly need additional information for processing. jABC's taxonomies and the corresponding concepts in the solutions provided by the other programming-oriented groups thus just represent in a systematic and organized way the same information contained in the interface descriptions of the services (the WSDL). Semantic information is however nice to have, as piece of documentation which may indeed also be used for guidance and validation e.g. via model checking.

Contrary to the original expectation, fully declarative approaches appeared only in a second phase: in 2007–2008 two solutions automatically generated the workflow implemented in the orchestration by means of planning (METEOR-S [30]) or LTL-guided synthesis [19] (incorporated as plugin in our jABC solution [9, 24]). The technical difficulty here is to deal automatically with complex control flows that include data-controlled loops. Here, the algorithms indeed use a semantically enriched description of the services, more correctly of the service functionalities, in order to compose the orchestration of components/service invocations that solves the problem. The solutions therefore require

- A goal that describes abstractly the desired product,
- Some implementations of the mediator's functionalities (we reused here the basic elements already implemented in our first approach) and
- Sufficient information on those functionalities and on the external services to steer the synthesis algorithm to produce a suitable composition for that goal.

Surprisingly, the Discovery scenario ended up containing orchestrations too: although the goal is the selection of the most adequate shipping service among a given selection, it turns out that not all the necessary information is provided statically by the shippers. Orchestration is necessary to request this information by invocation, or to negotiate e.g. pricing or delivery conditions. These ancillary orchestrations were addressed by the different groups with the same technical means used to solve the Mediation scenario.

In fact, it seems meanwhile very rare that any meaningful service-related problem can be solved in isolation: data or protocol mediation, interrogations prior to choice, or negotiation are always necessary, leading to an ubiquitous need for orchestration capabilities.

Both sets of orchestration solutions (explicit-style, as in the programmed or modeled approaches, or implicit-style, as in the synthesized approaches) directly depend on how we deal with the third aspect of complexity, the modeling of the application domain.

Domain Modelling

The organizers decided to not formalize the problems using any logical formalism, but rather to describe them using natural language documentation, in order to not influence (directly or indirectly) the freedom of choice of the participants by proposing any formalized reference description. As already observed in years of development of formal methods, a fair amount of the solution to a problems is its formal description, and having text based documentation as the only common specification is suboptimal: the availability of formal descriptions in the background could have improved the communication between the teams and with the testbed developers also in this case.

The semantical annotations adopted or introduced by the participating teams to adequately describe the application domain constitute the semantic modeling layer. They are the original primary target of the whole Challenge. The idea was to explore this way alternative annotations of functional and non-functional characteristics, to be taken into consideration by the mechanisms (automatic or not) that select adequate services during both mediation and discovery.

A popular model, mutated from the agent and AI communities, describes services in terms of inputs, outputs, preconditions, and effects (IOPE model). The issue here is what annotations can convey efficiently and understandably the notion of what the inputs and outputs really "mean" in the application domain, explicitating otherwise implicit or hidden knowledge. This is more than just the syntactic data type (like integer, string), and maybe also beyond the direct meaning often syntactically conveyed by the type names (like Volts, Address...).

- Preconditions can be attached both to the service and to single operations offered. They can accommodate assertion-style checks and also more vague context requirements.
- Effects can refer to a number of entities (internal state change, products and side effects, continuation in case one "consumes" some parts of a goal, and more), and are the model element with the biggest variance of interpretation and use in different approaches.

Strangely, the semantic annotation discussion is so far the aspect of the Challenge that made the least progress, and the one that shows the biggest spread and thus difficulty to compare.

- While several groups base on WSMO/WSML, which uses the IOPE model, and refer to huge pre-existing ontologies e.g. of time and geographic locations,
- Other approaches use simple self-contained taxonomies to express the few constraints really needed by the synthesis algorithms. Example which data must be available in order to be able to use a certain service operation, which is the (minimalistic and pragmatic, but self-contained and humanly understandable) approach used by both groups that provided a synthesis solution so far.

The synthesis approaches in fact need more refined information than the pure interfaces provided by the WSDL, therefore

- The METEOR solution uses SA-WSDL annotations and
- The jABC solution uses taxonomies of dataflow facts, of data types, and of operations expressed in a Datalog-like notation (a form of semantic triples) embeddable in Decision Logics.

All the discovery solutions need a finer characterization of the services than offered by the WSDL, for instance in order to deal with concrete values (price, pickup time, delivery location) and compare/rank the alternative solutions according to preference criteria. The reasoning behind these selections and ranking happens automatically, on the basis of the same semantic annotations and similar techniques as the the mediation scenario.

Coupling Complexities

Although the original goal of the SWS challenge was the evaluation of domain modeling approaches and languages, reified in two concrete scenarios that situated this modeling in a (pure) orchestration and in a (pure) matchmaking context, it turned out as just described that all three aspects deeply intermingle.

The normal case does not present three distinct and orthogonal dimensions at all: we are constantly facing issues of more or less complicated orchestrations in the presence of complex data, and in an application scenario with a blurred semantical definition. Therefore it is likely an illusion that a separate treatment of the individual facets of this trio is successful in practice. Rather, in order to be successful, proposals in one of these dimensions should continuously be evaluated in the light of the other two.

15.4.3 Conclusions and Future Work

Perhaps the very loose specification of the challenge's participation and evaluation criteria was both its major weakness and its major strength. It enlarged the potential audience, which is good for a new research direction in order not to suppress interesting solution. At the same time it made a comparison of the submitted solutions very difficult. The eventual decision to judge solutions on the basis of code reviews, which may look at first sight quite a flexible objective, unfortunately reflected only a very partial viewpoint. It did not consider how the code arose. In fact, structurally very different methods for generating equivalent solutions were not distinguished, and their merits concerning new synthesis and analysis methods with their specific degree of automation were not considered. This is very sad, because agility is one of the major promises of service-oriented methodologies and it cannot be achieved at the programming level. Rather it requires to leverage advanced generation technology to bridge between specifications and running code.

The decision to promote comparative contributions written in tandem by two participating teams in [33] may have been responsible for most of the impact of the SWS challenge, as it forced interaction, comparison of points of views, exchange of methods and technologies, as well as agreement of eventual formulation in the common publication. This was were most of the 'technology transfer' between the groups arose. One should keep this format in mind for future publications.

Structurally, the SWS treated three aspects separately, orchestration, matchmaking (discovery), and domain modeling. Even though focusing on these aspects separately was certainly a good decision for the start, during the challenge it turned out that these three aspects need to be considered in combination in order to obtain convincing solutions. This observation was the basis for the development of our loose programming paradigm, which leverages heterogeneous knowledge in terms of control flow skeletons, data flow information, ontologies, and goals specified in temporal logics [13]. The power of this approach could be already proved in the bioinformatics domain comprising ontologies with hundred of available (Web) services [13, 14]. For the future of the SWS Challenge this means that it would be important to explicitly take this issue into account, and to provide dedicated challenge scenarios, optimally with a concretized evaluation scheme.

We observed the power of a clear metric for challenges/competitions in the area of automata learning. Example the ZULU Challenge [37] provide a clear metric in terms of percentage of coverage by learned models, there simply measured relative to a huge test suite. This setup, although quite simple, motivated quite some research and let to surprising algorithmic advances [5]. For next year it is planned to refine the challenge scenario, perhaps in subdisciplines, in order to come closer to realistic application scenarios: abstraction will be addressed, as well as the treatment of automata carrying data. After its initial phase, the SWS challenge should perhaps move in a similar direction, by sketching dedicated challenge scenarios together with clear metrics that reflect progress. As for the automata learning challenges this requires of course an advanced experimentation environment comprising simulation and (quantitative) evaluation in order to provide competitors with a similar starting situation.

There is no doubt that the SWS Challenge triggered some important research, which otherwise would most probably have been delayed for quite some time. On the other hand it is also clear that its original format, which was adequate 4–5 years ago, has to be adapted to the current state of maturity. Clear standards should be established, tangible evaluation criteria should be applied, and also the technical backbone, the Challenge testbed, which often required code inspection to understand the provided functionality, should be improved. Otherwise the SWS initiative will be passed by the addressed research reality very soon.

15.5 Summary

We have addressed our XMDD (eXtreme Model Driven Design) approach to the development of large service-oriented applications and described how it was used to address the Semantic Web Services Challenge, which since 2006 aims at finding adequate domain modeling formalisms that help taming the complexity of service orchestration and service discovery.

Concretely, we provided a total of six solutions with different engines, methods, and profiles, most of which do not appear in the official SWS charts because the code-oriented criteria and methodology of the evaluation did not really fit the structure of the high-level approach taken by our groups. This observation has given rise to a series of discussions in the various committees about the principle of evaluation, which in the end led to three columns summarizing our work in the results table. Unfortunately this table does not reflect the fact that much of the technology needed to make automatic support of service evolution viable is already available today. Today's most advanced platforms might start introducing these concepts and technologies in real businesses, and this way realize the promise of a

Continuous Model-Driven Engineering approach [21]. This development is hardly visible from the low-level point of view taken by the SWS challenge evaluation, which consider service evolution as a matter of source code transformation rather than a matter of application model transformation. We are worried that this low level perspective, if continued, will prohibit the SWS challenge effort to leverage the real potential of the service methodology, which, in fact, is due to its power of virtualization. We therefore propose to explicitly address this potential in the future by posing a dedicated SWS scenario, supported by a high degree of virtualization, and aiming at a maximum of flexibility concerning service evolution exploiting in synergy orchestration, discovery, and domain modeling technology. Our experience with a related setting in the bioinformatics domain [12, 13] indicate that this may well revolutionize some of today's best practices in service engineering.

References

1. A. Efeoglu, *SAP Enterprise Service Workplace Handbook* (SAP, 2007)
2. E.A. Emerson, C.S. Jutla, A.P. Sistla, On model-checking for fragments of μ-calculus, in *Computer Aided Verification, 5th International Conference, CAV'93*, Elounda, Greece, June 28–July 1, 1993
3. GEAR: game-based, easy and reverse model-checking, http://jabc.cs.uni-dortmund.de/gear/
4. K. Gomadan, A. Ranabahu, Z. Wu, A. Sheth, J. Miller, A declarative approach using SAWSDL and semantic templates towards process mediation, in *Semantic Web Services Challenge – Results From the First Year*, (Springer, Dordrecht, 2008), pp. 101–118
5. F. Howar, B. Steffen, M. Merten, From ZULU to RERS – lessons learned in the ZULU challenge, Prof. ISoLA 2010. LNCS, vol. 6415 (Springer, Heidelberg, 2010), pp. 687–704
6. http://labh-curien.univ-st-etienne.fr/zulu/
7. S. Jörges, C. Kubczak, R. Nagel, T. Margaria, B. Steffen, Model-driven development with jABC, in *HVC – IBM Haifa Verification Conference*, Haifa, 23–26 Oct 2006. LNCS, IBM, Springer, 2006
8. M. Kaiser, Towards the realization of policy-oriented enterprise management. IEEE Comput. **40**(11), 57–63 (2007)
9. C. Kubczak, T. Margaria, B. Steffen, S. Naujokat, Service-oriented mediation with jeti/jabc: verification and export, in *Workshop on Service Composition & SWS Challenge, Part of WI-IAT'07, the IEEE/WIC/ACM International Conference on Web Intelligence*, Stanford, Nov 2007, IEEE CS. ISBN-10: 0-7695-3028-1
10. C. Kubczak, T. Margaria, M. Kaiser, J. Lemcke, B. Knuth, On-the-fly synthesis of the mediator scenario with jABC and POEM, in *Proceedings of EON-SWSC2008, 6th International Workshop on Evaluation of Ontology-Based Tools and the Semantic Web Service Challenge, with ESWC 2008*, Tenerifa (E), 2008
11. C. Kubczak, T. Margaria, B. Steffen, R. Nagel, Service-oriented mediation with jABC/jETI, in *Semantic Web Services Challenge – Results from the First Year*, ed. by C. Petrie, T. Margaria, M. Zaremba, H. Lausen (Springer, Heidelberg, 2009), pp. 71–99. ISBN: 978-0-387-72495-9
12. A.-L. Lamprecht, T. Margaria, B. Steffen, Seven variations of an alignment workflow – an illustration of agile process design/management in bio-jeti, in *ISBRA 2008, 4th International Symposium on Bioinformatics Research and Applications*, Atlanta, May 2008. LNBioinformatics, LNCS, vol. 4983, Springer, 2008, pp. 445–456
13. A.-L. Lamprecht, S. Naujokat, T. Margaria, B. Steffen, Synthesis-based loose programming, in *Proceedings of 7th International Conference on the Quality of Information and Communications Technology (QUATIC)* (IEEE Computer Society, Washington, 2010)

14. A.-L. Lamprecht, S. Naujokat, T. Margaria, B. Steffen, Constraint-guided workflow composition based on the EDAM Ontology, in *Proceedings 3rd Workshop on Semantic Web Applications and Tools for Life Sciences (SWAT4LS 2010)*, Berlin, 10 Dec 2010
15. T. Margaria, Service is in the eyes of the beholder. IEEE Comput. **40**(11), 33–37 (2007)
16. T. Margaria, The semantic web services challenge: tackling complexity at the orchestration level, in *Proceedings of ICECCS'08, 13th IEEE International Conference on Engineering of Complex Computer Systems*, Belfast, Apr 2008, (invited talk)
17. T. Margaria, B. Steffen, From the how to the what, in *VSTTE: Verified Software – Theories, Tools, and Experiments, Proceedings of IFIP Working Conference*, Zurich, Oct 2005
18. T. Margaria, B. Steffen, Towards the realization of policy-oriented enterprise management. IEEE Comput. **40**(11), 57–63 (2007)
19. T. Margaria, B. Steffen, LTL guided planning: revisiting automatic tool composition, in *ETI Proceedings of SEW2007, 31st IEEE Annual Software Engineering Workshop*, Loyola College, Baltimore, (IEEE CS Press 2007)
20. T. Margaria, B. Steffen, Agile IT: thinking in user-centric models, *ISoLA'08, Proceedings of 3rd International Symposium on Lev-eraging Applications of Formal Methods, Verification, and Validation*, Chalkidiki, Springer, 2008, CCIS N. 017,
21. T. Margaria, B. Steffen, Continuous model-driven engineering. IEEE Comput. **42**(10), 106–109 (2009), http://doi.ieeecomputersociety.org/10.1109/MC.2009.315
22. T. Margaria, B. Steffen, Business process modelling in the jABC: the One-thing-approach, *Handbook of Research on Business Process Modeling*, ed. by J. Cardoso, W. van der Aalst (IGI Global, Information Science Reference, Hershey, 2009), pp. 1–26
23. T. Margaria, C. Kubczak, B. Steffen, Bio-jETI: a service integration, design, and provisioning platform for orchestrated bioinformatics processes, in *BioMed Central (BMC) Bioinformatics Supplement Dedicated to Network Tools and Applications in Biology 2007 Workshop (NETTAB 2007)*, vol. 9/4 (2007), http://www.biomedcentral.com/1471-2105/9?issue=S4
24. T. Margaria, M. Bakera, C. Kubczak, S. Naujokat, B. Steffen, Automatic generation of the SWS-challenge mediator with jABC/ABC, in *Semantic Web Services Challenge: Results from the First Year*, ed. by C. Petrie, T. Margaria, M. Zaremba, H. Lausen (Springer, Boston, 2009), pp. 119–138. ISBN: 978-0-387-72495-9
25. T. Margaria, D. Meyer, C. Kubczak, M. Isberner, B. Steffen, Synthesizing semantic web service compositions with jMosel and golog, in *Proceedings of ISWS 2009, International Semantic Web Conference*, Chantilly, Oct 2009. LNCS, vol. 5823, Springer, 2009, pp.392–407
26. T. Margaria, B. Steffen, C. Kubczak, Evolution support in heterogeneous service-oriented landscapes. J. Braz. Comput. Soc. **16**(1), 35–47 (2010), Springer
27. OSA: parlay, http://www.parlay.org.
28. SAP Enterprise Service Website, http://www.sdn.sap.com
29. Semantic Web Service Challenge Website, http://www.sws-challenge.org
30. K. Sivashanmugam, J. Miller, A. Sheth, K. Verma, Framework for semantic web process composition. Int. J. Electron. Commer. Winter **9**(2), 71–106 (2004–2005)
31. Special Session on SerComp & SWS Challenge 2007 Workshop, in *IEEE/WIC/ACM International Conference on Web Intelligence (WI 2007)*, Silicon Valley, 2007
32. B. Steffen, P. Narayan, Full lifecycle support for end-to-end processes. IEEE Comput. **40**(11), 64–73 (2007)
33. C. Petrie, T. Margaria, H. Lausen, M. Zaremba (eds.), *Semantic Web Services Challenge – Results From the First Year*, Springer, 2008, ISBN: 978–0–387–72495–9
34. Plan-jETI website, http://plan-jeti.cs.tu-dortmund.de/opencms/en/home/
35. Protege' Webpage, http://protege.stanford.edu/
36. WSMO Working Drafts Online Site, http://www.wsmo.org/TR/
37. ZULU Active Automata Learning Competition, http://labh-curien.univ-st-etienne.fr/zulu/

Chapter 16
Service Offer Discovery in the SWS Challenge Shipment Discovery Scenario

Maciej Zaremba, Tomas Vitvar, Raluca Zaharia, and Sami Bhiri

Abstract In this chapter we describe the experience of applying our Service Offer Discovery approach to the SWS Challenge discovery scenario. At the early stage of the SWS Challenge initiative we have discovered a gap between coarse-grained conceptual frameworks of WSMO or OWL-S and fine-grained modeling requirements for search requests and service descriptions arising at the level of realistic and complex discovery scenarios. Our observations and experience resulted in a number of extensions of the original WSMO model. Our discovery approach operates on fine-grained service offer descriptions dynamically created for individual service consumers. Descriptions of service offers contain fine-grained details of service capabilities which are often input and context dependent. In order to deal with input-dependence of service capability we introduce rules and data-fetching interfaces as part of service descriptions. We focus on the lesson learnt from applying our approach to the SWS Challenge discovery scenario. We compare our approach along different structural dimensions to other solutions to the same scenario, namely: jABC/miAamics, SWE-ET and DIANE.

16.1 Introduction

Service discovery is one of the core tasks in Service Oriented Architectures (SOA) [4]. Service discovery matches search requests (goals) with available service descriptions. However, service descriptions are often incomplete and underspecified [16] what hinders the discovery process. The majority of service discovery

M. Zaremba (✉) · R. Zaharia · S. Bhiri
Digital Enterprise Research Institute, National University of Ireland, Galway, Ireland
e-mail: Maciej.Zaremba@deri.ie; Raluca.Zaharia@deri.ie; Sami.Bhiri@deri.ie

T. Vitvar
Institute of Computer Science, University of Innsbruck, Innsbruck, Austria
e-mail: tomas.vitvar@uibk.ac.at

M.B. Blake et al. (eds.), *Semantic Web Services*, DOI 10.1007/978-3-642-28735-0_16,
© Springer-Verlag Berlin Heidelberg 2012

approaches (e.g., [6, 12, 15]) operate on coarse-grained service descriptions which do not suffice for determining a service suitability for concrete needs of service consumers. A single service may provide a number of individual service offers dependent on inputs required from a service consumer. For example, a single shipping service provides a number of different shipping offers dependent on required shipping input details (e.g., the source and target locations, the package weight, dimension, etc.). Fine-grained details of service functionality (e.g., the shipping price or the package delivery time) which are highly relevant from a service consumer point of view are not present at the level of coarse-grained service descriptions.

In the current SOA world, search requests "discover a service that can ship a package of **30 lbs from New York, USA to Bristol, UK**, in the **maximum of two business days**, and with overall **cost below $120, the cheaper the better**" similar to the SWS Challenge discovery scenario goals[1] typically consist of two phases. First, a discovery engine *abstracts to a* service description suitable for a search of a shipping *service category*, and, in the second phase, a service consumer *manually checks on a finer level* if the resulting services can ship the given package and satisfy the constraints on the requested delivery time, the price and the location. Our service discovery approach focuses on phase two by supporting further automation in determining fine-grained and frequently changing details of service functionality which are currently determined manually.

Our Service Offer Discovery approach consists of: (1) goals descriptions which specify hard constraints, preferences and goal input parameters, (2) service descriptions with rules describing relationships between input and output parameters, (3) rule-based service interfaces for fetching dynamic parameters at discovery time, and (4) a discovery algorithm that utilizes all the above mentioned goal and service descriptions. We have implemented our model using the WSMO framework [18], and WSML ontology language [3] for modeling service and goal descriptions, and the WSMX execution middleware [20].

In the SWS Challenge discovery scenario, offers of shipping services depend on input parameters requested from service consumers. Our discovery approach addresses discovery of highly configurable services [11] such as the SWS Challenge shipping services, which are difficult to describe on the fine-grained level. We have evaluated our approach against a number of other service discovery approaches which address the same SWS Challenge discovery scenario.

16.2   Approach: Service Offer Discovery

Service descriptions are core artifacts used in the service discovery process. The quality of discovery results relies on the quality of the provided descriptions. Similar to [7, 11], and [16] we distinguish two types of service descriptions:

---

[1]http://sws-challenge.org/wiki/index.php/Scenario:_Shipment_Discovery

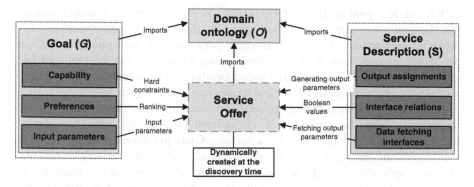

Fig. 16.1 Elements of conceptual model

(1) *coarse-grained abstract service descriptions* that represent service functionalities in terms of service category, execution effects, and types of input and outputs
parameters, and (2) *fine-grained service offer descriptions* that represent concrete
service offers created for an individual service consumer at the given point in time.
The majority of existing service discovery approaches operate on coarse-grained
abstract service descriptions, whereas our approach operates on dynamically created
fine-grained service offer descriptions.

Our service discovery approach is based on WSMO , which defines key elements
of Semantic Web services. However, as a purely conceptual framework, WSMO
does not prescribe how these elements should be utilized to address real world scenarios. We have found that there is a gap between coarse-grained WSMO definitions
and their applicability to solve problems arising in real world scenarios, such as the
SWS Challenge discovery scenario. In order to address requirements of the SWS
Challenge discovery scenario, we had to extend WSMO with dedicated elements
such as: *goal preferences, goal input parameters, service interface relations, service
output assignments* and *service data-fetching interfaces*.

The conceptual model of our approach contains: (1) a **domain ontology** O that
is a conceptualization of a domain, (2) a **goal** G that expresses service consumers'
needs, and (3) a **service description** S that represents the service functionality.
Figure 16.1 shows the elements of our conceptual model and the interplay between
them.

We use a **domain ontology** for the conceptualization which is shared between
goals and service descriptions. We define the ontology as $O = (C, R, E, I)$, where
the sets C, R, E, I in turn denote concepts (unary predicates), relations (binary
and higher-arity predicates), explicit instances (extensional definitions), and axioms
(intensional definition) which describe ontological rules. Input parameters P^I are
expected by a service, and output parameters P^O are provided by a service in
response to P^I. We denote a concept $P^I = \{p_1^I, \ldots, p_n^I\}$, $P^I \in C$ as a set of
input parameters, and a concept $P^O = \{p_1^O, \ldots, p_m^O\}$, $P^O \in C$ as a set of output
parameters, where $\{p^I\}$ and $\{p^O\}$ denote attributes of their respective concepts
(we call these parameters).

We define a **goal** as $G = (O, G_C, G_P, G_I)$, where O is the domain ontology that the goal references, G_C is a goal capability that specifies hard constraints, G_P are goal preferences, G_I are goal input parameters. **Goal capability** defines preconditions that must hold in a state before the service can be executed and effects that must hold in a state after the successful service execution. Preconditions and effects are defined using logical expressions with logical connectives such as conjunction, disjunction and negation. Preconditions and effects are evaluated respectively with the instances of P^I defined in the *goal input parameters*, and instances of P^O provided by a service. **Goal preferences** express service consumer's soft constraints that the discovery algorithm uses for service ranking. We use simple ordering criteria over input and output parameters, i.e., *LowerBetter* or *HigherBetter* constructs. Dynamically obtained output parameters such as *price* of *delivery* details can be used for ranking. **Goal input parameters** is a set of instance data that corresponds to input parameters defined in the domain ontology. We use the input data to create service offers on-the-fly during the discovery process.

We define a **service** as: $S = (O, R_A, R_I, X_f)$, where O is the domain ontology that the service references, R_A is a set of rules that define so called *output assignments*, R_I is a set of rules that define implementations of interface relations from O, and X_f is a data-fetching interface. The output assignments and data-fetching interface provide service values of output parameters during the discovery process and they allow domain experts to explicitly represent relationships between input parameters and output parameters. **Service output assignments** define sets of input parameters P^I and output parameters P^O and a rule body defined over a set of the output parameters. **Service interface relations** provide a boolean value under provided input parameters P^I. They are useful when sharing concepts and instances does not suffice to describe the service functionality. The abstract definition is part of the domain ontology and is shared between the goal and the service descriptions. The implementation of the interface relation is part of the service descriptions and defines service-specific implementation details. The **service data-fetching interface** is the public service interface, that is used during the discovery process to dynamically fetch output parameters. Not all dependencies between input and output parameters can be explicitly specified in service descriptions due to the dynamic character of service parameters, complexity of these dependencies, or business sensitivity of these dependencies. In such cases, output parameters P^O must be generated in the service provider's back-end system. Each rule in the data-fetching interface is a logical expression that must hold in a state before the service call can be performed.

In the discovery process we create service offer descriptions by augmenting service descriptions with values of service parameters generated on-the-fly. We execute service declarative parts (*service output assignments* and *service interface relations*) under provided *goal input parameters* in order to create actual values of service offer parameters (e.g., shipping price). Values of service offer parameters can be also dynamically obtained by communicating with services using *data-fetching interfaces* under provided *goal input parameters*. We have described the design-time tasks, architecture and algorithms of the Service Offer Discovery, that operates on presented conceptual model, in [21, 22].

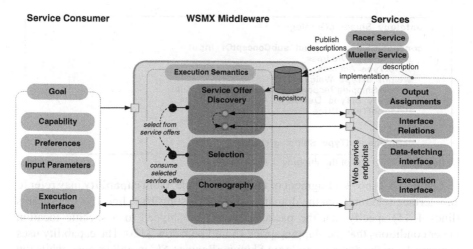

Fig. 16.2 Architecture of the service offer discovery approach to the SWS challenge discovery scenario

16.3   Solution: Service Discovery

Figure 16.2 presents the architecture of our solution in the context of the SWS Challenge discovery scenario. WSMX is used as a middleware to facilitate run-time discovery between service consumers and the SWS Challenge shipping services. The functionality of WSMX is defined using Execution Semantics. It can be customized to conform to particular integration needs through choosing and configuring appropriate middleware services. Semantic descriptions of services are provided and exposed in the Repository component. The following are the most relevant middleware services we use in the context of the SWS Challenge discovery scenario: (1) *Service Offer Discovery* – discovers services at a fine-grained offer level, (2) *Selection* – selects the most suitable service for the invocation, and (3) *Choreography Engine* – performs stateful invocation of the selected service.

The presented architecture operates on the conceptual model introduced in the previous section, with a domain ontology, goals and service descriptions. In this section we present the elements of our conceptual model (Listings 16.1–16.3) exemplified for the SWS Challenge discovery scenario.

Listing 16.1 shows a fragment of the **shipping domain ontology**. The input parameters are *ShippingRequest* = {*from, to, weight*}, and output parameters are *ShippingResponse* = {*price, delivery*}. Both shipping service descriptions and shipping goals use these input and output parameters. We distinguish the input and output parameters by the abstract concepts *Input* and *Output* respectively. The ontology also defines the *isShipped* interface relation (line 12). This relation is referred from goals and implemented in service descriptions.

```
 1    ontology ShippingOntology
 2
 3    concept ShippingRequest subConceptOf Input
 4      from ofType Address
 5      to ofType Address
 6      weight ofType Weight
 7    concept ShippingResponse subConceptOf Output
 8      delivery ofType Delivery
 9      price ofType Price
10
11    relation
12      isShipped(ofType ShippingRequest)
```

Listing 16.1 Fragment of the shipping domain ontology

Listing 16.2 shows a fragment of the **goal** example. **Goal capability** may refer to an interface relation from the domain ontology (Listing 16.1, line 12). Constraints (lines 4–11) specify that the package should be shipped to a specific location under conditions that the shipping price should be below \$120. The capability uses concepts from the domain ontology: *ShippingRequest*, *ShippingResponse*, while the logical expression *isShipped* (line 6) refers to the interface relation. Further, the *ShippingRequest* instance (lines 19–23), that *isShipped* uses, is part of the **goal input parameters**. Instance of the *ShippingResponse* is provided by the service during the discovery time.

Goal preferences (lines 13–15) define service consumers' preference for the lowest price and the fastest delivery and are specified as follows: *?price-LowerBetter*, *?delivery-LowerBetter*.

```
 1    Goal goalC3
 2    /* goal capability - logical hard constraints */
 3    capability goalC3Capability
 4      precondition goalC3Precondition definedBy
 5        (?request memberOf ShippingRequest and
 6        isShipped(?request)).
 7
 8      effect goalC3Effect definedBy
 9        (?resp[price hasValue ?price, delivery hasValue ?delivery]
10        memberOf ShippingResponse and ?price < 120).
11
12    /* goal preferences */
13    ontology goalC3Ranking
14    instance preference memberOf ranking#Preference
15      value hasValue "?price-LowerBetter, ?delivery-LowerBetter"
16
17    /* goal input parameters */
18    ontology goalC3InputParameters
19    instance shippingOrderReq1 memberOf ShippingRequest
20      from hasValue addressInUSA
21      to hasValue addressBristolInUK
22      weight hasValue 20.0
23      weightUnit hasValue units#LBS
```

Listing 16.2 An example of a shipping goal (Goal C3)

Listing 16.3 show a fragment of the **service description** of the SWS Challenge services. **Service output assignment** rule *shippingEuropeDef* (lines 2–9) produces a new instance of the *ShippingResponse* concept if the source, destination and weight constraints are satisfied. The shipping price formula is explicitly available in the service description (line 9). The price *price* is calculated as a fixed fee of $41 per package and $6.75 per each lb. *isShipped(ShippingRequest)* is an example of **service interface relation** (lines 12–15). It is declared in the domain ontology (see Listing 16.1, line 11–12) and *used* in the goal effect (see Listing 16.2, line 6). This relation specifies that the service only ships to Europe. **Service Data-fetching interface** (lines 18–24) describes how to obtain details of a shipping offer from the SWS Challenge Mueller service. The condition of the rule in lines 20–24 will be true if the service can ship to the specified addresses (determined through the *isShipped* interface relation), and the effect of the rule defines the *ShippingResponse* data that will be obtained from the service. Lines 18–19 show the grounding for *ShippingRequest* and *ShippingResponse* to the input and output messages of the Mueller service WSDL operation.

```
1    /* Output Assignment — price for Europe */
2    axiom shippingEuropeDef
3      definedBy
4        shippingToEurope [ price hasValue ?price ] memberOf ShippingResponse
5      impliedBy
6        ?req [ to hasValue ?to, weight hasValue ?weight ]
7        memberOf ShippingRequest and
8        isOnContinent (?to, Europe) and ?weight=<50 and
9        ?price = (( ?weight * 6.75) + 41).
10
11   /* Interface Relation — implementation of isShipped relation */
12   axiom isShippedDef
13     definedBy isShipped (?req) impliedBy
14       ?req [ to hasValue ?to ] memberOf ShippingRequest and
15       isOnContinent (?from, Europe).
16
17   /* Data-fetching interface */
18     in ShippingRequest withGrounding  _"http ://.../ muller . wsdl /..."
19     out ShippingResponse withGrounding _"http ://.../ muller . wsdl /..."
20     forall {?sReq} with (?sReq memberOf ShippingRequest and
21            isShipped (sReq))
22       do
23           add ( _# memberOf ShippingResponse )
24     endForall
```

Listing 16.3 An example of service description elements

16.4   Lessons Learned

In this section we compare our Service Offer Discovery [22] with other solutions to the SWS Challenge discovery scenario . We provide a qualitative evaluation by comparing different solutions on the same discovery scenario. We compare our Service Offer Discovery approach to **jABC/miAamics** [8], **SWE-ET** [19], **DIANE** [9]. In the following parts of this section, we describe and compare various aspects of the aforementioned approaches in a structured way according to the following criteria: data model, service description, goal description and discovery. We summarize our evaluation in Fig. 16.3.

Feature		jABC/miAamics	SWE-ET	DIANE	Service Offer Discovery
Data model	Expressivity	[-] limited expressivity of RDB model	[+] expressive logic-based formalism	[-] custom language (no well-defined semantics)	[+] expressive logic-based formalism
Service description	Handling input-dependent parameters	[-] only Boolean rules	[+] logical rules with arithmetic support	[-] no arithmetic support (external services are used)	[+] logical rules with arithmetic support
	Handling dynamic parameters	[-] pre-processing in orchestration	[-] unconditional data-fetching	[-] unconditional data-fetching	[+] conditional, rule-based data-fetching
Search request	Handling hard constraints	[-] not supported	[+] logical rules	[-] only on individual parameters	[+] logical rules
	Handling preferences	[-] only weighted rules		[-] only utility functions	[-] simple preferences
	Handling input parameters	[-] only fixed input data		[+] flexible input data	[-] only fixed input data
Discovery	Ranking	[-] limited ranking	[-] discrete ranking	[+] continuous ranking	[-] simple ranking

[+] advantage　　　　[-] disadvantage

Fig. 16.3 Evaluation summary

16.4.1　Overview of Other Approaches

jABC/miAamics combines a model-driven design approach using the jABC orchestration engine with the miAamics discovery module. It performs service discovery as a part of service orchestration using jABC Service Logic Graph (SLG). jABC provides a user interface for specifying search requests and for preprocessing data before the miAamics discovery module can be invoked. miAamics acts as a rule-based matcher operating on a relational data model.

SWE-ET is a combination of two components, namely: (1) Glue for service discovery and (2) WebRatio for service invocation and mediation. Glue is based on the WSMO [18] conceptual model, however it does not use WSML but models WSMO elements in the F-Logic Flora-2[2] language. It has support for modeling constructs of a standard logic language such as concepts, instances, relations and rules. WSMO wgMediators are used in Glue for connecting goals with Web service descriptions. wgMediators contain a domain specific notion of matching and generic matching preferences.

DIANE　provides a service matching algorithm based on a *set matching* operation. Both service descriptions and service requests are specified in a custom DIANE Service Description (DSD) language. DSD is modeled in a tree structure as a fuzzy set of possible service effects. DIANE aims at finding service offers with optimal input and output parameters, according to expressive preferences of a service requester. A DSD goal is specified as a fuzzy set of parameters' values with numerical preferences over acceptable service effects.

---

[2]http://flora.sourceforge.net

16.4.2   Evaluation Results

Data Model Expressivity

Service Offer Discovery and SWE-ET utilize ontological relationships and rules that go beyond the concept and attribute modeling offered by DIANE and jABC/mi-Aamics. Both SWE-ET and Service Offer Discovery can benefit from standard reasoning due to use of logic languages. DIANE has a graphical, tree-structured notation used for describing goals and service offers. DIANE Elements have no well-defined semantics, in contrast to the Datalog semantics used by Service Offer Discovery. The expressivity of DIANE Elements can be characterized as a subset of F-Logic without rules and quantifiers [9].

Service Descriptions: Handling Input-Dependent Parameters

jABC/miAamics supports only simple Boolean *if ... then ...* rules over database attributes without support for more complex rules, resulting in a limited support for modeling service dependencies on input parameters. Similar to Service Offer Discovery, SWE-ET also supports arithmetic calculations and rules which help in modeling service's dependency on input parameters. In contrast to Service Offer Discovery and SWE-ET, DIANE has no support for rules and arithmetic calculations. In the case of DIANE, it is necessary to create and use external services for arithmetic operations (e.g., calculate the price). Service Offer Discovery models service descriptions as a combinations of input-dependent rules (output assignments and interface relations) and data-fetching interfaces over service input and output parameters.

Service Descriptions: Handling Dynamic Parameters

In Service Offer Discovery, a data-fetching operation will only be triggered if the required input data conditions are satisfied. This is in contrast to the unconditional data-fetching performed by jABC/miAamics, SWE-ET and DIANE. In Service Offer Discovery, data-fetching operations are invoked only if a service is able to handle a given request following the rules specified in a choreography. For example, the price and the delivery information will be obtained only if the source, destination and weight constraints are satisfied.

Search Requests: Handling Hard Constraints

Hard constraints are not directly supported in jABC/miAamics matching module. However, higher weights can be assigned to the rules, such that they are unlikely to be overruled by lower-weighted rules. Hard constraints can be introduced in jABC orchestration. In SWE-ET, hard constraints are imposed as logical constraints in the goal capability, similar to Service Offer Discovery. In DIANE, hard constraints can only be modeled over single parameter (e.g., *price* < 100), while in Service Offer Discovery, hard constraints can be modeled over combinations of parameters (e.g., *price/weight* < 12), making it more powerful than hard constraints modeling supported by DIANE. A DIANE goal has to follow the same structure as a matching service structure. In the case of Service Offer Discovery, goals and service descriptions should refer to the same service input and output parameters, but do not need to have the same structure. Service Offer Discovery and DIANE approaches support hard constraints and preferences.

Search Requests: Handling Preferences

Both jABC/miAamics and SWE-ET, use only weighted rules for modeling preferences. Weighted rules are evaluated against a service and depending on a rule evaluation result, a weight (possibly negative) is assigned. Matching algorithm sums up assigned weights and ranks matched services according to the accumulated weights. However, it is not possible to apply linearly increasing or decreasing preferences over service parameters, in contrast to the min/max mechanism offered by DIANE. Multi-attribute preferences can be expressed using DIANE's *connective strategies*. Connective strategies can be specified as an additive function of weighted parameters. Multi-attribute preferences can be expressed using DIANE's *connective strategies*. Connective strategies can be specified as an additive function of weighted parameters. Service Offer Discovery used in the SWS Challenge uses a simple preference modeling where service offers can be ranked following values bound to input and output parameters.

Search Requests: Handling Input Parameters

Input parameters in DIANE can be specified as ranges or enumerations. SWE-ET, jABC/miAamics and Service Offer Discovery do not allow service consumers to specify flexible input data. Elements of DIANE's goals can be specified as ranges or as enumerations over service parameters.

Discovery: Ranking

jABC/miAamics calculates the discovery results by evaluating all the rules of a search request. Results are ranked by the accumulated weight of the matching service offers. In SWE-ET, depending on which rules in wgMediatiors are satisfied, a different discrete value indicating the matching level is returned. Generic preferences in wgMediators are disadvantageous, since different service consumers may have different preferences. DIANE support preferences over continuous parameters. Service Offer Discovery uses simple preferences to rank dynamically created service offers.

16.4.3   Advantages and Disadvantages

In this section we present advantages and disadvantages of our Service Offer Discovery in the context of the SWS Challenge Discovery.

Advantages

Sound conceptual model for the discovery of service offers. Our conceptual model is particularly suited for handling highly configurable services [11]. Our approach deals with scenarios where all possible offers of a service cannot be statically enumerated in the service description due to the considerable number of possible offers. Service offers are created on-the-fly by utilizing *goal input parameters* provided by service consumers. We proposed using interface relations, output assignments and data-fetching interfaces for describing services, and showed that they bring significant benefits to the discovery process. Our discovery operates on fine-grained service offers, in contrast to service discovery approaches operating on abstract service descriptions.

Fulfillment of the SWS Challenge evaluation criteria. Our approach satisfied multiple problem levels.[3] We have been able to deal with service dynamism, by using data-fetching interfaces, and with service input-dependence, by introducing output assignments and input dependent rules. Our approach supports modeling hard preferences as well as simple preferences, which contributed to fulfillment of SWS Challenge evaluation criteria (e.g., discovery based on destination, weight and price, requiring also an interaction with a service during discovery time).

Disadvantages

Difficulty with semantic modeling of goals and services. Our approach has been applied by ourselves to the SWS Challenge Scenario and we have not investigated the ease of use of our approach from the perspective of a typical user. Using our approach requires background knowledge in logics and ontology development. These skills are not yet common with typical software developers and therefore a special training would have to be provided first. Describing services and goals using Logic Programming or Description Logics based languages is a challenging task for an average user, as it requires detailed knowledge of the underlying logical formalisms. A library of reusable templates of service descriptions and goals created for different domains should reduce problems due to the lack of experience with logical languages. Web interfaces can greatly help inexperienced users to formalize their search requests into the required set of constraints and preferences.

---

[3]http://sws-challenge.org/wiki/index.php/Workshop_Innsbruck

16.4.4 Conclusions and Future Work

SWS Challenge gave us an opportunity and a testbed to validate our discovery approach. Thanks to SWS Challenge we were able to identify weaknesses and advantages of our approach and to work on extensions of our approach in order to satisfy SWS Challenge evaluation criteria. We were able to compare our approach to other semantic solutions to SWS Challenge within the same set of problems. Our discovery approach encompasses the practical experience we have gained applying semantics to realistic discovery scenarios. We have found that there is a gap between coarse-grained elements of WSMO and OWL-S [14] conceptual models, and their applicability to solve problems arising in realistic service discovery scenarios. In order to address the SWS Challenge discovery scenario, we had to extend WSMO with new conceptual elements.

We have observed that there was a very limited exchange of created artifacts (e.g., service descriptions, ontologies) among SWS Challenge participants. Every team used their own formalism for modeling ontologies, search requests and service descriptions, which considerably hindered exchange of these artifacts. The Semantic Web and its more lightweight version, Linked Data [1], are becoming more mature, and the use of Linked Data standards such as RDF [13], RDFS [2] and SPARQL [17] should have a significant impact on improving artefact reuse among the SWS Challenge participants.

For future work, we plan the following activities:

- **Changing the underlying formalism to Linked Data standards.** We have started to move our conceptual model to Linked Data standards. Domain ontologies can be expressed using RDFS, while parts of search requests and service descriptions can be expressed using SPARQL. Using Linked Data standards should significantly improve adoption of our conceptual model and promote reuse of created artifacts (domain ontologies, search requests and service descriptions).
- **Increasing expressivity of preferences.** To address the SWS Challenge discovery scenario, we have used simple preferences, however our approach can be easily extended with more complex preferences. We propose to use a combination of utility functions [5] and weighted rules [10] that provides more expressive preference modeling mechanism. It would allow service consumers to better express their flexibility in terms of what is more relevant for their requests. Utility functions are suitable for expressing min/max criteria over service parameters, whereas weighted rules are suitable for expressing various logical conditions over service parameters.
- **Flexibility in expressing input parameters.** To address the SWS Challenge discovery scenario we have used fixed goal input parameters. We plan to extend goal input parameters with a more flexible specification defined in terms of *enumerations* and *ranges*, which will bring much more flexibility into the service discovery process because flexibility in specifying input parameters results in a larger number of possible service offers.

The participation in the SWS Challenge and the evaluation activities were beneficial for us since it showed some weak points of our discovery approach. We have also discovered interesting future directions pointed out in terms of the second (*increasing expressivity of preferences*) and the third bullet points (*flexibility in expressing input parameters*) of the future work.

16.5   Summary

This chapter presented the Service Offer Discovery approach, its conceptual model, its application to the SWS Challenge discovery scenario and qualitative evaluation with respect to other solutions to the same scenario. We have focuses on the lessons learnt during the process of solving the SWS Challenge discovery scenario.

In this chapter we presented a conceptual model and architecture for our Service Offer Discovery. Our major contributions include: (1) modeling of goals descriptions that specify hard constraints, simple preferences and input parameters, (2) modeling of service descriptions with rules describing relationships between service input and output parameters, (3) modeling of rule-based service interfaces for fetching dynamic output parameters at discovery time, and (4) discovery algorithm that utilizes all above mentioned goal and service descriptions.

Our work addresses *service offer* discovery in contrast to *abstract service* discovery addressed by the majority of industry and research works [6, 12, 15]. From the point of view of service consumers, discovery that operates on fine-grained service offer descriptions created on-the-fly is far more beneficial than discovery of coarse-grained abstract services. While abstract service descriptions require further, often manual examination, our approach can verify on service offers descriptions whether the concrete needs of service consumers are satisfied.

Acknowledgements This work is supported by the Science Foundation Ireland under Grant No. SFI/08/CE/I1380 (Lion-2).

References

1. C. Bizer, T. Heath, T. Berners-Lee, Linked data – the story so far. Int. J. Semant. Web Inf. Syst. **5**(3), 1–22 (2009)
2. D. Brickley, R.V. Guha, RDF vocabulary description language 1.0: RDF schema. W3C Recommendation (2004)
3. J. de Bruijn, H. Lausen, A. Polleres, D. Fensel, The web service modeling language WSML: an overview, in *European Semantic Web Conference (ESWC)*, Budva, 2006
4. T. Erl, *SOA Principles of Service Design* (Prentice Hall PTR, Upper Saddle River, 2007)
5. R.L. Keeney, H. Raiffa, *Decisions with Mulitple Objectives: Preferences and Value Tradeoffs* (Cambridge University Press, Cambridge, 1999)
6. U. Keller, H. Lausen, M. Stollberg, On the semantics of functional descriptions of web services, in *European Semantic Web Conference (ESWC)*, Budva, 2006

7. J. J. Kopecký, E. Simperl, D. Fensel, Semantic web service offer discovery, in *Workshop on Service Matchmaking and Resource Retrieval in the Semantic Web (SMR2) Co-located with Internation Conference on Semantic Web (ISWC)*, Busan, 2007

8. C. Kubczak, T. Margaria, B. Steffen, C. Winkler, H. Hungar, An approach to discovery with miAamics and jABC, in *Semantic Web Services Challenge*, ed. by C. Petrie, H. Lausen, M. Zaremba (Springer, New York, 2008) pp. 217–234

9. U. Küster, B. König-Ries, Semantic service discovery with DIANE service descriptions, in *Semantic Web Services Challenge*, ed. by C. Petrie, H. Lausen, M. Zaremba (Springer, New York, 2008), pp. 199–216

10. U. Küster, B. König-Ries, T. Margaria, B. Steffen, Comparison: handling preferences with DIANE and miAamics, in *Semantic Web Services Challenge*, ed. by C. Petrie, H. Lausen, M. Zaremba (Springer, New York, 2008), pp. 217–234

11. S. Lamparter, A. Ankolekar, R. Studer, S. Grimm, Preference-based selection of highly configurable web services, in *World Wide Web Conference (WWW)*, Banff, 2007

12. L. Li, I. Horrocks, A software framework for matchmaking based on semantic web, in *World Wide Web Conference (WWW)*, Budapest, 2003

13. F. Manola, E. Miller, RDF Primer. W3C Recommendation (2004)

14. D.L. Martin, M.H. Burstein, D.V. McDermott, S.A. McIlraith, et al., Bringing Semantics to Web Services with OWL-S. World Wide Web **10**, 243–277 (2007)

15. M. Paolucci, T. Kawamura, T.R. Payne, K.P. Sycara, Semantic matching of web services capabilities, in *International Semantic Web Conference (ISWC)*, Sardinia, 2002

16. C. Preist, A conceptual architecture for semantic web services, in *International Semantic Web Conference (ISWC)*, Hiroshima, 2004

17. E. Prud'hommeaux, A. Seaborne, SPARQL query language for RDF. W3C Recommendation (2008)

18. D. Roman, U. Keller, H. Lausen, J. de Bruijn, et al., Web service modeling ontology. Appl. Ontol. IOS Press, **1**, 77–106 (2005)

19. A. Turati, E. Della Valle, D. Cerizza, F.M. Facca, Using glue to solve the discovery scenarios of the SWS-challenge, in *Semantic Web Services Challenge*, ed. by C. Petrie, H. Lausen, M. Zaremba (Springer, New York, 2008), pp. 185–197

20. T. Vitvar, A. Mocan, M. Kerrigan, M. Zaremba, M. Zaremba, M. Moran, et al., Semantically-enabled service oriented architecture: concepts, technology and application. Serv. Oriented Comput. Appl. **1**(2), 129–154 (2007)

21. M. Zaremba, T. Vitvar, M. Moran, Towards optimized data fetching for service discovery, in *European Conference on Web Services (ECOWS)*, Halle, 2007

22. M. Zaremba, M. Moran, T. Vitvar, Instance-based service discovery with WSMO/WSML and WSMX, in *Semantic Web Services Challenge*, ed. by C. Petrie, H. Lausen, M. Zaremba (Springer, New York, 2008), pp. 169–183

Chapter 17
A Solution to the Logistics Management Scenario with the Glue2 Web Service Discovery Engine

Alessio Carenini, Dario Cerizza, Marco Comerio, Emanuele Della Valle,
Flavio De Paoli, Matteo Palmonari, Luca Panziera, and Andrea Turati

Abstract In this chapter, we describe a solution to the Logistics Management Scenario based on the Web service discovery engine Glue2, which provides support for both functional and non functional discovery components. The solution addresses the two main aspects this scenario focuses on: (a) the radically different perspectives adopted by the final users to describe their goals and the service providers to describe the services; (b) the evaluation of soft constraints to rank a set of Web services that satisfy the hard constraints expressed in the goal. The solution is based on an extension of the WSMO conceptual model that (1) manages classes and instances of services and goals in a different way, and (2) supports a richer specification of the services' non functional properties in Web Service and Goal descriptions. The point (a) is solved by adopting a rule-based mediator-centric approach. The point (b) is solved by modeling some properties of the services and the soft constraints in the goals as Non Functional Properties adopting the Policy-Centered Meta-model (PCM); there properties are used by a Glue2 ranking component to rank the set of discovered services.

17.1 Introduction

A key problem to address in a Service Oriented Architecture (SOA) is supporting requesters to dynamically engage with (previously unknown) providers [1]. A requester is only supposed to know the functional criteria of the Web service

A. Carenini (✉) · D. Cerizza · E.D. Valle · A. Turati
CEFRIEL – Politecnico di Milano, via Fucini 2, 20133, Milano, Italy
e-mail: carenini@cefriel.it; cerizza@cefriel.it; dellavalle@cefriel.it; turati@cefriel.it

M. Comerio · F. De Paoli · M. Palmonari · L. Panziera
University of Milano – Bicocca, viale Sarca 336, 20126, Milano, Italy
e-mail: comerio@disco.unimib.it; depaoli@disco.unimib.it; palmonari@disco.unimib.it; panziera@disco.unimib.it

M.B. Blake et al. (eds.), *Semantic Web Services*, DOI 10.1007/978-3-642-28735-0_17,   263
© Springer-Verlag Berlin Heidelberg 2012

it wishes to interact with and it can find out suitable candidate services by inquiring a *discovery agency*. So the discovery agency decouples requester from providers. Quite often, decisions taken outside the organizational border involve complex negotiations on the base of different view points. We prefer to refer to such different view points with the notion of "polarization". In case there is "polarization", it is very difficult to agree on using a common terminology. For example, UDDI and ebXML, being syntactic, are very difficult to deploy in presence of polarization.

Our research on Web Service discovery lead us to believe that *semantics* is a key ingredient in handling polarization. Different *Ontologies* can be used to capture different points of views and *rules* can be used to encode domain-specific matching criteria. By using rules to mediate between different ontologies, the results of the Web Service discovery process can be more accurate; but more significantly, polarization can be handled by relaxing the unrealistic requirement that service requesters and service providers commit to a common ontology. We conceived as well as implemented such idea in a Web Service discovery engine named Glue2 [3].

The Logistics Management Scenario (LMS) has been recently introduced in the Semantic Web Service Challenge. The scenario provides a benchmark for discovery engines, involving important issues that need to be addressed by Web Service (WS) discovery technology to solve real world problems. The scenario focuses on two main issues. First, service providers (providers for short) and service requesters (requesters) often belong to different communities and have semantically heterogeneous perspectives when they describe their services or describe their requests. In the LMS, these problems are captured in the formulation of hard constraints in the goals' descriptions. Second, several services may match against a set of hard constraints specified in a request and a requester might want to express some preferences related to some service aspects. These preferences can be expressed as soft constraints that are used to select the best services among the set of services that satisfy the hard constraints. Soft constraints described in the LMS challenge WS discovery technology to provide techniques and tools to consider preferences expressed as soft constraints in the requests and to be able to rank services based on these preferences. Observe that soft constraints are often needed to codify preferences about the Quality of Service (QoS), or, more in general, about Non Functional Properties (NFPs).

In this chapter we present the only approach that has been officially evaluated in the Semantic Web Service Challenge by solving the LMS. However, a solution to this scenario based on another approach has been discussed in [5]. Among the problems addressed in this approach is that it focuses only on the evaluation of soft constraints; moreover, the experimental evaluation of the approach is not clear as not enough details about the implementation are provided.

17.2 Approach: The Glue2 Discovery Engine

The approach adopted by Glue2 to semantic Web service matchmaking extends the WSMO [6] approach. From the WSMO meta-model, we borrow the base concepts of *Web Services, Goal* and *Mediator*. We extend the WSMO meta-model by adding Web Services and Goals classes and instances. In our extended meta-model, instances of *Goal Class* describe specific parametrized and pre-defined goals, whereas instances of *Goal Instance* describe the instantiation of a specific goal class. Similarly, we introduce the concept *Web Service Class*, whose instances are parametrized and pre-defined Web Service descriptions that can be instantiated by the provider into instances of the concept *Web Service Instance*.

The Glue conceptual model for discovery considers the whole discovery process divided in three subsequent phases: *Set-up time*, when ontologies, classes of Web Services description and Goal and mediators are developed and loaded into the system. *Publishing time*, when the instances of Web Services description are created and published into the system. *Discovery time*, when an instance of Goal is created and submitted to the system.

During *set-up time*, the system is initialized by modeling and loading all the necessary knowledge in a specific domain **D** to perform automatic service discovery. This knowledge includes domain ontologies, Web Service Classes, Goal Classes and the required mediators. As discussed in the introduction, given a specific domain **D**, it is natural that provider's point of view is reflected in a particular polarized **D⁺** domain understanding and, on the other hand, requester's point of view is reflected in a differently polarized **D⁻** domain understanding.

Instead of developing one ontology, we suggest following the activities shown in Fig. 17.1. The Semantic Web service expert (SWS Expert) is actor who is able to understand the semantic notation of the system. Domain ontologies for **D⁺** and **D⁻** are developed (integrating already available sources) during separated engineering processes that involve the SWS Expert and the domain experts. When the ontologies are ready, a provider representative and the SWS Expert define the class of Web Service **X** using the ontology for domain **D⁺**. Meanwhile, a requester representative and SWS Expert define the class **Y** of goals. According to this approach, the providers and the requesters do not need to commit to on common ontology (which is unrealistic in many cases), and the SWS Expert does not need to develop a complete mediator between all the conflicting ontologies (which is unnecessary when only a small portion of such ontologies is involved in the matching process).

This process generally requires to model the rules that describe various WSMO mediators. For instance, the domain-specific rules for solving terminology mismatches between the involved portion of ontology **D⁺** and ontology **D⁻** are implemented as an ontology-to-ontology mediator (ooMediator). A goal-to-goal mediator (ggMediator), or a web service-to-web-service mediator (wgMediator) can encode rules that can mediate between instances of a goal class (or WS class)**Y** and semantically equivalent instances of a goal class (or WS class) **X**. Finally a wgMediator can be used to implement the domain-specific rules for matching instances of goal class **X** with instances of Web Service class **X**.

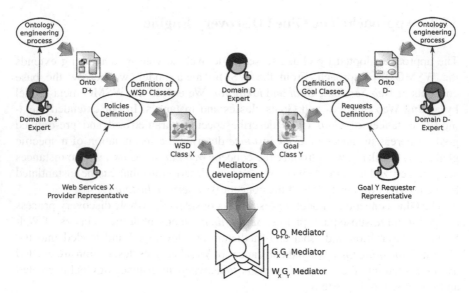

Fig. 17.1 The sequence of activities performed by actors at set-up time

At *publishing time*, providers publish instances of Web Service class simply by referring to the correct class of Web Service class and providing values to all the necessary parameters. The system creates the instances and register them in its internal repository in order to retrieve them when a wgMediator will require it.

Finally, *at discovery time*, when a goal instance is created and submitted, Glue uses a composite discovery procedure where the discovery of the appropriate mediators and the discovery of the appropriate services is combined. First ggMediators translate the users' goals in a goals expressed in the point of view of the provider, thus neutralizing polarization. Then, the domain specific notion of matching encoded as rules in the wgMediators can be used to match the translated goals against the instances of Web Service.

17.3   Solution: Glue2 Architecture and Execution Semantics

Figure 17.2 shows the architecture of Glue2 , which allows users both to publish their meta-model entities and to perform discovery through the submission of a Goal instance. The architecture takes advantages from the conceptual model of Glue2 to implement discovery tasks efficiently.

The **Resource Manager** is responsible to manage files describing entities like Web Service class, mediators and others, and store them in the internal Repository, so that they can be used by the discovery engine.

The **Execution Semantics** is the orchestrator of the discovery process that can be programmed to implement different discovery logics. One possible execution

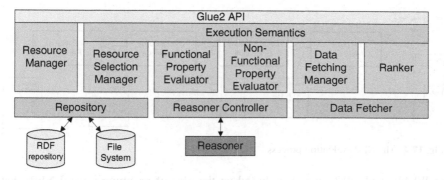

Fig. 17.2 The architecture of Glue2

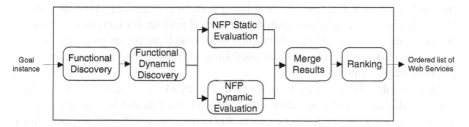

Fig. 17.3 NFP-based SWS discovery process

semantics could be the one depicted in Fig. 17.3, which includes the basic phases of the NFP-based Semantic Web Service discovery process.

The process starts with a user who creates and submit a Goal instance describing the functional and non-functional properties of the service she/he is looking for. The first action carried out by the Execution Semantics is the *Functional Discovery* to identify the Web Service instances that satisfy the functional properties described in the Goal instance. To do this, the Execution Semantics invokes the Resource Selection Manager and then the Functional Property Evaluator.

The next step is the invocation of the **Functional Property Evaluator**, which implements the core of the mediator-centric discovery process and discover the services that satisfy the hard constraints. Indeed, it compares the functional properties of all Web Service instances with the Goal instance by using the rules coded in the wgMediator. It extracts all the ontologies included in entities provided by the RSM, and feeds the Reasoner Controller with it. The Functional Property Evaluator finally extracts from the wgMediator the query that has to be submitted in order to trigger the rule checking the functional properties. This way, the Functional Property Evaluator gets a list of Web Service instances that satisfy all the rules of the wgMediator and match the functional properties of the Goal instance consequently.

The Non Functional Property Evaluator and the Ranker support the evaluation of soft constraints and rank the services consequently. In our approach, the service features that are considered in the user preferences and are modeled as soft constraint in the LMS, are represented by NFPs defined according to the Policy-Centered Meta-model (PCM) [4]. PCM is an expressive meta-model represented

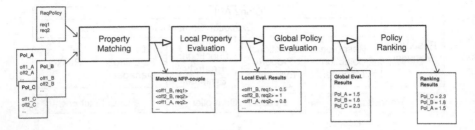

Fig. 17.4 The NFP evaluation process

in WSML and OWL, which is based on the idea of grouping several NFPs that are available under a same applicability condition (e.g. if the requester is a regular customer, he gets a discount on the price of a shipment service). According to the PCM, each service can be associated with several policies (in fact, several policies are associated with the services from the LMS), which are the elements that appear in the final ranking (e.g. two policies associated with a same service can occupy two positions of the ranking).

More in details, a *Policy* is defined in the PCM as a cluster of *PolicyNfps* (i.e., the offered NFPs) associated with a Web service that can be characterized by a *policyCondition* (i.e., a logical element that defines the conditions for the validity of the policy). A *RequestedPolicy* is a cluster of *Requests* (i.e., the requested NFPs) associated with a Goal where each *Request* states what values are acceptable for a certain property, and expresses the *relevance* of the property for the user.

Discovered services with their *Policies*, ooMediators and the Goal instance with its *RequestedPolicy* are inputs of both the *NFP Static Evaluation* and *NFP Dynamic Evaluation* phases (implemented by the **Non-Functional Property Evaluator**). These phases are in charge of evaluating the matching rules defined by ooMediators and computing the matching degree of pairs *<Request, PolicyNfp>*. The NFP Evaluation process is composed of four steps (see Fig. 17.4):

- **Property matching phase**: identifies the *PolicyNfp*s in the offered *Policies* that match with the *Requests* in the *RequestedPolicy*. The matching is performed using the matching rules stored in ooMediators. Such rules produce a result table such as the one depicted in Table 17.1 providing all the information needed for the next phases.
- **Local property evaluation phase**: for each identified *Request/PolicyNfp* couple, evaluates a *local satisfaction degree* (LSD) stating how the offered property satisfies the requested one. For details about local evaluation the reader can refer to [2].
- **Global policy evaluation phase**: for each policy, evaluates the results of the previous phase to compute a *global satisfaction degree* (GSD). An example of GSD formulas is the weighted sum where weights are the relevance that requesters have assigned to each requested NFP.
- **Policy ranking phase**: *Policies* are ranked according to their global satisfaction degree.

Table 17.1 A fragment of the table displaying the matching phase results for two *requests*

	Policy/Req Policy	hasNFP	hasOperator	hasParameter	hasUnit	has Relevance
Request:	reqInstance	reqHoursToDelivery	lessThan	48	hours	0.6
	PolicyInst4	offHoursToDelivery	interval	24, 48	hours	-
Offers:	PolicyInst3	offDeliveryTime	equal	48	hours	-
	...	...	...	...	...	-
Request:	reqInstance	reqPaymentMethod	exact	carriagePaid	null	0.7
	PolicyInst4	offPaymentMethod	exact	carriagePaid	null	-
Offers:	PolicyInst3	offPaymentMethod	exact	carriageForward	null	-
	...	...	...	...	...	-

17.4   Lessons Learned

We provide some examples about the way in which our technology is concretely applied to solve the LMS scenario. These examples are aimed to make the discussion about the lessons learned from the experience in the SWS challenge more effective.

Several ontologies have been developed to solve the scenario; an overview of such ontologies organized in terms of Glue2 meta-model objects, is shown in Fig. 17.5. The two main ontologies, imported respectively by the *Logistic Operator WS Class* and by the *Goal Class Transport Order* are the *Logistic Operator Ontology* and the *Transport Order Ontologies*. These two ontologies define the basic concepts and relations used by the service providers and by the requests. The other ontologies reported in figure deal with three different aspects involved in the logistic scenario: time, space and goods. *DateTime* ontology models concepts about defining time intervals and contains the axioms required to confront times and time intervals, whereas *Locations, Cities* and *Countries* ontologies deal with the definition of geographical locations. The remaining ontologies model goods and the different existing laws that regulates goods transportation, namely ADR (Accord européen relatif au transport international des marchandises Dangereuses par Route) and ATP (Accord Transport Perishable).

17.4.1   Hard Constraints Evaluation

Goal A3 can be used to show an example about how hard constraints have been implemented in the Glue2 solution to the logistic management scenario, as it requires the enforcement of the ATP rules, which regulates storage temperature of perishable goods during a transport. The Goal Class and the Web Service class have different point of views, as the Goal deals with just products, while the Web Service deals with the ATP regulations that have to be taken into account while delivering the goods. The implementation of such regulations is managed in three different steps. In *ATP_Goods* ontology, each of the goods is characterized by a

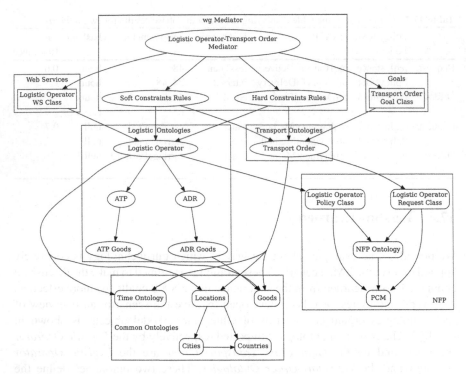

Fig. 17.5 Glue2 metamodel objects for the logistic scenario

minimum and a maximum storage temperature, while in *ATP* ontology, each storage class is characterized by a minimum and a maximum provided storage temperature. The first of the two axioms listed below then performs the matching between the temperatures required by the goods and the ones provided by the storage, characterizing the goods as requiring a particular storage type. Then, the fleet matching axiom already described checks whether a logistic operator has a truck to carry the provided goods. This particular implementation allows for a split between the customer's and the provider's point of views, as the former one just specifies the goods without knowing its storage temperature, and the latter specifies the features of his transport means without explicating which kind of goods he's able to carry.

```
1   axiom Goods_to_ATP_Category definedBy
2       ?g [goods#requires_storage hasValue ?v]:−
3       ?g [required_min_temp hasValue ?min, required_max_temp hasValue ?max] memberOf
            goods#Goods and
4       ?v [min_internal_temperature hasValue ?tmin, max_internal_temperature hasValue ?tmax]
            memberOf ?vc and
5       ?vc subConceptOf ATP_capable_storage and
6       ( ?min >= ?tmin ) and
7       (?max =< ?tmax ).
```

17.4.2   Soft Constraint Modeling

The first step to WS ranking consists of coding the soft constraints as NFPs defined according to the PCM. The soft constraints defined in each goal are coded as *Requests* and they are grouped into *RequestedPolicies*. As an example, the following listing shows the PCM-based WSML specification of the goal E1 *Insurance* soft constraint.

```
1   instance LORequestE1 memberOf pcm#RequestedPolicy
2       pcm#hasNfp hasValue requestedBasePrice
3       pcm#hasNfp hasValue requestedPaymentDeadline
4       pcm#hasNfp hasValue requestedInsurance
5       ...
6   instance requestedInsurance memberOf nfpo#InsuranceRequest
7       pcm#hasExpression hasValue requestedInsuranceExpression
8       pcm#hasRelevance hasValue 0.8
9   instance requestedInsuranceExpression memberOf nfpo#InsuranceExpression
10      pcm#hasOperator hasValue pcm#all
11      pcm#hasParameters hasValue {ins#refundForDamage,ins#refundForLoss}
```

The approach to evaluate the soft constraints is described in the Sect. 17.4.3.

The NFPs associated with the WS in the scenario are of two different types. *BasePrice*, *PriceForKm*, *PriceForKg* and *PaymentDeadline* are coded as quantitative *PolicyNfps*, instead *Insurance* and *PaymentMethod* are coded as qualitative *PolicyNfps*. Each WS of the scenario is associated with a *Policy* composed of the previous NFPs, except for WS1 and WS4 that are associated with two different policies, to express that two conditions hold on offered property. These conditions are coded as *policyConditions*. For example, the following listing shows an excerpt of the WSML PCM-based specification of WS4.

```
1    instance safePolicyA memberOf pcm#Policy
2        pcm#hasServiceReference hasValue "http://www.cefriel.it/logistic/operator/safe_transport#
             Safe_transport"
3        pcm#hasCondition hasValue policyCondition_safePolicyA
4
5        pcm#hasNfp hasValue offeredBasePriceA
6        ...
7    axiom policyConditionAxiom_safePolicyA
8        definedBy
9            pcm#satisfied(policyCondition_safePolicyA) :−
10               requestedShipments[nfpo#numberOfShipments hasValue ?n] memberOf nfpo#
                      Shipments
11               and(?n =< 5).
12       ...
13   instance offeredBasePriceA memberOf nfpo#BasePrice
14       pcm#hasExpression hasValue offeredBasePriceExpressionA
15   instance offeredBasePriceExpressionA memberOf nfpo#BasePriceExpression
16       pcm#hasOperator hasValue pcm#equal
17       pcm#hasParameter hasValue 170.0
18       pcm#hasUnit hasValue nfpo#euro
19       ...
```

17.4.3   Soft Constraints Evaluation

In order to evaluate the soft constraints coded as *RequestedPolicy* we adopt the NFP Evaluation processes described in Sect. 17.3.

Two different algorithmic techniques are exploited for evaluating couples of the form *<Request, PolicyNfp>* in the *local property evaluation phase*. The quantitative NFPs expressed by numerical values, are evaluated by specific mathematical functions; instead, the qualitative NFPs defined as instances of a domain ontology concept are evaluated with rules that tests the semantic equivalence between requested and offered values.

In the following, the solution for the two more relevant goals in the Scenario and the specific functions applied for the evaluation of the soft constraints are discussed. For the formal details about the whole set of functions designed in our approach for evaluating qualitative and quantitative properties the reader can refer to [7].

The former solution is related to Goal C1. The first soft constraint (*Payment-Method*) is coded as a qualitative *PolicyNfp*; the second constraint (*BasePrice*) is coded as a quantitative *PolicyNfp*. The *relevance* values are set to 0.8 for *PaymentMethod* and to 0.2 for *BasePrice*. This choice permits the requester to express the different levels of preference among the two constraints.

The local evaluation of *PaymentMethod* follows the same steps as for goal B1, while the computation of the *BasePrice* satisfaction degree is performed by using the following Gaussian function:

$$LSD = e^{-\frac{(r-o)^2}{r^2+1}},$$

where r is the requested value, o is the offered value and LSD is the local satisfaction degree.

The latter described solution is related to Goal D1. The *BasePrice* soft constraint, which state the preference for lower offered prices, is coded as a quantitative NFP by exploiting the *lessEqual* ($\leq\downarrow$) defined by the PCM, to express the operator $\leq$. Since the operator used in the *Request* is different respect to the one in goal C1 (i.e. close to, less equal) a different evaluation function is used:

$$LSD = \begin{cases} 1 - e^{-\frac{(r-o)^2}{r^2+1}} + \varepsilon & \text{if } r > o \\ 0 & \text{elsewhere} \end{cases},$$

where r is the requested value, o is the offered value and ε is the lesser non-negative floating point value that can be represented.

The LSDs obtained applying the above evaluation techniques are composed to compute the GSD applying a weighted sum (where weights are set as the relevance of the requests). Table 17.2 represents the sets of ranked policies returned by Glue2 for each goal of the scenario involving soft-constraints. Observe that according to this approach, Web Services associated with more than one policy occur in different positions in the rank.

Table 17.2 The ordered policies resulting from the soft constraints evaluation

Rank	Policy	WS	GSD	Rank	Policy	WS	GSD
	Goal B1				Goal C1		
#1	liteworldPolicyA	WS1	1.6	#1	helloPolicy	WS2	0.998
#1	liteworldPolicyB	WS1	1.6	#2	allAtHomePolicy	WS5	0.979
#2	allAtHomePolicy	WS5	0.8	#3	fast4UPolicy	WS6	0.195
#3	fandfPolicy	WS3	0	–	–	–	–
	Goal D1				Goal E1		
#1	safePolicyB	WS4	0.0141	#1	liteworldPolicyB	WS1	1.842
#2	gtlPolicy	WS7	0.0035	#2	fandfPolicy	WS3	1.390
#3	fast4UPolicy	WS6	$4.9 \cdot 10^{-324}$	#3	liteworldPolicyA	WS1	1.042
#4	safePolicyA	WS4	0	#4	gtlPolicy	WS7	0.541

17.4.4   Advantages and Disadvantages

The logistic scenario of the SWS Challenge proved that our approach based on Glue2 is able to deal with real world domains featuring complex domain rules and different points of view between service providers and requesters.

The polarization problem has been tackled by letting the actors define classes of Goals and of Web Services using radically different ontologies, and leaving the reconciliation to mediators written by domain experts. All the constraints specified in the Goals of the scenario can be represented by the model adopted by our engine; for all the test goals, the engine is therefore able to select the Web Service Instances that better match against the given constraints.

Moreover, the NFP evaluator module enables a parametric NFP-based ranking process, supporting the definition of custom mathematical functions for the *local property evaluation* and the *global policy evaluation* phases in order to be better adapted to specific domains. In fact, PCM allows the engine to perform the ranking process on NFP descriptions that can be grouped by applicability conditions, that are characterized by qualitative and quantitative values, and that make use of different constraint operators. Another relevant characteristic of our NFP evaluation approach is the possibility to perform the ranking process even when the descriptions present unspecified/missing values. This feature allows the requesters to obtain a complete list of the available *Policies* as results of the ranking process; this list includes also those *Policies* that do not specify some of the properties that are considered in the goal description, which is desirable when the missing NFPs are considered little relevant by the user.

The disadvantages of the Glue2 solution are mainly related to low flexibility and to the high effort required to model all the domain knowledge and entities.

A first drawback is related to the high level of precision and clarity that is required to design a solution for a given scenario. As constraints in Glue2 are expressed using logic, it is mandatory to have a sound and unambiguous domain description. The ontologies used by the various actors must not contain contradictions, and even if countermeasures can be put in place to prevent it, they must not assert false truths. This is a rather strong requirement, as it assumes a deep knowledge of both the principles of logic and the whole description of the scenario conceptualization. As a result, the learning curve for a new service provider is very steep, as a modeling error could lead to a failure of the whole discovery process. Therefore, the domain experts who take care of defining the service ontologies and the domain expert who maintain the mediators always have to work in close collaboration, as they have to ensure that the whole set of ontologies remains sound and consistent. Another aspect that limits the flexibility of a solution based on rich semantic models is the consensus that has to be reached while defining the conceptualization of the domain related to the scenario and the rules that the mediator applies at runtime.

The choice of modeling hard and soft constraints at design time is another cause of low flexibility. In fact, according to this approach, every requester must agree on the kind of properties that are considered functional (evaluated through hard constraints) and non functional (evaluated through soft constraints). The PCM does provide a partial solution to this problem, whereas a *Request* with relevance set to 1 actually models a hard constraint. Yet, *RequestedPolicies* modeling soft constraints of the goals are matched only against *Policies*. Being able to dynamically match soft constraints against the whole service descriptions, including functional specifications and policies would make the approach more flexible.

According to the above considerations we can conclude that the Glue2 approach is desirable when there is a large consensus over the domain conceptualizations (possibly more than one though until mediation rules are defined), the addressed problem, and the distinction between hard and soft constraints and the related properties. Instead, the high precision required in the modeling and matchmaking processes makes the approach not suitable for "emerging scenarios" resulting from the integration of independent and unrelated domains.

The performance of service discovery engines is not explicitly considered in the Semantic Web Service Challenge. Although we agree that the issues addressed by the challenge are very important, we believe that performance should deserve more consideration in the evaluation of semantic Web service technology. LMS provides goals with growing complexity involving both hard and soft constraints and can be used as a first benchmark for the Glue2 performances. The experiments have been carried out on an Intel Core2 CPU at 1.66 GHz with Linux 64-bit operating system. As shown in Fig. 17.6, we can notice that the overall time for completing a matchmaking process is between 30 and 50 s. The figure clearly shows that reasoning determines a major bottleneck for the discovery process.

One of the causes of the reasoning bottleneck is the WSML2Reasoner library adopted by Glue2 to manage the reasoner (KAON2 in our framework). The WSML2Reasoner library has been designed to offer WSML reasoning capabilities using different reasoning engines, but it does not provide a real storage solution with reasoning features. This means that there is no way of materialising the results of an inference process. A matchmaking scenario, in Glue2 terms, is composed of one Goal Instance, several Goal Classes, a wgMediator, and several Web Service Classes and Instances. All these entities are quite "stable" in time, with the exception of

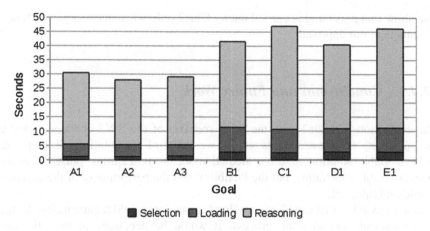

Fig. 17.6   Performance results of Glue2 with the LSM scenario

Table 17.3   Performance tests on NFP evaluation phase expressed in seconds

Goal	Loading	Matching	Local evaluation	Total time
B1	4.255	1.408	0.512	6.178
C1	4.333	1.393	0.262	5.988
D1	4.289	1.312	0.002	5.605
E1	4.413	1.481	0.743	6.639

the Goal Instance which is introduced at run-time. Automatic reasoning techniques based on forward-chaining algorithms can be applied to this more stable component of the knowledge base; in this way a large set of inferences can be precomputed and can be made available when a request is submitted to the engine. When the Goal Instance is submitted, a backward chaining could then be applied to activate the rules inside the wgMediator to return the final results. This solution would improve on the response time but cannot be implemented because of the limitations of the WSML2Reasoner library.

We also made further tests to analyze the NFP evaluation process. We decided to focus on the Property Matching and Local Property Evaluation phases because they make use of both semantic and algorithmic techniques. The *global policy evaluation* and the *policy ranking* were omitted because these phases are algorithmic only and are not significant in terms of performance. Table 17.3 shows the results for the two considered phases of the NFP evaluation process (for the Property Matching phase, which starts with loading the knowledge base, we analyze the loading and the matching time in two different columns). The first consideration is related to the time required to load the ontologies in the knowledge base. As showed in the second column, the time is similar for each goal because the ontologies are of similar size. Not surprisingly, reasoning is major cause of inefficiency also in the *local evaluation* phase. In fact, the local evaluation for goal D1, which considers only quantitative NFPs, requires few milliseconds since the reasoner is not used. However, the results also show that reasoning is carried out by Glue2 only when necessary, which is an advantage of our approach.

17.4.5   Conclusions and Future Work

The evaluation of Glue2 with the LSM scenario of the SWS challenge gave us the possibility to assess advantages and weakness of our solution. Glue2 proved to be a viable solution to solve mediation scenarios featuring polarization and expressive soft constraints, but the flexibility and the performance of the approach should be improved.

More flexibility in the evaluation of hard constraints would require major changes to the current matchmaking process. It would be necessary to treat the hard constraints contained in a Goal Class as a "restaurant menu" with multiple possible properties to choose from by describing a Goal Instance. In order to improve on this problem, we plan to define techniques to dynamic rewrite the wgMediator at run-time excluding the matching rules related to the constraints not expressed in the Goal Instance. In order to relax the rigid separation between functional and non functional descriptions of services; a new kind of mediator can be adopted to translate hard constraints to Requests and soft constraints to functional requirements.

Regarding performances, two possible improvements can be explored. The first one is pre-filtering the Web Service Classes that clearly don't match the rules in the wgMediator either at publishing time or during the selection of the services. The current implementation populates the set of entities required by a Goal Instance according to the declarations contained in the entities themselves. Filtering incomplete descriptions would diminish the number of Web Services Instances and their related ontologies, thus speeding up the evaluation process. A second improvement in performances could be achieved by modifying the reasoning step as described in Sect. 17.4.4, dividing the matchmaking process in two phases, one at publishing time with the materialisation of the partial reasoning (without the Goal Instance), and a second one activated by the user with the publishing of the Goal Instance. This could reduce the processing time perceived by the user, as the data obtained in the first step would be reused by multiple Goal Instances.

17.5   Summary

The Logistics Management Scenario addresses two main problems related to the discovery of Web services: (a) to overcome the semantic mismatches that arise when the points of view that requesters and providers have on a service domain are deeply different; (b) to evaluate requesters' preferences expressed by rich soft constraints in order to rank the discovered Web services. In this chapter, we describe how the

Web service discovery engine Glue2, which provides support for both functional and non functional discovery aspects, has been used to solve the scenario.

This solution is based on an extension of the WSMO conceptual model that (1) manages differently classes and instances of services and goals and (2) supports a richer specification of the services' non functional properties in Web Service and Goal descriptions. The point (a) is solved by adopting a rule-based mediator-centric semantic approach. The point (b) is solved by codifying some properties of the WSs, and the soft constraints in the goals as Non Functional Properties modeled according to the Policy-Centered Meta-model (PCM); a ranking component of Glue2 based on the PCM ranks the discovered services. The chapter presents the basic principles the Glue2 system is based on and its architecture. Moreover, the solution to the more relevant goals of the scenario is described, providing the reader with guidelines to solve the class of problems addressed by this scenario. All the constraints specified in the goals of the scenario can be represented by the model adopted by our engine; for all the goals, the engine is therefore able to select the Web Service Instances that better satisfy the set of constraints.

Glue2 is capable of mediating between mismatching perspectives between the final users and the service providers, e.g. when services are annotated using different ontologies. Moreover, the system handles expressive hard and soft constraint and is tolerant to underspecified service descriptions with respect to soft constraints required by the user. However, we also observe that the above functionalities come at the cost of a significant effort needed to design the SWS descriptions and the mediation rules. We also discuss the performance of the system, and some possible improvements that can be achieved by optimizing the exploitation of reasoner.

References

1. D. Booth, H. Haas, F. McCabe, E. Newcomer, M. Champion, C. Ferris, D. Orchard, Web services architecture. Technical report, W3C, 2004
2. M. Comerio, F. DePaoli, A. Maurino, M. Palmonari, Nfp-aware semantic web services selection, in *Proceedings of the Enterprise Computing Conference (EDOC)*, Annapolis, 2007
3. E. Della Valle, D. Cerizza, The mediators centric approach to automatic web service discovery of glue, in *MEDIATE2005, CEUR Workshop Proceedings*, CEUR-WS.org, vol. 168, Amsterdam, 2005, pp. 35–50
4. F. De Paoli, M. Palmonari, M. Comerio, A. Maurino, A meta-model for non functional property descriptions of web services, in *Proceedings of the IEEE International Conference on Web Services (ICWS)*, Beijing, 2008
5. J. Garca, D. Ruiz, A. Ruiz-Corts, A model of user preferences for semantic services discovery and ranking, in *The Semantic Web: Research and Applications*. Lecture Notes in Computer Science, vol. 6089 (Springer, Berlin/Heidelberg, 2010), pp. 1–14
6. U. Keller, R. Lara, H. Lausen, A. Polleres, D. Fensel, Automatic location of services, in *ESWC*, Heraklion, 2005, pp. 1–16
7. M. Palmonari, M. Comerio, F. De Paoli, Effective and flexible nfp-based ranking of web services, in *Proceedings of the 7th International Joint Conference on Service Computing (ICSOC-ServiceWave 2009), Nov 23–27, 2009*, Lecture Notes in Computer Science, (Stockholm, 2009)

Chapter 18
The COSMO Solution to the SWS Challenge Mediation Problem Scenarios: An Evaluation

Camlon H. Asuncion, Marten van Sinderen, and Dick Quartel

Abstract During the course of our participation in the Semantic Web Services (SWS) Challenge, we have shown how the concepts defined in the *CO*nceptual *S*ervices *MO*deling (COSMO) framework for the modeling, reasoning and analysis of services can be used to solve the Mediation Problem Scenarios of the Challenge. Along with the service-oriented refinement and composition paradigm of COSMO, our approach is also based on model-driven and goal-oriented principles where the semantic integration of applications is designed at a layer of abstraction higher than technology specifications. The objective of this paper is to evaluate our previous and current research efforts towards advancing our solution to the semantic integration of service-oriented applications, particularly, using the mediation problem scenarios of the Challenge. We do this by presenting the state of the art of our solution while reporting our experience with applying our solution to the scenarios including lessons learned and identified research challenges.

18.1 Introduction

In today's times, enterprises must adapt to a constant change in business demand in order to survive and stay competitive. A collaboration with other enterprises in order to add value to their products and/or services is therefore vital. Enterprise collaboration is now possible with current advances in information technology. However, achieving such collaboration effectively and efficiently is never an

C.H. Asuncion (✉) · M. van Sinderen
Center for Telematics and Information Technology (CTIT), University of Twente,
P.O. Box 217, 7500, AE, Enschede, The Netherlands
e-mail: c.h.asuncion@utwente.nl; m.j.vansinderen@utwente.nl

D. Quartel
Novay, P.O. Box 589, 7500, AN, Enschede, The Netherlands
e-mail: dick.quartel@novay.nl

M.B. Blake et al. (eds.), *Semantic Web Services*, DOI 10.1007/978-3-642-28735-0_18,   279
© Springer-Verlag Berlin Heidelberg 2012

easy task. For one, enterprises are faced with system interoperability problems as a result of using legacy systems, oversupply (or the lack) of standards, heterogeneous hardware and software platforms, etc. Integration solutions also need to be flexible so that enterprises can continuously adapt to current and future changes and demands from within and outside their business environment [27].

Our work with the SWS Challenge testifies to our continued interest in designing a reusable and flexible interoperability solution. Our approach over the years has evolved into combining goal-oriented, model-driven and service-oriented design principles in designing interoperability solutions in the context of service mediation. A goal-oriented approach keeps the solution problem-oriented rather than technology-oriented: A change in the business requirements should not adversely affect the underlying technology implementation. Model-driven techniques raise the problem and solution analysis spaces to a level of abstraction that is technology independent and more suited for business-level analysis. Service-oriented principles allow integration solutions to be specified by means of service interactions; i.e., technical details can be hidden during integration design thus providing a high degree of flexibility.

This chapter presents a reflection about our experience in solving the three mediation problem scenarios of the SWS Challenge; namely, the Purchase Order Mediation Scenarios (first and second), and the Payment Problem Scenario.[1] The scenarios require the design of a Mediator service that acts as an intermediary software in reconciling message protocol and semantic data mismatches. Service mediation is ideal when systems need to interoperate but have existing and often difficult-to-change services. In particular, this paper reviews how our solution was evaluated with respect to the requirements of the SWS Challenge. We also provide an analysis of our solution in terms of its advantages and disadvantages, and the future research work resulting from this evaluation.

The rest of the chapter is structured as follows: Sect. 18.2 provides an overview the COSMO framework and its relation to the modeling, refinement and composition of services in the context of service mediation. Section 18.3 discusses our solution's the state of the art. Section 18.4 provides an account of lessons learned through an evaluation of the solution and future research challenges. Finally, Sect. 18.5 provides a summary of this chapter.

18.2 Approach: Service Mediation and the COSMO Framework

Service mediation. We define *service mediation* as *"to act as an intermediary agent in reconciling mismatches between the services of two or more systems"*[18]. We distinguish two types of mismatches: *data mismatches* which occur when

---

[1]http://swschallenge.org/wiki/index.php/Scenarios

Fig. 18.1 Service mediation as service composition [20]

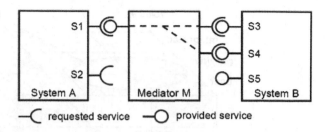

systems use different information models (vocabularies) to describe the messages that are exchanged by their services; *process mismatches* which occur when systems use services that define different messages or different orderings of message exchanges. Service mediation aims at resolving these mismatches [13, 20].

The need for an intermediary, hereafter denoted as *Mediator*, is imposed by the assumption that the mediated services can not be changed. The definition abstracts, however, who will perform the Mediator role, e.g., some of the existing systems or a 'third' system. We approach the design of the Mediator as a composition problem: each service that is requested by some system has to be composed from one or more services that are provided by the other systems and, possibly, by the same system. Figure 18.1 illustrates this for the case of two systems. Mediator M offers a mediation service that matches requested service S1 of system A by composing services S3 and S4 that are offered by system B. The Mediator should provide such a mediation service for each service that is requested by systems A and B [19].

We have developed an *integration framework* [19] that supports the design, implementation and validation of mediation services. Our framework consists of the following elements: the COSMO *conceptual framework* for modeling and reasoning about services, *languages* to express service models using COSMO, *techniques* to analyze the interoperability and conformance of service models, *transformations* from service design to service implementation level, *tools* supporting the editing, analysis and transformation of service models and a *methodology* for developing mediation services.

The COSMO framework. COSMO defines concepts to support the modeling, reasoning and analysis of services. In COSMO, we define a service as *"the establishment of some effect (or value) through the interaction between two or more systems"*. Figure 18.2 provides a graphical description of the COSMO framework.

We distinguish four service aspects, i.e., *information, behavior, structure*, and *quality*, representing categories of service properties that need to be modeled. The structure aspect is concerned with modeling the systems that provide or use services, and their interconnection structure. The interconnection structure comprises (amongst others) the interfaces at which services are offered. The behavioral aspect is concerned with the activities that are performed by systems as well as the relations among these activities. The information aspect is concerned with modeling the information that is managed and exchanged by systems. The quality aspect is concerned with modeling the non-functional characteristics of

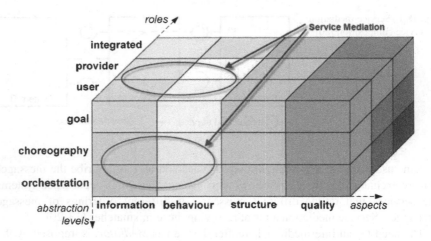

Fig. 18.2 The COSMO framework

services. These qualities often play an important role in the selection of services. Examples of quality aspects are the "cost" associated with a service or the "response time" of a service.

Besides service aspects, we distinguish three global abstraction levels at which a service can be modeled; namely, *goal*, *choreography* and *orchestration* level. A model at a goal level describes a service as a single interaction, where the interaction result represents the effect of the service as a whole. A model at choreography level refines the model at goal level by describing the service as a set of multiple related, more concrete interactions. A model at orchestration level describes the implementation of the service using a central coordinator that invokes and adds value to one or more other services.

Finally, we distinguish different roles of the systems involved in a service: the *user*, *provider* and *integrated roles*. The integrated role abstracts from the distinction between a user and provider by considering interactions as joint actions, thereby focusing on what the user and provider have in common.

Currently, our mediation solution mainly considers choreographies and orchestrations from the behavior and information aspect, and by distinguishing between a user and provider role. Furthermore, services are modeled close to the level at which they are described using WSDL, while abstracting from technology details [18,23].

18.3 Solution: Applying the COSMO Framework

As previously mentioned, we have developed an integration framework that consists of, among others, a *methodology* for developing mediation services. We discuss in this section a brief overview of the previous and current methodologies, hereafter termed version 1 and version 2, respectively. Separating the solutions

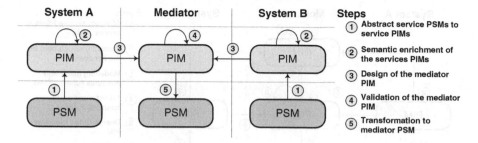

Fig. 18.3 The COSMO methodology for service integration [12]

into versions permits a more focused and targeted evaluation. Version 1 of the methodology largely draws from the service modeling, refinement, reasoning and analysis concepts of COSMO combined with Model Driven Architecture (MDA) principles. Version 2 seeks to extend the previous through a combination of goal-oriented requirements engineering and business rules approach to specification of the integration requirements. Version 1 of the methodology is used to solve the two Purchase Order Mediation Scenarios (cf. [12, 16, 19, 20, 22]), and version 2 of the methodology is used to solve the Payment Problem Scenario (cf. [1–3]).

18.3.1   Version 1

We have shown in [12, 16, 19, 20, 22] that in version 1 of the methodology (shown in Fig. 18.3), we start by "lifting" service description described in the WSDLs to a platform independent level which means, in MDA, transforming Platform Specific Models (PSM) to Platform Independent Models (PIM). Doing so avoids unnecessarily complicating the design space and thus provides more opportunity for business domain experts to be involved in the design. Business domain experts do not need to understand WSDLs to design the integration solution.

The second step involves semantically enriching PIM information which cannot be automatically derived from the WSDL. This is done because WSDLs do not inherently provide interaction protocols (i.e. how the sequence of message execution is specified), therefore, this information is supplemented through some text documentation in natural language, stakeholder interviews, or even code inspection. This enrichment is done so that the PIM is designed completely and precisely allowing better reasoning and generation of the mediation solution later on.

The third step involves the actual design of the Mediator at the PIM level. This usually involves splitting the integration solution in two areas which may be done in parallel: generating the behavior and information models. The information model unifies the differences in the data representations and interpretations between systems. The behavior model composes requested and provided mismatching service by relating their operations (i.e. matching the input of an operation call to the output of another and their constraints). The Mediator PIM is currently specified and designed using the Interaction System Design Language (ISDL) [17].

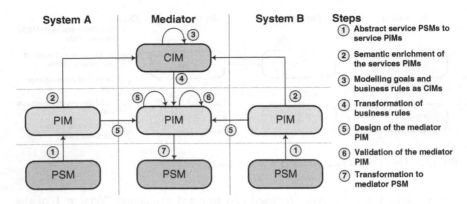

Fig. 18.4 The extended service mediation methodology [2]

The fourth step involves validation of the composed service Mediator using techniques such as interoperability assessment and simulation of generated behavior and information models [14, 15].

The fifth and sixth steps include transforming the designed PIM models of Mediator to PSM by mapping the integration solution to a specific service computing platform [5]. This is done by transforming the Mediator PIM in ISDL to the Mediator PSM using Business Process Execution Language (BPEL).[2]

18.3.2 Version 2

As version 1 of the methodology is only limited to the PIM level, we have looked into extending the methodology to the CIM (Computation-Independent Model) level. This is done so that we can abstract further in separating the business requirements from their technical implementation (i.e. essentially separating the "why" from the "how"). We argue that doing so gives business domain experts the opportunity to better understand, specify, and validate integration requirements without having to deal with their technical implementations. To do this, we treat requirements as goals and specifying them in some goal modeling language at the CIM layer. In turn, these goals are refined into rules which are encapsulated as services and incorporated into the Mediator service [1–3]. Figure 18.4 describes the extended methodology.

This required changes to the third step of version 1 where goal models are used to specify the requirements of the integration solution at the CIM layer. As Fig. 18.4 shows, the goal model depicts only the motivations of the integration (represented by the single rounded square under the Mediator column). Although the collaborating enterprises may have their own goals, we are only concerned with the goal of

---

[2]http://docs.oasisopen.org./wsbpel/2.0/wsbpel-v2.0.pdf

the integration. Currently, we model the goals using Architectural Modelling of Requirements (ARMOR) [21] an extension of ArchiMate [10] that seeks to add a goal-oriented requirements engineering aspect to architectural modeling.

The higher-level goals are then refined into lower-level goals which are then mapped to existing services identified in Step 1. Furthermore, business rules that constrain some aspect of the integration may also be derived from the lower-level goals. If no existing service can realize or satisfy these business rules, they may have to be transformed into an executable form, exposed as a service (as described in the fourth step) and integrated into the behavior model of the Mediator.

The fourth step transforms the business rules derived from the goal model into their equivalent rule specifications at the different layers of the MDA stack. At the CIM layer, we use Attempto Controlled English (ACE) [7] to specify the business rules in a near-natural controlled English language. These rules are then transformed into an XML-based rule specification for added rule interoperability at the PIM layer using Rule Markup Language (RuleML).[3] Finally, at the PSM layer, we transform these business rules into an executable form and expose them as a service to constrain the behavior of the Mediator using Java Expert System Shell (Jess) [6]. The generated Jess rules are then wrapped into one batch file and deployed as a Web service. This approach essentially separates the business rules of the Mediator from the business logic they constrain [8]. The next step involves the design of the integration specification at the PIM layer as described in Step 3 of version 1 (now, Step 5). The rest of the steps as outlined in version 1 follows as usual thereafter.

18.4   Lessons Learned

This section discusses the results of our solution as evaluated against the requirements of the SWS Challenge. The SWS Challenge evaluation criteria mostly focus on how the solution can cope with changes when new requirements are introduced. This section describes how our solutions respond to such changes. We also compare of COSMO with other approaches. Finally, we discuss the advantages and disadvantages of the solution.

18.4.1   Evaluation Results

18.4.1.1   Solving the Purchase Order Scenarios with Version 1

This section describes the required changes to version 1 of the solution when additional requirements are introduced from the second Purchase Order Scenario.

---

[3]http://ruleml.org/

The second Purchase Order Scenario is essentially an extension of the first. In particular, it requires the addition of Moon's Product Management System (PMS) to manage production capabilities requiring additional new services to be modeled in the Mediator PIM. Further details can be found in [16] as to how the changes to the solution have been carried out. Essentially, when changes are introduced at a higher abstraction level, model reuse can be done. Already existing abstract models need not be entirely redesigned or replaced. Furthermore, the PSM can simply be regenerated based on the existing abstract PIM model (and in fact, to another technology implementation of choice).

To illustrate, when the checkProductionCapability and confirm-Order services from Moon's PMS are added according to the requirements of the second Purchase Order Scenario, the steps outlined in Sect. 18.3.1 can be repeated minimally to accommodate such requirements: Step 1 requires the same abstraction of WSDL data and behavior information to UML and ISDL, respectively. The other PIMs of the first Purchase Order Scenario are simply reused. Step 2 requires no further behavior enrichment is necessary since the new services can be invoked independently of each other. However, new information mapping relations will have to be defined. Step 3 requires an update on the behavior and information models to reflect the changes in the requirements. This means that the new services will also need to be represented as complementary operation calls. The services of the first scenario are also reused. This only requires adding new relations between the services of the first and second scenarios. Step 4 requires that the same techniques be used to validate (e.g. simulation or conformance assessment) and analyze whether the integration solution still allows the systems to interoperate. Furthermore, we can also reuse the already existing information mappings of the first scenario to add new mappings between the Mediator PIM and Moon's PMS. Finally, Step 5 simply requires the reuse of the transformations between the Mediator PIM in ISDL to its an executable PMS in BPEL. This step is done automatically requiring only the addition of the endpoints of the newly added services.

18.4.1.2 Solving the Payment Problem Scenario with Version 2

This section describes how version 2 of the solution complies when changes are made in the authorization requirements of the Payment Problem Scenario. When changes are required in the Mediator PIM in ISDL, the same adjustments to the solution must be made as described previously in Sect. 18.4.1.1. However, version 2 is much more flexible when changes are confined within the requirements related to payment authorization since such requirements are separated, encapsulated and specified as business rules.

Version 2 of the solution was evaluated during the workshop against the different requirements that the authorize operation of Blue's Management Department System may have which included the following: Deny any request for authorization outright. Change the amounts that can be authorized by an authority. Return an authority that does not follow the original sequence of authorities. For example, the rule engine expects that `Arnold Black` is the next subsequent authority, but when the `authorize` operation returns `Peter Petrelli`, the response is still `denied`.

These changes in requirements did not trigger any change to the solution's code or data since they do not affect the interface constraints. However, the following change in requirements can introduce a change in the solution artifacts as they affect the logic behind the rules. The solution, however, is still flexible as the changes are confined only within the rule specifications. This was not evaluated during the workshop itself but through our own evaluation efforts: Adding other authorization response codes. Deleting an authorization response code. Adding or removing an authority from the list. Changing the original sequence of authorizations.

18.4.2   Comparison with Other Approaches

This section provides a comparison between other approaches that have solved the mediation problems and COSMO. In particular, we compare COSMO with Web Services Modelling Ontology (WSMO) [24], SWE-ET/WebML [4], and jABC [25]. This comparison is taken from a more detailed version in [11]. As a comparison criteria, we make use of DESMET [9] – a comprehensive methodology for planning and executing unbiased and reliable evaluation exercises. DESMET is a qualitative form of evaluation allowing the comparison to be described using a set of *features*. Feature analysis involves identifying requirements and mapping them to features that a method (or tool) must have to support such requirements.

We focus on the qualitative aspect of the comparison by using four features: *data mediation, process mediation, correctness* and *suitability of design concepts*. Data mediation refers to how an exchange data is mapped and transformed from a source schema into a target schema to solve the data mismatch. Process mediation refers to how the interaction behavior is expressed to solve the behavior mismatch. Data and process mismatches are evaluated against design and runtime aspects, as well. Correctness refers to how correct and reliable the Mediator is with respect to the requirements. Finally, suitability of design concepts mean how adequate the design concepts are in characterizing the system being modeled. Figure 18.5 shows the summary of the comparison between WSMO, WebML, jABC and COSMO.

WSMO uses the notion of goals, mediators, services and ontologies. The Mediator, a core concept, performs an ontology-to-ontology mediation through the use of adapters that provide mapping rules between ontologies. Goals specify requested capability and requested interfaces. The goal-oriented paradigm allows service discovery, selection of appropriate services, invocation of services, and composition of services for a common task.

WebML uses Business Process Modelling Notation (BPMN) to first specify a workflow at a high level of abstraction which is then transformed into hypertext diagrams that represent a service invocation order – a design concept that is adapted to model the mediation solution. Furthermore, in WebML, Adapter units that transform XML messages into WebML's internal ontology perform data mediation.

		WSMO	WebML	jABC	COSMO
Data mediation	**Design time aspects**	Ontologies manually created from analyzing the RosettaNet messages and WSDL service descriptions.	ER-model manually created from analyzing the RosettaNet messages and WSDL service descriptions.	SIBs and hierarchical parameters automatically generated from WSDL service descriptions.	Ontologies partially generated from RosettaNet messages and WSDL service descriptions.
		Ontology to Ontology mappings.	XML to Ontology mappings.	XML to SIB parameters mapping.	Ontology to Ontology mappings
	Runtime aspects	Mappings execution on the instance level.	Mappings execution on the instance level.	Reflected into the hierarchical parameter structure of the SIBs.	Mappings execution on the instance level.
Process mediation	**Design time aspects**	Defining services capability, choreography interfaces and goal templates. Behaviour modelled as Abstract State Machines by means of transformation rules.	Defining BPMN model, hypertexts and constraints. Behaviour specified at a high level of abstraction is transformed into a hypertext model for further manual refinement.	Defining a workflow explicitly describing the behaviour of the mediator. Behaviour modelled in terms of control flow graphs based on fork/join parallelism.	Defining a workflow explicitly describing the behaviour of the mediator. Behaviour modelled in terms of interactions, operation calls and causality relations.
	Runtime aspects	Execution based on abstract state machines and transformation rules defined by choreography.	WebML model is transformed into a WSMO specification and execution is delegated to a Semantic Execution Environment (WSMX).	Model-to-code transformations are defined to generate the implementation code and the execution tree is defined as the unfolding of the marking graph of the mediator.	Simulator tool able to execute the behaviour models. In addition, the Mediator was transformed into a BPEL process and its execution delegated to a BPEL engine.
Behaviour correctness		No explicit support.	No explicit support.	Formal verification capability based on temporal logic formulas expressed in mu-calculus.	Formal verification capability based on ISDL techniques.
Suitability of design concepts		Appropriate (mediators, goals, services and ontologies).	Sufficient, but not intuitive (pages, units, hypertexts, and links).	Appropriate (Service Independent Building Blocks and hierarchical parameters).	Appropriate (Goals, operations and Interactions).

Fig. 18.5 A comparison between COSMO, WSMO, WebML, and jABC (Taken from [11])

jABC uses basic service types, called SIBs (Service-Independent Building Blocks), from WSDL service descriptions which are then used to design behavior models, called SLGs (Service Logic Graphs), by composing the reusable SIBs into (flow-)graph structures. The behavior models can then be analyzed early on for correctness. Formal verification of the models allows simplification of debugging complex processes, reducing development time, and increasing robustness. Data mediation is achieved by mapping the messages structures from the WSDL into hierarchical SIB parameters. Finally, the Mediator can be made executable through model-to-code transformations.

COSMO uses ontologies as the underlying information model allowing analysis as to whether the relations defined between classes and properties are violated at the instance level or if a common interaction result can be established by matching input and output services parameters. Based on the selected match, the signature for the required data transformation can be obtained automatically. In particular, the approach focuses in applying reasoning techniques to automate parts of the mediator design process. The Mediator behavior is specified as a workflow explicitly modeling interactions between services, operation calls and causality relations between then.

18.4.3 Advantages and Disadvantages

Some of the salient *advantages* of the solution include the following:

Use of abstract models. In version 1, the use of model-driven and goal-oriented techniques to design the integration solution at varying abstraction levels provides flexibility to the solution. Here, the integration problem is solved at a higher level of abstraction bringing the solution closer to the problem domain and less on the solution technologies. Abstraction captures the semantics of the integration problem and the proposed solution without having to deal with technology-specific implementations yet, allowing decision makers to choose their own implementation technology later. Abstraction also captures changes in the requirements; i.e., the abstract solution specification is updated and a new solution implementation is generated without adversely affecting the implementation. Should the underlying implementation technology changes, the abstract requirements can still be reused.

Separation of business rules. In version 2, the solution allows the separation of business rules from the business process they constrain. The more dynamic aspects of the requirements are specified as business rules while keeping the more stable parts in the business process. Flexibility is again achieved since the dynamic parts of the business process are separated from the more stable ones so that a change between the either of them does not affect the other adversely. Furthermore, this separation allows business rules to be identified, changed, and managed better. Combined with model-driven techniques, we specify rules at various abstraction layers which again brings the integration solution closer to the problem domain. For example, low-level goals when operationalized as a controlled language can be validated better by business domain experts. Separating the business rules also allows their migration. For example, should there be some activities in the business process that change often, these activities can be migrated and specified as rules. Conversely, should there be rules that turn out not to change too often, they can then be migrated as an activity in a business process.

Better involvement of non-technical business domain experts. As a result of the abstracted view on the various specifications of the solution, non-technical business domain experts can participate better in integration solution by describing the goals of the integration, specifying and validating the business logic of the Mediator PIM, deriving the semantic mapping between the information models, and verifying the order of service invocations. This involvement is important in arriving at a more complete, accurate, and reliable integration solution.

Better requirements specification. With the use of goal-oriented requirements engineering, the solution provides better opportunity to specify the requirements of the integration solution. This can lead to a more precise, accurate, and complete specification of the requirements. Specifying the requirements in terms of goals also allows *early* verification without waiting for the implementation. With goals and business rules specifying the requirements at a higher abstraction, business domain experts have a better way of validating the requirements in a more structured manner as the models are intuitively understandable.

Some of the salient *disadvantages* of the solution include the following:

Manual modeling of integration solution. Although our solution uses information models to specify entities and their mappings, we still require designers to discover and represent these mappings from documentation, stakeholder interviews, or code inspection. This is a manual and error-prone process which requires understanding the meaning of all information models to be integrated. A large part work in the manual design of the Mediator is currently done during the design of the Mediator PIM in ISDL, data- and process-wise. Data-wise, matching the *semantic equivalence* between message elements is done by drawing on domain knowledge to determine the correct mapping which is then manually specified in a domain specific language. Data elements belonging to different vocabularies are semantically equivalent if they have similar meanings. Process-wise, the composition and refinement of the Mediator service is also done manually by determining the causal dependencies, including the mapping the sequence of invocations, between interaction contributions. Automating the data and process matching remains a challenging task since the knowledge to do this depends highly on the stakeholder requirements and domain knowledge.

Rule transformations. Version 2 of the methodology is limited in terms of the transformations between ACE, to RuleML and to Jess. Our prototype for transforming RuleML to Jess is rather specific only to the Payment Problem Scenario. Although we strive to create just one XSLT stylesheet to transform all the four RuleML Authority rules, we have not explored the possibility of applying our transformation to other possible rule structures. While doing the scenario, our experience has been that once a different Discourse Representation Structure (DRS) is generated by the ACE Parser Editor (APE)[4] for a given rule stated in ACE, necessary (and in fact time-consuming) changes need to be done to the XSLT stylesheet as well. Research related to rule transformation is lacking.

Limited goal-modeling methodology. ARMOR does not currently provide a standard "way of working" in the modeling of goals. More mature goal modeling approaches (e.g. KAOS [26]), propose a set of heuristic steps which include among others some best practice development techniques, and an extensive collection of formally-driven goal refinement techniques. Furthermore, ARMOR should be improved to allow translation of modeled business rules into a controlled language such as ACE. At the moment, although ARMOR supports business rules as one of its constructs, automatic translation is currently not supported. We have to manually specify the business rules in ACE.

Limited tooling support. Although there is an available tool support in terms of designing the goal models in ARMOR, specifying a valid ACE sentence using APE, transforming from ACE to RuleML and Jess (albeit prototypical), and from ISDL to BPEL, designing and simulating the Mediator PIM using Grizzle and Sizzle, deploying services in BPEL, and finally specifying information model mappings using Tizzle, an integrated environment where one can perform all the design, implementation and validation activities in one place is still absent. Such an integrated environment is important to reduce errors, development time, and provide debugging and deployment facilities.

18.4.4   Conclusions and Future Work

Aside from addressing the disadvantages described earlier; i.e., providing a more automated support for the integration design and implementation, improving the semantic equivalence between rule transformations, and developing an integrated tooling environment. Some future work include:

Support for non-functional properties. Our current work focuses solely on functional properties of integration requirements. Non-functional properties play an important role in the design and implementation of the integration solution. These non-functional properties can include, for example, security, response time, and economic value of provided and requested services.

Validation between CIM and PIM goal models. In version 2 of the methodology, we still have to explore the validation between the designed goal models at the CIM layer and their implementations in the PIM and PSM layers; i.e., we still need formal ways to verify if whether the overall effect of the Mediator service, when executed, does indeed satisfy the integration goal.

---

[4]http://attempto.ifi.uzh.ch/site/tools/

Use of other rule-based technologies. We shall be investigating the potential use of other rule-based specification such as the Semantics of Business Vocabulary and Business Rules (SBVR) as the controlled language to specify rules at the CIM layer. Unlike ACE, SBVR is more expressive: rules can be specified in other languages through a speech community. It also allows sharing of business vocabulary through a semantic community. It also supports some formalisms such as modalities which may add flexibility to specifying business rules. Other potential rule-based specifications include the W3C's Rule Interchange Format (RIF) and OMG's Production Rule Representation (PRR).

18.5 Summary

This chapter reviews the state of the art and evaluation of the COSMO framework in solving the Service Mediation Problems Scenarios of the SWS Challenge. We have demonstrated the use of goal-oriented requirements specification, coupled with model-driven techniques in the service-oriented design of integration solutions.

Several advantages can be drawn: Using model-driven techniques allows requirements to be specified at varying levels of abstraction bringing the solution closer to the problem domain. Separating business rules from the business process they constrain permits flexibility as those parts of the solution that change more often are isolated from those that do not. Several disadvantages also need to be addressed: the design largely remains manually performed, albeit the availability of tools. There is a need to develop better selection and transformations between rule-based technologies. Finally, there is still a need to develop an integrated development environment where technically and/or non-technically oriented designers can share participate better in the integration design.

Our participation in the SWS Challenge has been beneficial in improving, designing and validating the concepts behind the COSMO framework. Indeed, the Challenge has been an appropriate venue for exchanging and appreciating different solutions from other participants. Furthermore, this evaluation has allowed us to do a self reflection especially in terms of dealing with the limitations of our approaches and the future solutions at hand. Finally, a possible improvement that can be to the evaluation process is towards generalizing the results between various approaches. This could be possible since all approaches try to solve the same problems; therefore, a criteria for generalization may well be achievable.

Acknowledgements The authors are grateful to Rodrigo Mantovaneli Pessoa, Teduh Dirgahayu, and Stanislav Pokraev whose earlier works have been used in this book chapter.

References

1. C.H. Asuncion, Goal-driven service mediation solution, Master's thesis, University of Twente, 2009
2. C.H. Asuncion, M.E. Iacob, M.J. van Sinderen, Towards a flexible service integration through separation of business rules, in *14th IEEE International Enterprise Computing Conference*, Vitoria, IEEE Computer Society, 2010
3. C.H. Asuncion, D.A.C. Quartel, S.V. Pokraev, M.E. Iacob, M.J. van Sinderen, Combining goal-oriented and model-driven approaches to solve the payment problem scenario, in *8th Semantic Web Service (SWS) Challenge Workshop*, Eindhoven, 2010
4. M. Brambilla, I. Celino, S. Ceri, D. Cerizza, E. Della Valle, F. Facca, A software engineering approach to design and development of semantic web service applications, in *The Semantic Web – ISWC 2006*. LNCS, vol. 4273 (Springer, Berlin/Heidelberg, 2006), pp. 172–186
5. T. Dirgahayu, D.A.C. Quartel, M.J. van Sinderen, Development of transformations from business process models to implementations by Reuse, Technical report, CTIT, University of Twente, Enschede, 2007
6. E. Friedman, *Jess in Action: Rule-Based Systems in Java* (Manning Publications Co., Greenwich, 2003)
7. N.E. Fuchs, U. Schwertel, R. Schwitter, Attempto controlled english – not just another logic specification language, in *8th International Workshop on Logic Programming Synthesis and Transformation* (Springer London, 1990), pp. 1–20
8. M.E. Iacob, D. Rothengatter, J. van Hillegersberg, A health-care application of goal-driven software design. Appl. Med. Inform. **24**(1–2), 12–33 (2009)
9. B. Kitchenham, S. Linkman, D. Law, DESMET: a methodology for evaluating software engineering methods and tools. J. Comput. Control Eng. **8**(3), 120–126 (1997)
10. M. Lankhorst, *Enterprise Architecture at Work: Modelling, Communication and Analysis* (Springer, Berlin, 2009)
11. R. Mantovaneli Pessoa, D.A.C. Quartel, M.J. van Sinderen, A comparison of data and process mediation approaches, in *2nd Workshop on Enterprise Systems and Technology, I-WEST*, vol. 1, ed. by J. Cordeiro, M.J. Sinderen van, B.B. Shishkov (INSTICC Press, Portugal, 2008), pp. 48–63
12. S.V. Pokraev, *Model-driven semantic integration of service-oriented applications*, PhD thesis, University of Twente, Enschede, 2009
13. S. Pokraev, M. Reichert, M.W.A. Steen, R.J. Wieringa, Semantic and pragmatic interoperability: a model for understanding, in *Open Interop Workshop on Enterprise Modelling and Ontologies for Interoperability*, CEUR-WS, vol. 160, Porto, 2005, pp. 1–5
14. S.V. Pokraev et al., A method for formal verification of service interoperability, in *IEEE International Conference on Web Services*, Chicago, Sep 2006, IEEE Computer Society, 2006, pp. 895–900
15. S.V. Pokraev, D.A.C. Quartel, M.W.A. Steen, M.U. Reichert, Requirements and method for assessment of service interoperability, in *4th International Conference on Service Oriented Computing*, Chicago. LNCS, Springer, 2006, pp. 1–14
16. D.A.C. Quartel, M.J. Van Sinderen, Modelling and analysing interoperability in service compositions using COSMO. Enterp. Inf. Syst. **2**(4), 347–366 (2008)
17. D. Quartel, L.F. Pires, M. van Sinderen, On architectural support for behaviour refinement in distributed systems design. J. Integr. Des. Process Sci. **6**(1), 1–30 (2002)
18. D.A.C. Quartel, M.W.A. Steen, S.V. Pokraev, M.J. van Sinderen, COSMO: a conceptual framework for service modelling and refinement, Inf. Syst. Front. **9**(2–3), 225–244 (2007)
19. D.A.C. Quartel, S.V. Pokraev, R. Mantovaneli Pessoa, M.J. van Sinderen, Model-driven development of a mediation service, in *12th International IEEE Enterprise Computing Conference*, Munich, IEEE Computer Society, 2008, pp. 117–126
20. D. Quartel, S. Pokraev, T. Dirgahayu, R.M. Pessoa, M. van Sinderen, Model-driven service integration using the COSMO framework, in *7th Workshops Semantic Web Services Challenge*, Stanford Logic Group Technical Reports, Karlsruhe, 2008, pp. 77–88

21. D.A.C. Quartel, W. Engelsman, H. Jonkers, M.J. van Sinderen, A goal-oriented requirements modelling language for enterprise architecture, in *13th IEEE International Enterprise Computing Conference*, Auckland, IEEE Computer Society, 2009, pp. 3–13

22. D.A.C. Quartel et al., Model-driven development of mediation for business services using COSMO. Enterp. Inf. Syst. **3**(3), 319–345 (2009)

23. D. Quartel, T. Dirgahayu, M. Van Sinderen, Model-driven design, simulation and implementation of service compositions in COSMO. Int. J. Bus. Process Integr. Manag. **4**(1), 18–34 (2009)

24. D. Roman et al., Web service modeling ontology. Appl. Ontol. **1**, 77–106 (2005)

25. B. Steffen, T. Margaria, R. Nagel, S. Jörges, C. Kubczak, Model-driven development with the jABC, in *Hardware and Software, Verification and Testing*. LNCS, vol. 4383 (Springer, Berlin/Heidelberg, 2007), pp. 92–108

26. A. van Lamsweerde, Goal-oriented requirements engineering: a guided tour, in *5th IEEE International Symposium on Requirements Engineering*, Toronto, 2001, pp. 249–262

27. M.J. van Sinderen, Challenges and solutions in enterprise computing. Enterp. Inf. Syst. **2**(4), 341–346 (2008)

Part IV
Results from the Web Services Challenge

Chapter 19
Overview of the Web Services Challenge (WSC): Discovery and Composition of Semantic Web Services

Ajay Bansal, Srividya Bansal, M. Brian Blake, Steffen Bleul, and Thomas Weise

Abstract The capabilities of organizations can be openly exposed, easily searched and discovered, and made readily-accessible to humans and particularly to machines, using service-oriented computing approaches. Artificial intelligence and software engineering researchers alike are tantalized by the promise of ubiquitously discovering and incorporating services into their own business processes (i.e. composition and orchestration). With growing acceptance of service-oriented computing, an emerging area of research is the investigation of technologies that will enable the Discovery and Composition of Web Services. The Web Services Challenge (WSC) is a forum where academic and industry researchers can share experiences of developing tools that automate the integration of Web Services. Participating Software platforms address several new composition challenges. Requests and results are transmitted within SOAP messages, semantics represented as ontologies written in OWL, services are represented in WSDL, and service orchestrations are represented in WSBPEL. In addition, non-functional properties (Quality of Service) of a service are represented using WSLA format.

A. Bansal (✉) · S. Bansal
Arizona State University – Polytechnic Campus, Mesa, AZ, USA
e-mail: ajay.bansal@asu.edu; srividya.bansal@asu.edu

M.B. Blake
University of Miami, Coral Gables, FL, USA
e-mail: M.Brian.Blake@miami.edu

S. Bleul
Tetralog Systems AG, Munich, Germany
e-mail: stbleul@gmx.de

T. Weise
University of Science and Technology of China, Hefei, Anhui, China
e-mail: tweise@ustc.edu.cn

M.B. Blake et al. (eds.), *Semantic Web Services*, DOI 10.1007/978-3-642-28735-0_19,
© Springer-Verlag Berlin Heidelberg 2012

19.1 Introduction

Inter-organization collaboration resulting in enterprise integration is experiencing a promising advancement considering the recent inception and potential acceptance of network-accessible services, or Web Services. Commercial, academic, and government organizations alike are beginning to share their capabilities via the exposition of their underlying software services. The notion of millions or even billions of universally accessible service-based capabilities is not only promising to the individual looking for a specific consumer-based service but also to organizations hoping to enhance their own capabilities by incorporating the services of external entities. In addressing the latter, there are several specific open issues in the strategy-based composition of such underlying services from both theoretical and applied perspectives. Potential semantic and syntactic mismatch among services, performance constraints on service discovery, and fault tolerance are just a few issues. The International Web Service Discovery and Composition competition [5], the WS-Challenge, has helped to identify, evaluate, and baseline approaches. The first event took place at the IEEE International Conference on e-Technology, e-Commerce and e-Service held on March 2005 in Hong Kong [3]. The succeeding events were supported by National Science Foundation (NSF) and took place at CEC/EEE 2006 in San Francisco, CA [4], CEC/EEE 2007 in Tokyo, Japan [21,23], CEC/EEE 2008 in Washington, D.C. [22], CEC/EEE 2009 in Vienna, Austria [6], and CEC 2010 in Shanghai China [24] respectively.

WSC continues to provide a forum where researchers can collaborate on approaches, methods, and algorithms in the domain of Web Service Discovery and automated Composition. This forum provides quantitative and qualitative evaluation results on the performance of participating matchmaking and automated composition software and facilitates the dissemination of results that advance this field. It extends the original criteria of the first two competitions which focused on service discovery and service composition based on the syntactic matching of WSDL part names. It also further extends the third and fourth competition in 2006 and 2007 which provided taxonomy of parameter types represented using the natural hierarchies that are captured using simple and complex types within XML documents. WSC further evolved with the adoption of ontologies written in OWL to provide semantics. The challenge also considers non-functional properties of a Web Service. The Quality of Service of a Web service is expressed by its response time and throughput. It has been the tradition of the WSC events to adhere to technology-independent approaches to semantics. In this way, the competition attempts to circumvent debates on representations, such as differences between approaches like OWL-S [15], WSML [12], and WSDL-S [27]. In 2006, the use of pure XML-based semantics allowed for a bi-partisan approach. In 2007, we have evolved the challenge by mirroring the XML-based semantics with equivalent representations using OWL ontology. During the previous 3 years, Web Service challenge focused on optimizing the discovery and composition process solely using abstractions from real-world situations. The taxonomies of semantic concepts as well as the involved data formats were purely artificial. We have further evolved the challenge by using data formats and contest data based on OWL, WSDL, and WSBPEL schemas for ontologies, services, and service orchestrations in 2009 and 2010. Especially in the 2010 competition, an extremely comprehensive and thorough benchmarking, was performed jointly by all participants at the conference site.

19.2 Approach

There are several scientific challenges when designing and developing systems that discover, interpret, and combine multiple services into higher-order systems. The standard routine for service composition can be separated into six steps as shown in Fig. 19.1.

The first step in service composition is to capture the requirements while the second step is to seek potential services to fulfill those requirements. One significant research concern is to determine the most effective method when specifying the request then developing approaches to generally understand these specifications. There are a number of approaches used where businesses request service capabilities from other businesses (e.g. RosettaNet, EbXML, WSFL, WSCI, BPML/BPEL4WS, etc. [8, 11, 18, 25, 26]). There are few existing studies that evaluate these approaches for the purpose of requesting service capabilities. While seeking service capabilities as in the second step, automated software must efficiently search repositories of potentially hundreds of thousands of services. Another significant research concern is to understand how to effectively and efficiently search and identify candidate services such that the solution set consists of high quality matches.

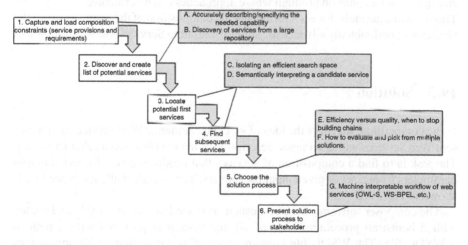

Fig. 19.1 Web service composition

In steps 3 and 4, automated tools must identify the first service for a service composition chain then build a solution with all the subsequent services involved in composition. Although the list of candidate services, at this point, is smaller than the original open repository, effective techniques to traverse the designated search space are still required at this stage. In addition, identifying adequate services is a both a syntactic and semantic matching problem. Semantic Web Services research represents much of the on-going project work in this area [1, 7, 14, 16, 17] however it is just one component of the full service composition problem. Finally in steps 5 and 6, a solution must be picked to fulfill the new capability and it must be presented to the stakeholders as a machine-interpretable workflow such as WS-BPEL. Automated techniques must be designed with "just-in-time" approaches to determine when to stop building the solution chains. If multiple solutions are constructed, then there must be techniques to choose the most effective solution [10]. Finally, the solution chain must be converted into a business-oriented workflow that is integrated with domain-specific directives.

Although WSC is perhaps the first venue, other unique venues have been established to investigate the need for solutions to the Service Composition Problem. The Semantic Web Services (SWS) Challenge [19] is a venue where both business cases and solution applications are the focus. Participants are placed in a forum where they can incrementally and collaboratively learn from each other. While WSC venues are more driven by application, the SWS venues concentrate more on the environment. As such, the SWS venues place more focus on semantics where the WSC favors applied, short-term solutions. Alternatively, the SOA Contest [20] held at the International Conference on Services Computing (SCC2006, SCC2007, and SCC2008) allows participants to openly choose the problems that best demonstrate their approach. The benefit of this venue is that participants can show the best approach for a particular domain-specific problem. In contrast, the WSC venue attempts to set a common problem where approaches can be evaluated side-by-side. There is a unique niche for each forum and the composition of the results from all the venues will undoubtedly advance the state-of-the-art in Service-oriented computing.

19.3   Solution

In the competition, we adopt the idea of so-called Semantic Web Services that represent Web Services with a semantic description of the interface and its characteristics. The task is to find a composition of services that produces a set of queried output parameters from a set of given input parameters. The overall challenge procedure is shown in Fig. 19.2.

The composer software of the contestants is placed on the server side and started with a bootstrap procedure. First of all, the system is provided with a path to a WSDL file. The WSDL file contains a set of services along with annotations of their input- and output parameters. The number of services will change from challenge to challenge. Every service will have an arbitrary number of parameters.

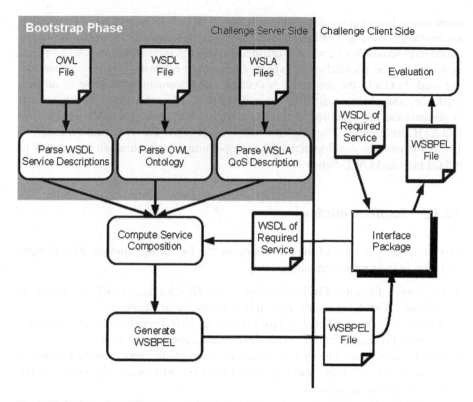

Fig. 19.2 Web service challenge – procedure

Additional to the WSDL file, we also provide the address of the OWL file during the bootstrapping process. This file contains the taxonomy of concepts used in this challenge in OWL format. The bootstrapping process includes loading the relevant information from these files. The challenge task will then be sent to the composer via a client-side GUI. After the bootstrapping on the server side is finished, the GUI queries the composition system with the challenge problem definition. The contestant's software computes a solution – one or more service compositions – and answer in the solution format which is a subset of the WSBPEL schema. When the WSBPEL document is received by the GUI, time measurement is stopped the compositions themselves are evaluated.

19.3.1 Semantics

Ontologies are usually expressed with OWL [2], an XML format [9]. We used the OWL format in the challenge last couple of years, but like in the previous years, we limit semantic evaluation strictly to taxonomies consisting of sub and super class relationship between semantic concepts only. OWL is quite powerful. In addition to semantic concepts (OWL-Classes), OWL allows to specify instances of classes called individuals. While we also distinguish between individuals and classes in the competition, the possibility to express equivalence relations between concepts is not used. In OWL, the semantics is defined with statements consisting of subject, predicate, and object, e.g. ISBN-10 is a ISBN (ISBN subsumes ISBN-10). Such statements can be specified with simple triplets but also with XML-Hierarchies and XML-References. The implementation of an OWL-Parser is hence not trivial. In order to ease the development of the competition contributions, so far we stick to a fixed but valid OWL-Schema.

19.3.2 Implementation

The composer software of the contestant use the following representation formats and rules in their implementation.

- Document formats: OWL Ontologies, WSDL-Queries, WSBPEL solutions schemas, WSLA for representation of non-functional attributes.
- XSD-types: The challenge includes matching XSD-Type definitions like arrays, simple types, complex types with substructures and enumerations.
- Parallel execution: The WSBPEL schema supports the specification of parallel execution of services. Valid parallel execution will positively influence the systems challenge score.
- No results: The challenge will include sets of services that actually deliver no solution. The system should act accordingly and cancel the discovery in time.

19.3.3 Quality of Service

The Quality of Service for a service can be specified using the Web Service Level Agreements (WSLA) [13], language from IBM. In contrast to the Web Service Agreements (WS-A) language, WSLA is in its final version. Furthermore, WSLA offers more specific information than WS-A. We can not only specify the Service Level Objectives (SLO) of a service and its service operations, but also the measurement directives and measurement endpoints for each quality dimension. WSLA represents a configuration for a SLA management and monitoring system. In contrast to WS-A, WSLA enables the automated discovery and deployment of service contracts inside SOAs. In WSC-09, we defined the following quality dimensions for a Web Service. They can be accessed in this document format and must be calculated for a whole BPEL process.

- Response Time: In a data system, the system response time is the interval between the receipt of the end of transmission of an inquiry message and the beginning of the transmission of a response message to the station where the inquiry originated. Example: 200 ms.

- Throughput: In communication networks such as Ethernet or packet radio, throughput is the average rate of successful message delivery over a communication channel. Example: 10,000 (successful) invocations per minute.

We define one WSLA document containing the specification of the average response time in milliseconds and the throughput (invocations per minute) of each service in a challenge set. Metrics can be omitted as they do not contain relevant information for the service composition. They are interesting nonetheless as they present the capabilities of WSLA.

19.4   Lessons Learned

In the initial year, the competition was limited to syntactical matching using the Web Services Description Language (WSDL). Participants were required to identify and compose WSDL-specified services based on their input and output messages as specified in directory of WSDL documents. In 2006, the competition added a new challenge where participants must semantically link Web Services using additional XML-based semantic notations. Participants for each year are required to submit a technical description of their software agent or component of no more than four pages. This description is used to judge and rate the design of the entry. The 4-page description follows the IEEE Computer Society format as specified by the main conference, and they are published as a poster papers in the general proceedings for all accepted entries. The Web Services challenge evolved based on lessons learnt from previous years. The different variants of this competition are described in the following sections.

19.4.1   Competition A (2005 and 2006): Service Discovery Capabilities

Participants were provided with a directory of Web Service specifications. The directory contained multiple WSDL files. Each participant was given a specific discovery request as represented by the provided input messages and the required output messages. The participant's component or agent was required to find all services that met the requirements. The service repositories contained services that did not meet the requirements, services that partially met the requirements, services that exactly met the requirements, and services that met the requirements but also provide additional information. Competition A was evaluated by the number of services retrieved that either exactly met the requirements or exceeded the requirements. In addition, the entries were evaluated on their performance in gathering the list of services.

19.4.2 Competition B (2005 and 2006): Syntactical Service Composition Capabilities

Given the same service repositories provided in Competition A, the participants were provided with another discovery request. In this part of competition, the request could only be fulfilled by the composition of multiple services. The participants were required to supply the sequence and list of services that met the requirements. In this competition the input and output messages of multiple services matched syntactically. Competition B was evaluated by the number of correctly composed services in addition to the performance of the software agent or component. We realized that performing composition based on syntactic matching of input and output parameters was very limited and hence decided to enhance the challenge in the coming years.

19.4.3 Competition C (2006 Onwards): Semantic Service Discovery and Composition Capabilities

With National Science Foundation support in 2006, we extended the competition to have Semantic Service Discovery and Composition. We decided not to use OWL-S which is evolving quickly, but in the first year we used a hierarchical feature present in all XML documents. In this approach, participants had to use parent-child relationships in the XML schemas supporting the Web Service descriptions to determine when two terms were equivalent or originated from the same type. A taxonomy of parameter types represented using the natural hierarchies that are captured using simple and complex types within XML documents was provided to the participants in 2006. With further feedback from the participants and organizers ontologies written in OWL were adopted in 2008 to provide semantics.

Ontologies are usually expressed with OWL [2], an XML format [9]. We started using OWL format in the 2008 challenge, but like in the previous years, we limited semantic evaluation strictly to taxonomies consisting of sub and super class relationship between semantic concepts only. OWL is quite powerful. In addition to semantic concepts (OWL-Classes), OWL allows to specify instances of classes called individuals. While we also distinguish between individuals and classes in the competition, the possibility to express equivalence relations between concepts is not used. In OWL, the semantics is defined with statements consisting of subject, predicate, and object, e.g. ISBN-10 is a ISBN (ISBN subsumes ISBN-10). Such statements can be specified with simple triplets but also with XML-Hierarchies and XML-References. The implementation of an OWL-Parser is hence not trivial. In order to ease the development of the competition contributions, we will stick to a fixed but valid OWL-Schema.

The challenge now also considers non-functional properties of a Web Service. The Quality of Service of a Web Service is expressed by its response time and throughput. We define one document containing the specification of the average response time in milliseconds and the throughput (invocations per minute) of each service in a challenge set. Elements like Metrics can be omitted as they do not contain relevant information for the service composition. They are interesting nonetheless as the present the capabilities of WSLA. Below is an example WSLA document.

```
<SLA
   xmlns ="http://www.ibm.com/wsla"
   xmlns:xsi="http://www.w3.org/2001/XMLSchema-instance"
            name="WSCServiceSLA">

   <!-- Definition of the Involved Parties, the signatory
        parties as well as the supporting ones -->

   <Parties >
       <ServiceProvider name=" ACMEServiceProvider">
           <Contact >
               <Street >Vienna XPress Services </Street >
               <City >Vienna </City >
           </Contact >
       </ServiceProvider >
       <ServiceConsumer
           name=" WebServiceChallengeCompositionClient "/>
   </Parties >

   <!-- The definition of the service in terms of
        the service parameters and their measurement. -->

   <ServiceDefinition name=" SLAMonitorTestServiceA ">
   ...
   </ServiceDefinition >

   <ServiceDefinition name=" SLAMonitorTestServiceN ">
   ...
   </ServiceDefinition >

   <!-- The obligations of the parties,
        referring to the services above. -->
   <Obligations >
   ...
   </Obligations >

</SLA >
```

19.4.4   Competition D (2007 Onwards): Architecture Challenge

We extended the competition repositories with services and queries that produced multiple solutions. The participants were required to discover the shortest composition chains. We also built large XML schemas with nested parent-child relationships. As a result of this, participants had to build their components with efficient techniques to determine if two terms were equivalent or originated from the same type. Their components also had to be equipped with techniques to process large XML Schema documents efficiently as the overall performance of the composition engine relied on it. Along with performance, teams were also evaluated based on the architecture and design of their engine to handle all the challenges involved in a composition task.

19.4.5 Evaluation Results

The Web Service Challenge awards the most efficient system and also the best architectural solution. The best architectural effort is awarded according to the contestant's presentation and system features. The evaluation of efficiency consists of two parts as described below and shown in Fig. 19.3.

1. Time measurement: The time measurement is done by the interface package. We take the time after submitting the query and the time when the composition result is fully received. The bootstrap mechanism is excluded from the assessment. There will be a time limit for bootstrapping after which a challenge is considered as failure.
2. Composition evaluation: Evaluation of the composition solutions was based on the following criteria.

   • Completeness: The amount of compositions discovered by the system.
   • Composition length: The shortest composition.
   • Composition efficiency: Parallel versus sequential execution of services.

The organizers created a BPEL checking software that evaluates the results of the participant's composition system. The BPEL file is examined for a solution path and its correctness with respect to the challenge task.

1. Four challenge sets and each composition system can achieve up to 18 points and no less than 0 points per challenge set. Three challenge sets will have at least one feasible solution and one challenge set will have no solution at all.
2. The time limit for solving a challenge is 5 min. Every composition system replying with a solution later than 5 min will receive 0 points for the challenge set.
3. The task is to find the service composition with the lowest response time which solves the challenge of the challenge set. Additionally the composition system which also finds the service composition with the highest throughput in the fastest time will be rewarded.

Score per challenge set:

• +6 Points for finding the service composition with the lowest response time that solves the challenge.
• +6 Points for finding the service composition with the highest throughput that solves the challenge.

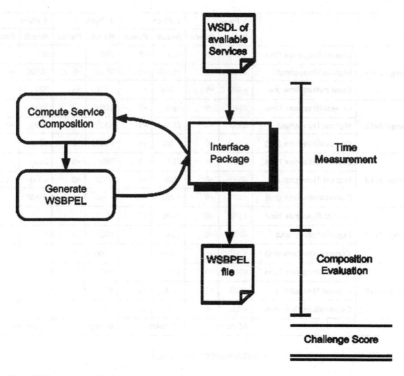

Fig. 19.3 Web services challenge – evaluation

- +6 Points for the composition system which finds the service composition with
  the lowest response time or highest throughput that solves the challenge in the
  fastest time.
- +4 Points for the composition system which finds the service composition with
  the lowest response time or highest throughput that solves the challenge in the
  second fastest time.
- +2 Points for the composition system which finds the service composition with
  the lowest response time or highest throughput that solves the challenge in the
  third fastest time.

The results of last year's challenge are shown in Fig. 19.4.

19.4.6   The Solution Format

During the WS-Challenge 2007, many participants encouraged the usage of a
process language like BPEL as the output format for the composition solutions.
A process language has more expressiveness than an XML solution format. It can
be used to connect the challenge implementation to real world technologies and,
hence, improves the reusability of the challenge implementations. The challenge

A. Bansal et al.

		1. Place		2. Place		3. Place		4. Place	
		Result	Points	Result	Points	Result	Points	Result	Points
Challenge Set 1	Lowest Response Time	500	+6	500	+6	780		880	
	Highest Throughput	15000	+6	15000	+6	15000	+6	15000	+6
	Composition Time (ms)	< 300	+6	< 300	+6	< 300	+6	531	
Challenge Set 2	Lowest Response Time	1690	+6	1690	+6	2100		2110	
	Highest Throughput	6000	+6	6000	+6	6000	+6	6000	+6
	Composition Time (ms)	< 300	+6	< 300	+6	< 300	+6	2219	
Challenge Set 3	Lowest Response Time	760	+6	760	+6	760	+6	950	
	Highest Throughput	4000	+6	4000	+6	4000	+6	4000	+6
	Composition Time (ms)	< 300	+6	< 300	+6	< 300	+6	21438	
Challenge Set 4	Lowest Response Time	1470	+6	1470	+6	2070			
	Highest Throughput	4000	+6	2000		4000	+6		
	Composition Time (ms)	< 300	+6	< 300	+6	< 300	+6		
Challenge Set 5	Lowest Response Time	4070	+6	4070	+6	4500			
	Highest Throughput	4000	+6	4000	+6	4000	+6		
	Composition Time (ms)	< 300	+6	938	+2	< 300	+6		
Sum		90 Points		80 Points		66 Points		18 Points	

Fig. 19.4 Web services challenge – performance scoreboard

uses OWL to represent semantics and an extension to WSDL standard to represent Web Services in the repository. A subset of WSBPEL is used to represent the composition solutions. An example solution is shown below in WSBPEL format:

```
<WSChallenge type="solutions ">

    <!-- First solution -->
    <case name="SolutionA ">
        <service name="serviceA "/>
        <serviceSpec name="2.1">
            <service name="serviceB "/>
            <serviceSpec name="2.2">
                <service name="serviceC "/>
                <service name="serviceD "/>
            </serviceSpec >
            <service name="serviceE "/>
        </serviceSpec >
    </case >

    <!-- Second alternative solution -->
    <case name="SolutionB ">
    ...
    </case >
</WSChallenge >
```

In this example we have two possible solutions.

1. SolutionA: First we invoke the serviceA then invoke serviceB. Afterward we execute step 2.2 or serviceE. In step 2.2 we can freely choose between serviceC and serviceD. Additionally, we can (dependent on the query and test set) execute serviceB and serviceE concurrently. But this cannot be expressed with this solution format.
2. SolutionB is omitted here.

19.4.7   Advantages and Disadvantages

The competition database evolved over the years as well as WSC evolved. It was a significant effort creating the test sets the first couple of years. As the competition evolved and started incorporating XML schemas followed by OWL schemas, a taxonomy of concepts used by the services in the repository had to be created. Further the WSDL descriptions of services had to be updated to use concepts from the XML schema for a couple of years. The descriptions were then updated again to use concepts from the OWL schema as opposed to XML Schema. Initially the queries were provided in XML format. Over the years the challenge started provided queries also in WSDL data format instead of XML and the solutions had to be produced in WS-BPEL format. Sample queries and solutions were created that participants could use for testing their work. In addition, sample template code was provided that contestants could use to build their software. This template code had to be refactored every year to handle new and complex challenges.

19.4.8   Conclusions and Future Work

In 2005, we learned that there is a great deal of interest in a Web Services Composition competition. We also discovered that orchestrating the Web Services is a difficult problem, even if data mismatch is not an issue. In the first year, the challenge was a syntactic Web Service Discovery and Composition competition. Participation by teams from various countries had greatly increased in a couple of years. The WSC was further enhanced with semantics provided by XML-Schemas followed by OWL in subsequent years. The repositories with services and queries resulted in compositions of different lengths. The XML-Schema files were large sized files with further nesting of parent-child relationships of terms. This challenged the participants to build sophisticated engines to handle such data. WSBPEL is used to represent the composition solutions.

The future challenges would also have repository and environment that is dynamic in nature where services are changing and hence could be added, removed, or updated in the repository. Besides QoS, semantics, and large-scale tasks, in future we will also consider service mashups, cross-domain integration, and security mediation.

19.5 Summary

The Web Services Challenge (WSC) is a SOA venue that looks to benchmark software applications that automatically manage Web Services. It continues to provide a forum where researchers can collaborate on approaches, methods, and algorithms in the domain of Web Service discovery and automated composition. This forum provides quantitative and qualitative evaluation results on the performance of participating matchmaking and automated composition software and facilitates the dissemination of results that advance this field.

WSC continues to evolve with the adoption of new representations to provide semantics, compose Web Services, and non-functional attributes. It has been the tradition of the WSC events to adhere to technology-independent approaches to semantics. In earlier competitions, Web Service composition applications (i.e. participant entries) were constructed as stand-alone applications. Participating software now have to be implemented as Web Services. As such, requests and results of composition routines are transmitted as SOAP messages to and from the participating software applications. This natural progression in the WSC allow the competition itself to take place within a SOA environment. The composition problems include the requirement to handle concurrent threads for composition routines. The combination of complex, workflow-based heuristics with semantically-rich representations required participants to create new software that is both robust and efficient.

References

1. P. Albert, L. Henocque, M. Kleiner, Configuration-based workflow composition, in *Proceedings of the 3rd IEEE International Conference on Web Services (ICWS 2005)*, Orlando, 2005
2. S. Bechhofer, F. Harmelen, J. Hendler, I. Horrocks, D. McGuinness, P. Patel-Schneider, L. Stein, OWL web ontology language reference, in *World Wide Web Consortium (W3C)*, 2004, Available at http://www.w3.org/TR/2004/REC-owl-ref-20040210/
3. M.B. Blake, K.C. Tsui, W. Cheung, The EEE-05 challenge: a new web service discovery and composition competition, in *Proceedings of the IEEE International Conference on E-Technology, E-Commerce, and E-Services (EEE-05)*, Hong Kong, 2005
4. M.B. Blake, W. Cheung, M.C. Jaeger, A. Wombacher, WSC-06, the web service challenge, in *Joint Proceedings of the CEC/EEE 2006*, San Francisco, 2006
5. M.B. Blake, W. Cheung, A. Wombacher, Web services discovery and composition systems. Int. J. Web Serv. Res. **4**(1), iii–viii (2007)
6. M.B. Blake, S. Bleul, T. Weise, A. Bansal, S. Bansal, WSC-09: the web services challenge (2009), http://ws-challenge.georgetown.edu/wsc09/index.html
7. W. Blanchet, E. Stroulia, R. Elio, Supporting adaptive web-service orchestration with an agent conversation framework, in *Proceedings of the 3rd IEEE International Conference on Web Services (ICWS 2005)*, Orlando, 2005
8. BPML-BPEL4WS (2005), www.bpmi.org/downloads/BPML-BPEL4WS.pdf
9. T. Bray, J. Paoli, C. Sperberg-McQueen, E. Maler, F. Yergeau, Extensible Markup Language (XML) 1.0 (4th edn.), in *World Wide Web Consortium (W3C)*, 2007, Available at http://www.w3.org/TR/2006/REC-xml-20060816

10. G. Canfora, M. Di Penta, R. Esposito, M.L. Villani, QoS-aware replanning of composite web services, in *Proceedings of the 3rd IEEE International Conference on Web Services (ICWS 2005)*, Orlando, 2005
11. ebXML (2005), http://www.ebxml.org/
12. D. Fensel, C. Bussler, The web service modeling framework. Electron. Commer. Res. Appl. **1**(2), 113–137 (2002)
13. A. Keller, H. Ludwig, The WSLA framework: specifying and monitoring service level agreements for web services. J. Netw. Syst. Manag. **11**(1), 57–81 (2003)
14. D.J. Mandell, S.A. McIlraith, Adapting BPEL4WS for the semantic web: the bottom-up approach to web service interoperation, in *International Semantic Web Conference*, Sanibel Island, 2003, pp. 227–241
15. D. Martin, et al., Bringing semantics to web services: the OWL-S approach, in *Proceedings of the First International Workshop on Semantic Web Services and Web Process Composition (SWSWPC-04)*, San Diego, 2004
16. MindSwap at University of Maryland, College Park (2005), http://www.mindswap.org/
17. S.R. Ponnekanti, A. Fox, SWORD: a developer toolkit for web service composition, in *Proceedings International WWW Conference*, Honolulu, 2002
18. RosettaNet (2005), http://www.rosettanet.org/
19. The Semantic Web Services Challenge (2007), http://sws-challenge.org/wiki/index.php/Main_Page
20. The Services Computing Contest (2007), http://iscc.servicescomputing.org/2007/
21. The Web Services Challenge (2007), http://www.wschallenge.org/wsc07/
22. The Web Services Challenge (2008), http://cec2008.cs.georgetown.edu/wsc08/
23. The Web Services Challenge at the IEEE Conference on E-business Engineering (2007), http://www.comp.hkbu.edu.hk/simctr/wschallenge/
24. M.B Blake, T. Weise, S. Bleul, Web Services Composition and evaluation, in *Proceedings of the IEEE International Conference on Service-Oriented Computing and Applications (SOCA)*, Perth, 2010
25. Web Service Choreography Interface (WSCI) (2005), http://www.w3.org/TR/wsci/
26. Web Service Flow Language (WSFL) (2005), www-3.ibm.com/software/solutions/webservices/pdf/WSFL.pdf
27. WSDL-S (2007), http://www.w3.org/Submission/WSDL-S/

Chapter 20
Effective QoS Aware Service Composition Based on Forward Chaining with Service Space Restriction

Peter Bartalos and Mária Bieliková

Abstract Several approaches dealing with the performance of QoS aware semantic web service composition have been proposed. We describe an approach which took part at Web Services Challenge 2009. It showed good performance even if large service repositories were processed. We discuss the main principles of the used approach and also its further enhancement. The enhancement includes shorter composition time, consideration of the pre-/post-conditions of services, and adaptation to real conditions where changes of the service set, or the QoS attributes must be effectively managed. Moreover, the lessons learned during the development and the participation of the competition is discussed too.

20.1 Introduction

Automatic dynamic web service composition is showing to be an effective way how to deal with the dynamic character of the web service, and business environment, while providing a mechanism capable to supply varying composition goals [6]. Several research results concerning different aspect of the overall problem had been proposed. These present promising results and also address existing problems.

Several tasks, required to perform during the service composition, are NP-hard in general. These include for example the construction of the control-/data-flow together with the QoS optimization and evaluation of the compatibility between the pre- and post-conditions of services. To be able to handle large service repositories, sophisticated methods must be developed. These must provide good performance and scale well as the number of web services in the repository rises. There are

P. Bartalos (✉) · M. Bieliková
Faculty of Informatics and Information Technologies, Institute of Informatics and Software
Engineering, Slovak University of Technology in Bratislava, Ilkovičova 3, 842 16 Bratislava,
Slovakia
e-mail: bartalos@fiit.stuba.sk; bielik@fiit.stuba.sk

M.B. Blake et al. (eds.), *Semantic Web Services*, DOI 10.1007/978-3-642-28735-0_20,   313
© Springer-Verlag Berlin Heidelberg 2012

already several works presenting promising results considering effective QoS aware service composition [1, 5, 8, 10, 13].

In this chapter, we deal with our approach for QoS aware web service composition. Our work focuses on issues related to the description of the functional aspects of the web services, QoS optimization, reaction to the changes in the service environment, performance, and development of a composition system able to handle continuing arrival of the composition queries.

20.2   Approach: QoS and Pre-/Post-condition Aware Web Service Composition in Dynamic Environment

The overall web services composition process is a complex task including several sub-processes. The general aim of service composition is to arrange multiple web services into a composite service to supply more complex functionality. Beyond this basic objective, there are a lot of aspects of the problem, which are showing to be inevitable, or have the potential to make the composition much usable. These include the consideration of the QoS, pre-/post-conditions [2, 5, 9], user preferences, constraints and context [11, 15], user assistance [14], and transactional behavior of service compositions [7, 12]. The main objectives of our work, presented in [2–5], are related to the following issues:

* *Functional aspects of web services.* Proper representation of the functional aspects of web services is crucial for automatic web service composition. The existing approaches exploit additional meta-data depicting the semantics of the I/O parameters to describe the service behavior. This approach is showing to be insufficient. The proposed solutions are oriented to express the pre-/post-conditions of web services. Our work deals with the pre-/post-conditions aware composition and shows the feasibility of this approach.
* *QoS optimization.* Beside the functional requirements, the user is usually interested also in non-functional properties of web services. Hence, the QoS optimization during service composition is important. We deal with a service composition aware of the QoS and capable to find the best solution considering them.
* *Changes in the service environment.* The web service environment is frequently changing in time. New services are deployed, some of them are removed. The changes relate also to the QoS attributes, whose values might evolve in time. We developed a composition approach capable to react to these changes and thus providing a solution reflecting the actual situation in the service environment.
* *Effectiveness.* As the Web in general grows, also the set of web services which are available in repositories is rising. We deal with the problem of performance and scalability of the composition process considering large number of services to be searched and composed.
* *Composition system.* Our aim is not only to develop a composition method, but also to design a composition system realizing it.

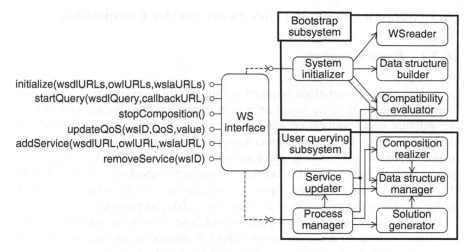

initialize(wsdlURLs,owlURLs,wslaURLs) ○—
startQuery(wsdlQuery,callbackURL) ○—
stopComposition() ○—
updateQoS(wsID,QoS,value) ○—
addService(wsdlURL,owlURL,wslaURL) ○—
removeService(wsID) ○—

Fig. 20.1 Composition system architecture

- *Continuing composition query arrival.* In real scenarios, the composition system must dynamically compose services based on the actual composition goal. The composition queries may arrive from multiple users. To handle multiple queries, our composition system stands as a querying system able to process continuing arrival of composition queries, while reacting also to possible frequent changes in the service environment.

Our composition system is built according to the requirements defined in the rules of *Web Services Challenge 2009*. However, it provides more functionality than required in the challenge. The additional requirements, which are not stated in the challenge rules, are: consideration of the pre-/post-conditions of the web services, processing multiple composition queries arriving independently, and reaction to the changes in the service environment.

Based on the defined requirements, we designed software architecture of the composition system as presented in Fig. 20.1. The system is divided into two main subsystems. The first includes components responsible for the preprocessing (bootstrap) phase. The second is responsible for the user querying phase.

The *Bootstrap subsystem* is coordinated by the *System initializer* realizing the preprocessing based on the web service set available at the startup time. The *User querying subsystem* is managed by the *Process manager* coordinating the composition. *Composition realizer* is responsible to run the composition method. It operates over the data structures managed by the *Data structure manager*. In the case of a change in a service environment, the *Process manager* initializes the *Service updater* to process the request.

20.3   Solution: Realizing QoS Aware Service Composition

20.3.1   Basic Concepts

In general, several operations required during service composition have a complexity exponentially rising based on certain parameters. The main issues making our solution good performing are preprocessing, effective data structures, and algorithms. The preprocessing is crucial to quickly respond to composition queries. In our approach, we perform preprocessing before responding to composition queries, see top of Fig. 20.2. During it, we analyze the actual service set and build effective data structures. All the important computations, which can be done without the knowledge of the composition goal, are realized during preprocessing.

The most important is that we evaluate which services are compatible and can be chained. Based on the compatibility check a directed acyclic graph (DAG) of services is built. Each service is represented by a node. If two services can be chained, there is a directed edge from the ancestor to the successor service.

The remaining task during composition is to find the initial/final services, and the design of the data-/control-flow, see bottom of Fig. 20.2. The initial services are those having provided all inputs in the composition query. The final services are those directly producing the outputs defined in the composition goal. The search for the initial, final services, and the design of the data-/control-flow can be completely realized only when the goal and the provided inputs are known. However, the effective data structures, built during preprocessing, are used here to realize them quickly.

Our composition method is based on two processes. The first selects services which have provided all inputs and thus can be used in the composition. The second selects services which cannot be used because they do not have provided all inputs. The inputs are provided in the composition query, or as an output of another usable service. The second process is not necessary to find the composition. It is used only to faster the selection of the usable services, which is a necessary process.

To select usable services, forward chaining is performed, starting with the initial services. During it, we realize also the QoS optimization. After, the solution is read backward, starting with the final services. The reading continues through each input, which is not provided in the composition query, over all the services already included in the composition. Considering QoS, we select those providers of the inputs which have the best aggregated value of a particular QoS attribute. We do not deal with calculation of the overall unified quality measure of the composite service.

The selection of the usable services becomes a high computation demanding task as the number of services, their inputs, and number of input providers rises. The complexity of the computation is also strongly dependent on the interconnections between the services. To speed up the process, we propose *service space restriction* selecting the *unusable services*, i.e. a service with at least one unprovided input. The process lies on identification of such services, for which there is at least one input not provided by any available service, i.e. the only case when it is usable is when the

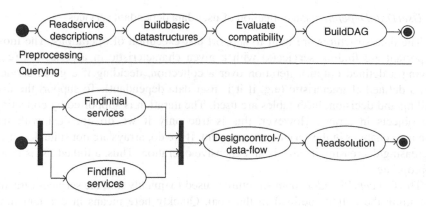

Fig. 20.2 Overview of the composition process

respective input is provided in the composition query. These services are identified during preprocessing. We call them *user data dependent services*.

20.3.2   Data Structures

In our solution, we focused on a design of such data structures, which can be built during preprocessing and then effectively used during the querying phase. To do this, it was necessary to analyze which calculations, required during the composition, can be realized without the knowledge of the composition goal. The most important of them are: the processing of the semantic meta-data associated with the web services, the evaluation of which services can be chained (i.e. which services provide/consume inputs/outputs from the other services), and the search for services having an input/output associated with a defined concept or its sub-/super-class. To support these calculations, the following data structures are built:

- *Service*: represents a service including its attributes and reference to other *Services* providing/consuming its inputs/outputs (i.e. the collection of *Services* represents the directed acyclic graph of services). The *Service* data structure is the basic item in the other data structures.
- *AllServices*: a collection of all available services.
- *ConceptProviders*: a collection, where an element is a key-value pair of (1) *concept* and (2) list of services having an output associated with *concept* or a concept subsuming *concept*.
- *ConceptConsumers*: a collection, where an element is a key-value pair of (1) *concept* and (2) list of services having an input associated with the *concept* or a concept subsumed by the *concept*.
- *InputDependents*: the same as *ConceptConsumers*, but contains only user data dependent services.

- *UserDataDependents*: a collection of user data dependant services.

The data structures are built to support fast execution of operations. The most important are finding service(s) with a given characteristic in a collection (e.g. having a defined output), iteration over a collection, deciding if a given service has a defined characteristic (e.g. if it is user data dependant). To support the fast finding and decision, hash tables are used. The iteration is supported by collecting the objects in arrays. However, this is true only if we do not deal with the dynamic changes in the service environment. If we do, arrays are not suitable, since increasing/decreasing its size is an expensive operation. Thus, a linked list is more appropriate.

The *ConceptProviders* data structure is used to quickly find the services directly providing the outputs defined in the goal. Quickly here means in constant time for each output. Analogically to the *ConceptProviders*, the *ConceptConsumers* is used to find the services consuming the inputs provided in the composition query. Notice that during the look for the initial, or final service, it is not necessary to deal with evaluation of the subsumption relations between concepts. The elements in the *ConceptProviders* and *ConceptConsumers* do already consider this.

The *AllServices*, *InputDependents*, and *UserDataDependents* data structures are used during the design of the control-/data-flow. During the selection of the usable services, the directed acyclic graph is traversed, starting with the initial services. Its creation during preprocessing showed to be crucial. The actual composition can be seen as a selection of a subgraph. It is already not required to find services providing, or consuming a defined input/output (i.e. the interconnections).

20.4   Lessons Learned

20.4.1   Evaluation Results

Our experiments were realized using data sets generated by a generator tool used at *Web services Challenge 2009*. We used service sets consisting from 10,000 up to 100,000 services. For each set, the solution requires at least 50 services to compose. The ontology consists from 30,000 to 190,000 concepts. The test sets are available at http://semco.fiit.stuba.sk/compositiontestsets/. Our experiments were realized using a Java implementation of our composition system on a machine with two 64-bit Quad-Core AMD Opteron(tm) 8354 2.2 GHz processors with 64 GB RAM.

Control-/Data-Flow Design

The aim of evaluating the control-/data-flow design phase is to show the: efficiency and scalability of our composition approach, and a dramatic improvement of the composition time due to the service space restriction.

Table 20.1 Experimental results

Services	Composition time (msec)			Number of code line crosses					
	Par	Seq	NoUnusab	Par A	Seq A	NoUnusab A	Par B	Seq B	NoUnusab B
10,000	6	7	97	991	976	30,767	552	149	5,079
20,000	11	19	336	1,728	1,611	53,686	831	263	9,249
30,000	42	49	718	3,041	3,018	72,825	539	319	12,325
40,000	29	44	932	1,144	1,136	52,368	606	204	8,438
50,000	22	49	1,022	1,674	1,661	55,542	376	248	12,023
60,000	60	94	1,454	2,613	2,581	62,142	1,361	199	11,645
70,000	82	106	2,070	1,577	1,413	76,288	751	254	12,713
80,000	76	75	2,806	2,194	2,174	76,390	602	290	11,230
90,000	173	222	2,613	3,299	3,262	50,183	471	329	11,025
100,000	121	179	3,009	2,711	2,667	75,202	895	256	14,589

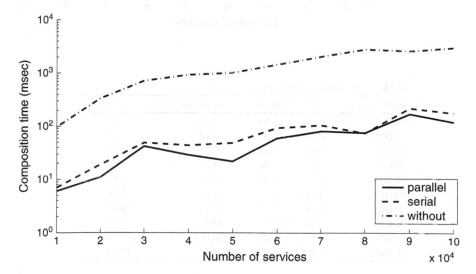

Fig. 20.3 Composition time

During experiments we tested three configurations of the composition system:

1. The service space restriction runs in parallel with selection of the usable services, denoted as *Par*,
2. The selection of the usable services starts after the service space restriction finishes, denoted as *Seq*,
3. The service space restriction is not applied, denoted as *NoUnusab*.

The results are summarized in Table 20.1, Figs. 20.3 and 20.4. To be able to clearly state the difference between the composition with/without service space restriction, we provide also measurements depicting the number of crosses through

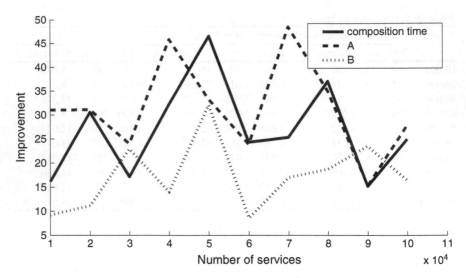

Fig. 20.4 Improvements

Table 20.2 Operation times (in ms)

Web services	Add	Remove	Reinitialization	Composition
10,000	0.84	1.68	1.86	4.95
20,000	0.92	2.84	4.46	14.8
30,000	1.02	4.82	10.2	46.3
40,000	1.53	7.88	13.8	35.9
50,000	1.13	5.81	19.6	37.3
60,000	2.12	10.3	25.6	93.6
70,000	1.39	9.11	27.1	88.0
80,000	1.48	13.3	29.5	64.3
90,000	1.86	9.46	30.0	271.8
100,000	1.89	12.0	51.1	152.4

two steps of the selection of usable services process. These two steps, denoted as
A and B, are the most critical steps considering the performance (appear in the most
inner loop). For other details, see [4].

Dynamic Changes in the Service Environment

The evaluation of our approach, in the context of dynamic changes in the service
environment, focuses on the time required to add/remove services, compose services, and reinitialize the system, which is required after each composition (note
that the QoS changes are managed in constant time). The results are presented in
Table 20.2 and Fig. 20.5. During the experiment, we measured the time of adding

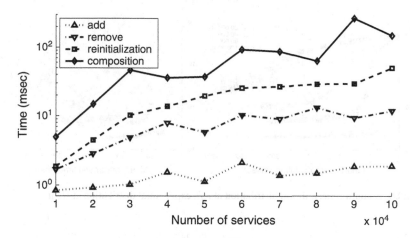

Fig. 20.5 Add/remove, reinitialization, and composition time

1,000 new services into a repository and permanently removing the same services.
The added/removed services are selected randomly.

As we see, removing a service is more time demanding as adding. The composition and update times do not necessary rise as the number of services rises.
This is because they are strongly affected also by the interconnections between the
services and their QoS parameters. Based on this, the hardest test set is the set with
90,000 services. The reinitialization time is linearly dependent on the number of
all services and the number of user data dependent services. In our experiments, it
reached maximum of 53% of the composition time, 33% in average.

Continuing Query Arrival

The evaluation of the composition system focuses on its behavior due to continuing
query arrival, without or with the dynamic changes in the service environment. We
measured the sojourn time and the queue sizes. The sojourn time is the time between
the generation of the update, or composition request and the end of its processing.
We assume that the arrivals of both the update requests and composition queries are
continuous, independent, and occur according to a *Poisson process*. Hence, the inter
arrival times follow exponential distribution. Since there is no real application, we
cannot verify these assumptions. Due to this, we present also results where the inter
arrival times follow uniform distribution, to see the effect of the different distribution
on the measured parameters.

Figure 20.6 presents the dependency between the mean inter arrival time and
the sojourn time, for data sets with 20,000 up to 100,000 services. Note that the
sojourn time and the mean queue size are linearly dependent. As we see, there is
a significant difference between the results when different distributions are used.
In the exponential case, the standard deviation of the results is higher. Moreover, it

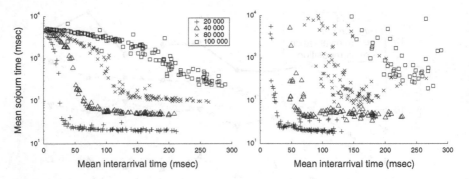

Fig. 20.6 Sojourn time: uniform distribution at *left*, exponential distribution at *right*

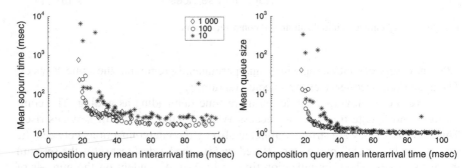

Fig. 20.7 Effect of dynamic changes in the service environment

presents rising tendency as the complexity of the data set and the sojourn time rises. The system tends to be in a stable state if the mean inter arrival time is more than a double of the composition time.

Figure 20.7 presents the effect of the dynamic changes in the service environment. We had been simulating arrival of requests to add a new, or permanently remove a service, with various inter arrival times, with exponential distribution. We used the test set with 20,000 services.

The experiments show that the sojourn time is not significantly enlarged, even if the update requests are frequent. We had dramatically decreased the inter arrival time of the update requests, from 1,000 to 10 ms. Even in this case, we observed only a little delay in the composition. The mean composition query queue size remained low and the stability of the system was not upset.

20.4.2 *Important Observations*

The issues affecting the effectiveness of the composition system can be divided into two categories: technical and conceptual solution. The technical issues include the chosen technologies and the way how they are used. Our experience is that these cannot be neglected. The performance of the system is significantly affected by the chose of the programming language and platform, relational database, external libraries, and other technical issues. On the other side, the performance characteristics of the standard technologies are usually known and a skilled developer should be able to choose the right technology and use it in an effective manner. Hence, however it can be a time and knowledge demanding task, the proper technical solution can be designed straightforwardly. This is not true for the conceptual solution whose bases are the proper methods and algorithms. These must be designed specifically for the web service composition problem. The most important issues, which had been shown to be important in our composition system, are: data structures, preprocessing, state space restriction, and parallel execution.

Data Structures and Preprocessing

The proper selection of the built-in data structures, or those available in external libraries, is important if the performance is an issue. Beside this, if we build our own data structure, it is crucial to know which operations, performed over it, can become a potential performance bottle-neck. In this context it is very important to realize what can be done before we actually respond to composition queries. We believe that preprocessing is necessary to make the actual composition fast and do not waste time by realizing calculations which could be done already before.

A preliminary version of our composition system used relational databases to store some data and perform certain operations over them. During the composition, the relational database was queried to find relevant services (for example services consuming/requiring some data). Since the mentioned version of our composition system considers also the pre-/post-conditions of the services, the search for these services is a quite complex task. It requires evaluating logical implication between two formulae. The relational database showed to be a useful tool to realize this task. The declarative approach helped to relatively easily develop a method evaluating if a post-condition of some service implicates the pre-condition of another one (i.e. if they can be chained). Although the approach was convenient and feasible to realize the required task, the performance was poor when more complex logical formulae were processed. Due to this, we left the idea of using relational databases during service composition. Our new approach is based on encoding of the formulae and is realized purely programmatically [5].

Restricting the Service Space

One of the most important conceptual solutions in our composition system is the application of the service space restriction. It removes services which cannot be used in the composition, because they have not provided all inputs. The reduced

service space is much easier to traverse and thus we can find the services required
in the composition much faster.

We had been experimenting with different configurations of the composition
system (as introduced in Sect. 20.4.1). The best results, considering the composition
time, are achieved with the *Par* configuration. In this case the selection of the usable
services runs in parallel with the service space restriction. The *Ser* configuration
performs slightly slower. According to *NoUnusab* configuration, both *Par* and *Ser*
perform faster in more than one order of magnitude. The results considering the *Par*
configuration show that even with the hardest test set, the composition time is below
200 ms, which can be still considered as acceptable from the user point of view.

Figure 20.3 shows the significant difference between the cases when service
space restriction is applied, and if not. The measurements of how much times did the
execution of the *select usable* services process cross those steps which appear in the
most inner loops (denoted as A and B) clarifies the reason of the improvement, see
Table 20.1. The decrease of the crosses, when service space restriction is applied,
explains the improvement of the composition time. The *Par* configuration presents
an improvement from 15 to 46 times in terms of composition time and adequate
improvement in terms of the number of crossing steps A, B, see Fig. 20.4.

Parallel Execution

The difference in performance between the *Par* and *Seq* configurations is minor
(in contrast to the situation when no service space restriction is applied). During
our experiments the *Seq* configuration performed in average 27% slower than the
Par configuration. The differences between the composition times showed high
deviation, from which we can conclude that the difference is significantly affected
by the service set (e.g. the interconnections between the services based on their
inputs/outputs). The experiments showed that, to achieve good results, it is not
necessary to realize full service space restriction (remove all unusable services).
The full service space restriction is realized during the *Seq* configuration. In this
case, the selection of the usable services executes the fastest. However, since it must
wait until the restriction is done, the overall composition time is not the lowest.

In the *Par* configuration, the selection of the usable services runs in parallel with
service space restriction. The composition finishes when the usable services are
selected. It is not necessary to wait until the service space restriction finishes too
(since it is not a necessary process). This causes that the *Par* configuration performs
better than *Seq* also on single-core computers. On multi-core computers, the benefits
of parallel execution are even more significant.

Despite the fact that, the selection of the usable services and the service
space restriction operate over the same data structure (the directed acyclic graph
of services and the services themselves), no synchronization is required. In our
implementation, due to the guaranteed atomicity of the access and assignment of
the program variables, no conflicts can occur. The variable, to which both processes
perform assignments, is the variable holding the information about the usability of

the service. In any case, for a particular service, a value to this variable is assigned only once and only by one of the processes (it is once set as usable or unusable). Hence, the overall composition process does not suffer from synchronization overhead.

As we mentioned earlier, to realize the composition, we use forward chaining selecting the usable services. Note that in general, the solution for a particular composition goal does not require using all the usable services. This means that it is not necessary to find all the usable services. The selection of them can stop if the actual usable service set provides a solution for a composition goal and it is the optimal one considering the QoS. Hence, we can stop the selection of the usable services earlier and thus potentially save execution time. However, in this case, there is an additional overhead in the process because of the check if we already found a solution. Our experiments with the service sets, generated by the WS-Challenge generator tool, showed that it is not useful to perform a check and stop the selection of the usable services earlier. The reason is that, to find a solution, it was required to select almost all the usable services. We believe that this is only a special case of the data sets generated by the WS-Challenge generator tool. We expect that, in real scenarios with real services, it would be better to check whether we already have a solution for a composition goal and stop the selection of the usable services in this case and thus save execution time.

In the context of improving the performance of our composition system, we have been experimenting with executing the service space restriction in multiple, parallel threads. If the composition system operates on a computer with more than two threads, this could potentially lead to faster composition. It is important that in this case, the synchronization is already an issue. Conflicts may occur if multiple threads try to access the same object at the same time. Hence, the threads must be synchronized during those steps, when they may potentially manipulate the same object.

During our experiments, we tried to run the selection of usable service in two up to six threads, on a computer with eight cores. The results showed that the synchronization overhead is too high. Comparing with the situation when the usable services selection runs in one thread, i.e. no synchronization was required, the results with multiple threads were worse.

20.4.3 Conclusions and Future Work

The automation of the service composition is crucial to be able to supply varying composition goals. Several problems must be addressed and solved to achieve fully automatic service composition. In the last years, the research of service composition automation tended to be focused on the issues related to the QoS, performance, and semantic matching problem. There is a tremendous amount of work concerning these. On the other side, there are plenty of problems without interest.

The performance in the context of service composition aware of the QoS showed to be a challenging task. Even though, there already are approaches showing promising results. Several papers showed that it is possible to realize a service composition even if the number of services considered during the composition rises to thousands, ten-thousands, or even some hundred-thousands. To make an imagination about the number of currently available web services, we made an overview of some public repositories. The number of services which can be found in these repositories varies from some thousands up to some ten thousands. The largest one, called *Seekda* (http://webservices.seekda.com/), included in August 2010 about 28,000 service descriptions, as claimed by the repository provider. Based on this, we believe that the performance of the current solutions is sufficient to handle the real situation.

The research regarding QoS aware service composition is noticeably farther as for example the research dealing with the pre-/post-conditions. We suppose that the research attention in future should move to other problems than the efficiency of QoS aware composition. Since there is still no practical application of service composition, we should analyze what are the real scenarios where it could be applied and which problems have to be solved before this can be achieved.

More attention should be given to those issues which are not related to the actual arrangement of services into a composite one. The whole life-cycle of web services, and their composition should be covered. More interest is required to the design of web services. The design decisions significantly affect the further possibility to compose the developed services. Semantic annotation of web services is also a subject of further research. Methodologies and tool should be developed to support this process. Finally, it should be analyzed if the description focusing on the I/O and pre-/post-conditions is sufficient.

20.5 Summary

In this chapter we presented a QoS and pre-/post-condition aware web service composition system able to handle changes in the service repository and continuing arrival of the composition queries. The composition system showed to be effective and scalable. We have presented experimental results showing good performance even if the number of services, which have to be considered during the composition, rises to 100,000 services. Even during the hardest test set, the system was able to perform the composition below 200 ms.

The main sources of the effectiveness of our solution are: effective data structures built during preprocessing and service space restriction. We have analyzed what calculations are required to be performed during service composition and which ones of them do not rely on the knowledge of any composition query. These calculations should be realized as preprocessing. Moreover, we have precisely designed data structures which supply fast operations performed during the composition.

One of the most important issues of our approach is a service space restriction. Its aim is to speed up the composition process by restricting the number of services which must be considered when looking for a solution. Our experiments showed that the restriction is very beneficial. It improved the composition time in more than one order of magnitude.

Another important issue of our approach is the parallel execution of processes realizing the composition. Our composition approach is based on two processes, the selection of the usable services and the service space restriction. These can run in parallel without additional synchronization overhead. The parallel execution showed to be useful on single-core and also multi-core computers. We have been experimenting also with running the selection of the usable services in multiple threads. This approach did not show usefulness, since in this case the synchronization is required and the caused overhead leads to slower execution.

Our approach showed to be effective and scalable even in large-scale situations. We believe that our and also other composition systems proved to be effective enough to be able to operate over the amount of services which are available nowadays. Moreover, they show good scalability, thus, even if we expect that the number of services will raise, the performance will not be a problem.

We believe that the web services composition research should move its focus from performance to other important issues. The existing approaches to automatic service composition base on semantic meta-data. It is known that the idea of semantic web services and the Semantic Web in general is not practically applied. There is a lack of methodologies and tools supporting the creation, processing, and management of semantic metadata. Our future work is to move our focus from performance issues and deal with other aspect of the service composition, which are important to achieve practical applicability.

Acknowledgements This work was supported by the Scientific Grant Agency of SR, grant No. VG1/0675/11 and it is a partial result of the Research & Development Operational Program for the project Research of methods for acquisition, analysis and personalized conveying of information and knowledge, ITMS 26240220039, co-funded by the ERDF. We would like to thank to the organizers of the WS-Challenge 2009 to provide a great forum progressing the research of web services composition.

References

1. M. Alrifai, T. Risse, P. Dolog, W. Nejdl, A scalable approach for qos-based web service selection, in *Service-Oriented Computing Workshops* (Springer, Berlin/Heidelberg/New York, 2009), pp. 190–199
2. P. Bartalos, M. Bieliková, Fast and scalable semantic web service composition approach considering complex pre/postconditions, in *Proceedings of the 2009 IEEE Congress on Services, International Workshop on Web Service Composition and Adaptation*, (IEEE CS, Washington, 2009), pp. 414–421
3. P. Bartalos, M. Bieliková, Semantic web service composition framework based on parallel processing, in *International Conference on E-Commerce Technology 2009* (IEEE CS, Los Alamitos, 2009), pp. 495–498
4. P. Bartalos, M. Bieliková, Effective qos aware web service composition in dynamic environment, in *International Conference on Information Systems Development 2010*, Prague, Springer, 2010

5. P. Bartalos, M. Bieliková, Qos aware semantic web service composition approach considering pre/postconditions, in *International Conference on Web Services 2010*, Miami, Fl, pp. 345–352, IEEE CS, 2010
6. S. Dustdar, W. Schreiner, A survey on web services composition. IJWGS **1**(1), 1–30 (2005)
7. J. El Haddad, M. Manouvrier, M. Rukoz, Tqos: transactional and qos-aware selection algorithm for automatic web service composition. IEEE Trans. Serv. Comput. **3**(1), 73–85 (2010)
8. W. Jiang, C. Zhang, Z. Huang, M. Chen, S. Hu, Z. Liu, Qsynth: A tool for qos-aware automatic service composition, in *International Conference on Web Services 2010*, Miami, Fl, pp. 42–49, IEEE CS, 2010
9. S. Kona, A. Bansal, M. Brian Blake, G. Gupta, Generalized semantics-based service composition, in *ICWS 08: Proceedings of the 2008 IEEE International Conference on Web Services*, Beijing, pp. 219–227, IEEE CS, 2008
10. F. Lécué, N. Mehandjiev, Towards scalability of quality driven semantic web service composition, in *International Conference on Web Services 2009*, Los Angeles, CA, pp. 469–476, IEEE CS, 2009
11. M. Mrissa, C. Ghedira, D. Benslimane, Z. Maamar, F. Rosenberg, S. Dustdar, A context-based mediation approach to compose semantic web services. ACM Trans. Intern. Tech. **8**(1), 23 (2007)
12. M.P. Papazoglou, Web services and business transactions. WWW'03 **6**(1), 49–91 (2003)
13. F. Rosenberg, M.B. Muller, P. Leitner, A. Michlmayr, A. Bouguettaya, S. Dustdar, Meta-heuristic optimization of large-scale qos-aware service compositions, in *IEEE International Conference on Services Computing*, Miami, 2010, pp. 97–104
14. V. Rozinajova, M. Kasan, P. Navrat, Towards more effective support of service composition: utilizing ai-planning, semantics and users assistance, in *International Conference on Next Generation Web Services Practices*, Prague, 2009, pp. 50–55
15. H.Q. Yu, S. Reiff-Marganiec, A backwards composition context based service selection approach for service composition, in *International Conference on Services Computing 2009*, Bangalore, pp. 419–426, IEEE CS, 2009

Chapter 21
Semantics-Based Web Service Composition Engine

Srividya K. Bansal, Ajay Bansal, and Gopal Gupta

Abstract Service-oriented computing (SOC) has emerged as the eminent market environment for sharing and reusing service-centric capabilities. For Web services to become practical, an infrastructure needs to be supported that allows users and applications to discover, deploy, compose and synthesize services automatically. This automation can take place effectively only if formal semantic descriptions of Web services are available. In this chapter we report on an implementation of a semantics-based automated service discovery and composition engine that we have developed. This engine employs a multi-step narrowing algorithm and is efficiently implemented using the constraint logic programming technology. The salient features of our engine are its scalability, i.e., its ability to handle very large service repositories, and its extremely efficient processing times for discovery and composition queries. This implementation was evaluated at the Web Services Challenge (WSC) in 2006 and 2007 (Blake et al. (2006) WSC-06: the web service challenge. In: Joint proceedings of the CEC/EEE, San Francisco, The Web Services Challenge (2007) http://www.wschallenge.org/wsc07/).

S.K. Bansal (✉)
Arizona State University, Polytechnic Campus, Mesa, AZ, USA
e-mail: srividya.bansal@asu.edu

A. Bansal
Georgetown University, Washington, DC, USA
e-mail: bansal@cs.georgetown.edu

G. Gupta
The University of Texas at Dallas, Richardson, TX, USA
e-mail: gupta@utdallas.edu

M.B. Blake et al. (eds.), *Semantic Web Services*, DOI 10.1007/978-3-642-28735-0_21,
© Springer-Verlag Berlin Heidelberg 2012
329

21.1   Introduction

A Web service is a program accessible over the web that may effect some action or change in the world (i.e., causes a side-effect). Examples of such side-effects include a web-base being updated because of a plane reservation made over the Internet, a device being controlled, etc. The next milestone in the Web's evolution is making *services* ubiquitously available. As automation increases, these Web services will be accessed directly by the applications rather than by humans [2]. In this context, a Web service can be regarded as a "programmatic interface" that makes application to application communication possible. An infrastructure that allows users to discover, deploy, synthesize and compose services automatically is needed in order to make Web services more practical.

In order to make services ubiquitously available, a semantics-based approach is required such that applications can reason about a services capability to a level of detail that permits their discovery, deployment, composition and synthesis [7]. Informally, a service is characterized by its input parameters, the outputs it produces, and the side-effect(s) it may cause. The input parameter may be further subject to some pre-conditions, and likewise, the outputs produced may have to satisfy certain post-conditions. For discovery and composition, one could take the syntactic approach in which the services being sought in response to a query simply have their inputs syntactically match those of the query. Alternatively, one could take the semantic approach in which the semantics of inputs and outputs, as well as a semantic description of the side-effect is considered in the matching process. Several efforts are underway to build an infrastructure for service discovery and composition [5, 9, 10]. These efforts include approaches based on the semantic web (such as USDL [1], OWL-S [8], WSML [15], WSDL-S [16]) as well as those based on XML, such as Web Services Description Language (WSDL [14]). Approaches such as WSDL are purely syntactic in nature, that is, they only address the syntactical aspects of a Web service. In this chapter, we present our approach for automatic service composition which was evaluated at Web Services Challenge 2006 and 2007 [4].

21.2   Approach

Discovery and Composition are two important tasks related to Web services. In this section we formally describe these two tasks.

21.2.1   The Discovery Problem

Given a repository of Web services, and a query requesting a service (we refer to it as the query service in the rest of the text), automatically finding a service from the

Fig. 21.1 Substitutable
service

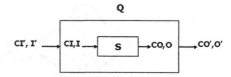

repository that matches these requirements is the Web service Discovery problem. Valid solutions to the query satisfy the following conditions:

1. They produce at least the query output parameters and satisfy the query post-conditions;
2. They use only from the provided input parameters and satisfy the query pre-conditions;
3. They produce the query side-effects. Some of the solutions may be over-qualified, but they are still considered valid as long as they fulfill input and output parameters, pre/post conditions, and side-effects requirements.

Definition (Service): A service is a 6-tuple of its pre-conditions, inputs, side-effect, affected object, outputs and post-conditions. $S = (CI, I, A, AO, O, CO)$ is the representation of a service where CI is the pre-conditions, I is the input list, A is the service's side-effect, AO is the affected object, O is the output list, and CO is the post-conditions.

Definition (Repository of services): Repository is a set of Web services.

Definition (Query): The *query service* is defined as $Q = (CI', I', A', AO', O', CO')$ where CI' is the pre-conditions, I' is the input list, A' is the service affect, AO' is the affected object, O' is the output list, and CO' is the post-conditions. These are all the parameters of the requested service.

Definition (Discovery): Given a repository R and a query Q, the Discovery problem can be defined as automatically finding a set S of services from R such that $S = \{s|s = (CI, I, A, AO, O, CO), s \in R, CI' \Rightarrow CI, I \sqsubseteq I', A = A', AO = AO', CO \Rightarrow CO', O \sqsupseteq O'\}$. The meaning of $\sqsubseteq$ is the subsumption (subsumes) relation and $\Rightarrow$ is the implication relation. For example, say x and y are input and output parameters respectively of a service. If a query has $(x > 5)$ as a pre-condition and $(y > -x)$ as post-condition, then a service with pre condition $(x > 0)$ and post-condition $(y > x)$ can satisfy the query as $(x > 5) \Rightarrow (x > 0)$ and $(y > x) \Rightarrow (y > -x)$ since $(x > 0)$.

In other words, the discovery problem involves finding suitable services from the repository that match the query requirements. Valid solutions have to produce *at least* those output parameters specified in the query, satisfy the query pre and post-conditions, use *at most* those input parameters that are provided by the query, and produce the same side-effect as the query requirement as shown in Fig. 21.1.

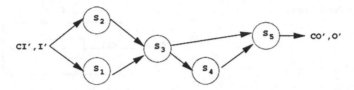

Fig. 21.2 Example of a composite service as a directed acyclic graph

21.2.2   The Composition Problem

Given a repository of service descriptions, and a query with the requirements of the requested service, in case a matching service is not found, the composition problem involves automatically finding a directed acyclic graph of services that can be composed to obtain the desired service. Figure 21.2 shows an example composite service made up of five services S_1 to S_5. In the figure, I' and CI' are the query input parameters and pre-conditions respectively. O' and CO' are the query output parameters and post-conditions respectively. Informally, the directed arc between nodes S_i and S_j indicates that outputs of S_i constitute (some of) the inputs of S_j.

Definition (Composition): The Composition problem can be defined as automatically finding a directed acyclic graph $G = (V, E)$ of services from repository R, given query $Q = (CI', I', A', AO', O', CO')$, where V is the set of vertices and E is the set of edges of the graph. Each vertex in the graph represents a service in the composition. Each outgoing edge of a node (service) represents the outputs and post-conditions produced by the service. Each incoming edge of a node represents the inputs and pre-conditions of the service. The following conditions should hold on the nodes of the graph:

1. $\forall i\ S_i \in V$ where S_i has exactly one incoming edge that represents the query inputs and pre-conditions, $I' \sqsupseteq \bigcup_i I_i$, $CI' \Rightarrow \wedge_i CI_i$.
2. $\forall i\ S_i \in V$ where S_i has exactly one outgoing edge that represents the query outputs and post-conditions, $O' \sqsubseteq \bigcup_i O_i$, $CO' \Leftarrow \wedge_i CO_i$.
3. $\forall i\ S_i \in V$ where S_i has at least one incoming edge, let $S_{i1}, S_{i2}, \ldots, S_{im}$ be the nodes such that there is a directed edge from each of these nodes to S_i. Then $I_i \sqsubseteq \bigcup_k O_{ik} \cup I'$, $CI_i \Leftarrow (CO_{i1} \wedge CO_{i2} \ldots \wedge CO_{im} \wedge CI')$.

The meaning of the $\sqsubseteq$ is the subsumption (subsumes) relation and $\Rightarrow$ is the implication relation. In other words, a service at any stage in the composition can potentially have as its inputs all the outputs from its predecessors as well as the query inputs. The services in the first stage of composition can only use the query inputs. The union of the outputs produced by the services in the last stage of composition should contain all the outputs that the query requires to be produced. Also the post-conditions of services at any stage in composition should imply the pre-conditions of services in the next stage.

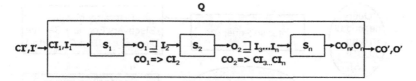

Fig. 21.3 Sequential web service composition

Figure 21.3 explains one instance of sequential composition problem pictorially. When the number of nodes in the graph is equal to one, the composition problem reduces to the discovery problem. When all nodes in the graph have not more than one incoming edge and not more than one outgoing edge, the problem reduces to a sequential composition problem (i.e., the graph is a linear chain of services).

21.3 Solution: A Multi-step Narrowing Solution

We assume that a directory of services has already been compiled, and that this directory includes semantic descriptions for each service. In this section we describe our Service Composition algorithm.

21.3.1 Service Composition Algorithm

For service composition, the first step is finding the set of composable services. The correct sequence of execution of these services can be determined by the pre-conditions and post-conditions of the individual services. That is, if a subservice S_1 is composed with subservice S_2, then the post-conditions of S_1 must imply the pre-conditions of S_2. The goal is to derive a single solution, which is a directed acyclic graph of services that can be composed together to produce the requested service in the query. Figure 21.4 shows a pictorial representation of our composition engine.

In order to produce the composite service which is represented by a graph as shown in Fig. 21.2, we filter out services that are not useful for the composition at multiple stages. Figure 21.5 shows the filtering stages for the particular instance shown in Fig. 21.2. The composition routine starts with the query input parameters. It finds all those services from the repository which require a subset of the query input parameters. In Fig. 21.5, CI, I are the pre-conditions and the input parameters provided by the query. S_1 and S_2 are the services found after step 1. O_1 is the union of all outputs produced by the services at the first stage. For the next stage, the inputs available are the query input parameters and all the outputs produced by the previous stage, i.e., $I_2 = O_1 \cup I$. I_2 is used to find services at the next stage, i.e., all those services that require a subset of I_2. In order to make sure we do not end up in cycles, we get only those services which require at least one parameter from the

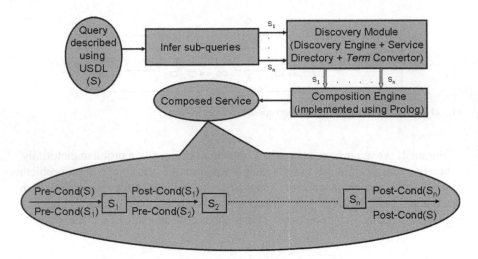

Fig. 21.4 Web service composition

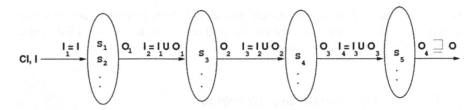

Fig. 21.5 Multi-step narrowing solution

outputs produced in the previous stage. This filtering continues until all the query output parameters are produced. At this point we make another pass in the reverse direction to remove redundant services which do not directly or indirectly contribute to the query output parameters. This is done starting with the output parameters working our way backwards.

Algorithm: Composition
Input: QI - QueryInputs, QO - QueryOutputs, QCI - Pre-Cond, QCO - Post-Cond
Output: Result - ListOfServices
1. L ← NarrowServiceList(QI, QCI);
2. O ← GetAllOutputParameters(L);
3. CO ← GetAllPostConditions(L);
4. While Not ($O \sqsupseteq QO$)
5.   I = QI ∪ O; CI ← QCI ∧ CO;
6.   L' ← NarrowServiceList(I, CI);
7. End While;
8. Result ← RemoveRedundantServices(QO, QCO);
9. Return Result;

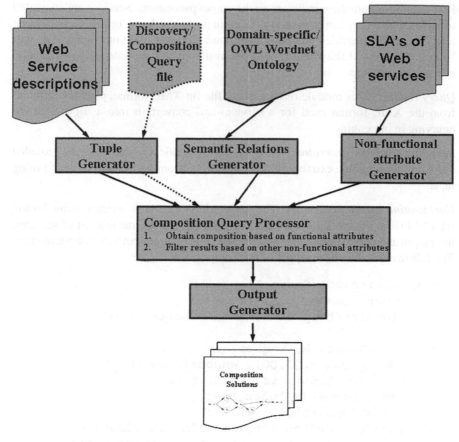

Fig. 21.6 High-level design of composition engine

21.3.2   *Implementation*

Our composition engine is implemented using Prolog [11] with Constraint Logic Programming over finite domain [6], referred to as CLP(FD) hereafter. The high-level design of our prototype is shown in Fig. 21.6. In this section we briefly describe our software system and its modules.

Triple generator: The triple generator module converts each service description into a triple as follows:

   (Pre-Conditions, affect-type(affected-object, I, O), Post-Conditions)

The function symbol affect-type is the side-effect of the service and affected-object is the object that changed due to the side-effect. I is the list of inputs and O is the list of outputs. Pre-Conditions are the conditions on the input parameters and

Post-Conditions are the conditions on the output parameters. Services are converted to triples so that they can be treated as terms in first-order logic. In case conditions on a service are not provided, the Pre-Conditions and Post-Conditions in the triple will be null. Similarly if the affect-type is not available, this module assigns a generic affect to the service.

Query reader: This module reads a query file (in XML format, possibly different from the XML format used for a service) and converts it into a triple used for querying in our engine.

Semantic relations generator: We obtain the semantic relations from the provided ontology. This module extracts all the semantic relations and creates a list of Prolog facts.

Composition query processor: The composition engine is written using Prolog with CLP(FD) library. It uses a repository of facts, which contains list of services, their input and output parameters and the semantic relations between the parameters. The following is the code snippet of our composition engine:

```
composition(sol(Qname,A)) :-
    dQuery(Qname,_,_),
    minimize(compTask(Qname,A,SeqLen),SeqLen).

compTask(Qname, A, SeqLen) :-
    dQuery(Qname,QI,QO), encodeParam(QO,OL),
    narrowO(OL,SL), fd_set(SL,Sset),
    fdset_member(S_Index,Sset),
    getExtInpList(QI,InpList),
    encodeParam(InpList,IL), list_to_fdset(IL,QIset),
    serv(S_Index,SI,_), list_to_fdset(SI,SIset),
    fdset_subtract(SIset,QIset,Iset),
    comp(QIset,Iset,[S_Index],SA,CompLen),
    SeqLen #= CompLen + 1,   decodeS(SA,A).

comp(_, Iset, A, A, 0) :- empty_fdset(Iset),!.
comp(QIset, Iset, A, SA, SeqLen) :-
    fdset_to_list(Iset,OL),
    narrowO(OL,SL), fd_set(SL,Sset),
    fdset_member(SO_Index,Sset), serv(SO_Index,SI,_),
    list_to_fdset(SI,SIset),
    fdset_subtract(SIset,QIset,DIset),
    comp(QIset,DIset,[SO_Index|A],SA,CompLen),
    SeqLen #= CompLen + 1.
```

The query is converted into a Prolog query that looks as follows:

composition(queryService, ListOfServices).

The engine will try to find a *ListOfServices* that can be composed into the requested *queryService*. Our engine uses the built-in, higher order predicate "bagof" to return all possible *ListOfServices* that can be composed to get the requested *queryService*.

Output Generator: After the Composition Query processor finds a matching service, or the graph of atomic services for a composed service, the results are sent to the output generator in the form of triples. This module generates the output files in any desired XML format. For the WS-Challenge, this module will produce output files in the format provided [13].

21.4 Lessons Learned

21.4.1 Requirements of an Ideal Engine

Our initial prototype implementation was evaluated at the Web services Challenge. We realized that some of the features of an ideal Discovery/Composition engine are correctness, small query execution time, ability to perform incremental updates, and ability to use cost functions to rank solutions.

Correctness: An important requirement for an ideal engine is to produce correct results, i.e, the services discovered and composed by it should satisfy all the requirements of the query. Also, the engine should be able to find all services that satisfy the query requirements.

Small query execution time: Querying a repository of services for a requested service should take a reasonable amount of (small) time, i.e., a few milliseconds. Here we assume that the repository of services may be pre-processed (indexing, change in format, etc.) and is ready for querying. In case services are not added incrementally, then time for pre-processing a service repository is a one-time effort that takes considerable amount of time, but gets amortized over a large number of queries.

Incremental updates: Adding or updating a service to an existing repository of services should take a small amount of time. A good Discovery/Composition engine should not pre-process the entire repository again, rather incrementally update the pre-processed data (indexes, etc.) of the repository for this new service added.

Cost function: If there are costs associated with every service in the repository, then a good Discovery/Composition engine should be able to give results based on requirements (minimize, maximize, etc.) over the costs. We can extend this to services having an attribute vector associated with them and the engine should be able to give results based on maximizing or minimizing functions over this attribute vector.

These requirements have driven the design and development of our semantics-based Web service Composition engine. Also our initial implementation and entries

Q

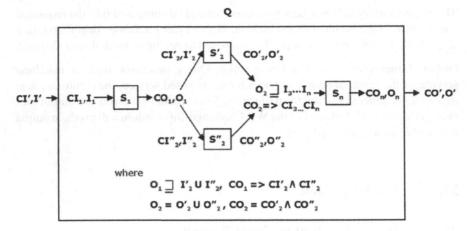

Fig. 21.7 Non-sequential composition

to the challenge performed a sequential composition. We realized that a generalized composition that can handle non-sequential composition and conditional composition would be of great value. We further refined our design and formulated a generalized Web service composition as shown in Fig. 21.7.

Definition (Generalized composition): The generalized Composition problem can be defined as automatically finding a directed acyclic graph $G = (V, E)$ of services from repository R, given query $Q = (CI', I', A', AO', O', CO')$, where V is the set of vertices and E is the set of edges of the graph. Each vertex in the graph either represents a service involved in the composition or post-condition of the immediate predecessor service in the graph, whose outcome can be determined only after the execution of the service. Each outgoing edge of a node (service) represents the outputs and post-conditions produced by the service. Each incoming edge of a node represents the inputs and pre-conditions of the service. The following conditions should hold on the nodes of the graph:

1. $\forall i\ S_i \in V$ where S_i has exactly one incoming edge that represents the query inputs and pre-conditions, $I' \sqsupseteq \bigcup_i I_i$, $CI' \Rightarrow \wedge_i CI_i$.
2. $\forall i\ S_i \in V$ where S_i has exactly one outgoing edge that represents the query outputs and post-conditions, $O' \sqsubseteq \bigcup_i O_i$, $CO' \Leftarrow \wedge_i CO_i$.
3. $\forall i\ S_i \in V$ where S_i represents a service and has at least one incoming edge, let $S_{i1}, S_{i2}, \ldots, S_{im}$ be the nodes such that there is a directed edge from each of these nodes to S_i. Then $I_i \sqsubseteq \bigcup_k O_{ik} \cup I'$, $CI_i \Leftarrow (CO_{i1} \wedge CO_{i2} \ldots \wedge CO_{im} \wedge CI')$.
4. $\forall i\ S_i \in V$ where S_i represents a condition that is evaluated at run-time and has exactly one incoming edge, let S_j be its immediate predecessor node such that there is a directed edge from S_j to S_i. Then the inputs and pre-conditions at node S_i are $I_i = O_j \cup I'$, $CI_i = CO_j$. The outgoing edges from S_i represent the outputs that are same as the inputs I_i and the post-conditions that are the result of the condition evaluation at run-time.

The post-conditions of services at any stage in composition should imply the pre-conditions of services in the next stage. When it cannot be determined at compile time whether the post-conditions imply the pre-conditions or not, a *conditional* node is created in the graph. The outgoing edges of the conditional node represent the possible conditions which will be evaluated at run-time. Depending on the condition that holds, the corresponding services are executed. That is, if a subservice S_1 is composed with subservice S_2, then the postconditions CO_1 of S_1 must imply the preconditions CI_2 of S_2. The following conditions are evaluated at run-time:

if $(CO_1 \Rightarrow CI_2)$ then execute S_1;
else if $(CO_1 \Rightarrow \neg CI_2)$ then no-op;
else if (CI_2) then execute S_1;

21.4.2 Efficiency and Scalability Issues

In this section we discuss implementation strategies of our system that were important and necessary for creating an efficient and scalable system. After our participation in the challenge in 2006, we realized that incorporating these strategies in our system was important and guided us towards a Multi-step narrowing solution that was implemented using Constraint Logic Programming.

Pre-processing of data: Our system initially pre-processes the repository and converts all service descriptions into Prolog terms. In case of semantic approach, the semantic relations are also processed and loaded as Prolog terms in memory. Once the pre-processing is done, then discovery or composition queries are run against all these Prolog terms and hence we obtain results quickly and efficiently. The built-in indexing scheme and constraints in CLP(FD) facilitate the fast execution of queries. During the pre-processing phase, we use the term representations of services to set up constraints on services and the individual input and output parameters. This further helped us in getting optimized results.

Execution efficiency: The use of CLP(FD) helped significantly in rapidly obtaining answers to the discovery and composition queries. We tabulated processing times for different size repositories and the results are shown in the next section. As one can see, after pre-processing the repository, our system is quite efficient in processing the query. The query execution time is insignificant.

Programming efficiency: The use of Constraint Logic Programming helped us in coming up with a simple and elegant code. We used a number of built-in features such as indexing, set operations, and constraints and hence did not have to spend time coding these ourselves. This made our approach efficient in terms of programming time as well. Not only the whole system is about 200 lines of code, but we also managed to develop it in less than 2 weeks.

Scalability: Our system allows for incremental updates on the repository, i.e., once the pre-processing of a repository is done, adding a new service or updating an existing one will not need re-execution of the entire pre-processing phase. Instead we can easily update the existing list of CLP(FD) terms loaded in the memory and run discovery and composition queries. Our estimate is that this update time will be negligible, perhaps a few milliseconds. With real-world services, it is likely that new services will get added often or updates might be made on existing services. In such a case, avoiding repeated pre-processing of the entire repository will definitely be needed and incremental update will be of great practical use. The efficiency of the incremental update operation makes our system highly scalable.

Use of external database: In case the repository grows extremely large in size, then saving off results from the pre-processing phase into some external database might be useful. This is part of our future work. With extremely large repositories, holding all the results of pre-processing in the main memory may not be feasible. In such a case we can query a database where all the information is stored. Applying incremental updates to the database will be easily possible thus avoiding re-computation of the pre-processed data.

Searching for Optimal Solution: If there are any properties with respect to which the solutions can be ranked, then setting up global constraints to get the optimal solution is relatively easy with the constraint based approach. For example, if each service has an associated cost, then the discovery and the composition problem can be redefined to find the solutions with the minimal cost. Our system can be easily extended to take these global constraints into account.

21.4.3   Evaluation Results

We evaluated our approach on different size repositories and tabulated the Pre-processing time and the Query Execution time. We noticed that there was a significant difference in the pre-processing time between the first and the subsequent runs (after deleting all the previous pre-processed data) on the same repository. What we found is that the repository was cached after the first run and that explained the difference in the pre-processing time for the subsequent runs. We used repositories from the WS-Challenge web site [13].

Table 21.1 shows performance results for our Discovery Algorithm and Table 21.2 shows results for Composition. The times shown in the tables are the wall clock times. The actual CPU time to pre-process the repository and execute the query should be less than or equal to the wall clock time. The results are plotted in Fig. 21.8. The graphs exhibit behavior consistent with our expectations: for a fixed repository size, the preprocessing time increases with the increase in number of input/output parameters. Similarly, for fixed input/output sizes, the preprocessing time is directly proportional to the size of the service repository. However, what is surprising is the efficiency of service query processing, which is negligible (just 1–3 ms) even for complex queries with large service repositories.

Table 21.1 Performance of discovery algorithm

Repository Size (number of services)	Number of I/O parameters	Non-cached pre-processing time (in secs)	Cached pre-processing time (in secs)	Query execution time (in msecs)
2,000	4–8	36.5	7.3	1
2,000	16–20	45.8	13.4	1
2,000	32–36	57.8	23.3	2
2,500	4–8	47.7	8.7	1
2,500	16–20	58.7	16.6	1
2,500	32–36	71.6	29.2	2
3,000	4–8	56.8	12.1	1
3,000	16–20	77.1	19.4	1
3,000	32–36	88.2	33.7	3

Table 21.2 Performance of our composition algorithm

Repository Size (number of services)	Number of I/O parameters	Non-cached pre-processing time (in secs)	Cached pre-processing time (in secs)	Query execution time (in msecs)
2,000	4–8	36.1	7.2	1
2,000	16–20	47.1	15.1	1
2,000	32–36	60.2	24.7	1
3,000	4–8	58.4	11.0	1
3,000	16–20	60.1	17.8	1
3,000	32–36	102.0	42.1	1
4,000	4–8	71.2	13.4	1
4,000	16–20	87.9	25.3	1
4,000	32–36	129.2	43.1	1

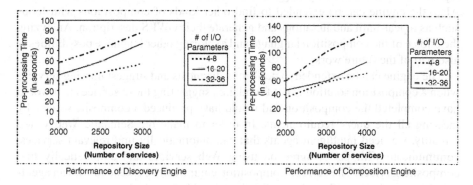

Performance of Discovery Engine   Performance of Composition Engine

Fig. 21.8 Performance of discovery/composition engine

21.4.4   Advantages and Disadvantages

Our implementation pre-processes the repository data first and then executes queries on the pre-processed data. This was an important step towards creating a scalable system that can perform incremental updates instead of reprocessing the entire dataset in response to repository updates. Though this was an important feature in our design, it turned out to be a disadvantage in the Web services challenge where total execution time was being measured. Systems that processed data in-memory on-the-fly performed faster though they were not scalable. In the initial years of the challenge the test data sets were not too large and hence the in-memory processing turned out to be a better approach to creating a fast engine. The competition has now evolved over time to use large test data sets and measures both pre-processing time and query execution time individually.

21.4.5   Conclusions and Future Work

Our semantics-based Web Service Composition engine finds substitutable and composite services that best match the desired service. Given semantic description of Web services, our engine produces optimal results (based on criteria like cost of services, number of services in a composition, etc.). The composition flow is determined automatically without the need for any manual intervention. Our engine finds any sequential or non-sequential composition that is possible for a given query. Use of Constraint Logic Programming helped greatly in obtaining an efficient implementation of this system.

The Composition engine can be further extended to support an external database to save off pre-processed data. This will be particularly useful when service repositories grow extremely large in size which can easily be the case in future. Also, the engine can be extended to find other kinds of compositions with loops such as repeat-until and iterations and generate their OWLS description. Analyzing the choice of the composition language and exploring other language possibilities is also part of the future work.

The engine can be extended to perform a diagnosis and suggest missing services when a composition solution is not found, i.e., suggesting those services that would have completed the composition and would have produced a composite service by meeting all the query requirements. In order to make the Semantic Web vision a reality, we need intelligent agents that can automatically find relevant services, communicate with peers, agree on using Web services and automatically find composite services. The current Composition engine can be extended with an agent-based approach that will work in a distributed and heterogeneous environment.

21.5   Summary

To catalogue, search and compose services in a semi-automatic to fully-automatic manner we need infrastructure to publish services, document services, and query repositories for matching services. We presented our approach for Web service composition. Our composition engine can find a graph of atomic services that can be composed to form the desired service as opposed to simple sequential composition in our previous work [4]. Given semantic description of Web services, our solution produces accurate and quick results. We are able to apply many optimization techniques to our system so that it works efficiently even on large repositories. The use of Constraint Logic Programming (CLP) helped greatly in obtaining an efficient implementation of this system. We used a number of built-in features such as indexing, set operations, and constraints and hence did not have to spend time coding these ourselves. These CLP(FD) built-ins facilitated the fast execution of queries.

References

1. A. Bansal, S. Kona, L. Simon, A. Mallya, G. Gupta, T. Hite, A universal service-semantics description language, in *Proceedings of European Conference On Web Services (ECOWS)*, Växjö, 2005, pp. 214–225
2. A. Bansal, K. Patel, G. Gupta, B. Raghavachari, E.D. Harris, J.C. Staves, Towards intelligent services: a case study in chemical emergency response, in *International Conference on Web Services (ICWS)*, Orlando, 2005, pp. 751–758
3. M.B. Blake, W. Cheung, M.C. Jaeger, A. Wombacher, WSC-06: the web service challenge, in *Joint Proceedings of the CEC/EEE*, San Francisco, 2006
4. S. Kona, A. Bansal, G. Gupta, T. Hite, Web service discovery and composition using USDL. in *Proceedings of CEC/EEE*, San Francisco, 2006
5. D. Mandell, S. McIlraith, Adapting BPEL4WS for the semantic web: the bottom-up approach to Web service interoperation, in *International SemanticWeb Conference (ISWC)*, Sanibel Island, 2003
6. K. Marriott, P.J. Stuckey, *Programming with Constraints: An Introduction* (MIT Press, Cambridge, 1998)
7. S. McIlraith, T.C. Son, H. Zeng, Semantic web services. IEEE Intell. Syst. **16**(2), 46–53 (2001)
8. OWL-S. www.daml.org/services/owl-s/1.0/owl-s.html. Accessed 1 May 2012
9. M. Paolucci, T. Kawamura, T. Payne, K. Sycara, Semantic matching of web service capabilities, in *International Semantic Web Conference (ISWC)*, Sardinia, 2002, pp. 333–347
10. J. Rao, D. Dimitrov, P. Hofmann, N. Sadeh, A mixed-initiative approach to semantic web service discovery and composition, in *International Conference on Web Services (ICWS)*, Chicago, 2006
11. L. Sterling, S. Shapiro, *The Art of Prolog* (MIT Press, Cambridge, 1994)
12. The Web Services Challenge (2007), http://www.wschallenge.org/wsc07/
13. Web Services Challenge, http://www.wschallenge.org/. Accessed 1 May 2012
14. Web Services Description Language, http://www.w3.org/TR/wsdl. Accessed 15 Mar 2001
15. WSML – Web Service Modeling Language, http://www.wsmo.org/wsml/
16. WSDL-S: Web Service Semantics http://www.w3.org/Submission/WSDL-S. Accessed 7 Nov 2005

Chapter 22
Efficient Composition of Semantic Web Services with End-to-End QoS Optimization

Bin Xu and Sen Luo

Abstract The efficiency of QoS-aware service composition is important since most service composition problems are known to be NP-hard. With the growing number of Web services, service composition is like a decision problem on selecting services or/and execution plans to satisfy the users end-to-end QoS requirements (e.g. response time, throughput). Composite services with the same functionality may have different execution plans, which may cause different end-to-end QoS. A model combining semantic data-links and QoS is proposed, which leads to an efficient approach to automatic construction of a composite service with optimal end-to-end QoS. The approach is based on a greedy algorithm to select both services and execution plans for composite services. Empirical and theoretical analysis of the approach show that its time complexity is $O(mn^2)$ for a repository with n services and an ontology with m concepts. Moreover, the approach takes linear time in practice when using an index to search services in the repository.

22.1 Introduction

In the service-oriented computing paradigm, single web services can be combined to create value-added services for business applications. Service compositions have put into industrial practice in many areas like e-commerce, supply chain management, finance, and travel. With the growing number of web servers with different quality parameters (QoS), the service composition problem becomes a QoS-aware service composition problem, which is to find a composite service with the optimal end-to-end QoS.

The QoS-aware service composition problem has been discussed in many studies [1, 11–13]. Given an abstract composition request (execution plan), which can be

B. Xu (✉) · S. Luo
Department of Computer Science and Technology, Tsinghua University, Beijing, China
e-mail: xubin@keg.cs.tsinghua.edu.cn; luos@keg.cs.tsinghua.edu.cn

M.B. Blake et al. (eds.), *Semantic Web Services*, DOI 10.1007/978-3-642-28735-0_22,
© Springer-Verlag Berlin Heidelberg 2012

stated in a work flow language (e.g. BPEL [8]), each abstract service (task node) in the execution plan has a candidate service list. The goal is to select one concrete service for each abstract service such that the aggregated QoS satisfies the user's end-to-end QoS requirement.

However, the problem we discuss about, The QoS-aware service composition with data-links, is not based on an abstract composition. The first goal of the service composition is to find a proper execution plan. The execution plan may contain many kinds of relationships between services such as sequence, parallel and switch. The services in the composite service should be linked by data, which requires that former services' output can satisfy successive service's input by semantics. In practice, several composite services may satisfy the request, but with different QoS. Thus, the second goal is to find the composite service with the best end-to-end QoS. The QoS attributes include response time, throughput, cost, availability, reliability and etc.

22.2   Approach: QoS-Aware Service Composition

The abstract composition based QoS-aware service composition problem can be mapped to a Multi-Choice Multidimensional Knapsack problem , which is known to be NP-hard in the strong sense [5]. Consequently, an optimal solution may not be expected to be found in a reasonable amount of time [4]; so many approximation algorithms have been proposed. Zeng et al. [12,13] used global planning to optimize multiple QoS criteria. Yu et al. [11] proposed a broker-based architecture as well as a heuristic algorithm to optimize the end-to-end QoS with multiple QoS constrains. Alrifai and Risse [1] gave a method to handle the global QoS requirements through combining global optimization with local selection.

The QoS-aware service composition model with the data-links is shown in Fig. 22.1. The composition request includes a provided data list and a required data list. The goal is to find an execution plan with data-links from the service repository and to get the optimal end-to-end QoS. Followings are some basic definitions:

Definition 22.1. Service $S = \{D_{in}, D_{out}, Q_s\}$ where
$D_{in}(S) = \{d_i(S)|d_i(S)$ is an input data type of service S, defined by one specific concept in an ontology}
$D_{out}(S) = \{d_j(S)|d_j(S)$ is an output data type of service S, defined by one specific concept in an ontology}
$Q_s(S) = \{q_r(S)|q_r(S)$ is a QoS attribute of service S, such as cost or response time}

The most important features of a service include the I/O parameters and QoS. Each I/O parameter of a service can be mapped to a concept of some ontology to express semantic information about the service. Thus, the QoS can represent any kind of non-functional property.

Request: Provided Data and Required Data

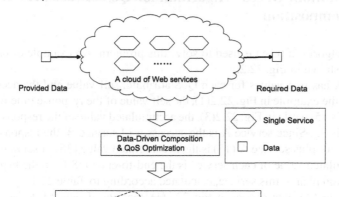

Solution: Execution Plan with Data-Link and Optimal end-to-end QoS

Fig. 22.1 Conceptual overview

Definition 22.2. Composite Service $CS = \{D_{in}, D_{out}, P, Q_{cs}\}$ where

$D_{in}(CS) = \{d_i(CS) | d_i(CS)$ is an input data type of CS, defined by one specific concept in an ontology$\}$

$D_{out}(CS) = \{d_j(CS) | d_j(CS)$ is an output data type of CS, defined by one specific concept in an ontology$\}$. If CS is composed by S_1 to S_n, then $D_{out}(CS) = \{D_{out}(S_1), D_{out}(S_2), \ldots\ldots, D_{out}(S_n)\}$

P: The implementation of the CS as an execution plan (such as BPEL) where services can be invoked following certain dependency rules to perform certain tasks.

$Q_{cs}(CS) = \{q_r(CS) | q_r(CS)$ is end-to-end QoS attribute of CS, such as total cost or total response time$\}$

The problem of QoS-aware service composition with data-links can be stated as follows:

For a given composition request $R = \{D_{in}(R), D_{out}(R), q_r\}$ and a given service repository $SS = S_1, S_2, \ldots\ldots, S_n$, find a composite service CS such that:

1. $D_{in}(R) \supseteq D_{in}(CS), D_{out}(R) \subseteq D_{out}(CS)$;
2. The end-to-end QoS attribute $q_r(CS)$ is optimal.

This problem is concerned with a single QoS attribute of a composite service, not the integration of all the QoS attributes. The system can find the composite service with the minimum response time or maximum throughput. A utility function to weight different QoS attributes is not discussed in this paper.

22.3   Solution: Greedy Algorithm for QoS-Aware Service Composition

A greedy algorithm (GA) is used to solve this problem. An example of GA search process is shown in Fig. 22.2.

The GA has two values for each QoS attribute, self value and the accumulated value. For the example in Fig. 22.2(1), the self value of the response time for service A (Srv A) is 15; while in Fig. 22.2(3), the accumulated value of the response time for service A is 35. Since service A is the successor of service B, the response time of service B (20) plus service A (15) is the accumulated value (35) of service A. Thus, the accumulated value of each service is the end-to-end QoS from the beginning of the execution plan to this service, calculated according to Table 22.1

The given I/O data shown in Fig. 22.2(1) consists of data #1, #2, #3 *and* #4, while the required output data type is data #8, #9 *and* #10. In Fig. 22.2(2), the

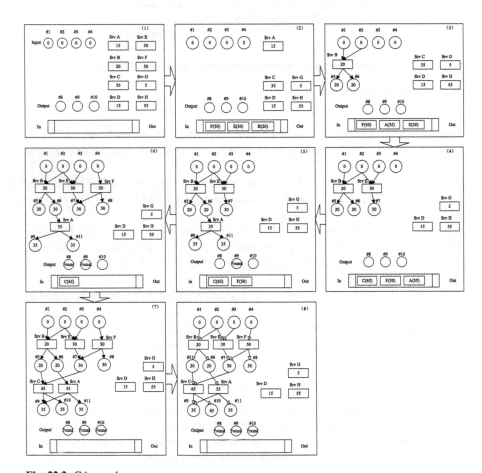

Fig. 22.2 GA search process

Table 22.1 QoS calculation for various composite structures

QoS attribute	Composition structure	Calculation
Response time	Parallel	$R = max\{R_i\}$
	Sequence	$R = \sum_{i=1}^{n}\{R_i\}$
	Switch	$R = min\{R_i\}$
Throughput	Parallel	$T = min\{T_i\}$
	Sequence	$T = min\{T_i\}$
	Switch	$T = max\{T_i\}$

satisfied services (B, E, F) are pushed into the queue sorted by the accumulated response times. In Fig. 22.2(3), the service with the minimum accumulated response time is popped and added into the solution (execution plan), with newly satisfied service A pushed into the queue. Then in Fig. 22.2(4), the first service in the queue, service E, is popped. The procedure is repeated in Fig. 22.2(5, 6) until all the required output data types are found in Fig. 22.2(7). Then, a trace back procedure helps to find the solution shown in Fig. 22.2(8).

22.4 Lessons Learned

22.4.1 Algorithm Description

The key idea is to select the service with the best accumulated QoS. A priority queue is defined to record all the satisfied services. A service becomes satisfied only when all of its inputs are satisfied. The priority of a service is determined by its accumulated QoS. A smaller accumulated response time gives a higher priority. A larger accumulated throughput also gives a higher priority.

The DataType in the algorithm is defined in Listing 22.1.

The main procedure is shown in Listing 22.2.

A trace back function is used at the end of the main process to generate BEPL format solution, which is described in Listing 22.3.

22.4.2 Algorithm Correctness Analysis

If the algorithm has proposed a solution, the solution must have the minimum accumulated response time. The solution is denoted as $Solution_1$ (with accumulated response time R_1). Suppose there is another solution with a smaller accumulated response time which will be denoted as $Solution_2$ (with a smaller accumulated response time R_2). If service S_{last} is the last popped service of $Solution_1$, then when S_{last} is pushed into the queue, its accumulated response time

```
 1   struct DataType
 2   {
 3        //the concept the data type belongs to
 4        Concept concept_of_data type;
 5        //the accumulated response time for producing it
 6        float response_time;
 7        //point to the service which generates it
 8        Service ptr_response_time_generator;
 9   }
10   struct Service
11   {
12        String name;
13        //the least response time for invoking it
14        float response_time;
15        //time interval between start and complete
16        float self_response_time;
17        List<DataType> input;
18        List<DataType> output;
19   }
```

Listing 22.1 Definition of DataType

```
 1   for each Service S_i
 2     S_i.response_time = S_i.self_response_time
 3   for each DataType D_j
 4     D_j.response_time = infinity
 5   for each DataType D_k in the provided DataTypes
 6     D_k.response_time = 0
 7     available_data.add(D_k)
 8   available_service = getAvalblSrv(available_data)
 9   for each Service S_m in available_service
10     priority_queue.push(S_m)
11   while(priority_queue is not empty and required data are not covered){
12     Service s = priority_queue.pop()
13       for each DataType D_o in s.output
14         if(D_o.response_time > s.response_time)
15           D_o.response_time = s.response_time
16         available_data.add(D_o)
17       available_service =getAvalblSrv(available_data)
18       for each Service S_n in available_service
19         S_n.response_time+=maxResponseTime(S_n.input)
20         priority_queue.push(S_n)
21       if all required DataType are found
22         for each required DataType D_r
23             traceback(D_r);
24   }
```

Listing 22.2 Main GA process

```
 1   traceback(D_r){
 2       if D_r belongs to the provided DataTypes
 3           return
 4       print("<sequence>\n<parallel>")
 5       for each DataType D_m in D_r.ptr_response_time_generator.input
 6           traceback(D_m);
 7       print(" </parallel>")
 8       print("invoke " + D_n.ptr_response_time_generator.name)
 9       print(</sequence>)
10   }
```

Listing 22.3 Trace back Search

is R_1. When S_{last} is popped, at least one of the services in $Solution_2$, denoted as S_0, must not have been popped from the queue; otherwise all the services in $Solution_2$ would have been popped to get $Solution_2$ rather than $Solution_1$. Then at least one of services that produce the inputs of S_0 is not popped, otherwise S_0 would be popped. A trace back (a service is not popped because at least one of services that produce the inputs of it is not popped) will show a service that is satisfied by the provided data but not popped. However this is impossible, since this service was pushed into the queue when the queue was initialized and its accumulated response time was smaller than R_1 (otherwise R_2 will not be smaller than R_1). There is a contradiction so $Solution_1$ must be the optimal solution.

22.4.3 Algorithm Correctness Analysis

Suppose n is the number of the overall services and m is the number of the overall concepts in the ontology.

The algorithm has several main operations, denoted as SCAN (scan unused services to find satisfied services), POP (pop out a service from the priority queue) and PUSH (push a service into the priority queue).

For the POP operation, every service is popped from the queue at most once, so there are at most n POP operations. Every POP operation takes $O(1)$ time, so POP operations take $O(1)n = O(n)$ time.

The PUSH operation also has at most n PUSH operations. Each PUSH operation takes $O(m)$ time to update the corresponding response times and takes $O(logn)$ time to put the service at the right position. Thus all the Push operations take $(O(m) + O(logn))n = O(mn + nlogn)$ time.

The SCAN operation takes place at most n times regardless of the original SCAN, since there are n services overall and the SCAN operation is executed right after a POP operation. In each SCAN operation, the time to determine whether a service is satisfied is $O(m)$ and there are at most n unused services. So each SCAN operation takes $O(m)n = O(mn)$ time. All the SCAN operations take $O(mn) * O(n) = O(mn^2)$ time.

An index is used to record all the relationships between the I/O data types and the services. Assume a data type has a constant number of services, c, on average. Then $O(c)$ time is needed to update the response time in PUSH and to determine whether a service is satisfied in SCAN. The SCAN operation needs only to test at most c services to determine the satisfied services. The time complexity is then $O(cn + nlogn)$ for PUSH and $O(c^2n)$ for SCAN.

In summary, the time complexity is $O(n) + O(mn + nlogn) + O(mn^2) = O(mn^2)$. If an index is used, the time complexity becomes $O(n) + O(cn + nlogn) + O(c^2n) = O(nlogn)$. This is a very loose upper bound, which only happens in the worst case. In the best case, all the popped services are services in the optimal solution and the algorithm takes only a constant amount of time (assume the number of service in the optimal solution is n_0 and there are at most cn_0 PUSH operations, n_0 POP operations and n_0 SCAN operations. The total time is then $O(cn_0) + O(cn_0 + n_0logn_0) + O(c^2n_0)$, which is constant).

Table 22.2 Concepts and services increase with the same ratio

TestSet	Test set properties		Time cost (ms)	
	Number of concepts	Number of web services	QDA	GA
1	37,500	500	125	78
2	75,000	1,000	300	78
3	112,500	1,500	600	93
4	150,000	2,000	800	109
5	187,500	2,500	950	109
6	225,000	3,000	1,040	78

22.4.4 Performance Evaluation

The algorithm performance was tested based on the requirements of the annual Web Service Challenge(WS-Challenge) [9] which focuses on the semantic composition of Web services with QoS. WS-Challenge provides a set of standard testing tools and data sets.

WS-Challenge uses a generator to generate a test set. Each test set includes four input files: (1) Services.wsdl provides the available Web services; (2) Taxonomy.owl [6] provides all the concepts in the ontology with every input/output data type of the Web services defined as an instance of a concept; (3) Servicelevelagreements.wsla [7] provides the self QoS values (response time and throughput) of the Web services; and (4) Query.wsdl gives the user requests including the provided and required data types. The generator also gives a standard result for each test set.

The tests first used the generator to generate 18 test sets. Then the composition algorithm and other algorithm are used to evaluate on the 18 test sets with the time cost recorded during the composition procedure. The results are checked against the results provided by WS-Challenge.

The GA performance is compared to that of QDA (QoS-driven algorithm) [10] which placed second in the WS-Challenge 2009 performance evaluation.

The tests are on a machine with Intel Core 2 CPU 1.83 GHz, 1 GB RAM, running Windows XP.

The 18 test sets generated by the generator each has different scale of Web services and ontology concepts. There are about 20,000 Web services available on the Internet [2], with the most widely used "OpenCyc" ontology [3] having about 150,000 concepts.

The 1–6 test sets are designed with different numbers of concepts and Web services but a constant ratio between them. Table 22.2 lists the settings for these six test sets and the time cost for the QDA and GA algorithms.

The results in Table 22.2 show that the QDA time cost increases with the scale of the test sets, while the GA time cost is constant at about 100 ms, even for 225,000 concepts and 3,000 services. In test set 6, the GA is more than ten times faster than the QDA.

The 7–12 test sets fixed the number of Web services at 20,000 and changed the ontology concepts from 50,000 to 300,000 with the interval of 50,000. These sets

Table 22.3 Concepts increase while the services remain constant

TestSet	Test set properties		Time cost (ms)	
	Number of concepts	Number of web services	QDA	GA
7	50,000	20,000	600	234
8	100,000	20,000	800	141
9	150,000	20,000	1,100	140
10	200,000	20,000	1,220	188
11	250,000	20,000	1,440	219
12	300,000	20,000	1,680	210

Table 22.4 Services increase while the concepts remain constant

TestSet	Test set properties		Time cost (ms)	
	Number of concepts	Number of web services	QDA	GA
13	150,000	2,000	580	78
14	150,000	4,000	620	78
15	150,000	6,000	750	94
16	150,000	8,000	880	109
17	150,000	10,000	960	125
18	150,000	12,000	1,040	125

are closer to development trends on the real Web, with the semantic Web expanding rapidly and more ontologies appearing, the number of Web services has remained stable in recent years. Table 22.3 lists the results for these six test sets, and the time costs.

The results in Table 22.3 show that the QDA time cost increases linearly with the increasing number of concepts. The GA is more efficient with the time cost constant at about 200 ms. With test set 12, the GA was about eight times faster than the QDA.

In the 13–18 test sets, the number of concepts was held constant while the number of Web services increased. In the future, when most concepts are well described by ontologies, the number of Web services may increase because of new businesses. Table 22.4 lists the results for these six test sets, and the time costs.

The results in Table 22.4 show that when the number of concepts is constant, the QDA time cost changes linearly with the increasing number of services. The GA is again stable and efficient at about 100 ms. In test set 18, the GA is about eight times faster than the QDA.

For all 18 test sets, the QoS values in the composition result are the same as the standard results with the optimal QoS.

In all 18 test sets, the GA algorithm was very efficient, performing the composition in no more than 219 ms. Test sets 1–6 and 13–18 had time less than 125 ms. The GA is two to ten times faster than the QDA with the GA performance very stable even with large number of services and concepts. The GA always selects the service with the best accumulated QoS, so the services in the solution need not be updated in the following search process which improves the efficiency. The QDA

Table 22.5 Trace back search overhead

TestSet	Test set properties		Time cost (ms)	
	Number of concepts	Number of web services	GA	Trim-GA
1	5,000	500	55	47
2	40,000	4,000	85	78
3	60,000	8,000	95	93
4	60,000	8,000	165	156
5	100,000	15,000	550	159

is an iterative search process with new services added to the solution layer by layer until all the output data is found, so many redundant services are included. The GA search space is also much smaller than that of the QDA.

22.4.5 Advantages and Disadvantages

In context of service composition, we have found the following advantages in our algorithm:

- A QoS-aware service composition model with semantic data-links is proposed. Unlike the QoS-aware service composition problem having an abstract composition as a request, this model uses provided data and required data as request. Service composition request can be given out more easier by provided and required data than by an abstract composition. The QoS optimization in this model finds the execution plan as well as selects the services for the optimal end-to-end QoS.
- An efficient data-driven, QoS-optimized service composition algorithm is given. A greedy algorithm is used to select services from a repository of services and to construct execution plan to ensure the optimal end-to-end QoS. A theoretical analysis of the algorithm shows its time complexity is $O(mn^2)$, with linear time dependence in practice by using indexing. Test data sets from the Web Service Challenge [9] are used to compare with other algorithms [10]. Tests show that the algorithm significantly outperforms existing algorithms in terms of composition efficiency while achieving optimal end-to-end QoS.

22.4.6 Conclusions and Future Work

Trace back search is indeed a heavy overhead as shown in Table 22.5 (Trim-GA denotes GA algorithm without trace back search part). Test sets used here are the five test sets used in the WS-Challenge 2009.

To further improve the efficiency, an optimized trace back search is necessary to reduce the quantity of the services appeared in the solution. So our future work will be trace back search optimization.

22.5 Summary

This chapter presents a QoS-aware service composition model with data-links. The end-to-end QoS optimization in this model finds the execution plan and selects services with the optimal accumulated QoS. A greedy algorithm is used to select services for a given composition request. Tests show that the algorithm significantly outperforms existing algorithms in terms of composition time cost while still achieving the optimal end-to-end QoS. The algorithm was on problems having the scale of a real Web (20,000 services and 300,000 concepts). The algorithm will be applied to Web services with dynamic QoS in future work to satisfy real-time composition requests. A run-time composition engine will be developed to integrate real services.

References

1. M. Alrifai, T. Risse, Combining global optimization with local selection for efficient qos-aware service composition, in *WWW*, Madrid, Spain, 2009
2. E. Al-Masri, Q.H. Mahmoud, Investigating web services on the world wide web, in *WWW*, 2008
3. Cyc Ontology (2010), http://www.cyc.com/cyc/
4. I. Maros, *Computational Techniques of the Simplex Method*. International Series in Operations Research & Management Science, Vol. 61 (Kluwer, Boston, 2003)
5. D. Pisinger, *Algorithms for Knapsack Problems*, PhD thesis, University of Copenhagen, 1995
6. Web Ontology Language (2004), http://www.w3.org/TR/owl-features/
7. Web Service Level Agreements (2003), http://www.research.ibm.com/wsla/
8. Web Services Business Process Execution Language (2007), http://docs.oasis-open.org/wsbpel/2.0/wsbpel-v2.0.pdf
9. Web Service Challenge (2010), http://ws-challenge.georgetown.edu/wsc10/
10. B. Xu, Y. Yan, An efficient qos-driven service composition approach for large-scale service oriented systems, in *SOCA*, Taipei, 2009
11. T. Yu, Y. Zhang, K.J. Lin, Efficient algorithms for web services selection with end-to-end qos constraints. ACM Trans. Web 1(1), 6-es (2007)
12. L. Zeng, B. Benatallah, Qos-aware middleware for web service composition. IEEE Trans. Softw. Eng. 30(5), 311–327 (2004)
13. L. Zeng, B. Benatallah, M. Dumas, J. Kalagnanam, Q.Z. Sheng, Quality driven web services composition, in *WWW*, Budapest, Hungary, 2003

Index

M.B. Blake et al. (eds.), *Semantic Web Services*, DOI 10.1007/978-3-642-28735-0,
© Springer-Verlag Berlin Heidelberg 2012